Promotion Cramme[r]
for Sergeants' and Inspe[ctors']
Part 1 Exams – 2011

Tom Barron
Julianna Mitchell

No part of this publication may be reproduced or transmitted in any form or by any means, or stored in any retrieval system of any nature, without prior written permission, except the permitted fair dealing under the Copyright, Designs and Patents Act 1988, or in accordance with the terms of a licence issued by the Copyright Licensing Agency in respect of photocopying and/or reprographic reproduction.

Application for permission for other use of copyright material including permission to reproduce extracts in other published works shall be made to the publishers.

Full acknowledgement of author, publisher and source must be given.

Published by IHS (Global) Limited (IHS Jane's)

© IHS (Global) Limited 2010

13th Edition 2010

ISBN 978 0 7106 2930 2

IHS Jane's, IHS (Global) Limited
Sentinel House, 163 Brighton Road,
Coulsdon, Surrey CR5 2YH

www.janes.com   www.policereview.com

This book was produced using FSC certified paper
Printed and bound in the UK by Polestar Wheatons

While every care has been taken in compiling (and checking) the suggested answers and other information contained in this book, no responsibility can be accepted by the publishers or the author for any error, inaccuracy, or omission which remains, or for any loss or injury sustained to any (person/reader) as a result.

About the authors

Tom Barron was born in Glasgow in 1945. He joined the army at the age of 15 and served in Germany, Cyprus (United Nations), Singapore, Malaya and in Borneo where he saw active service with the Royal Corps Of Transport (Air Despatch).

He joined the Police Service in 1969 serving for 27 years in various operational and training roles including two years teaching crammer courses for officers taking the Sergeants' and Inspectors' exams. He was also in charge of the Avon & Somerset interview technique training unit.

Tom has had a number of articles published in newspapers and journals including the *Daily Telegraph*, and the *Daily Mail*. He enjoys lecturing in colleges and universities on his subject of choice: the Anatomy of a Lie. He is the author of *The Special Constable's Manual*.

Julianna Mitchell LLB (Hons), BCL (Oxon) is a barrister practising from chambers in The Temple, London and a contributing author of *Halsbury's Laws of England*.

To Isobel

Contents

THE RULES AND SYLLABUSES
Rules for the Sergeants' and Inspectors' Exams

ON STUDYING

PART 1 - GENERAL POLICE DUTIES ... 1
Police ... 1
Complaints, misconduct and performance ... 3
Human rights ... 19
Policing powers and powers of arrest ... 25
Stop and search ... 31
Powers of entry, search & seizure ... 43
Harassment, hostility and anti-social behaviour ... 51
Nuisance ... 55
Offences involving communications ... 59
Terrorism and associated offences ... 63
Public disorder ... 69
Offensive weapons ... 91
Civil disputes ... 97
Trade disputes ... 99
Offences related to land ... 101
Licensing and offences related to alcohol and gambling ... 111
Offences involving information ... 123
Diversity, discrimination and equality ... 129

PART 2 - CRIME ... 131
Introduction ... 131
Defences ... 135
Homicide ... 137
Misuse of drugs ... 145
Firearms and gun crime ... 153
Offences against the person ... 167
Sexual offences ... 175
Offences against children and vulnerable persons ... 197
Theft and related offences ... 205
Fraud ... 223

CONTENTS

Criminal damage 231
Offences against the administration of justice 239
Immigration offences 243

PART 3 - ROAD POLICING 245
Standards of driving 245
Notice of intended prosecution 251
Accidents 253
Drink, drugs and driving 257
Insurance 267
Traffic safety measures 269
Construction and use 279
Driving licensing 283
Fixed penalty systems 289
Forgery and falsification of documents 293

PART 4 - EVIDENCE AND PROCEDURE 297
Instituting criminal proceedings 297
Bail 301
Court procedure and witnesses 307
Youth crime and disorder 313
Sentencing 317
Evidence 319
Exclusion of admissible evidence 331
Disclosure of evidence 333
Custody officer duties 339
Identification 353
Interviews 359

www.janes.com

The Rules and Syllabuses
Rules for the Sergeants' and Inspectors' exams

1. Admission to the Sergeants' exam is currently restricted to regular constables who, by 30th November of the calendar year in which they take the exam, will have completed not less than 2 years service; been confirmed in their appointment, and have not previously obtained a pass in a Sergeants' promotion exam. Admission to the Inspectors' exam is currently restricted to sergeants who, on 1st July of the calendar year in which they take their exam, will have attained the substantive rank and have not previously obtained a pass in an Inspectors' promotion exam.

2. Part I consists of a single multiple choice paper of 3 hours duration, which is normally held in March for sergeants and September for inspectors. The exam will comprise 150 questions.

3. There is now a set pass mark for each exam. This is 55% for the Sergeants' exam and 65% for the Inspectors'.

Notes

It is always important, before beginning any revision programme, to familiarise yourself with the current rules and syllabus applicable to your exam. Don't assume that these will be the same as previous years - double check! Candidates are advised to obtain a copy of the official rules booklet (which is available online via www.npia.police.uk).

Sergeants' and Inspectors' Syllabus
[a summary]

Part 1 - Crime
State of mind
Criminal conduct
Incomplete offences and police investigations
General defences
Homicide
Misuse of drugs
Firearms and gun crime
Non-fatal offences against the person
Miscellaneous offences against the person
Sexual offences
Control of sex offenders
Child protection
Theft and related offences
Fraud
Criminal damage
Offences against the administration of justice and public interest
Offences arising from immigration, asylum and people exploitation

Part 2 - Evidence and Procedure
Sources of law
The Courts
Instituting criminal proceedings
Bail
Court procedure and witnesses
Youth justice, crime and disorder
Evidence
Exclusion of admissible evidence
Disclosure of evidence
Custody officer's duties
Identification
Interviews

Part 3 - Road Policing
Classifications and concepts
Offences involving standards of driving
Notices of intended prosecution
Accidents and collisions
Drink, drugs and driving
Insurance
Protection of drivers and passengers
Highway and safety measures
Construction and use
Driver licensing
Fixed penalty system
Forgery and falsification of documents

Part 4 - General Police Duties
Police
Complaints and misconduct
Unsatisfactory performance and attendance
Extending the policing family
Human rights
Policing powers and powers of arrest
Stop and search
Entry, search and seizure
Harassment, hostility and anti-social behaviour
Offences involving communications
Terrorism and associated offences
Public disorder
Sporting events
Weapons
Civil disputes
Offences relating to land and premises
Licensing, offences related to alcohol, and gambling
Offences and powers relating to information
Diversity, discrimination and equality

On Studying...
THE NEED TO KNOW PRINCIPLE

The need to know principle is summed up thus:

'If you don't need to know it, don't study it'

This book is designed to help you pass the Sergeants' and Inspectors' exams at the first attempt.

It is a 'no nonsense - no frills' book aimed at people who want to get as much as possible from their time spent studying, with all the verbiage thrown overboard together with everything else that seems to cloud the issues with facts, leaving only the bare bones of what you **need to know** to pass the exam. The bare bones are laid out in manageable bite-size portions which you can digest with relative ease and regurgitate when necessary. Why read the whole of the Bible if you can achieve a pass mark with a good knowledge only of the 10 Commandments? There are no semantic somersaults or linguistic limbo dancing in this book - just what you **need to know**.

MEMORY IS REPETITION

I know a three-year-old who can speak Chinese. Surprised? You shouldn't be, he lives in China.

We are all born with a blank sheet [our brain where we keep our memory]. That sheet has things imprinted on it, like language, and we learn the most difficult things possible with apparent ease - how come? By repetition. By hearing the same thing over and over again we memorise something as difficult as a language. Police officers fail exams, not because they have misunderstood a section of legislation when they **read it**, but because they did not **learn it**. Reading and learning are two different things. Learning takes place when you can remember or write down what you have read. By constant repetition, information is memorised and when memorised it is learned. Why do you have to write down other people's telephone numbers but not your own? Repetition has caused you to memorise your number and therefore it is learned. Read this book over and over again until you reach a point whereby you know what is on the next page. When you reach that point you have learned it. The enormity of what you have to learn seems daunting. It actually begs the question 'How do you eat an elephant?'

Any elephant eater will tell you, one piece at a time. Learn 10 pages and have your partner test your knowledge. He or she needs no police knowledge because the pages are set as questions and answers. Once you have

ON STUDYING...

satisfactorily mastered the first 10 pages, go on to the next. Remember, one piece at a time. Stick to basic facts, don't allow anything to cloud the issue with facts.

Do not stray from the concept of **KISS** – Keep It Simple **Stupid**!
And remember the elephant.

Tom Barron
Cannington
Somerset

Part 1 - General Police Duties

POLICE

Q What is the jurisdiction of a police officer?

A A member of a police force shall have all the powers and privileges of a constable throughout England and Wales and the adjacent United Kingdom waters.

s.30 POLICE ACT 1996

Q What are the principal functions of the Serious Organised Crime Agency (SOCA)?

A Preventing and detecting serious organised crime, and contributing to the reduction of such crime and mitigating its consequences.

Q What is the general duty of chief officers of police in relation to SOCA?

A Chief officers must keep SOCA informed of any information relating to crime in his/her police area that appears to him/her to be likely to be relevant to the exercise by SOCA of any of its functions.

s.36 SERIOUS ORGANISED CRIME AND POLICE ACT 2005

Q What is the general duty of police to assist SOCA?

A It is the duty of every constable, officer of Her Majesty's Revenue and Customs, member of Her Majesty's armed forces or Her Majesty's coastguard to assist SOCA in the exercise of its functions in relation to serious organised crime.

s.37 SERIOUS ORGANISED CRIME AND POLICE ACT 2005

Q What is the jurisdiction of a special constable?

A Special constables have the same powers and privileges as regular constables. Although formerly restricted to exercising them in their own and contiguous (neighbouring) force areas, the Police and Justice Act 2006 extended their jurisdiction to match that of the regular constabulary, thus enabling them to exercise their powers throughout England and Wales and adjacent United Kingdom waters.

s.30(2) POLICE ACT 1996

POLICE

Q Can a police officer be a member of a trade union?

A   No. Section 64(1) of the Police Act 1996 states that a member of a police force shall not be a member of any trade union, or of any association having for its objects, or one of its objects, to control or influence the pay, pensions or conditions of service of any police force. The only exception to this rule is where the officer was a member of a trade union *before* becoming a member of the police service, in which case he or she may continue to be a member of that union *with the consent of the chief officer of police.*

Q What is the Police Federation?

A   The Police Federation is a staff association for all constables, sergeants, inspectors and chief inspectors which represents the interests of police officers in lieu of a union and which is permitted to represent officers in disciplinary proceedings.

Q Are police officers employees?

A   No, police officers are not employed under a contract of employment but are public office holders (the office of constable).

COMPLAINTS, MISCONDUCT AND PERFORMANCE

Q In relation to police disciplinary matters, what does 'misconduct' mean?

A Misconduct means a breach of the Standards of Professional Behaviour.

Q In relation to police disciplinary matters, what does 'gross misconduct' mean?

A Gross misconduct means a breach of the Standards of Professional Behaviour which is so serious that dismissal would be justified.

Q In relation to police disciplinary matters, what does 'unsatisfactory performance' mean?

A Unsatisfactory performance means an inability or failure of a police officer to perform the duties of the role or rank he/she is currently undertaking to a satisfactory standard.

The Standards of Professional Behaviour

Q What are 'the Standards of Professional Behaviour'?

A These are the code of ethics which provides the standard by which the conduct of all police officers, from chief constables to constables including special constables and those subject to suspension, is to be judged. They are intended to be modern, positive in tone and to enshrine values of fairness and equality in policing. They are also intended to be easy to understand and reflective of how the public expects police officers to behave, thus ensuring greater public confidence in the police service.

Q Outline the Standards

A The standards are:

- **Honesty and Integrity:** Police officers are honest, act with integrity and do not compromise or abuse their position.
- **Authority, Respect and Courtesy:** Police officers act with self-control and tolerance, treating members of the public and colleagues with respect and courtesy. Police officers do not abuse their powers or authority and respect the rights of all individuals.
- **Equality and Diversity:** Police officers act with fairness and impartiality. They do not discriminate unlawfully or unfairly.
- **Use of Force:** Police officers only use force to the extent that it is necessary, proportionate and reasonable in all the circumstances.

COMPLAINTS, MISCONDUCT AND PERFORMANCE

- **Orders and instructions:** Police officers only give and carry out lawful orders and instructions. Police officers abide by police regulations, force policies and lawful orders.
- **Duties and Responsibilities:** Police officers are diligent in the exercise of their duties and responsibilities.
- **Confidentiality:** Police officers treat information with respect and access or disclose it only in the proper course of police duties.
- **Fitness for Duty:** Police officers when on duty or presenting themselves for duty are fit to carry out their duties and responsibilities.
- **Discreditable Conduct:** Police officers behave in a manner which does not discredit the police service or undermine public confidence, whether on or off duty. Police officers report any actions taken against them for a criminal offence, conditions imposed by a court or the receipt of any penalty notice.
- **Challenging and Reporting Improper Conduct:** Police officers report, challenge or take action against the conduct of colleagues which has fallen below the standards of professional behaviour.

Q **What is the role of a 'police friend'?**

A Police officers who are subject to any misconduct or performance proceedings are entitled to consult with and be accompanied by a 'police friend' during any stage of such proceedings. The police friend may do any of the following:

- Advise the police officer throughout any proceedings under the Police (Conduct) Regulations 2008 or Police (Performance) Regulations 2008.
- Unless the police officer has the right to, and chooses to be, legally represented, represent the police officer at the misconduct proceedings, performance proceedings, appeal meeting, a special case hearing or at a police appeals tribunal.
- Make representations to the 'appropriate authority' concerning any aspect of the proceedings under the Conduct or Performance Regulations.
- Accompany the police officer to any interview, meeting or hearing which forms part of any proceedings under the Conduct or Performance Regulations.

Q **Who is the 'appropriate authority' under the Performance Regulations?**

A The chief officer of police (who may delegate any of his/her functions to an officer of at least the rank of chief inspector, or a police staff member of equivalent seniority).

COMPLAINTS, MISCONDUCT AND PERFORMANCE

Q Must the 'police friend' be a police officer?

A Not necessarily. The police friend can be a police officer, a police staff member, or a person nominated by the police officer's staff association. The police friend must not have had any involvement in that particular case. Police friends will be considered to be 'on duty' when attending interviews, meetings or hearings under the disciplinary procedures and are entitled to take a reasonable amount of duty time to fulfil their responsibilities.

Misconduct Procedures

Q What is a 'complaint'?

A Under the Police Reform Act 2002 it is any complaint (in writing or otherwise) about the conduct of a person serving with the police. It may be about, for example, behaviour, inappropriate language, actions or omissions or an allegation of criminal behaviour.

Q Who can make a complaint?

A A complaint can be made by:

- Any member of the public who alleges that police misconduct was directed at them.
- Any member of the public who alleges that they have been adversely affected by police misconduct, even if it was not directed at them.
- Any member of the public who claims that they witnessed misconduct by the police.
- A person acting on behalf of someone who falls within any of the categories above.

Q What is a 'recordable conduct matter'?

A Where a matter is not the subject of a complaint, but it appears that a member of the police service has committed a criminal offence or behaved in a manner that justifies the bringing of disciplinary proceedings then it should be recorded and will be 'a recordable conduct matter'.

Q How do the misconduct procedures begin?

A Where conduct is linked to a complaint or is a recordable conduct matter, or death or serious injury matter, the appropriate authority is required to follow the misconduct procedures set out in the Police Reform Act 2002 and accompanying regulations. These *misconduct*

COMPLAINTS, MISCONDUCT AND PERFORMANCE

procedures should not be used to deal with *unsatisfactory performance*, which is governed by its own set of rules (see below).

Q Are student police officers (probationer constables) subject to the misconduct procedures?

A   Yes. (They are not subject to the unsatisfactory performance procedures, see below).

Q Outline the misconduct procedure

A   1. ***Initial assessment.***
Following an allegation of misconduct, the appropriate authority should conduct an *initial assessment* in order to:

   [a] ensure a timely response to the allegation
   [b] identify the police officer subject to the allegation and eliminate those not involved
   [c] ensure that the most appropriate procedures are used.

   2. ***Written notification.***
Where the initial assessment determines that an *investigation* into the alleged misconduct is required, written notification will be given to the officer concerned by the appointed investigator, advising that their conduct is under formal investigation. The written notice will:

   [a] Inform the officer that there is to be an investigation of their potential breach of the Standards of Professional Behaviour, and of the name of the appointed investigator.
   [b] Describe the conduct to be investigated and how it is alleged to have fallen below the Standards.
   [c] Inform the officer whether the conduct (if proved) would be considered to be misconduct (and likely to be dealt with by a misconduct meeting) or gross misconduct (and likely to be dealt with by a misconduct hearing).
   [d] Inform the officer that if the likely form of the proceedings changes they will be notified, and given the reasons.
   [e] Inform the officer of his/her right to seek advice, and to be represented by a police friend (or by a lawyer in the case of gross misconduct hearings or special case hearings).
   [f] Inform the officer that he/she may provide, within 10 working days of receipt of the notice (which may be

COMPLAINTS, MISCONDUCT AND PERFORMANCE

extended by the investigator), a statement (written or oral) relating to the investigation, together with any relevant documents.

[g] Caution the officer that whilst he/she does not have to say anything, it may harm his/her case if he/she does not mention when interviewed or when providing any information within the relevant time limits something which he/she later relies on at any meeting/hearing.

When should the written notification be given? As soon as is practicable, unless to do so would prejudice the investigation (or any other investigation e.g. a criminal investigation). Any decision not to inform must be recorded and kept under review, so that the officer can be notified as soon as appropriate.

3. **Investigation.**
The appropriate authority should ensure that investigations into the alleged misconduct are proportionate and carried out as soon as possible after the allegation comes to light. The purpose of the formal investigation is to:

[a] Gather evidence to establish the facts and circumstances of the alleged misconduct.
[b] Assist the appropriate authority to establish on the balance of probabilities, based on the evidence and taking into account all of the circumstances, whether there is a case to answer.
[c] Identify any learning for the individual or organisation.

If the investigation concludes that the matter is one of performance rather than misconduct, the officer should be informed that the performance procedures now apply (see below).

Interviews. The investigator may choose to carry out formal interviews, giving the officer written notice of the date, time and place. The officer may propose an alternative time, and the interview will be postponed to this time provided that it is reasonable and within 5 working days of the original time. The officer must attend and it will be a further misconduct matter to fail to do so. A record of the interview should be made and given to the interviewee.

Conclusion? At the conclusion of the investigation the investigator must as soon as is practicable submit a report of the investigation attaching any relevant documents. The appropriate authority must decide, based on the report, whether there is a case to answer. If no, no further action will be taken against the officer

COMPLAINTS, MISCONDUCT AND PERFORMANCE

(although management/organisational action may be considered appropriate). If it is decided that there is a case to answer, the appropriate authority must decide whether to proceed to a misconduct meeting (for cases of misconduct) or misconduct hearing (for cases of gross misconduct). This must be arranged and the officer notified and given a copy of the investigation report (or relevant parts), any relevant documents and a copy of his/her statement.

4. ***Preparation for Meeting/Hearing.***
    Within 14 working days (which may be extended in exceptional cases) after being notified, the officer must submit, in writing:

    [a] whether or not he/she accepts that his/her behaviour amounts to misconduct/gross misconduct
    [b] if so, any written submission in mitigation
    [c] if not, or if any part of the case is disputed, written notice of the dispute and his/her account of the relevant events and any points of law to be relied upon. The officer should also provide copies of any documents to be relied upon.

    The officer should be notified of the name of the person appointed to conduct the meeting/hearing, and may object, within 3 working days, giving reasons.

5. ***Misconduct Proceedings.***
    There are two types:

    [a] A misconduct *meeting* for cases where there is a case to answer in respect of misconduct and where the maximum outcome would be a final written warning.
    [b] A misconduct *hearing* for cases where there is a case to answer in respect of gross misconduct or where the officer already has a final written warning and there is a case to answer in respect of a further act of misconduct. The maximum outcome at this hearing is dismissal without notice.

    Misconduct Meetings. Should take place no later than 20 working days after documents are supplied to the officer. This time limit can be extended if appropriate in the interests of justice. *For officers up to and including chief superintendent* the meeting will be chaired by a police officer (or other member of a police force) of at least one rank above the officer concerned. *For special constables*, it will be a sergeant (or above) or senior human resources professional.

Misconduct Hearings. Should take place no later than 30 working days after documents are supplied to the officer. This time limit can be extended if appropriate in the interests of justice. The hearing will have a 3 person panel, the chair being a senior officer or senior human resources professional. If the senior human resources professional is chair then the panel must also include an independent member (appointed from a list held by the police authority) and a police officer of the rank of superintendent or above. If the senior officer is chair, the other panel members will be an independent member and a superintendent or above or a senior human resources professional. The officer can be legally represented.

Conduct of meetings/hearings. Chair to determine, in accordance with principles of fairness and natural justice. Standard of proof: civil (balance of probabilities).

6. **Outcome.**
If the conclusion is that the officer's conduct did fail to meet the Standards, then the most appropriate outcome will be determined by the chair. The officer may make representations.

Outcomes available:

[a] No further action
[b] Management advice
[c] Written warning
[d] Final written warning

and, in addition, at misconduct hearings

[a] dismissal with notice
[b] dismissal without notice

The officer must be notified of the outcome as soon as is practicable and in any event within 5 working days of the conclusion of the meeting/hearing. The officer will be informed of his/her right to appeal.

COMPLAINTS, MISCONDUCT AND PERFORMANCE

Unsatisfactory Performance and Attendance Procedures

Q What are 'UPPs'?

A UPPs are the formal procedures to deal with unsatisfactory performance and attendance set out in the Police (Performance) Regulations 2008. Unsatisfactory performance or attendance is defined in reg.4 of the Regulations as 'an inability or failure of a police officer to perform the duties of the role or rank he is currently undertaking to a satisfactory standard or level'.

Q What is the primary aim of the procedures?

A To improve poor performance and attendance in the police service.

Q To whom do the procedures apply?

A To police officers up to an including chief superintendent, including special constables.

Q Do the procedures apply to student police officers (probationer constables)?

A No. The procedures do not apply to student police officers during their probationary period, instead issues of student performance and attendance will be determined by local force policies.

Q What standard of proof applies during the procedures?

A When deciding matters of fact the standard of proof will be the civil standard (balance of probabilities) i.e. it must be more likely than not that the performance or attendance in question is unsatisfactory. The more serious the allegation, and the more serious the potential consequence for the officer, the more persuasive the evidence will have to be to meet this standard.

Q What is a 'PDR'?

A A performance and development review. This is a performance appraisal by which the officer's performance and attendance can be monitored by his/her line manager, who may be a police officer or police staff member. Performance objectives should be set by line managers and be 'SMART': Specific, Measurable, Achievable, Relevant and Time-related. Officers should know what standard is expected of them and be given support to maintain that standard.

COMPLAINTS, MISCONDUCT AND PERFORMANCE

Q How do the UPPs begin?

A Unsatisfactory performance or attendance is most likely to be identified by line managers, but may also be identified following information from a member of the public e.g. a formal complaint. Ideally concerns will be dealt with informally as part of ongoing performance appraisal but where this is not possible the formal process may be initiated.

Q Outline the formal UPP process

A There are 3 stages to the UPPs.

 1. *First stage meeting.* Line manager will notify officer that he/she is required to attend a first stage meeting. Notice will be accompanied by relevant documents and the evidence relied on by the line manager in support of their view of underperformance. Where possible the meeting should be agreed, but if that is not possible the line manager must specify time and place. The purpose of the meeting is to hear evidence of unsatisfactory performance and give the officer an opportunity to respond. Officer may be accompanied by a police friend. Maximum outcome: improvement notice.

    If line manager considers performance satisfactory: no further action. If unsatisfactory: improvement notice which should clearly identify the areas of underperformance.

    The officer may submit written comments within 7 days or appeal. If they choose not to appeal, an action plan should be agreed and performance monitored. If the officer appeals, it should be submitted in writing to second line manager within 7 days of receipt of improvement notice. An appeal meeting will take place, at which the officer can be accompanied by a police friend and make representations. The second line manager will either confirm or reverse the original finding or endorse or vary the improvement notice. Written notice of the appeal decision should be given within 3 days of the appeal meeting.

 2. *Second stage meeting.* If performance or attendance is still considered unsatisfactory at the end of the period specified in the improvement notice, the second line manager will notify the officer in writing that he/she is required to attend a second stage meeting. The notice must include the documents to be relied upon. (Only matters raised in first stage meeting can be considered, not new matters. New matters must be dealt with by a new stage one meeting). A second meeting, similar in format to

the first, will be held, at which the officer may be accompanied by a police friend and make representations. Maximum outcome: final improvement notice.

Final improvement notice. This will require the officer to improve his/her performance and must set out in what way that performance is unsatisfactory, the improvement required, specify a time period in which the improvement is to be made (normally no longer than 3 months, or 12 months in exceptional cases. May be extended by appropriate authority) and how long the notice is valid for (12 months, during which time the improved performance must be maintained). Must also notify of possible consequences of failure to improve i.e. next stage of process will be initiated.

Officer may submit written comments within 7 days, or appeal. May be accompanied by police friend at second stage appeal meeting.

3. *Third stage meeting.* The process may proceed to or even commence at this stage in severe cases of gross incompetence (which is defined in the Regulations as *'... a serious inability or serious failure of a police officer to perform the duties of the rank or role he is currently undertaking to a satisfactory standard or level, to the extent that dismissal would be justified'*). The officer may be accompanied by a police friend (and/or legally represented in cases of gross incompetence). Potential outcome may be dismissal, reduction in rank (performance cases only), redeployment to alternative duties or an extended improvement notice (in exceptional cases).

Procedure. Where, after the specified period of the final improvement notice, performance is still not satisfactory, the line manager must notify the officer in writing that he/she is required to attend a third stage meeting. Copies of documents relied on should be supplied. A panel will be appointed by the appropriate authority to hear representations. Panel consists of chair and two other members. At least one panel member must be a police officer. Chair: senior police officer or senior human resources professional. First panel member: superintendent (or above) or equivalent human resources professional. Second panel member: superintendent (or above) or police staff member of equivalent rank. All members must be at least of the same rank or senior to the officer concerned and the chair should be senior in rank. All must be independent of the case. The officer may object, in writing to the appropriate authority, to any proposed panel member within 3 days of notification of the panel. If objection is accepted, a new panel member will be appointed (to whom officer can object as before).

Third stage meeting should take place within 30 days of notification (can be extended if appropriate).

Within 14 days of notification the officer must provide written notice of whether or not he accepts the allegations, and any written submission in mitigation. Where the officer disputes the allegations, he/she must provide written notice of the matters in dispute and any legal arguments. Documents to be relied upon should be supplied.

Within 3 days of the officer's notice, lists of witnesses (if any) must be exchanged. Panel chair will decide if any are to attend meeting and may call any other witness to attend if the chair considers it necessary in the interests of fairness for them to do so.

At the meeting representations may be made and the panel will make a finding as to whether the performance or attendance has been unsatisfactory, or whether the behaviour was grossly incompetent. Their decision will be in writing, stating reasons. A copy will be sent to the officer and his/her line manager as soon as reasonably practicable, and within 3 days. Officer may appeal against any negative finding.

Q   What is meant by 'vicarious liability of chief officer of police'?

A   The chief officer of police is legally responsible for the actions of his/her officers and employees when acting in the course of their duties. He/she may have to pay any damages arising out of civil claims against such officers/employees for any *unlawful conduct* (but not officers seconded to central services such as the SOCA or the Central Police Training and Development Agency, where liability rests with the Home Office or relevant Director).

COMPLAINTS, MISCONDUCT AND PERFORMANCE

Other Regulations

Q What restrictions are imposed on the private life of officers?

A The Police Regulations 2003 impose a number of restrictions on officers' private lives. A member of a police force:

1. Shall at all times abstain from any activity which is likely to interfere with the impartial discharge of his duties or which is likely to give rise to the impression among members of the public that it may so interfere.

2. Shall in particular –

    [a] not take any active part in politics;
    [b] not belong to any organisation specified or described in a determination by the Secretary of State. [The British National Party, Combat 18 and the National Front are currently specified for this purpose].

3. Shall not reside at premises which are not for the time being approved by the chief officer of police.

4. Shall not, without the previous consent of the chief officer of police, receive a lodger in a house or quarters with which he/she is provided by the police authority, or sub-let any part of the house or quarters.

5. Shall not, unless he/she has previously given written notice to the chief officer of police, receive a lodger in a house in which he/she resides and in respect of which he/she receives a rent allowance, or sub-let any part of such a house.

6. Shall not wilfully refuse or neglect to discharge any lawful debt.

Q What are the rules regarding 'business interests'?

A If a member of a police force or one of their relatives (being a spouse, parent, son, daughter, brother or sister) proposes to have, or has, a 'business interest', the member shall forthwith give written notice of that interest to the chief officer of police (unless they did so when appointed). The chief officer shall then determine whether or not the interest in question is compatible with their membership of the force, and shall notify the member of that decision in writing within 28 days. Within 10 days of notification (which may be extended by the police authority) the member may make a written appeal to the police authority against the chief officer's decision. If a business interest is still considered to be incompatible with membership of the force following the appeal, and following any representations being made by the member, the chief officer may dispense with the member's services.

POLICE REGS 2003, REG 7

Q What is meant by 'business interests'?

A Regulation 8 states that a member of a police force or relative has a 'business interest' if:

1. the member holds any office or employment for hire or gain or carries on any business;

2. a shop (or like business) is kept or carried on by the member's spouse (not being separated) at any premises in the area of the police force in question or by any relative living with them;

3. the member, his/her spouse (not being separated) or any relative living with them has a pecuniary interest in any licence or permit granted in relation to

   [a] liquor licensing
   [b] refreshment houses
   [c] betting and gaming
   [d] regulating places of entertainment

   in the area of the police force in question.

Offences

Q What is the offence of misconduct in a public office?

A It is an offence at common law for the holder of a public office to do anything that amounts to a malfeasance or a culpable misfeasance (*R v Wyatt* (1705)).

Purpose. Essentially to deal with cases of abuse of public power (rather than, for example, the misbehaviour of public officials whilst 'off-duty'). **Mal**feasance requires *action* with a wrongful motive or intention (bad faith), whilst a wilful (deliberate) *neglect* of duty would be a culpable **mis**feasance.

COMPLAINTS, MISCONDUCT AND PERFORMANCE

Q What is the offence of impersonating a police officer?

A

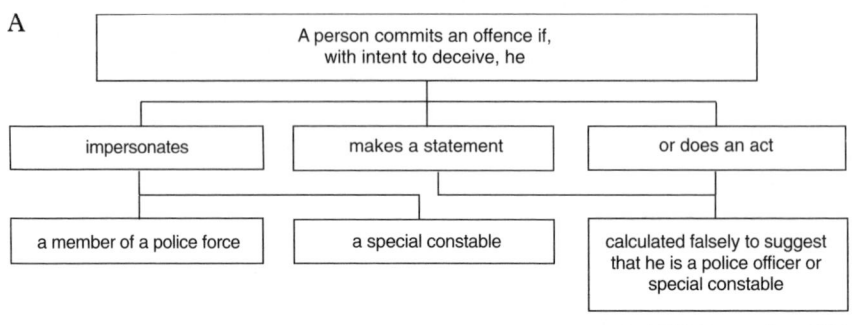

A person commits an offence if, with intent to deceive, he:
- impersonates a member of a police force
- impersonates a special constable
- makes a statement calculated falsely to suggest that he is a police officer or special constable
- or does an act calculated falsely to suggest that he is a police officer or special constable

S. 90(1) Police Act 1996

Q What is the offence of wearing or possessing uniform?

A

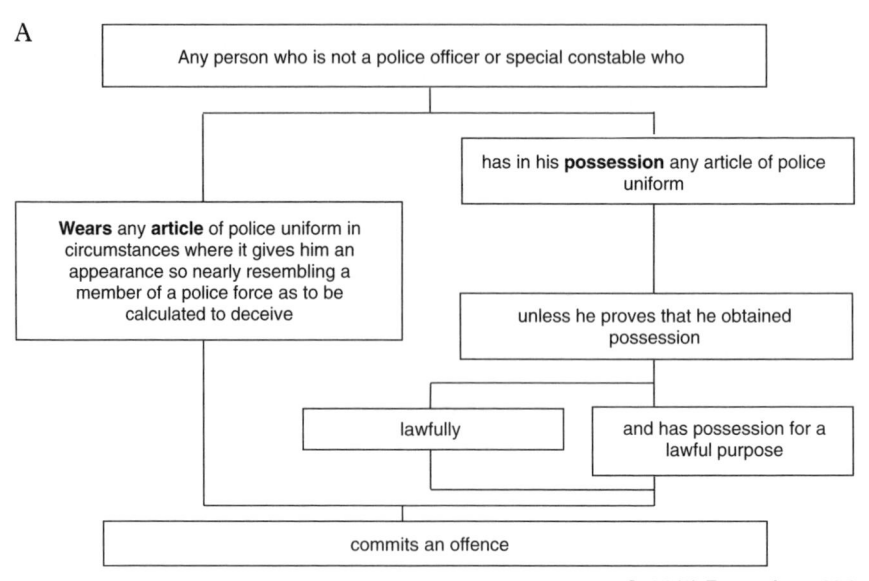

Any person who is not a police officer or special constable who:

- **Wears** any **article** of police uniform in circumstances where it gives him an appearance so nearly resembling a member of a police force as to be calculated to deceive

- has in his **possession** any article of police uniform, unless he proves that he obtained possession lawfully and has possession for a lawful purpose

commits an offence

S. 90(2) Police Act 1996

Q What is an 'article'?

A An 'article of police uniform' means:

- uniform
- a distinctive badge or mark, or
- documents of identification

COMPLAINTS, MISCONDUCT AND PERFORMANCE

Q What is the offence of impersonating a designated/accredited person?

A Any person who, with intent to deceive,

[a] impersonates a designated person, an accredited person or an accredited inspector,
[b] makes any statement or does any act calculated falsely to suggest he is such a person, or inspector
[c] makes any statement or does any act calculated falsely to suggest that he has powers as a designated or accredited person or inspector that exceed the powers he actually has is guilty of an offence.

S. 46(3) POLICE REFORM ACT 2002

Q What is the offence of causing disaffection?

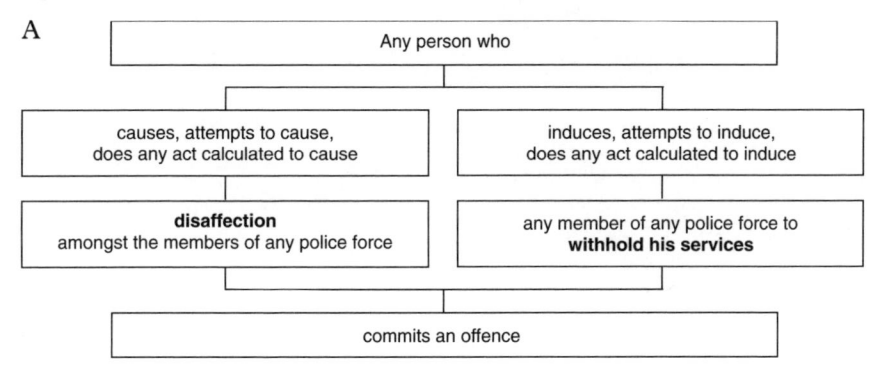

A

Any person who

causes, attempts to cause, does any act calculated to cause	induces, attempts to induce, does any act calculated to induce
disaffection amongst the members of any police force	any member of any police force to **withhold his services**

commits an offence

s.91(1) POLICE ACT 1996

HUMAN RIGHTS

Q Outline the key features of the European Convention on Human Rights (ECHR).

A The ECHR protects certain rights which are considered by many to be fundamental civil liberties (i.e. human rights) within a democratic society. There are five key features:

1. the balancing of individual rights against the needs of democratic society;

2. the three tests of legitimate limitations on Convention rights;

3. the ECHR as a 'living instrument' [i.e. it must be interpreted by courts in the light of present-day conditions];

4. the 'margin of appreciation' [i.e. the recognition that because of social, political, economic and cultural differences throughout Europe some latitude in national interpretation of the ECHR must be given]; and

5. derogations and reservations [Art. 15 allows States to derogate (i.e. restrict or disapply) aspects of the ECHR in time of war or public emergency].

Q Under the Human Rights Act 1998 and ECHR, what is meant by the three tests of legitimate limitations on a Convention right?

A Any limitation must be:

[a] Prescribed by law;
[b] intended to achieve a legitimate objective, and
[c] proportionate to the end that is to be achieved.

Q Summarise test 1 - 'prescribed by law'

A An individual has the right to ask 'where did you get the power to act as you did?' and the public body concerned must be able to give an answer e.g. 'from the Regulation of Investigatory Powers Act 2000'. So that where an illegal telephone tap is made on a person at work, his employer may have breached his human rights (as occurred in *Halford v. UK (1997)*, which pre-dated the Act authorising such activities).

HUMAN RIGHTS

Q Summarise test 2 - 'intended to achieve a legitimate objective'

A Any limitation must be directed at achieving a legitimate goal, as set out in the ECHR itself e.g. the prevention of crime. The public body concerned must always be acting lawfully however.

Q Summarise test 3 - 'proportionate to the end that is to be achieved'

A The state cannot use a sledgehammer to crack a nut. The test is 'were the measures taken necessary in a democratic society?' Where police officers enter and search premises using more force than was necessary they might argue that they intended to:

[a] achieve a legitimate objective by preventing crime; and
[b] the objective was prescribed by law, ie PACE; but
[c] the means employed by the officers would have to be in proportion to the crime that was to be prevented for the behaviour to be a legitimate limitation on the right to respect for private life.

Q Under the Human Rights Act 1998, when is a public authority acting unlawfully?

A It is unlawful for a public authority to act in a way that is incompatible with a Convention right.

S. 6 HRA 1998

Q Under the Human Rights Act 1998, what is meant by a public authority?

A A public authority includes:

[a] a court or tribunal, including the House of Lords in its judicial capacity;
[b] police, fire and ambulance service; and
[c] any person or body whose functions are of a public nature (but not including Parliament or persons exercising functions in connection with Parliamentary proceedings).

Q Under the Human Rights Act 1998, who can bring proceedings?

A Any 'victim' ie. person or organisation who believes that a public authority has acted unlawfully (i.e. breached their Convention rights).

HUMAN RIGHTS

To be a victim the person/organisation must show that they are either directly affected or at risk of being directly affected by the behaviour complained of.

S. 7 HRA 1998

Q **Under the Human Rights Act 1998, what are the time limits for commencing proceedings?**

A **One year** from the time of the act complained of, or a longer period if the court considers it equitable having regard to all the circumstances (subject to any stricter national time limits).

S. 7 HRA 1998

Q **Under the Human Rights Act 1998, what are the Convention Rights?**

A 1. *The right to life*. A life may be taken only by:

   [a] execution by order of a court;
   [b] when it results from the use of force which is *no more than absolutely necessary*:

   [i] in defence of any person from unlawful violence;
   [ii] in order to affect a lawful arrest or prevent escape from lawful detention; or
   [iii] in action lawfully taken to quell a riot or insurrection.

   [ART. 2]

2. *Freedom from torture*. No one shall be subjected to torture or to inhuman or degrading treatment or punishment. Oppressive interrogation techniques such as sleep deprivation, exposure to continuous loud noise and forcing suspects to adopt uncomfortable postures have been held to be degrading and inhuman.

   [ART. 3]

3. *Freedom from slavery and forced labour*. This does not include:

   [a] work done in the ordinary course of detention;
   [b] military service;
   [c] service exacted during an emergency; or
   [d] work done as a civic obligation.

   [ART. 4]

HUMAN RIGHTS

4. ***The right to liberty and security.*** This does not include:

    [a] lawful arrest; and
    [b] lawful detention.

    [ART. 5]

5. ***The right to a fair trial.*** Everyone is entitled to:

    [a] a fair and public hearing;
    [b] held within a reasonable time;
    [c] by an independent and impartial legal tribunal

    [ART. 6]

6. ***No punishment without crime.*** This effectively prohibits governments passing retrospective legislation making an offence of what was previously no offence, thus making crimes of otherwise lawful behaviour.

    [ART. 7]

7. ***Right to a private life.*** People are entitled to 'respect' for their:

    [a] private life,
    [b] family life,
    [c] home, and
    [d] correspondence.

    However, these may be interfered with if the three tests can successfully be applied:

    [i] there is a legal authority allowing the interference;
    [ii] there is a legitimate objective behind the actions; and
    [iii] there is a 'pressing social need' for the interference.

    [ART. 8]

8. ***Freedom of thought.*** This gives people the right to the freedom of:

    [a] thought,
    [b] conscience, and
    [c] religion.

    [ART. 9]

HUMAN RIGHTS

9. *Freedom of expression.* This gives people the right to the freedom:

    [a] of expression,
    [b] to have opinions, and
    [c] to receive and impart information and ideas.

    [ART. 10]

10. *Freedom of Assembly and Association.*

    [ART. 11]

11. *The right to marry.*

    [ART. 12]

12. *The right to an effective remedy.* This Article is not incorporated into the HRA 1998 but UK courts will be obliged to take case-law considering this right into account when interpreting the ECHR.

    [ART. 13]

13. *Prohibition of discrimination in Convention rights.* This provides a guarantee that access to the ECHR is enjoyed equally by everyone, regardless of:

    [a] sex;
    [b] race, colour;
    [c] language;
    [d] religion;
    [e] political or other opinion;
    [f] national or social origin;
    [g] association with a national minority;
    [h] property, birth or other status.

    [ART. 14]

14. *Derogation in time of emergency.* This means that a State can derogate from some of its obligations (i.e. those rights which are qualified not absolute) under the convention during:

    [a] times of **war,** or
    [b] other public emergency **threatening the life of the nation.**

    [ART. 15]

15. *Restrictions on political activities of aliens.* This permits limitations to be imposed upon certain non-European citizens.

    [ART. 16]

HUMAN RIGHTS

Q **What are the Convention Protocols?**

A   The original Convention has been extended by the addition of a number of Protocols concerning matters such as rights to property, education and participation in democratic elections.

Q **Summarise Article 1 of Protocol 1**

A   **Article 1.** *Protection of property*. Every person is entitled to the peaceful enjoyment of his possessions. To prove a breach of this Article it must be shown that the State has:

- [a] interfered with the applicant's peaceful enjoyment of his possessions; or
- [b] deprived him of his possessions; or
- [c] subjected those possessions to some sort of control.

However, the State is entitled to enforce such laws as it deems necessary to control the use of property 'in the general interest' or to secure payment of taxes, contributions or penalties.

POLICING POWERS AND POWERS OF ARREST

Q What is an 'arrest'?

A An arrest is the depriving of a person's liberty to go where he pleases (*Lewis v. CC of South Wales (1991)*).

Q When does an arrest begin?

A At the time the arresting officer informs the person of it, or when his/her words or conduct suggests that the person is under arrest (*Murray v Ministry of Defence (1988)*).

S.24 PACE ACT 1984

Q What information must be given on arrest?

A [a] That the person is under arrest and
   [b] the grounds for arrest

However, the above does not apply if it is impracticable to inform him by reason of his having escaped arrest before the information could be given.

S. 28 PACE ACT 1984

Q What did *Christie v. Leachinsky* (1947) decide?

A The reason given for the arrest must be the **real reason** in the officer's mind at the time, and he/she must clearly indicate the reason for arrest at the time of the arrest.

Q What does Article 5(2) of the European Convention on Human Rights add?

A That everyone who is arrested shall be informed promptly, *in a language which he understands*, of the reasons for his arrest and of any charge against him.

Q What is a constable's power of arrest?

A Under s. 24 PACE 1984 (as substituted by the Serious Organised Crime and Police Act 2005) a constable may arrest without warrant

   [a] anyone who is **about to commit** an offence;
   [b] anyone who is **in the act of committing** an offence;
   [c] anyone whom he has **reasonable grounds for suspecting to be about to commit** an offence;
   [d] anyone whom he has **reasonable grounds for suspecting to be committing** an offence.

POLICING POWERS AND POWERS OF ARREST

[e] where he has reasonable grounds for suspecting that an offence has been committed, anyone whom he has **reasonable grounds to suspect of being guilty** of it;

[f] where an offence has been committed, anyone who **is guilty** of it, and anyone whom he has **reasonable grounds for suspecting to be guilty** of it

provided that the constable has reasonable grounds for believing that it is *necessary* to arrest the person in question.

Q What are the 'necessity' criteria?

A An arrest may be considered necessary

[a] to enable the person's name or address to be ascertained (where such is unknown and cannot readily be ascertained or where there are reasonable grounds for doubting that a name given is genuine);

[b] to prevent the person -

   [i] causing physical injury to himself or another;
   [ii] suffering physical injury;
   [iii] causing loss or damage to property;
   [iv] committing an offence against public decency (where members of the public going about their normal business cannot reasonably avoid him)
   [v] causing an unlawful obstruction of the highway;

[c] to protect a child or other vulnerable person from him;
[d] to allow the prompt and effective investigation of the offence or conduct of the person;
[e] to prevent any prosecution for the offence being hindered by his disappearance.

Q With regard to a person's address, when is an address considered sufficient?

A When the person will be at it for a sufficiently long period for a summons to be served upon him/her, or if some other person at that address specified by the person will accept service on their behalf: Code G, para 2.9(b). This may mean that the address of a person's solicitor is sufficient.

POLICING POWERS AND POWERS OF ARREST

Q What is the power of arrest by citizens?

A A person other than a constable may arrest

[a] anyone who **is committing** an indictable offence;
[b] anyone whom he has **reasonable grounds for suspecting to be committing** an indictable offence;
[c] where an indictable offence has been committed, anyone who **is guilty**, or whom he has **reasonable grounds for suspecting to be guilty** of it

provided that the person making the arrest has reasonable grounds for believing that it is necessary to arrest and that it is not reasonably practicable for a constable to make the arrest instead.

In this case it may be 'necessary' to arrest in order to prevent the person

[a] causing physical injury to himself or another;
[b] suffering physical injury;
[c] causing loss or damage to property; or
[d] making off before a constable can assume responsibility for him.

S. 24A PACE ACT 1984

Q What power of arrest exists for failure to answer police bail?

A Persons who are in breach of a duty to surrender to police bail may be arrested and taken to the original bailing police station where they will be treated as if arrested for the original offence.

S. 46A PACE ACT 1984

POLICING POWERS AND POWERS OF ARREST

Q Explain cross-border arrest without warrant.

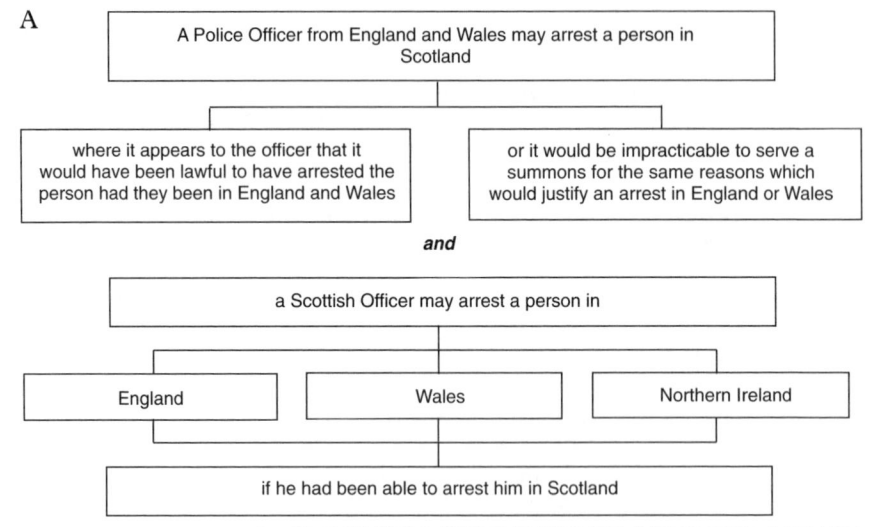

A

A Police Officer from England and Wales may arrest a person in Scotland

- where it appears to the officer that it would have been lawful to have arrested the person had they been in England and Wales
- or it would be impracticable to serve a summons for the same reasons which would justify an arrest in England or Wales

and

a Scottish Officer may arrest a person in

- England
- Wales
- Northern Ireland

if he had been able to arrest him in Scotland

S. 137 CRIMINAL JUSTICE AND PUBLIC ORDER ACT 1994

Q Outline the powers concerning removal of mentally disordered persons to a place of safety

A If, in a public place, a constable finds a person who appears to him/her to be suffering from a mental disorder and to be in immediate need of care or control, the constable may, if he thinks it necessary to do so in the interests of that person or for the protection of others, remove that person to a place of safety.

s.136 MENTAL HEALTH ACT 1983

Q What is a 'mental disorder'?

A
- [a] Mental illness;
- [b] arrested or incomplete development of mind;
- [c] psychopathic disorder (a persistent disorder or disability resulting in abnormally aggressive or seriously irresponsible conduct);
- [d] any other disorder or disability of mind.

s.1(2) MENTAL HEALTH ACT 1983

Q What is a 'place of safety'?

A
- [a] Residential accommodation provided by social services;
- [b] a hospital;
- [c] a police station;

POLICING POWERS AND POWERS OF ARREST

[d] an independent hospital or care home for mentally disordered persons, or

[e] any other suitable place where the occupier is willing to receive the person temporarily.

s.135(6) MENTAL HEALTH ACT 1983

Q For how long may a person removed to a place of safety be detained there?

A   For no more than 72 hours. This is to enable the person to be examined by a doctor and interviewed by an approved social worker, and arrangements to be made for further treatment or care.

Q Is a person detained under these provisions in police detention?

A   No, the power to remove to a place of safety is not a power of arrest and the person removed is not in police detention, even if they are taken to a police station. They are, however, treated as being 'in legal custody' for the purpose of provisions relating to escaping and assisting an escape. It is an offence to assist someone removed under s.136 to escape.

Q When may a magistrate issue a warrant to search for patients?

A   Where there is reasonable cause to suspect that a person believed to be suffering from a mental disorder ['the patient'] has been, or is being ill-treated or neglected, or is unable to care for himself/herself and is living alone, a magistrate may issue a warrant permitting a constable to enter any specified premises and remove the patient to a place of safety. The constable exercising this power must be accompanied by a doctor and a social worker.

s.135 MENTAL HEALTH ACT 1983

Q What are the rules concerning voluntary attendance at a police station?

A   Where a person voluntarily attends a police station [or anywhere where a constable is present] and is assisting with an investigation and is not under arrest he shall be:

[a] entitled to leave at will, and
[b] informed at once that he is under arrest if a decision has been made to prevent him from leaving, and

POLICING POWERS AND POWERS OF ARREST

[c] if he is under arrest at a police station and it appears that if he were released from that arrest, he would be liable to arrest for another offence, he shall be arrested for that other offence.

SS. 29, 31 PACE ACT 1984

Q After arrest, where shall a person be taken?

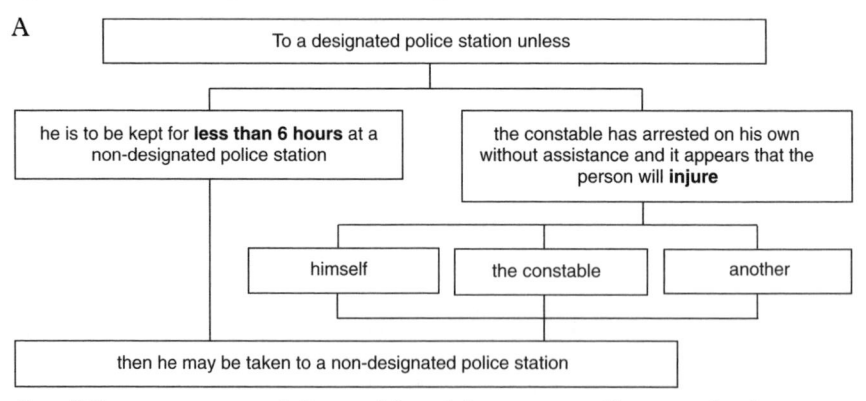

A

```
                 To a designated police station unless
                                 │
              ┌──────────────────┴──────────────────┐
   he is to be kept for less than        the constable has arrested on his own
   6 hours at a non-designated           without assistance and it appears that the
   police station                        person will injure
                                                 │
                                    ┌────────────┼────────────┐
                                 himself    the constable   another

              then he may be taken to a non-designated police station
```

Q When can you delay taking him to a police station?

A When his presence is necessary to carry out investigations that are reasonable to carry out **immediately**, e.g. checking an alibi, recovering property etc. The reason for any such delay must be recorded upon arrival at the police station.

S. 30 PACE ACT 1984

STOP AND SEARCH

Q What is the primary purpose of stop and search powers?

A To enable police officers to allay or confirm any suspicions about individuals without exercising their powers of arrest.

Q What principles govern the use of stop and search?

A Powers to stop and search must be used fairly, responsibly, with respect for people being searched and without unlawful discrimination. The Race Relations (Amendment) Act 2000 makes it unlawful for police officers to discriminate on the grounds of race, colour, ethnic origin, nationality or national origins when using their powers. The intrusion on the liberty of the person stopped or searched must be brief and detention for the purposes of a search must take place at or near the location of the stop.

CODE A PARA 1.1-1.2

Q Where there is no power to search, may an officer conduct a search if the person consents to it?

A NO. This should not be done, notwithstanding the person's agreement to it. Para 1.5 Code A states that an officer must not search a person, even with his/her consent, where no power to search is applicable. The only exception, where an officer does not require a specific power, applies to searches of persons entering sports grounds or other premises carried out with their consent given as a condition of entry.

STOP AND SEARCH

Q What are the general search powers under s.1 PACE 1984?

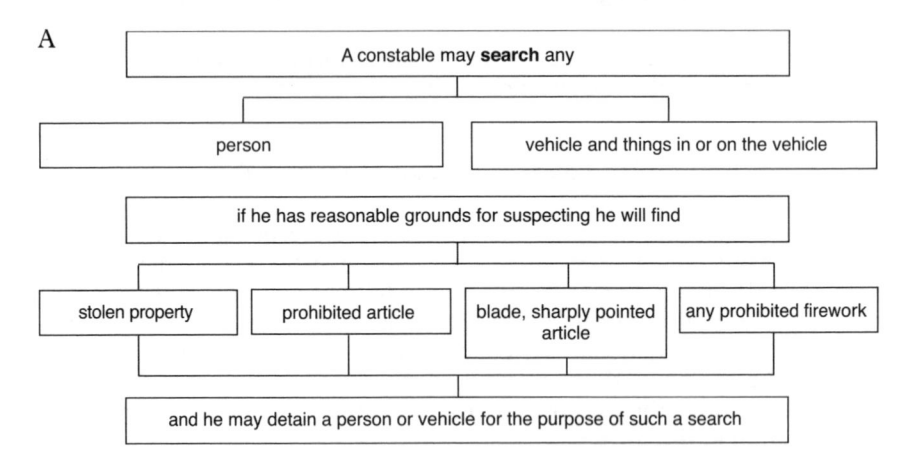

A

```
                    A constable may search any
                    ┌──────────────┴──────────────┐
                  person              vehicle and things in or on the vehicle
                    └──────────────┬──────────────┘
              if he has reasonable grounds for suspecting he will find
       ┌──────────────┬────────────┴────────────┬──────────────┐
  stolen property  prohibited article   blade, sharply pointed   any prohibited firework
                                              article
       └──────────────┴────────────┬────────────┴──────────────┘
       and he may detain a person or vehicle for the purpose of such a search
```

Q Does s.1 PACE 1984 provide a power to *stop* vehicles?

A No, only to search.

STOP AND SEARCH

Q What is meant by a 'prohibited article'?

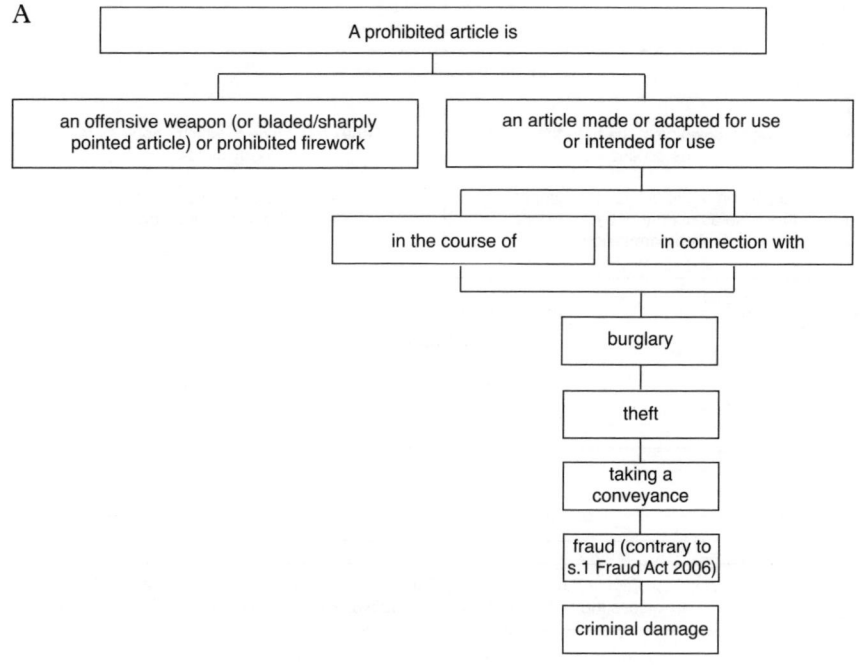

A

A prohibited article is:
- an offensive weapon (or bladed/sharply pointed article) or prohibited firework
- an article made or adapted for use or intended for use
  - in the course of
  - in connection with
    - burglary
    - theft
    - taking a conveyance
    - fraud (contrary to s.1 Fraud Act 2006)
    - criminal damage

S. 1(7) PACE ACT 1984

Q What is meant by an 'offensive weapon'?

A   Offensive weapon means any article:

    [a] made or adapted for use for causing injury to any person, or
    [b] intended for such use by the person having it with him or another.

S. 1(9) PACE ACT 1984

STOP AND SEARCH

Q Where can the power to search be exercised?

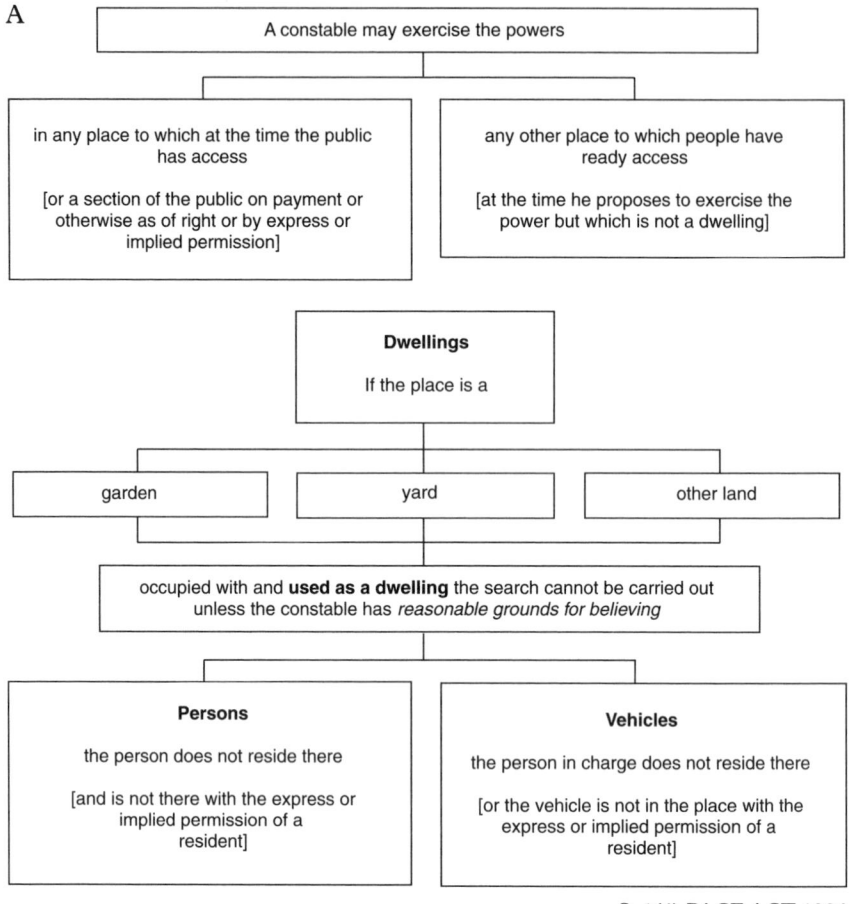

A

```
A constable may exercise the powers
```

- in any place to which at the time the public has access

  [or a section of the public on payment or otherwise as of right or by express or implied permission]

- any other place to which people have ready access

  [at the time he proposes to exercise the power but which is not a dwelling]

Dwellings

If the place is a

- garden
- yard
- other land

occupied with and **used as a dwelling** the search cannot be carried out unless the constable has *reasonable grounds for believing*

Persons

the person does not reside there

[and is not there with the express or implied permission of a resident]

Vehicles

the person in charge does not reside there

[or the vehicle is not in the place with the express or implied permission of a resident]

S. 1(4) PACE ACT 1984

STOP AND SEARCH

Q What must be done before a search is carried out?

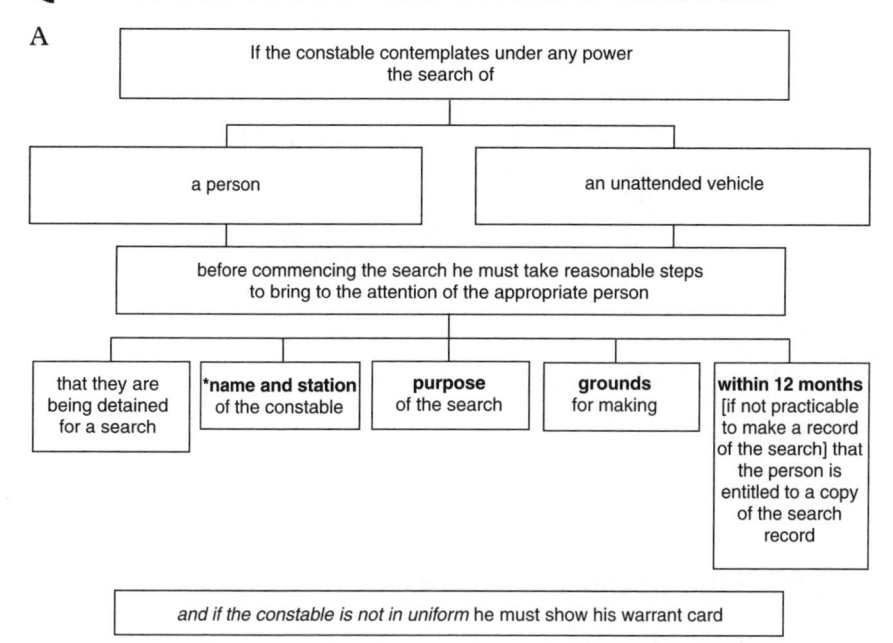

A

```
If the constable contemplates under any power
             the search of
                  │
         ┌────────┴────────┐
      a person      an unattended vehicle
         └────────┬────────┘
   before commencing the search he must take reasonable steps
        to bring to the attention of the appropriate person
```

| that they are being detained for a search | *name and station of the constable | purpose of the search | grounds for making | within 12 months [if not practicable to make a record of the search] that the person is entitled to a copy of the search record |

and if the constable is not in uniform he must show his warrant card

*In terrorism cases the requirement to provide his/her name is removed: Code A para 3.8

S. 2/3 PACE ACT 1984

Q What is meant by the 'appropriate person'?

A [a] Where a person is searched, that person.
[b] Where a vehicle is searched [or anything in or on it] the person in charge of the vehicle.

S. 2(5) PACE ACT 1984

Q What if the person does not appear to understand?

A Under para 3.11 Code A if the person to be searched, or in charge of a vehicle to be searched, does not appear to understand what is being said, or there is any doubt about the person's ability to understand English, the officer must take reasonable steps to bring information regarding the person's rights and any relevant code provisions to his/her attention. If the person is deaf or cannot understand English and is accompanied by someone, then the officer must try to establish whether that person can interpret or otherwise help the officer to give the required information.

STOP AND SEARCH

Q What should be left on a searched unattended vehicle?

A A notice stating:

[a] the vehicle has been searched;
[b] the police station to which the officer is attached [not his name];
[c] an application for compensation for damage to the vehicle can be made at [b], and
[d] the owner and person in charge of the vehicle are entitled to a copy of the search record for up to 12 months.

S. 2(6) PACE ACT 1984

Q Where should the notice be left?

A Inside the vehicle (unless it is not reasonably practicable to do so without damaging the vehicle).

S. 2(7) PACE ACT 1984

Q What does 'vehicle' include?

A Vessels, aircraft and hovercraft.

S. 2(10) PACE ACT 1984

Q What clothing can be removed in public for the purpose of a person check?

A Outer coat, jacket and gloves. (This restriction does not apply to searches elsewhere.) The Terrorism Act 2000 also allows for removal of footwear and headgear.

S. 2(9) PACE ACT 1984

Q How long can a person be detained for the purposes of a search?

A Such time as is reasonable to carry out the search at the scene or nearby.

S. 2(8) PACE ACT 1984

STOP AND SEARCH

Q What shall a search record contain?

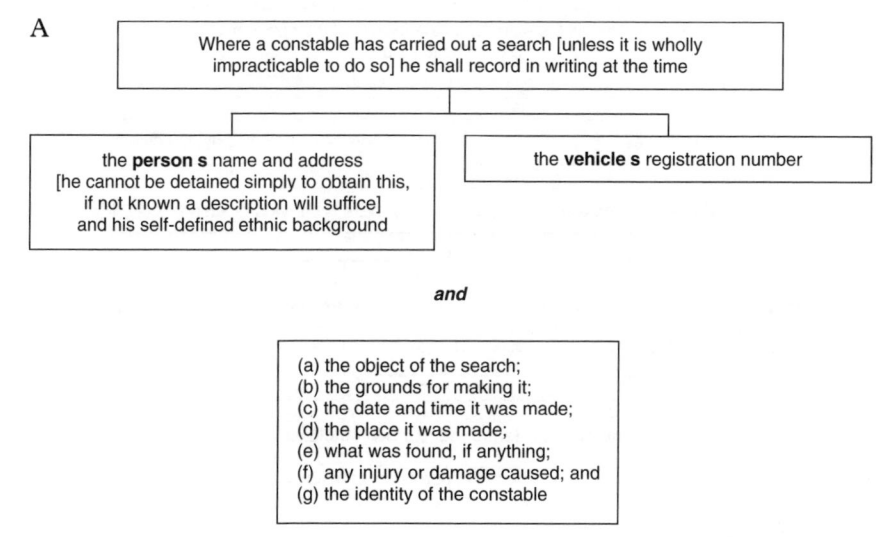

A

> Where a constable has carried out a search [unless it is wholly impracticable to do so] he shall record in writing at the time

- the **person's** name and address [he cannot be detained simply to obtain this, if not known a description will suffice] and his self-defined ethnic background
- the **vehicle's** registration number

and

> (a) the object of the search;
> (b) the grounds for making it;
> (c) the date and time it was made;
> (d) the place it was made;
> (e) what was found, if anything;
> (f) any injury or damage caused; and
> (g) the identity of the constable

S. 3 PACE ACT 1984

Q When might it be 'wholly impracticable' to make a search record at the time?

A In circumstances where there was realistically no real opportunity for the officer to make the record e.g. in situations of public disorder or where his presence was urgently required elsewhere. In such cases the officer must make the search record as soon as practicable after the search has been completed.

S. 3(2) PACE ACT 1984 & CODE A PARA 4.1

Q What record has to be kept when searching people entering football grounds?

A None. Records are required to be made only when searches are carried out in the exercise of any power to which the Codes apply. Nothing in the Codes affects the routine searching of persons entering sports grounds or other premises where their consent is a condition of entry.

STOP AND SEARCH

Q   What is a road check?

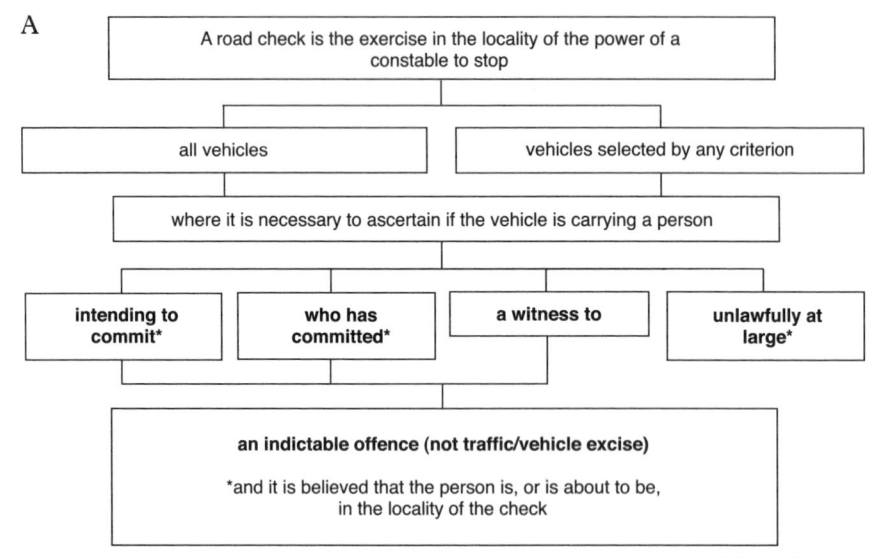

A

```
                A road check is the exercise in the locality of the power of a
                                    constable to stop

         ┌──────────────────────────┴──────────────────────────┐
              all vehicles                vehicles selected by any criterion

         where it is necessary to ascertain if the vehicle is carrying a person

   ┌──────────────┬──────────────┬──────────────┐
   intending to    who has        a witness to   unlawfully at
   commit*         committed*                    large*

                an indictable offence (not traffic/vehicle excise)

              *and it is believed that the person is, or is about to be,
                             in the locality of the check
```

S. 4 PACE ACT 1984

Q   Give an example of vehicles selected by any criterion

A   Stopping all yellow Escorts carrying three youths ... all blue VWs ... all white vans etc.

Q   Who may authorise a road check?

A   **A superintendent** (or above), in writing. Or an officer of **any rank in the case of urgency**, in which case he must, as soon as possible, make a written record of the time at which the authorisation is given and cause a superintendent (or above) to be informed.

S. 4(5)-(7) PACE ACT 1984

Q   Can a superintendent discontinue the road check when reported to him?

A   Yes, he may

   [a]   authorise it to continue, in writing, or
   [b]   discontinue the check and record in writing:

         [i]   the fact that it took place, and
         [ii] its purpose (including the relevant indictable offence).

STOP AND SEARCH

Q What are the time limits on non-urgent road checks?

A Seven days, which can be renewed (in writing) if it appears to the superintendent that it ought to continue. The check may be:

[a] continuous, or be
[b] conducted at specified times.

S. 4(11) PACE ACT 1984

Q What shall the written authorisation of a road check state?

A [a] The name of the authorising officer;
[b] the purpose of the road check; and
[c] the locality in which the vehicles are stopped.

S. 4(13) PACE ACT 1984

Q What entitlement have persons who are stopped at road checks?

A A person in charge of a vehicle stopped at a road check shall be entitled to a written statement of the purpose of the check if he applies for it not later than **12 months** from the date of being stopped.

S. 4(15) PACE ACT 1984

Q What is not a road check?

A Stopping vehicles for road traffic offences, excise offences, or the stopping of vehicles for any purpose other than those mentioned in Section 4.

STOP AND SEARCH

Q What stop powers are there under the Criminal Justice & Public Order Act 1994?

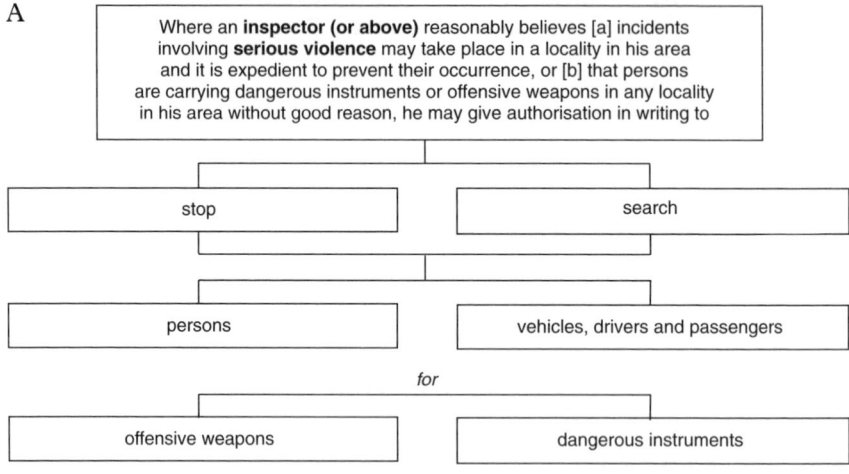

A

> Where an **inspector (or above)** reasonably believes [a] incidents involving **serious violence** may take place in a locality in his area and it is expedient to prevent their occurrence, or [b] that persons are carrying dangerous instruments or offensive weapons in any locality in his area without good reason, he may give authorisation in writing to

- stop
- search

- persons
- vehicles, drivers and passengers

for

- offensive weapons
- dangerous instruments

S. 60 CJ & PO ACT 1994

Q How long does the authorisation last?

A For no longer than appears reasonably necessary to prevent, or seek to prevent incidents of serious violence, or to deal with the problem of carrying weapons/instruments and in any event for no longer than 24 hours.

Q Can this period be extended?

A Yes, by a superintendent (or above) if

[a] violence or the carrying of instruments/weapons has occurred, or is suspected to have occurred, and
[b] the continued use of the powers is considered necessary to prevent or deal with further such activity.

The extension can be for a further 24 hours, and must be in writing.

Q Does the officer stopping and searching need reasonable suspicion to act?

A **No**. The authorisation to search is enough. The officer must be in uniform.

STOP AND SEARCH

Q What are 'dangerous instruments'?

A Bladed or sharply pointed instruments.

Q Who is entitled to a statement?

A The driver of any vehicle stopped under S. 60 is entitled to demand a written statement that the vehicle was stopped (not of 'the purpose of the check' - compare S. 4(15) PACE re road checks) provided s/he applies for one within 12 months of the day on which the vehicle was stopped. Additionally any person searched is entitled to a statement stating that s/he was searched if they apply within 12 months.

Q What are the powers to require removal of disguises?

A Where any S. 60 authorisation is in force in any locality, or if an inspector or above reasonably believes (a) that activities may take place in any locality in his area that are likely to involve the commission of offences, and (b) that it is expedient in order to control or prevent the activities, he may authorise any constable in uniform:

[a] to require any person to remove any item which the constable reasonably believes is being worn to conceal his identity;
[b] to seize any such item.

S. 60AA CJ & PO ACT 1994

Q For how long can the authorisation last?

A For no longer than appears reasonably necessary to prevent, or seek to prevent the commission of offences and in any event for no longer than 24 hours. If an inspector gives an authorisation s/he must inform a superintendent or above as soon as reasonably practicable, and this officer may direct an extension of the authorisation for a further 24 hours if crimes have been committed or suspected, and the continued use of the power is considered necessary to prevent further such activity.

Q What is the offence of failing to comply with a requirement to remove items?

A It is an offence for a person to fail to remove an item worn by him when required to do so by a constable exercising his S. 60 powers.

S. 60AA CJ & PO ACT 1994

STOP AND SEARCH

Q What is the power to set up a cordon under the Terrorism Act 2000?

A A superintendent or above may authorise the setting up of a cordon if it is considered expedient to do so for the purpose of a terrorist investigation. In cases of urgency, an officer below that rank may make the designation, but s/he must make a written record of the time at which it was made and ensure that a superintendent or above is informed as soon as reasonably practicable.

S. 33/34 TERRORISM ACT 2000

Q What directions may be given when a cordon is in place?

A A constable in uniform (including a PCSO) may

[a] order a person in a cordoned area to leave it immediately, or
[b] order a person immediately to leave premises in or adjacent to a cordoned area, or
[c] order a driver or person in charge of a vehicle in a cordoned area to immediately move it, or
[d] arrange for the removal of a vehicle from a cordoned area, or
[e] arrange for the movement of a vehicle within a cordoned area, or
[f] prohibit or restrict access to a cordoned area by pedestrians/vehicles.

S. 36 TERRORISM ACT 2000

POWERS OF ENTRY, SEARCH & SEIZURE

Q What is the procedure for applying for a search warrant?

A The application must be made with the written authority of an **inspector** unless he is not readily available and the case is **urgent** in which case the senior officer on duty may authorise the application.

The constable who makes the application must state:

[a] the grounds for the application;
[b] the Act under which it would be issued;
[c] the premises to be entered and searched;
[d] the identity of the articles/persons sought.

The application must be supported by written information. Where the application is for a warrant to enter and search on more than one occasion (multiple entry warrant) it must additionally state the ground for such a warrant and whether it is sought for an unlimited number of entries, or (if not) the maximum number of entries desired. Where the application is for an 'all premises' warrant (a warrant authorising entry to any premises occupied or controlled by a specified person) it must additionally state the ground for such a warrant, specify as many sets of premises it is desired to enter as is reasonably practicable to specify (and if not all can be specified, explain why) and identify the person in occupation/control.

SS. 15 & 16 PACE ACT 1984 & CODE B, PARA.2

Q What if the application is refused?

A Then no further application may be made unless it is supported by additional grounds.

Q How many entries may be made under a search warrant?

A One only, unless the warrant in question is a 'multiple entry' warrant, in which case it must state whether it authorises an unlimited number of entries, or is limited to a specific number.

Q For how long does a warrant last?

A Entry and search under a warrant must be within 3 months from the date of issue. After this date (or sooner if the warrant has already been executed) it should be returned to the appropriate court official.

POWERS OF ENTRY, SEARCH & SEIZURE

Q What shall the warrant specify?

A
[a] The name of the person applying for it;
[b] the date of issue;
[c] the Act under which it is issued;
[d] the premises to be searched, (and person in occupation/control in the case of all premises warrants), and
[e] identify the articles/persons sought [if possible].

Q What is the procedure for executing a search warrant?

A It shall be executed by a constable (who may be accompanied by any person so authorised by the warrant and who will have the same powers as the constable he accompanies) at a reasonable hour unless that would frustrate its purpose.

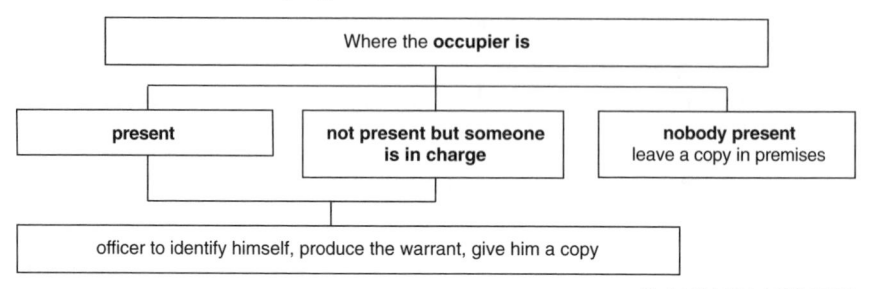

```
                    Where the occupier is
        ┌──────────────────┼──────────────────┐
     present       not present but someone   nobody present
                      is in charge         leave a copy in premises

officer to identify himself, produce the warrant, give him a copy
```

S. 16 PACE ACT 1984

Q When is an inspector's authority required for entry?

A If the warrant is an 'all premises' warrant, any premises which are not actually specified in the warrant may only be entered or searched if an inspector (or above) has so authorised, in writing. Additionally, if the warrant is a 'multiple entry' warrant, an inspector's (or above) written authority is required for second or any subsequent entries to the premises.

Q What shall be endorsed on the warrant after execution?

A
[a] Whether the articles or persons sought were found; and
[b] apart from what was sought, whether anything else was seized.

Q If a warrant is wrongly addressed can it be executed?

A No.

POWERS OF ENTRY, SEARCH & SEIZURE

Q What is the procedure for applying for a search warrant for an indictable offence?

A The constable must satisfy a JP that there are reasonable grounds for believing:

[a] an indictable offence has been committed; and
[b] there is material on the premises likely to be of substantial value to the investigation of the offence; and
[c] it is likely to be relevant evidence [ie. admissible at trial]; and
[d] that it does not consist of:

    [i] items subject to legal privilege;
    [ii] excluded material; or
    [iii] special procedure material, and
    [iv] a condition at [e] below applies

[e] [i] it is not practicable to communicate with any person entitled to grant **entry to the premises**;
    [ii] a person at [i] can be found but it is not practicable to communicate with any person entitled to grant **access to the evidence**;
    [iii] entry will not be granted unless a warrant is produced;
    [iv] the search may be frustrated or seriously prejudiced unless the constable arriving at the premises can **secure immediate entry**.

If so satisfied, the JP may grant a search warrant.

S. 8 PACE ACT 1984

POWERS OF ENTRY, SEARCH & SEIZURE

Q   What is the power to search for indictable offences?

A   This is a power to search premises following arrest for an indictable offence:

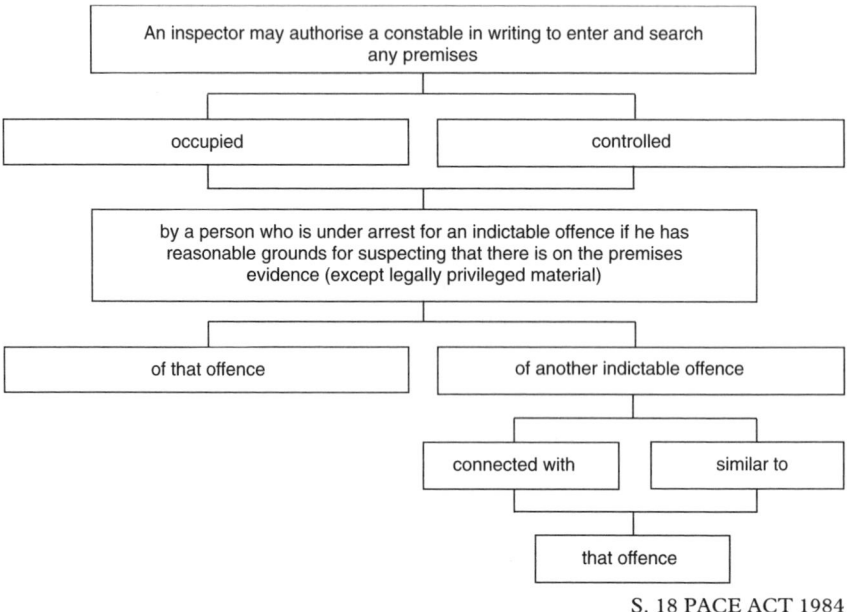

```
        An inspector may authorise a constable in writing to enter and search
                                   any premises
                          │                              │
                    ┌─────┴─────┐              ┌─────────┴─────────┐
                    │ occupied  │              │    controlled     │
                    └─────┬─────┘              └─────────┬─────────┘
                          │                              │
                          └──────────────┬───────────────┘
                                         │
        by a person who is under arrest for an indictable offence if he has
        reasonable grounds for suspecting that there is on the premises
                  evidence (except legally privileged material)
                          │                              │
                  ┌───────┴───────┐          ┌───────────┴──────────────┐
                  │ of that offence│          │ of another indictable offence│
                  └────────────────┘          └───────────┬──────────────┘
                                                          │
                                              ┌───────────┴───────────┐
                                              │                       │
                                      ┌───────┴───────┐       ┌───────┴───────┐
                                      │ connected with│       │   similar to  │
                                      └───────┬───────┘       └───────┬───────┘
                                              └───────────┬───────────┘
                                                   ┌──────┴──────┐
                                                   │ that offence│
                                                   └─────────────┘
```

S. 18 PACE ACT 1984

Q   Can a constable conduct an S. 18 search without authorisation?

A   Yes. A constable can conduct the search before taking the person to the police station if his presence is necessary for the effective investigation of the offence. He must inform an inspector as soon as practicable after the search.

Q   What must be recorded in writing regarding the search authority?

A   The grounds for the search and the nature of the evidence sought. If the occupier/controller of the premises searched is in police custody at the time the record is made it shall form part of his/her custody record.

POWERS OF ENTRY, SEARCH & SEIZURE

Q Must the occupier be informed of the reason for the search?

A Yes, so far as is possible to do so in the circumstances. Any search carried out without attempting to explain the reason to the occupier may mean the officers are not acting in the execution of their duty so that their entry may be lawfully resisted.

Q What are the powers to search after arrest for other offences?

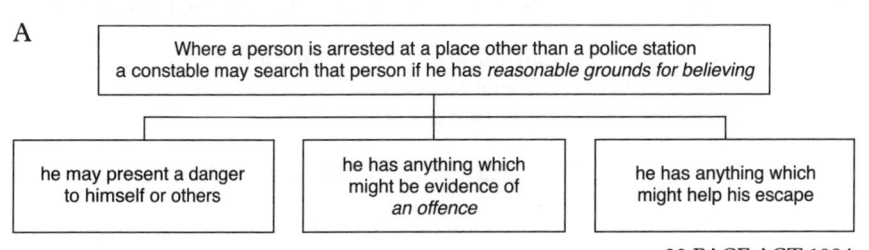

A

Where a person is arrested at a place other than a police station a constable may search that person if he has *reasonable grounds for believing*

- he may present a danger to himself or others
- he has anything which might be evidence of *an offence*
- he has anything which might help his escape

s32 PACE ACT 1984

Q What items may be seized under this power?

A A constable exercising the s.32 power may seize and retain anything he finds (other than items subject to legal privilege) if he has reasonable grounds for believing (a) the person might use it to escape from lawful custody or (b) it is evidence of an offence, or has been obtained in consequence of the commission of an offence.

s.32(9) PACE ACT 1984

Q When may premises be searched under s.32?

A A constable may enter and search any premises in which the person was when arrested or immediately before being arrested *for an indictable offence*, in order to find evidence relating to the offence for which he was arrested. The constable must have reasonable grounds for believing that such evidence is on the premises (and this must be a genuine belief, this is not a 'fishing' license).

s.32(2)(B) PACE ACT 1984

POWERS OF ENTRY, SEARCH & SEIZURE

Q What about premises containing two or more separate dwellings?

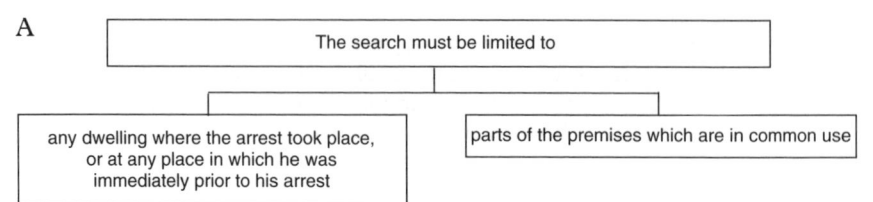

A The search must be limited to:
- any dwelling where the arrest took place, or at any place in which he was immediately prior to his arrest
- parts of the premises which are in common use

Q Outline the powers of entry under s.17 of PACE

A A constable may enter and search any premises for the purpose of:

[a] executing a warrant for arrest or committal;
[b] arresting for an indictable offence;
[c] arresting for offences under

   [i] s.1 Public Order Act 1936 (prohibition of political uniforms);
   [ii] ss.6,7,8,10 Criminal Law Act 1977 (entering and remaining on premises) **[Must be in uniform]**;
   [iii] s.4 Public Order Act 1986 (fear or provocation of violence);
   [iv] s.4 RTA 1988 (driving under influence) or s.163 RTA 1988 (failing to stop);
   [v] s.27 Transport and Works Act 1992 (drink/drugs offences);
   [vi] s.76 Criminal Justice and Public Order Act 1994 (failure to comply with interim possession order) **[uniform]**;
   [vii] the Animal Welfare Act 2006;

[d] arresting any child or young person remanded into local authority care (CYPA 1969);
[e] arresting for an offence under s.61 Animal Health Act 1981;
[f] recapturing a person unlawfully at large;
[g] saving life or limb or preventing serious damage to property

Q Must the constable have reasonable grounds for believing that the person is on the premises before entering?

A Yes (except when entering to save life or limb).

POWERS OF ENTRY, SEARCH & SEIZURE

Q May force be used under this power?

A Yes, when necessary to do so.

Q Is there a power of entry for a breach of the peace?

A Yes, where officers have a genuine and reasonable belief that a breach of the peace is happening or about to happen in the immediate future (*McLeod v. Cmr of Police for Metropolis (1994)*) and if need be by force.

Q What emergency powers of entry do employees of a fire and rescue authority have?

A Employees of a fire and rescue authority, who are authorised in writing by their authority, have the power to do anything they reasonably believe to be necessary, if they reasonably believe a fire has broken out (or is about to break out) in order to extinguish or prevent the fire. This will clearly include entering premises, if need be by force.

Q What are your powers of seizure under S. 19 of PACE?

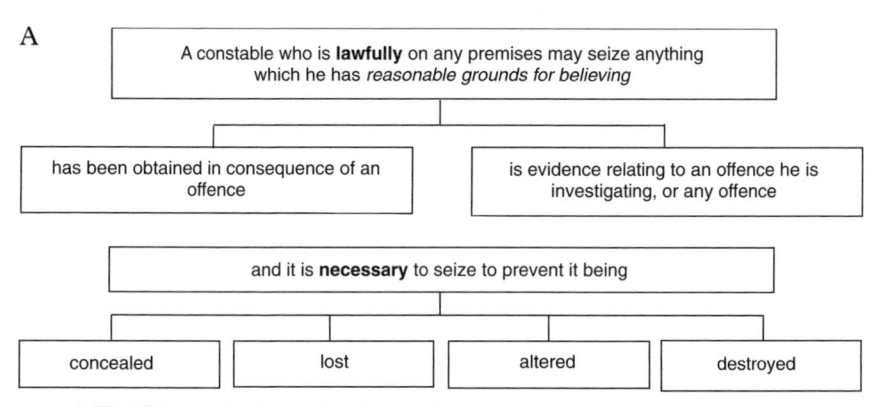

A

> A constable who is **lawfully** on any premises may seize anything which he has *reasonable grounds for believing*
>
> - has been obtained in consequence of an offence
> - is evidence relating to an offence he is investigating, or any offence
>
> and it is **necessary** to seize to prevent it being
>
> - concealed
> - lost
> - altered
> - destroyed

NB. Where the 'premises' searched are a vehicle, it can be seized.

Q Which material cannot be seized?

A [a] Legally privileged material;
[b] excluded material; and
[c] special procedure material.

POWERS OF ENTRY, SEARCH & SEIZURE

Q What is 'excluded material'?

A [a] Personal records acquired or created in the course of any trade, business, profession or other occupation or in any paid or unpaid office and which are held in confidence [eg. medical records, records made by counsellors, priests or religious advisers];
   [b] human tissue or tissue fluid which has been taken for the purpose of diagnosis or medical treatment and which are held in confidence;
   [c] journalistic material held in confidence.

Q How can access to excluded material be obtained?

A By applying to a judge for a production order under the Schedule 1 PACE procedure and PACE Code B

HARASSMENT, HOSTILITY AND ANTI-SOCIAL BEHAVIOUR

Q   Define the offence of harassment

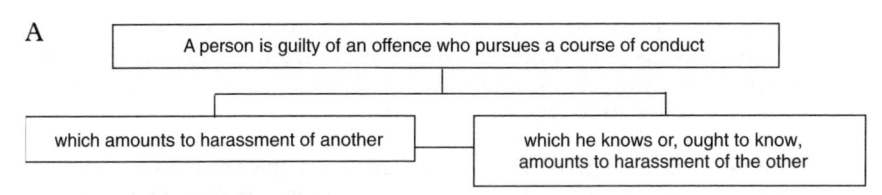

A

> A person is guilty of an offence who pursues a course of conduct
>
> — which amounts to harassment of another
> — which he knows or, ought to know, amounts to harassment of the other

Course of conduct. On at least two occasions.

Harassment. Includes alarming the person or causing them distress.

Another. Does not include companies or corporations. However individual employees etc are covered.

The test. Is objective. Did the defendant know, *or ought he have known*, that his conduct amounted to harassment? He ought to have known if a reasonable person in possession of the same information would think it amounted to harassment.

Defence. If done for the purposes of preventing or detecting crime, under a rule of law or if the conduct was reasonable.

SS. 1 & 2 PROTECTION FROM HARASSMENT ACT 1997

Q   Outline the offence of harassment of two or more people

A   A person must not pursue a course of conduct

[a]   which involves harassment of 2 or more persons, and
[b]   which he knows or ought to know involves harassment of those persons, and
[c]   by which he intends to persuade any person (whether or not one of those mentioned above)

  [i]   not to do something that he is entitled or required to do, or
  [ii] to do something that he is not under any obligation to do.

S.1A PROTECTION FROM HARASSMENT ACT 1997

Course of conduct. In relation to two or more people, this means conduct on at least one occasion in relation to each of those people. E.g. where an animal rights extremist sends a threatening letter to an employee of an animal research company and on another occasion

HARASSMENT, HOSTILITY AND ANTI-SOCIAL BEHAVIOUR

sends a threatening e-mail to another employee of the same company, intending to persuade those persons not to work for that company.

Q **Outline the offence of putting people in fear of violence**

A A person whose course of conduct causes another to fear, on at least **two occasions**, that violence will be used against him is guilty of an offence if he knows or ought to know that his course of conduct will cause the other so to fear *on each occasion*.

The test. Is objective. The defendant must know or ought to have known that his conduct would cause the other person to fear violence.

Defence. If done for the purposes of preventing or detecting crime, under a rule of law, or was reasonable for the **protection of himself/another or protection of property**.

S. 4 PROTECTION FROM HARASSMENT ACT 1997

The Secretary of State may issue a certificate that the conduct was carried out by a specified person on a specified occasion relating to:

[a] national security;
[b] the economic well-being of the UK; or
[c] the prevention and detection of serious crime

on behalf of the Crown. Such a certificate negates any offence under the 1997 Act.

S. 12 PROTECTION FROM HARASSMENT ACT 1997

Q **Who may apply for a harassment injunction?**

A Anyone who fears an actual or potential breach of S. 1 (i.e. a course of conduct amounting to harassment) or S. 1A (i.e. harassment of two or more persons) may apply to a civil court for an injunction prohibiting such conduct. Following any breach of such an injunction the claimant may apply for the issue of a warrant for the arrest of the defendant.

Ss.3 AND 3A PROTECTION FROM HARASSMENT ACT 1997

Q **Outline the breach of injunction offence under S. 3(6).**

A Where a court has granted an injunction to restrain any harassment by the defendant, if, without reasonable excuse, he does any act which is prohibited by the injunction, he is guilty of an offence.

HARASSMENT, HOSTILITY AND ANTI-SOCIAL BEHAVIOUR

Q What is a restraining order?

A An order made by a court dealing with a person convicted of a harassment offence and which is made for the purpose of protecting the victim, or any other specified person, from further harassment. It has a similar effect to a civil injunction, but can be made by a criminal court. Breach of a restraining order, without reasonable excuse, is an offence.

S. 5 PROTECTION FROM HARASSMENT ACT 1997

Q Who can apply for an anti-social behaviour order [ASBO]?

A The 'relevant authority', which is either:

[a] the local authority, or
[b] the chief officer of police of any police area forming part of the local authority, or
[c] the chief constable of the British Transport Police, or
[d] any registered social landlord providing housing in the area. They **must consult** each other before making the application.

Q When can an ASBO be applied for?

A When it appears to the relevant authority that a relevant person acted in a manner that caused, or was likely to cause, harassment, alarm or distress to one or more people who are not of the same household as the relevant person, **and** such an order is necessary to protect people in the local government area in which the consequence of that person's behaviour was suffered from further anti-social acts by that person.

Q At least how old must the 'relevant person' be?

A 10 years.

Q Can an ASBO be applied for by someone in the same household?

A No, only relevant authorities can apply, and only in relation to acts against people of a different household. The ASBO cannot be used to solve domestic disputes.

Q At which court should the application for an ASBO be made?

A Usually by way of complaint to a magistrates' court in the local government or police area concerned (which need not necessarily be where the anti-social behaviour occurred). ASBOs may also be sought in county courts when the relevant authorities are a party to the proceedings therein.

Q   What standard of proof is required?

A   ASBOs are *civil* not criminal matters but case law suggests that although generally the civil standard of proof (balance of probabilities) should apply to these proceedings, where allegations are made which might have serious consequences for the defendant the criminal standard (beyond reasonable doubt) should apply: *R (on the application of McCann) Manchester Crown Crown Court (2003)*

Q   How long does an ASBO last?

A   A minimum period of two years. It may be discharged before then with the consent of both parties.

Q   What can the ASBO prohibit?

A   Anything considered necessary to prevent further misconduct. E.g. communicating with a particular person, or creating noise (either generally or in a particular place or between particular times).

Q   Who can appeal in the case of a magistrates' court ASBO?

A   Only the defendant to the Crown Court. The applicant cannot appeal against a refusal to make an order (though it may ask the court to 'state a case' for the consideration of the Divisional Court).

Q   What power does a constable have under S. 50 Police Reform Act 2002 to require name and address?

A   If a constable in uniform has reasonable cause to believe that a person has been, or is, acting in an anti-social manner, he may require the person to give their name and address. Any person who fails to do so, or who gives false or inaccurate details, commits an offence.

NUISANCE

Q Outline the offences of dangerous activities on highways

A [a] Any person who [without lawful authority or excuse] **deposits** anything on a highway whereby a user is **injured or endangered** commits an offence;
  [b] any person who [without lawful authority or excuse] **lights a fire, discharges a firearm or firework, within 50 feet** of the centre of the highway whereby a user is **injured, interrupted or endangered** commits an offence;
  [c] any person who plays **games** on a highway to the **annoyance** of a user commits an offence;
  [d] any person who [without lawful authority or excuse] allows **offensive matter** to flow onto a highway from adjoining premises commits an offence;
  [e] any person who **lights a fire on land [not a highway]**, or directs or permits it whereby a user is **injured, interrupted or endangered** by the fire or smoke, commits an offence; and
  [f] any person who places any **rope, wire or anything** across a highway whereby it is likely to cause **danger** to a user commits an offence, unless he proves he has given adequate warning of the danger.

Fire defence. At the time the fire was lit he was satisfied that it was unlikely that users would be injured, interrupted or endangered by the fire or smoke and either:

  [i] both before and after the fire was lit he did what he reasonably could to prevent users being injured etc, or
  [ii] he had a reasonable excuse for not doing so.

SS. 161-162 HIGHWAYS ACT 1980

Q Give some examples of the common law offence of causing a public nuisance

A [a] Allowing a rave to take place in a field: *R v Shorrock* (1994);
  [b] making hundreds of nuisance telephone calls to at least 13 women: *R v Johnson* (1996);
  [c] contaminating 30 houses with noise and quarry dust: *AG v PYA Quarries Ltd.* (1957);
  [d] selling meat unfit for human consumption: *R v Stephens* (1866).

NUISANCE

Q Define the offence of exceeding noise level after service of notice

A Where a warning notice has been served in respect of noise from a dwelling, any person responsible for noise which is emitted from the dwelling during the **period specified** and exceeding the prescribed limit **measured from the complainant's dwelling**, commits an offence.

S. 4(1) NOISE ACT 1996

Defence. To show that there was a reasonable excuse for the noise.

Q Define the offence of leaving litter

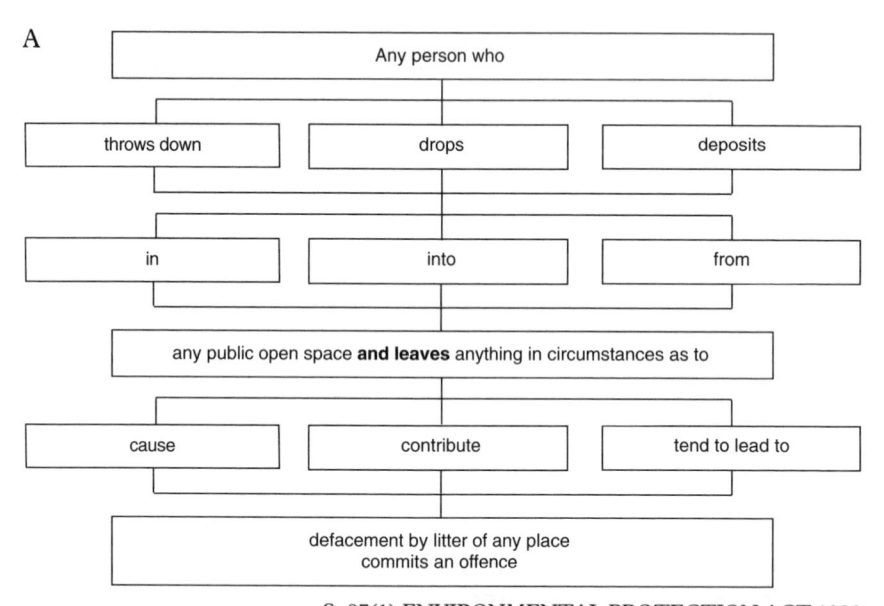

A

```
                    Any person who
                          │
       ┌──────────────────┼──────────────────┐
   throws down          drops            deposits
       └──────────────────┼──────────────────┘
                          │
       ┌──────────────────┼──────────────────┐
        in                into              from
       └──────────────────┼──────────────────┘
                          │
       any public open space and leaves anything in circumstances as to
                          │
       ┌──────────────────┼──────────────────┐
       cause            contribute       tend to lead to
       └──────────────────┼──────────────────┘
                          │
            defacement by litter of any place
                   commits an offence
```

S. 87(1) ENVIRONMENTAL PROTECTION ACT 1990

Public open space. Means where the public are entitled to access **without payment** and any **covered space** open to the public **open to the air on at least one side.**

Note. This offence can also be committed on relevant land belonging to: local authority, the Crown, statutory undertakers [railway, tramway, docks etc] and designated educational institutions.

NUISANCE

Defence. When authorised by law or with the consent of the land owner.

Litter. Includes animal droppings.

Q **Define the offence of throwing fireworks into a highway or street**

A If any person throws, casts or fires any fireworks in or into any highway, street, thoroughfare, or public place, he shall be guilty of an offence.

S. 80 EXPLOSIVES ACT 1875

Q **Outline the possession of fireworks offences**

A It is an offence for any person under 18 to possess (unless exempted) an adult firework in a public place. It is also an offence for any person (of any age) to possess (unless exempted) a category 4 firework.

REGS 3 & 4 FIREWORKS REGULATIONS 2003

Fireworks. The definitions and categories of fireworks are set out in the British Standards Specification BS 7114. Adult fireworks are generally those which have some explosive material except, for example, caps, cracker snaps, party poppers, sparklers etc. Category 4 fireworks are certain large powerful fireworks. General exemptions are provided for those who have such fireworks in the course of their work or business, or are properly authorised to conduct displays.

Q **Outline the offence of begging**

A It is a summary offence under the Vagrancy Act 1824 to beg or gather alms in a street or public place. Caselaw indicates that the Act is intended to deal with conduct that forces passers-by to deal with the defendant's activities rather than simply ignoring it (e.g. 'aggressive' begging), and it is necessary to prove more than a single act of approaching a person and asking for money.

OFFENCES INVOLVING COMMUNICATIONS

Q Outline the offence of bomb threats (placing or sending articles)

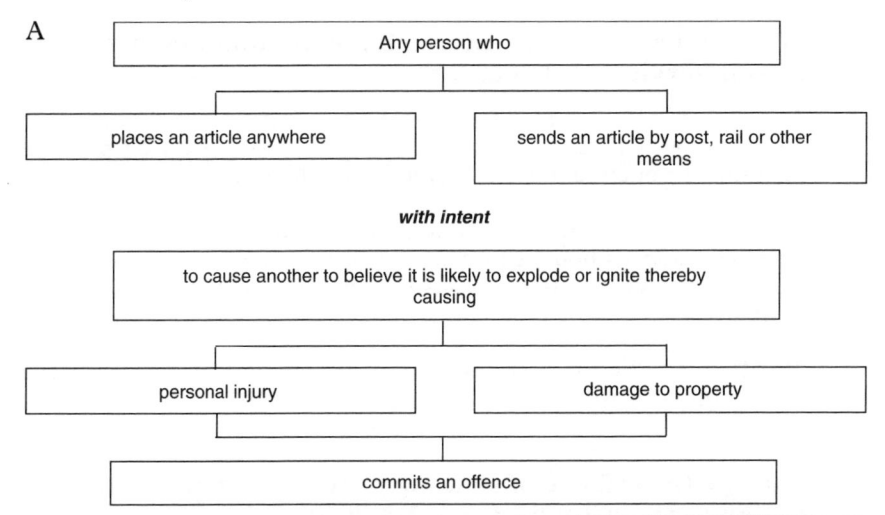

A

```
                        Any person who
                              │
            ┌─────────────────┴─────────────────┐
   places an article anywhere        sends an article by post, rail or other
                                                 means
            └─────────────────┬─────────────────┘
                        with intent
                              │
        to cause another to believe it is likely to explode or ignite thereby
                            causing
                              │
            ┌─────────────────┴─────────────────┐
       personal injury                    damage to property
            └─────────────────┬─────────────────┘
                      commits an offence
```

S. 51(1) CRIMINAL LAW ACT 1977

Q Define the offence of communicating hoax bomb threats

A A person who communicates information which he knows or believes to be false intending to induce in any person a belief that a bomb or anything liable to explode is in any place, commits an offence.

S. 51(2) CRIMINAL LAW ACT 1977

Q Outline the offence of placing or sending substances under the Anti-terrorism, Crime and Security Act 2001

A

S. 114(1) ANTI-TERRORISM, CRIME AND SECURITY ACT 2001

Q Outline the offence of hoax threats involving noxious substances

A A person is guilty of an offence if he communicates any information which he knows or believes to be false with the intention of inducing in a person anywhere a belief that a noxious substance or other noxious thing is likely to be present (whether at the time of the communication or later) in any place and thereby endanger human life or create a serious risk to human health.

S. 114(2) ANTI-TERRORISM, CRIME AND SECURITY ACT 2001

OFFENCES INVOLVING COMMUNICATIONS

Future threats. Note that this offence covers both present and future threats, whereas the equivalent offence concerning bomb hoaxes covers only present threats (e.g. 'there is a bomb in the city' not 'there will be a bomb next week').

Q **Outline the offence of interfering with mail under the Postal Services Act 2000**

A Any person who, without reasonable excuse, intentionally delays or opens a postal packet in the course of its transmission by post, or intentionally opens a mailbag, commits an offence.

Further, a person commits an offence if, intending to act to a person's detriment and without reasonable excuse, he opens a postal packet which he knows or reasonably suspects has been incorrectly delivered to him.

No offence. Where the actions were carried out under a lawful warrant or statutory provision.

S. 84 POSTAL SERVICES ACT 2000

Q **Outline the offence of sending prohibited articles by post under S. 85 Postal Services Act 2000**

A It is an offence to send by post a postal packet which encloses any creature, article or thing of any kind which is *likely to injure* other postal packets in the post or any postal operator (unless the contents are permitted by the postal operator concerned).

It is also an offence to send by post a postal packet which encloses:

[a] any indecent or obscene print, painting, photograph, lithograph, engraving, cinematograph film or other record of a picture or pictures, book, card or written communication, or
[b] any other indecent or obscene article

or to send any postal packet which has on the cover any words, marks or designs which are of an indecent or obscene character.

Q **Outline the postal obstruction offences**

A A person who, without reasonable excuse, obstructs a postal worker, or whilst in any post office or related premises obstructs the business of a postal provider, commits an offence. It is also an offence to fail to leave postal premises when required to do so by a postal worker who reasonably suspects him of committing an obstruction offence.

S. 88 POSTAL SERVICES ACT 2000

OFFENCES INVOLVING COMMUNICATIONS

Q Outline the offence under S. 1 of the Malicious Communications Act 1988

A Any person who sends to another a letter, electronic communication or any other article which he intends should cause distress or anxiety to the recipient or another conveying:

[a] a message which is indecent or grossly offensive;
[b] a threat; or
[c] information which he knows or believes is false
[d] any article or e-communication which is, in whole or part, of an indecent or grossly offensive nature commits an offence.

Defence. It is a defence to prove that the threat was used to reinforce a demand which he had reasonable grounds for making and the threat was the proper means of reinforcing demand.

Sends. Includes transmitting and would cover putting dog faeces through a neighbour's letterbox.

Q Outline the offence of improper use of public electronic communications network

A A person who:

[a] sends by means of a **public** electronic communications network, a message or matter that is grossly offensive or indecent, obscene or menacing; or
[b] for the purpose of causing annoyance, inconvenience or needless anxiety to another, sends (or causes to be sent) a message or matter that he knows to be false, or persistently makes use of a public electronic communications network for that purpose commits an offence.

S. 127 COMMUNICATION ACT 2003

Note. This offence applies to 'nuisance' calls on public systems such as the public telephone system or internet. It does not apply to internal calls in the workplace.

Persistent misuse. Requires proof of sufficient occasions to amount either to a pattern of behaviour, or recklessness as to whether someone suffers anxiety etc.

OFFENCES INVOLVING COMMUNICATIONS

Q **Outline the offence of sending unsolicited publications**

A It is a summary offence to send unsolicited material or advertising material which describes or illustrates human sexual techniques.

Prosecution. The consent of the DPP is required for prosecution.

S. 4 UNSOLICITED GOODS AND SERVICES ACT 1971

TERRORISM AND ASSOCIATED OFFENCES

Q   What is 'terrorism'?

A   The use or threat of action, whether inside or outside the UK, designed to influence government or intimidate the public (or a section of it) and made to advance a political, religious, racial or ideological cause which (a) involves serious violence against a person, or (b) involves serious damage to property, or (c) endangers another person's life, or (d) creates a serious risk to the health or safety of the public or a section of it, or (e) is designed seriously to interfere with or seriously to disrupt an electronic system.

s.1 Terrorism Act 2000

Q   Is there any difference when firearms or explosives are used?

A   Where the 'action' involves the use of firearms or explosives it is not necessary that it be designed to influence government or intimidate the public, merely that it be made to advance a cause. The shooting of a high-profile public figure might therefore be covered. 'Firearm' here includes air weapons.

Q   What are 'proscribed' organisations?

A   'Proscribed' means 'prohibited' and the Terrorism Act 2000 allows the Secretary of State to proscribe certain organisations because of their terrorist activity or support for terrorism. A number of offences under the Act relate to such organisations and are punishable by ten years' imprisonment on indictment.

TERRORISM AND ASSOCIATED OFFENCES

Q Summarise the principal offences concerning proscribed organisations

A [a] Belonging or professing to belong to a proscribed organisation (s.11(1));
[b] inviting support for a proscribed organisation (s.12(1));
[c] arranging or managing (or assisting) a meeting of 3 or more people (in public or private) which the defendant knows is

  [i] to support a proscribed organisation;
  [ii] to further the activities of a proscribed organisation, or
  [iii] to be addressed by a person who belongs or professes to belong to a proscribed organisation (s.12(2))

[d] addressing a meeting to encourage support for, or to further the activities of, a proscribed organisation (s.12(3)).

Terrorism Act 2000

Q Outline the offence of failing to disclose information about acts of terrorism

A Where a person has information which *he knows or believes* might be of material assistance (a) in preventing the commission by another of an act of terrorism, or (b) in securing the apprehension, prosecution or conviction of another person, in the UK, for an offence involving the commission, preparation or instigation of an act of terrorism, he commits an offence if he does not disclose the information as soon as reasonably practicable.

s.38B Terrorism Act 2000

Q To whom should relevant information be disclosed?

A To a police officer. (In Northern Ireland it may alternatively be disclosed to a member of HM forces).

Q What is the defence to failing to disclose?

A Reasonable excuse for not making the disclosure.

Q Outline the two 'tipping off' offences under the Terrorism Act 2000

A [1] Where a person *knows or has reasonable cause to suspect* that a constable is conducting (or proposes to conduct) a terrorist investigation, it is an offence to disclose to another anything likely to prejudice the investigation, or interfere with material which is likely to be relevant. [2] Where a person *knows or has reasonable cause to suspect* that a disclosure has been or will be made, it is an offence to disclose to another anything likely to prejudice any resulting investigation, or interfere with material likely to be relevant.

s.39 Terrorism Act 2000

Q **What are the defences to the tipping off offences?**

A That the person did not know and had no reasonable cause to suspect that the disclosure/interference was likely to affect a terrorist investigation; or that they had a reasonable excuse for the disclosure/interference.

Q **Certain offences under the Terrorism Act 2006 require proof that acts 'glorify' terrorism. What does this mean?**

A Glorification includes any form of praise or celebration which suggests to the public that the conduct being glorified should be emulated by them.

Q **Outline the power to arrest given by s.41 Terrorism Act 2000**

A A constable may arrest without warrant (anywhere in the UK) a person whom he reasonably suspects to be a terrorist.

Q **What is a 'terrorist'?**

A A person who (a) has committed one of the main terrorism offences under the Act; or (b) is or has been concerned in the commission, preparation or instigation of acts of terrorism.

Q **What additional powers does s.43 of the Act provide?**

A The power to stop and search anyone whom the constable reasonably suspects to be a terrorist to discover whether they have anything in their possession which may constitute evidence that they are a terrorist; and to seize and retain any such thing.

Q **The Prevention of Terrorism Act 2005 introduced 'control orders'. What are they?**

A Orders which are designed to impose restrictions on an individual's ability to engage in any terrorism-related activity. Restrictions might concern, for example, the person's movement to or within specified areas, their place of abode, their communications and associations, and their possession or use of certain property. It is an offence to contravene an obligation imposed by a control order.

TERRORISM AND ASSOCIATED OFFENCES

Q Outline the offence of causing an explosion likely to endanger life or property

A A person in the UK (or a UK citizen in the Republic of Ireland) who unlawfully and maliciously causes by any explosive substance an explosion of a nature likely to endanger life or to cause serious injury to property (whether or not any such injury is actually caused), is guilty of an offence.

s.2 EXPLOSIVE SUBSTANCES ACT 1881

Explosive substance. Includes any materials for making any explosive substance, and any apparatus used. Also includes fireworks, petrol bombs, shotguns, electronic timers, gelignite with a fuse and detonator.

Prosecution. The consent of the Attorney-General (or Solicitor-General) is required.

Q Outline the offence of attempting to cause an explosion or keeping explosive with intent

A A person in the UK or a dependency (or a UK citizen elsewhere) who unlawfully and maliciously (a) does any act with intent to cause, or conspires to cause, by an explosive substance an explosion of a nature likely to endanger life, or cause serious injury to property (whether in the UK or elsewhere), or (b) makes or has in his possession/control an explosive substance with intent by means thereof to endanger life, or cause serious injury to property (in the UK or elsewhere), or to enable any other person so to do, commits an offence (whether or not any explosion actually occurs).

s.3 EXPLOSIVE SUBSTANCES ACT 1883

Prosecution. The consent of the Attorney-General (or Solicitor-General) is required.

Q Outline the offence of making or possessing explosive under suspicious circumstances

A Any person who makes or knowingly has in his possession/control any explosive substance under such circumstances as to give rise to a reasonable suspicion that he is not making it or does not have it in his possession/control for a lawful object, is guilty of an offence (unless he can show that he did in fact make/have it for a lawful object).

s.4 EXPLOSIVE SUBSTANCES ACT 1883

Reasonable suspicion. Means would give rise to suspicion in a reasonable and objective bystander.

Lawful object. Requires a positive object that is lawful. 'Mere curiosity' not sufficient (in a case where defendant claimed he had made a pipe bomb using explosives taken from fireworks just out of curiosity and not for a criminal purpose. Court rejected the idea that curiosity could be a lawful object in making a lethal bomb). It is not necessary to show that the defendant had any criminal intent or unlawful purpose in having the items.

Prosecution. The consent of the Attorney-General (or Solicitor-General) is required.

Q   **Summarise the gunpowder offences under the Offences Against the Person Act 1861**

A   It is an offence to explode gunpowder to cause bodily harm; to throw or place gunpowder or corrosive fluid with intent to cause bodily harm; to place gunpowder or explosives near buildings or vessels with intent to cause bodily injury; and to possess or make gunpowder, explosives or other noxious things, with intent to enable any other person to commit an offence under the Act.

Q   **Outline the offence of interfering with contractual relationships so as to harm animal research organisations**

A   A person ('A') commits an offence if, with the intention of harming an animal research organisation, he –

   [a]   does a criminal act (or a civil wrong causing loss or damage), or
   [b]   threatens that he or somebody else will do such an act,

   in circumstances in which that act or threat is intended or likely to cause a second person ('B') to take any of the following steps:

   [i]   not to perform any contractual obligation owed by B to a third person ('C');
   [ii] to terminate any contract B has with C;
   [iii] not to enter into a contract with C.
         s.145(1) SERIOUS ORGANISED CRIME AND POLICE ACT 2005

   Prosecution. The consent of the DPP is required.

PUBLIC DISORDER

Q **What is a Breach of the Peace?**

A This is a common law 'complaint' (not a criminal offence) which concerns minor disturbances to public order. According to *R v. Howell (1982)* a breach is occasioned when an act is done or threatened which

  [a] harms a person or, in his presence, his property; or
  [b] which is likely to cause such harm; or
  [c] which puts someone in fear of such harm.

Q **What are the consequences of it not being a criminal offence?**

A Although the common law does provide a power of arrest for breach of the peace (and also the power to intervene or detain, if necessary by force, in order to prevent likely breaches) any person arrested for a breach of the peace is not technically in police detention and there is no power to bail. However, case law suggests that it is good practice for people arrested and detained for breach of the peace to be treated in accordance with PACE, and also cautioned. A person may be held until any likelihood of a recurrence of the breach has gone or be brought before a court as soon as possible to be 'bound over'.

Q **What is the power of arrest for a Breach of the Peace?**

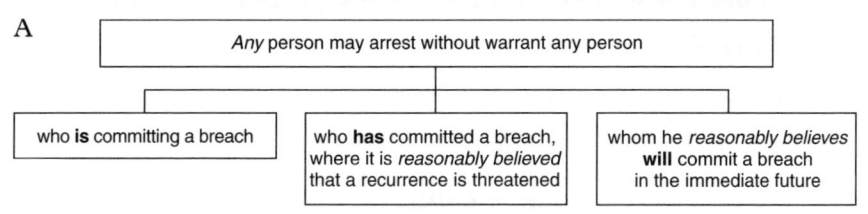

A

Any person may arrest without warrant any person

- who **is** committing a breach
- who **has** committed a breach, where it is *reasonably believed* that a recurrence is threatened
- whom he *reasonably believes* **will** commit a breach in the immediate future

Q **When can the power of arrest be exercised?**

A In *Bibby v. CC of Essex (2000)* the Court of Appeal held that the power to arrest for breach of the peace must only be exercised in the following circumstances:

  [a] where there is clearly a real and present threat to the peace;
  [b] the threat is coming from the person to be arrested;
  [c] their conduct must be clearly interfering with the rights of another; and
  [d] that conduct is unreasonable.

PUBLIC DISORDER

Q Can a Breach of the Peace take place on private premises?

A Yes. Breaches can take place anywhere, public or private (and if in private there is no requirement to show that the disturbance affected members of the public outside the property: *McQuade v. CC of Humberside Police (2001)*), and the power to arrest can be exercised anywhere. A constable may enter premises to prevent a breach and remain on site in order to do so. This is a completely separate power of entry to those contained in PACE.

Q Define riot

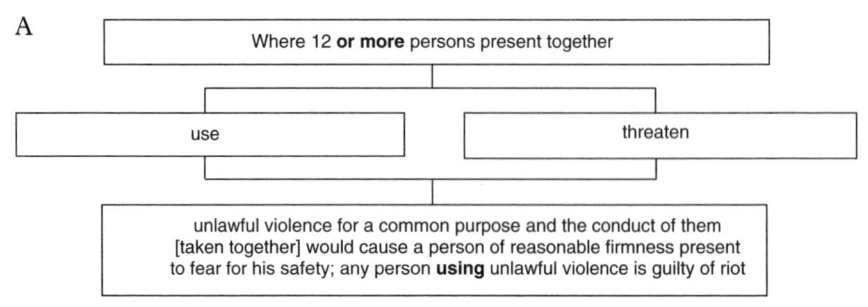

A

```
            Where 12 or more persons present together
                           │
              ┌────────────┴────────────┐
             use                      threaten
              └────────────┬────────────┘
    unlawful violence for a common purpose and the conduct of them
    [taken together] would cause a person of reasonable firmness present
    to fear for his safety; any person using unlawful violence is guilty of riot
```

S.1 PUBLIC ORDER ACT 1986

Q Whose consent is required for the prosecution of riot?

A The DPP's.

Q Where can riot take place?

A Anywhere, public or private.

Q What does 'violence' include?

A Violence towards persons or property. It is not restricted to conduct causing or intended to cause injury or damage but includes any other violent conduct, e.g. throwing a missile of a kind capable of causing injury to a person.

S. 8 PUBLIC ORDER ACT 1986

PUBLIC DISORDER

Q Does 'a person of reasonable firmness' need to be present at the scene?

A No. The Act makes it clear that the 'person of reasonable firmness present at the scene' referred to in the offence does not actually need to exist. The Act simply requires the violent conduct in question to be of the kind that *would* cause an ordinary person of reasonable fortitude to be frightened *had* they been present.

Q What mens rea must be proved to convict a person of riot?

A Not only must it be proved that the defendant *used* unlawful violence for a common purpose (rather than merely threatened it) but also that he ***intended*** to use such violence or was ***aware*** that his conduct may have been violent.

Q What if the defendant was unaware of what he was doing because he was drunk?

A Section 5 of the Public Order Act 1986 states that 'a person whose awareness is impaired by intoxication shall be taken to be aware of that which he would be aware if not intoxicated, unless he shows either that his intoxication was *not self-induced* or that it was caused solely by the taking or administration of a substance in the course of *medical treatment*.' In other words, a drunken person (whether drunk through alcohol, drugs or other means) will be treated as if he had been sober, and if a sober person would have been aware then the drunk will be taken to have been aware, and will not escape liability. However, if the drunkenness can be proved to have been non-voluntary e.g. the result of spiked drinks (Mickey Finns) or a consequence of medication, then the required mens rea will be negated and the drunken defendant cannot be convicted.

PUBLIC DISORDER

Q Define violent disorder

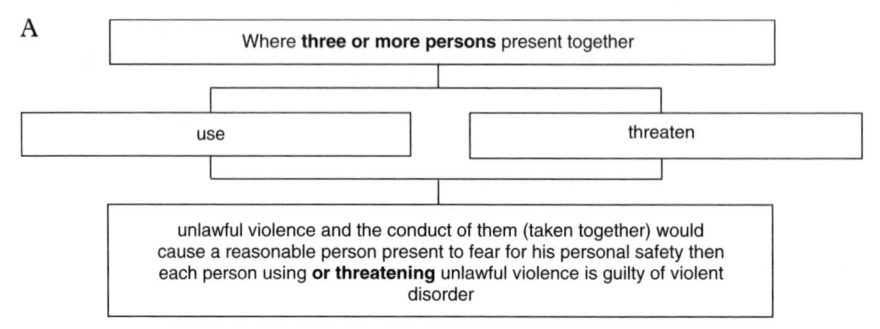

A Where **three or more persons** present together — **use** or **threaten** unlawful violence and the conduct of them (taken together) would cause a reasonable person present to fear for his personal safety then each person using **or threatening** unlawful violence is guilty of violent disorder

S. 2 PUBLIC ORDER ACT 1986

Q Define affray

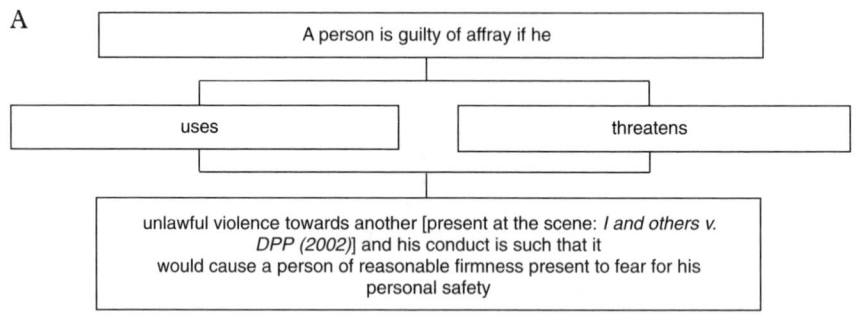

A A person is guilty of affray if he **uses** or **threatens** unlawful violence towards another [present at the scene: *I and others v. DPP (2002)*] and his conduct is such that it would cause a person of reasonable firmness present to fear for his personal safety

S. 3 PUBLIC ORDER ACT 1986

Q Can words alone constitute a threat?

A No. But words accompanied by action e.g. shaking fist or threatening with a dog, would be sufficient. Compare this with violent disorder, where words alone may well amount to a sufficient threat.

Q What is different about the definition of 'violence' in the context of affray?

A Unlike for the offences of riot and violent disorder, 'violence' here does not include violence towards property.

PUBLIC DISORDER

Q Compare riot, violent disorder and affray

A

Attribute	Riot	Violent disorder	Affray
Minimum number	12	3	1
Present together	Yes	Yes	N/A
Common purpose	Yes	Not required	N/A
Unlawful violence property	Person or property	Person or property	Personal only
Reasonable person who fears for his safety	Need not be present	Need not be present	Need not be present but the threat of unlawful violence must be towards a person present
Who is guilty?	those who actually use violence	those who use or threaten with violence	those who use or threaten with violence
Intoxication defence?	Only if medication or Mickey Finns	Only if medication or Mickey Finns	Only if medication or Mickey Finns
Private or public	Yes	Yes	Yes

PUBLIC DISORDER

Q Define S. 4 fear or provocation of violence

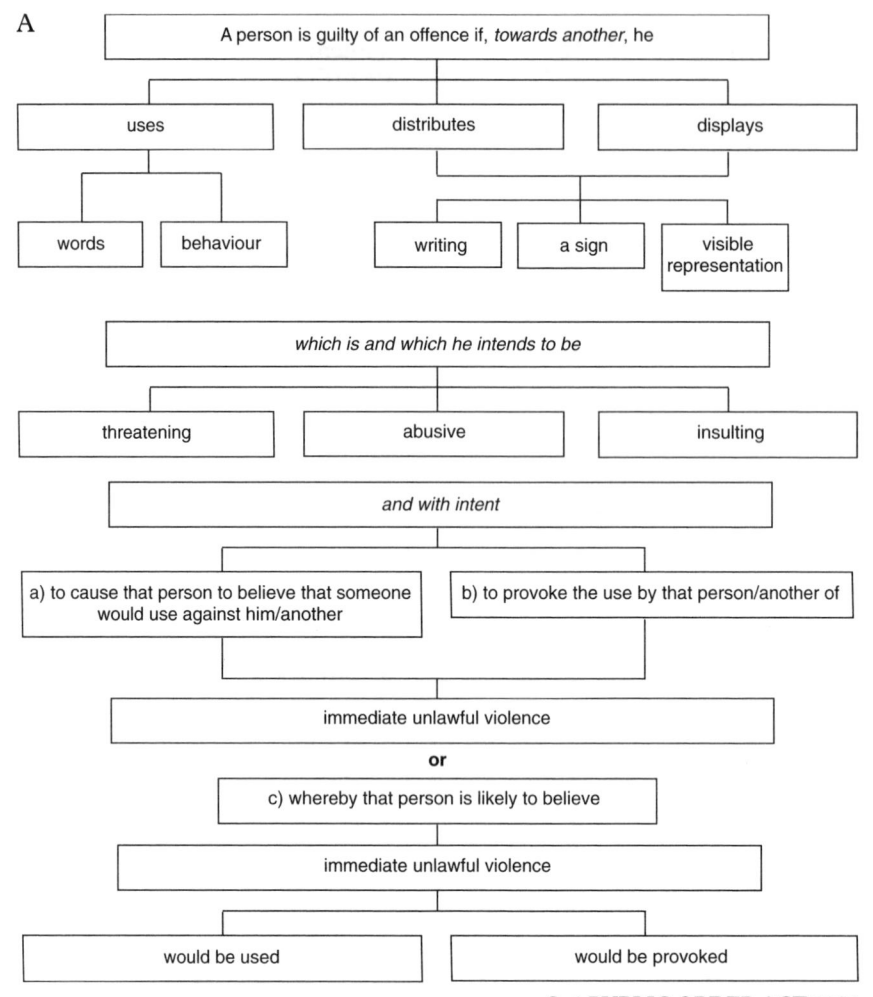

A

A person is guilty of an offence if, *towards another*, he

- **uses**
  - words
  - behaviour
- **distributes**
  - writing
  - a sign
  - visible representation
- **displays**
  - writing
  - a sign
  - visible representation

which is and which he intends to be

- threatening
- abusive
- insulting

and with intent

a) to cause that person to believe that someone would use against him/another

b) to provoke the use by that person/another of

immediate unlawful violence

or

c) whereby that person is likely to believe

immediate unlawful violence

- would be used
- would be provoked

S. 4 PUBLIC ORDER ACT 1986

No offence where the things are done **inside a dwelling** and the other person is inside that or *another* dwelling.

PUBLIC DISORDER

Q Define a 'dwelling'

A Any structure or part thereof **occupied as a person's home** or as living accommodation (whether the occupation is separate or shared with others), but not any parts not so occupied (e.g. communal landings, stairwells, lobbies, garages etc.).

Structure includes tent, caravan, vehicle, vessel or other temporary or moveable structure, e.g. a treehouse occupied by an eco-protestor.

Q Define the S. 4A intentional harassment, alarm or distress offence

A It is an offence, **with intent** to cause a person harassment, alarm or distress, to:

[a] use threatening, abusive or insulting words or behaviour, or disorderly behaviour, or
[b] display any writing, sign or other visible representation which is threatening, abusive or insulting, *thereby causing* a person harassment, alarm or distress.

S. 4A PUBLIC ORDER ACT 1986

Defence. To prove that he was inside a dwelling and had no reason to believe that the activities would be heard or seen by a person outside that or any other dwelling, or his conduct was reasonable.

No offence. If the activity is by a person inside a dwelling and the other person is inside that or another dwelling.

Q Define the S. 5 harassment, alarm or distress offence

A It is an offence to:

[a] use threatening, abusive or insulting words or behaviour, or disorderly conduct;
[b] display any writing, sign or other visible representation which is threatening, abusive or insulting **within the hearing or sight** of a person likely to be caused harassment, alarm or distress.

Mens rea. The offender must **intend** his actions or **be aware** of their likely consequences (but it is not necessary for them to actually cause any harassment, alarm or distress [compare the S. 4A offence]).

No offence if the activity is by a person **inside a dwelling** and the other person is inside that or another dwelling.

PUBLIC DISORDER

Defence:
- [a] he had no reason to believe that anyone likely to be caused harassment, alarm or distress could **hear or see** his activities;
- [b] he was **inside a dwelling** and he had no reason to believe he would be heard or seen by anyone outside that or any other dwelling; or
- [c] his conduct was reasonable.

Q What effect has the Crime and Disorder Act 1998 made on racially aggravated offences?

A The Act does not create new offences but instead sets out the circumstances when an offence is racially aggravated. Post 11 September 2001, the Anti-terrorism, Crime and Security Act 2001 has extended the definition to include religiously aggravated offences.

Q How does the Powers of Criminal Courts (Sentencing) Act 2000 relate to the above?

A The Act can increase the penalties for offences where they are shown to be racially or religiously aggravated.

Q Which offences can be deemed to be racially or religiously aggravated?

A
- [a] Wounding and GBH: Crime & Disorder Act 1998 S. 29(1) (a);
- [b] ABH: Crime & Disorder Act 1998 S. 29(1)(b);
- [c] common assault: Crime & Disorder Act 1998 S. 29(1)(c);
- [d] simple criminal damage: Crime & Disorder Act 1998 S. 30(1);
- [e] causing fear or provocation: S. 4 Public Order Act 1986;
- [f] intentional harassment, alarm or distress: S. 4A Public Order Act 1986;
- [g] causing harassment, alarm or distress: S. 5 Public Order Act 1986;
- [h] harassment and putting in fear of violence (Protection from Harassment Act 1997 offences): Crime & Disorder Act 1998 SS. 32(1)(a) & (b).

PUBLIC DISORDER

Q Define racially or religiously aggravated

A [a] A **demonstration of hostility** by the defendant based on the victim's membership or presumed membership of a racial or religious group:

  [i]   immediately before the offence;
  [ii] at the time of the offence; or
  [iii] immediately after committing the offence; or

  [b] **motivation by hostility** of the defendant based on the victim's membership of a racial or religious group.

Q What is a S. 42 direction?

A A power under the Criminal Justice & Police Act 2001 to deal with harassment of people in their homes. The **senior officer at the scene** may give directions to people in the vicinity to do anything the officer specifies as being necessary to prevent harassment, alarm or distress of the resident, such as leaving the vicinity (either immediately or after a specified time). The direction may be given orally and the officer giving it need not be in uniform. It is an offence to knowingly fail to comply with a requirement in a s. 42 direction or to return to the vicinity of the premises in question within the period of the direction (being up to three months, the precise length of time having been specified in the direction).

Q When does the power to give a S. 42 direction arise?

A Where a person is outside or in the vicinity of any premises used by any individual (not a company) as his/her dwelling, and a constable reasonably believes

  [a] the person is there to persuade the resident to

  [i]   not do something they are entitled to do, or
  [ii] do something they are not obliged to do, and

  [b] that that person's presence amounts to or may result in harassment of the resident or is likely to cause them alarm or distress.

PUBLIC DISORDER

Q Outline the offence of causing a nuisance on NHS premises.

A A person commits an offence if –

[a] the person causes, without reasonable excuse and while on NHS premises, a nuisance or disturbance to an NHS staff member who is working there or otherwise there in connection with work,
[b] the person refuses, without reasonable excuse, to leave the NHS premises when asked to do so by a constable or an NHS staff member, and
[c] the person is not on the NHS premises for the purpose of obtaining medical advice, treatment or care for himself or herself.
s.119 CRIMINAL JUSTICE AND IMMIGRATION ACT 2008

Power to remove. A constable may remove from the NHS premises (using reasonable force if necessary) anyone he reasonably suspects of committing or having committed this offence.

Q Define the racial hatred offence under S. 18 Public Order Act 1986

A A person who uses threatening, abusive or insulting words or behaviour, or displays any written material which is threatening, abusive or insulting commits an offence if:

[a] **he intends** thereby to stir up racial hatred, or
[b] **it is likely** to stir up racial hatred.

No offence where the activity is **inside a dwelling** and is not heard or seen except by persons in that or *another* dwelling.

Defence. For the accused to prove he was inside a dwelling and had no reason to believe the behaviour would be heard or seen by a person outside that or any other dwelling.

Prosecution. The consent of the Attorney-General (or Solicitor-General) is required.

Q Define the S. 19 racial hatred- publishing, distributing written material offence

A A person who publishes or distributes written material which is threatening, abusive or insulting commits an offence if:

[a] **he intends** to stir up racial hatred, or

PUBLIC DISORDER

[b] **it is likely** to stir up racial hatred.

S. 19 PUBLIC ORDER ACT 1986

Defence. For a person who is not shown to have intended to stir up racial hatred to prove **he was not aware of the contents** of the material and did not suspect, or have a reason to suspect, it was threatening, abusive or insulting.

Prosecution. The consent of the Attorney-General (or Solicitor-General) is required.

Q What are the requirements of the written notice to be given for public processions?

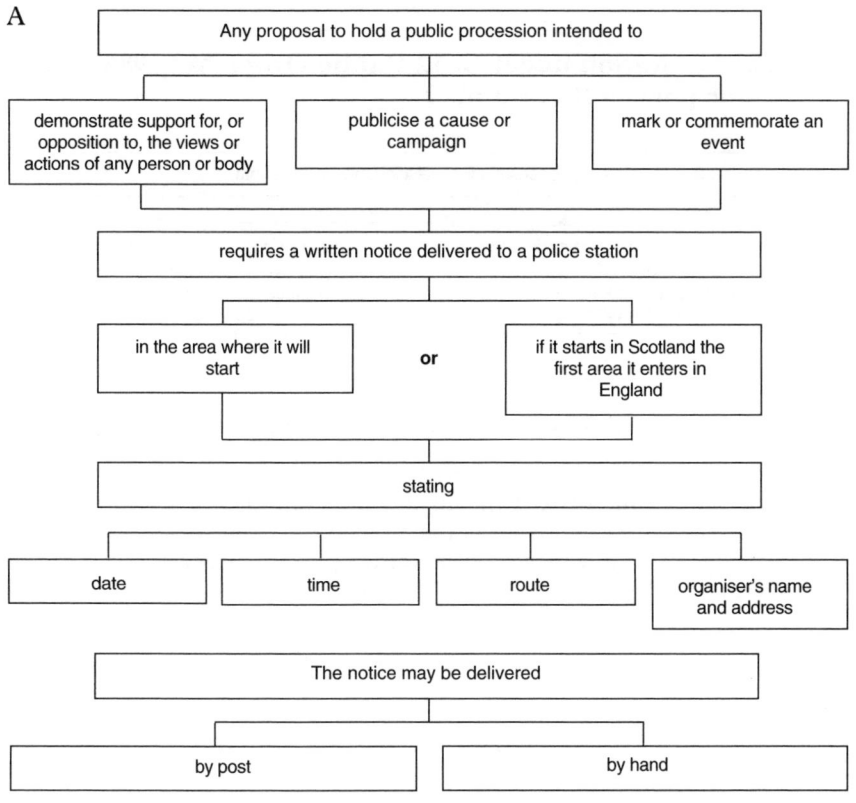

A

Any proposal to hold a public procession intended to

- demonstrate support for, or opposition to, the views or actions of any person or body
- publicise a cause or campaign
- mark or commemorate an event

requires a written notice delivered to a police station

- in the area where it will start

  or

- if it starts in Scotland the first area it enters in England

stating

- date
- time
- route
- organiser's name and address

The notice may be delivered

- by post
- by hand

S. 11 PUBLIC ORDER ACT 1986

PUBLIC DISORDER

By post. Not less than **six clear days** by **recorded delivery**. [S. 7 of the Interpretation Act 1978 under which a document sent by post is deemed to have been served when posted and to have been delivered in the ordinary course of post does not apply]; or

By hand. Not less than **six clear days**, or as soon as is practicable.

Offence. Is committed by any organiser who fails to comply with the above.

Defence. To prove that he did not know and neither suspected nor had reason to suspect of the failure to satisfy the requirements. In the case of providing the wrong date, time or route, it is a defence to prove the difference arose from circumstances beyond his control or with the agreement of a police officer.

Q **What condition under S. 12 Public Order Act 1986 can a senior police officer make?**

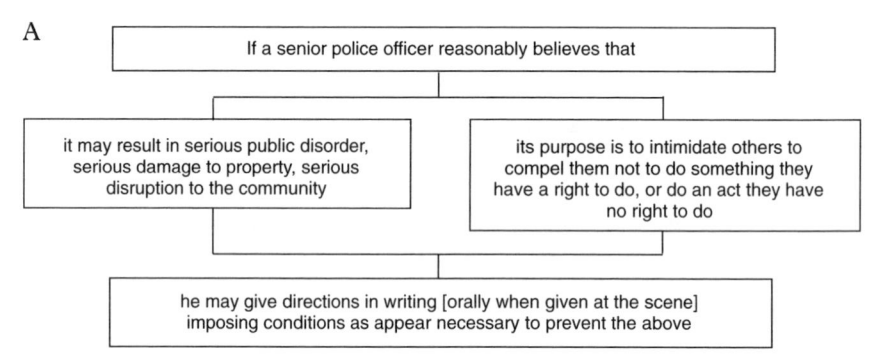

A

If a senior police officer reasonably believes that

- it may result in serious public disorder, serious damage to property, serious disruption to the community
- its purpose is to intimidate others to compel them not to do something they have a right to do, or do an act they have no right to do

he may give directions in writing [orally when given at the scene] imposing conditions as appear necessary to prevent the above

A senior police officer means the chief officer of police, unless the procession or meeting is in the process of being held, e.g. people forming up etc, in which case the **senior police officer present at the scene**.

PUBLIC DISORDER

Q Define the offence under S. 13 Public Order Act 1986 of taking part in a prohibited procession

A Any person who:

[a] organises a prohibited procession; or
[b] who takes part in; or
[c] incites another to take part in a prohibited procession knowing it is prohibited

commits an offence.

Q Define the offence under S. 14 Public Order Act 1986 of organising a public assembly

A Any person who:

[a] organises a public assembly and knowingly fails to comply with a condition; or
[b] takes part in an assembly and knowingly fails to comply with a condition; or
[c] incites another to take part in a public assembly which he knows does not comply with a condition commits an offence.

Defence. To prove that the failure to comply arose from circumstances beyond his control.

Q What is a public assembly?

A An assembly of two or more people in a public place that is wholly or partly open to the air (S. 16 Public Order Act 1986).

PUBLIC DISORDER

Q Outline the power under S. 14A Public Order Act 1986 to prohibit a trespassory assembly

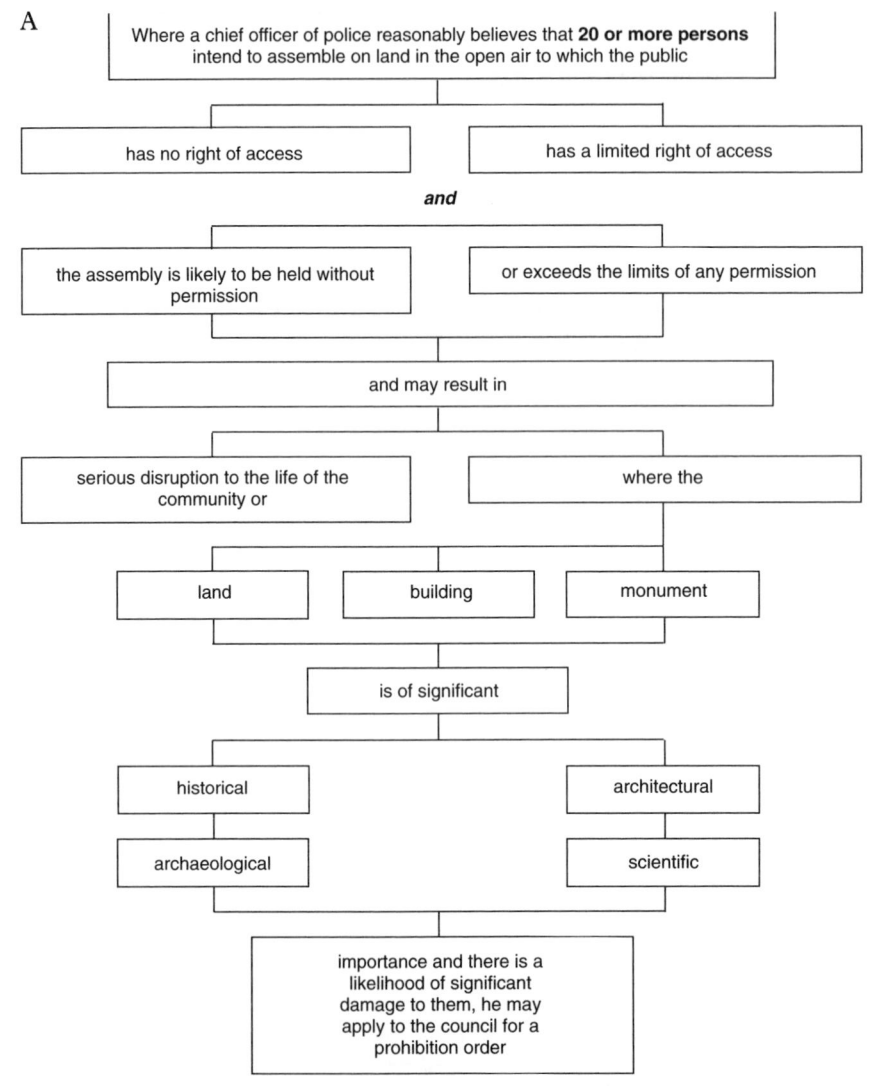

A

Where a chief officer of police reasonably believes that **20 or more persons** intend to assemble on land in the open air to which the public

- has no right of access
- has a limited right of access

and

- the assembly is likely to be held without permission
- or exceeds the limits of any permission

and may result in

- serious disruption to the life of the community or
- where the
  - land
  - building
  - monument

is of significant

- historical
- architectural
- archaeological
- scientific

importance and there is a likelihood of significant damage to them, he may apply to the council for a prohibition order

The order. May be granted by the council **with the consent of the Secretary of State**. It shall not exceed four days nor apply to more than a five mile radius from a specified centre.

PUBLIC DISORDER

Offence. Any person who organises or takes part in an assembly they know is prohibited, or incites another to, commits an offence.

Police powers. If a constable *in uniform* reasonably believes that a person is on his way to an assembly which is prohibited, he may:

[a] stop that person; and
[b] direct him not to proceed in the direction of the assembly.

The power must be exercised only in the area of the prohibitory order. Note that it applies to persons not vehicles. Use Road Traffic Act 1988 powers to stop vehicles.

Offence. Failure to comply is an offence.

Q Outline police powers under S. 1 Public Meeting Act 1908

A Where a person at a lawful public meeting acts in a disorderly manner for the purpose of preventing the business of the meeting or incites another to do so, he is guilty of an offence. If a constable reasonably suspects any person of committing this offence, he may *if requested by the chairman of the meeting*, require him to declare his name and address immediately. Failure to do so is a summary offence.

Public meeting. Not defined in the Act and therefore there is no specific number of persons required to be present. Public election meetings are excluded from this offence (but are covered by a similar specific offence under the Representation of the People Act 1983).

Q Outline the power to order dispersal of groups

A Where a superintendent or above has reasonable grounds to believe

[a] that any members of the public have been

[i] intimidated
[ii] harassed
[iii] alarmed or
[iv] distressed

as a result of the presence or behaviour of groups of two or more persons in public places in any locality in his police area, and

PUBLIC DISORDER

[b] that anti-social behaviour is a significant and persistent problem in that locality

s/he may, with the consent of the local authority(s) for that area, give an authorisation in writing conferring powers on constables **in uniform** who reasonably believe that ground (a) above has been or is likely to be satisfied, to direct

[i] dispersal of the group
[ii] any of those persons who do not reside in the locality to leave it, and
[iii] any such persons not to return within 24 hours of the direction to leave.

S. 30 ANTI-SOCIAL BEHAVIOUR ACT 2003

Offence. It is an offence knowingly to contravene any such direction.

Q How must the authorisation be notified to the group?

A The authorisation must be published, either in a local newspaper or by posting a notice in some conspicuous place(s) in the locality (or both). The direction to disperse may then be given (orally or otherwise) to any person individually or to two or more people together, and it may subsequently be withdrawn or varied by the person who gave it, or by another officer of the same or higher rank. The local authority must be consulted in advance.

Q Outline the power to remove under 16s

A If, between the hours of 9 pm and 6 am, a constable **in uniform** finds in any public place a person under 16 who is not under the effective control of a parent or a responsible person aged 18 or over, s/he may remove the person to their place of residence (unless s/he has reasonable grounds for believing that the person would, if removed to that place, be likely to suffer significant harm. [In which case s/he should exercise police protection powers under S. 46 Children Act 1989]). In the event that an officer exercises this power, the local authority must be notified. It is an offence to knowingly contravene a direction given under this power.

S. 30(6) ANTI-SOCIAL BEHAVIOUR ACT 2003

PUBLIC DISORDER

Q Can a constable use force in removing an under 16 from a dispersal area?

A Yes. In *R (on the application of W) v Commissioner of Police (2006)* it was held by the court that the word *'remove'* in S.30(6) should be interpreted as meaning 'take away using reasonable force if necessary'.

Q Outline the three offences of misbehaviour at designated football matches

A [a] **Throwing**. It is an offence to throw anything at or towards:

  [i] the playing area or any area adjacent to it where spectators are not admitted;
  [ii] any area in which spectators or other persons may be present [without lawful authority or lawful excuse - onus of proof [on a balance of probabilities] lies on him].

[b] **Chanting**. It is an offence to engage or take part in chanting of an **indecent or racist** nature.

  [i] 'Chant' means the *repeated* uttering of words or sounds whether alone or in concert with others; and
  [ii] 'racist' means threatening, abusive or insulting to a person by reason of colour, race, nationality or ethnic origins.

[c] **Entering playing area**. It is an offence to go on to the playing area or place adjacent to it where spectators are not normally allowed [without lawful authority or lawful excuse - onus of proof lies on him].

SS. 2,3,4 FOOTBALL (OFFENCES) ACT 1991

Q What is the purpose of the Football (Disorder) Act 2000?

A The regulation of Football Banning Orders.

Q In what two ways can a Banning Order be obtained?

A [a] Upon conviction for a 'relevant' offence under S. 14A Football Spectators Act 1989. Courts are under a duty to make an Order when satisfied that there are reasonable grounds to believe that an Order would help prevent violence or disorder at or in connection with a regulated football match. An order is in addition to any sentence imposed by the court for the relevant offence, and may be made even if the offence is dealt with by an absolute or conditional discharge.

PUBLIC DISORDER

[b] Following complaint by a chief officer of police, or the DPP, under S. 14 B Football Spectators Act 1989, if the court is satisfied that the person has, at any time, caused or contributed to any violence or disorder in the UK or elsewhere.

Q What power has the court in relation to banning orders?

A The court can impose any appropriate conditions and [save in exceptional circumstances] must require the **surrender of the person's passport** in connection with matches **outside the UK**.

Q When must a person who is the subject of a banning order first report to a police station?

A Within five days of the day on which the order was made (or five days of release if in custody).

Q What is the duration of a Banning Order?

A [a] A minimum of six years and a maximum of 10 years, where the order is imposed in addition to an immediate custodial sentence;
[b] a minimum of three years and a maximum of five years when imposed in addition to a non-custodial sentence;
[c] a minimum of three years and a maximum of five years when imposed following a police/DPP complaint.

Q What powers of detention exist in relation to Banning Orders?

A During any 'control period' in relation to any match or tournament outside the UK a constable in uniform who has reasonable cause to suspect that a person has caused/contributed at any time to any violence or disorder in the UK or elsewhere, and reasonable cause to believe that making a Banning Order would help prevent violence or disorder at or in connection with a regulated football match, may detain a **British citizen** for a maximum of **four hours** (**six hours** if authorised by an **inspector** or above) in order to decide whether to issue him with a S. 21B notice.

PUBLIC DISORDER

Q What is a S. 21B notice?

A A constable in uniform who is authorised by an inspector or above may give a person a written notice requiring him

  [a] to appear before a magistrates' court at a specified time (within 24 hours of the notice or detention, whichever is earlier);
  [b] not to leave England and Wales before that time, and
  [c] to surrender his passport.

Q What is the 'control period' during which these powers may be exercised?

A In relation to any match/tournament outside England and Wales, the period commencing five days before the match/tournament begins and ending when the match/tournament ends.

Q Is there any power of arrest?

A Yes, a constable may arrest the person to whom he is giving the notice if he has reasonable grounds to believe that it is necessary in order to secure compliance with the notice. It is also an offence to fail to comply with the notice once it is given.

Q To which vehicles does S. 1 of the Sporting Events (Control of Alcohol etc.) Act 1985 apply?

A Public service vehicles (PSVs) and trains being used for the *principal purpose* of carrying passengers to or from a designated sporting event.

Q Who commits alcohol-related offences in relation to such vehicles?

A [a] The operator of a PSV, or his servant/agent, who knowingly causes or permits alcohol to be carried on it;
  [b] the hirer of any PSV or train, or his servant/agent, who knowingly causes or permits alcohol to be carried on it;
  [c] any person who has intoxicating liquor in his possession while on the vehicle;
  [d] any person who is drunk on the vehicle.

Police powers. A constable may stop and search a PSV (or search a railway carriage, *not* stop the train) if he has reasonable grounds to suspect an offence under this section is being or has been committed on the vehicle.

PUBLIC DISORDER

Q Outline the power to ban sale of alcohol on trains.

A Following an application by an inspector (or above), a magistrates' court which is satisfied that a ban is necessary to prevent disorder, may make an order prohibiting the sale of alcohol, during any specified period, on any railway vehicle (a) at specified stations in their area or (b) travelling between such stations. The officer who applied for the order must immediately serve a copy on any affected train operators. It is an offence to knowingly contravene such a ban.

S. 157 LICENSING ACT 2003

Q Outline the alcohol-related offences at sports grounds

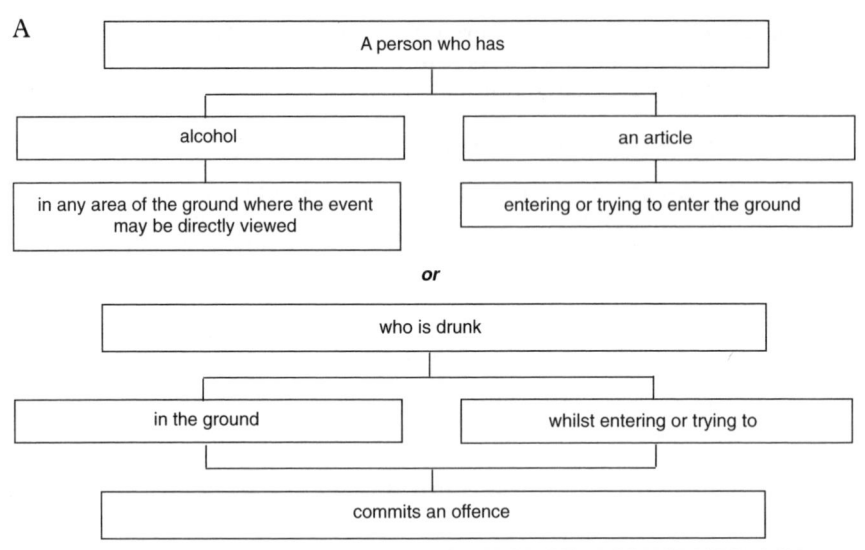

A

```
                    A person who has
                   /                  \
               alcohol              an article
                  |                     |
   in any area of the ground    entering or trying to enter the ground
   where the event may be
   directly viewed
                          or
                     who is drunk
                   /              \
            in the ground    whilst entering or trying to
                   \              /
                  commits an offence
```

S. 2 SPORTING EVENTS (CONTROL OF ALCOHOL ETC) ACT 1985

Q Define an 'article'

A It must be capable of **causing injury** to a person struck by it, being:

[a] a bottle, can or portable container, or part of such [whether crushed or broken] which

  [i] is for holding any drink, and
  [ii] is normally discarded or returned when empty.

But not medical containers.

PUBLIC DISORDER

Q During what times may these offences be committed?

A During the period beginning two hours before the start of the event or (if earlier) the advertised time, and ending one hour after the event. Where the event is postponed to a later date the time limits still apply on the originally advertised date [because spectators may have attended the ground].

Q Define the offence of Ticket Touting

A It is an offence for an unauthorised person to

[a] sell a ticket for a designated football match, or
[b] otherwise to dispose of such a ticket to another person.

S. 166 CRIMINAL JUSTICE AND PUBLIC ORDER ACT 1994

Unauthorised. Someone who does not have *written* authority to sell/dispose from the organisers of the match.

Sell. 'Selling' a ticket includes offering to sell, exposing for sale, making available for sale, advertising that it is available for purchase, giving a ticket to a person who pays/agrees to pay for some other goods or services or offering to do so.

Ticket. Anything purporting to be a ticket (whether or not it is genuine).

OFFENSIVE WEAPONS

Q Outline the offence of having an offensive weapon in a public place

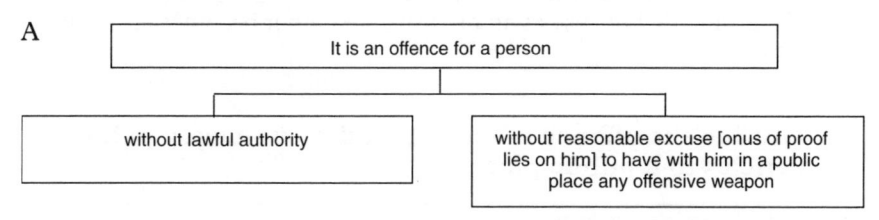

A

```
                 It is an offence for a person
        ┌──────────────────┴──────────────────┐
 without lawful authority      without reasonable excuse [onus of proof
                                lies on him] to have with him in a public
                                   place any offensive weapon
```

S. 1 PREVENTION OF CRIME ACT 1953

Lawful authority. Police officers, members of the military. **Not security guards** although they may have reasonable excuse on a particular occasion.

Reasonable excuse. Possession of tools of your trade, fancy dress incorporating, say, a policeman's truncheon. It **is not reasonable** to carry an offensive weapon 'just in case'. It may be reasonable if you have good grounds for fearing an unlawful attack, e.g. whilst guarding money in transit.

Has with him. Means actual physical possession or at least readily accessible.

Q Define an offensive weapon

A

```
              An offensive weapon is any article
       ┌─────────────────┬─────────────────┐
      made            adapted           intended
                         │
                  for causing injury
```

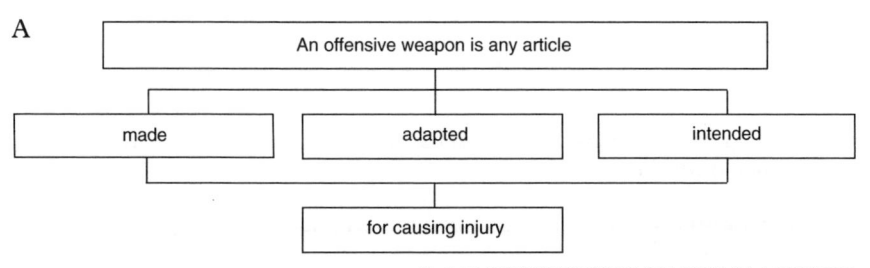

S. 1(4) PREVENTION OF CRIME ACT 1953

Made. Articles made for causing injury, e.g. knuckle dusters, swordsticks, bayonets, flick-knives etc are offensive per se [without further proof] and there is no need for the prosecution to show further proof of intent, possession is enough.

OFFENSIVE WEAPONS

Adapted. Where an article is adapted for causing injury, e.g. broken bottle, chair leg containing nails, etc, the prosecution must show that injury was intended.

Intended. An article may be inoffensive in itself, e.g. an umbrella, but if it is intended for use as an offensive weapon it becomes an offensive weapon.

S. 1 PREVENTION OF CRIME ACT 1953

Q Outline the offence of having blades or sharply pointed articles in a public place

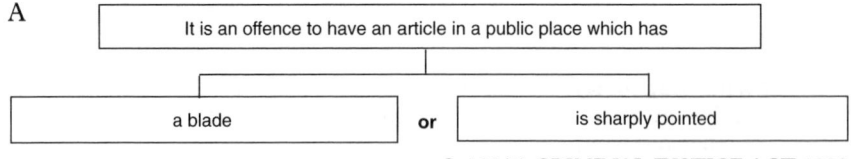

A It is an offence to have an article in a public place which has

- a blade
- **or**
- is sharply pointed

S. 139(1) CRIMINAL JUSTICE ACT 1988

Blade. Folding pocket knives with a blade which does not exceed 3 inches are exempt. If the folding pocket knife locks in the open position, it is not exempt.

Defence

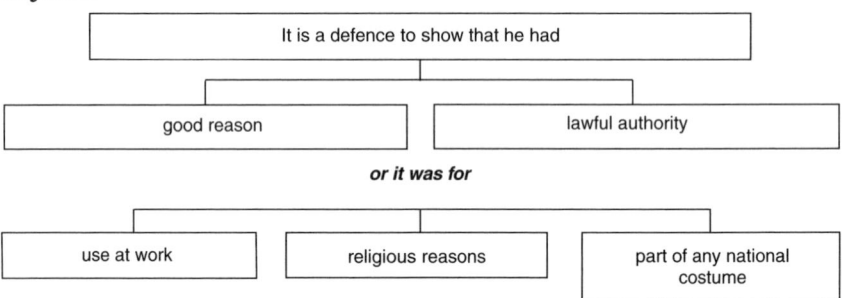

It is a defence to show that he had

- good reason
- lawful authority

or it was for

- use at work
- religious reasons
- part of any national costume

Religious reasons. E.g. a member of the Sikh religion may carry a small knife (kirpan).

National costume. E.g. someone in Highland dress with a skean dhu [knife in sock].

OFFENSIVE WEAPONS

Q Define the offence of having bladed or sharply pointed articles on school premises

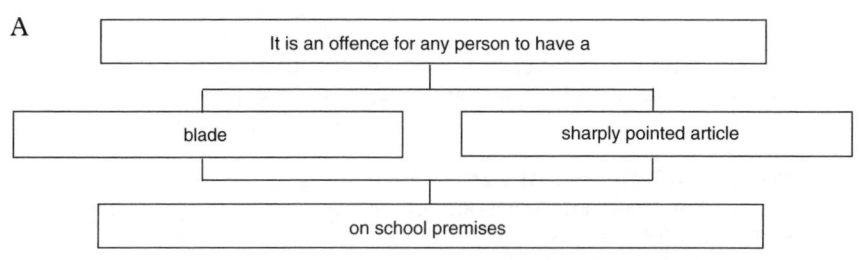

A

```
It is an offence for any person to have a
         │
    ┌────┴────┐
  blade   sharply pointed article
    └────┬────┘
  on school premises
```

S. 139A(1) CRIMINAL JUSTICE ACT 1988

School premises. Means land used for primary or secondary education. Not further or higher education. Land occupied solely as a dwelling by a person employed at the school (eg. caretaker's house) is excluded.

Defence. It is a defence to show that he had good reason or lawful authority or that he had it for use at work, for religious reasons or as part of any national costume.

Offensive weapons. Note that s.139A(2) extends this offence to cover offensive weapons as well as blades and sharps.

Q What is the power of entry for the above offence?

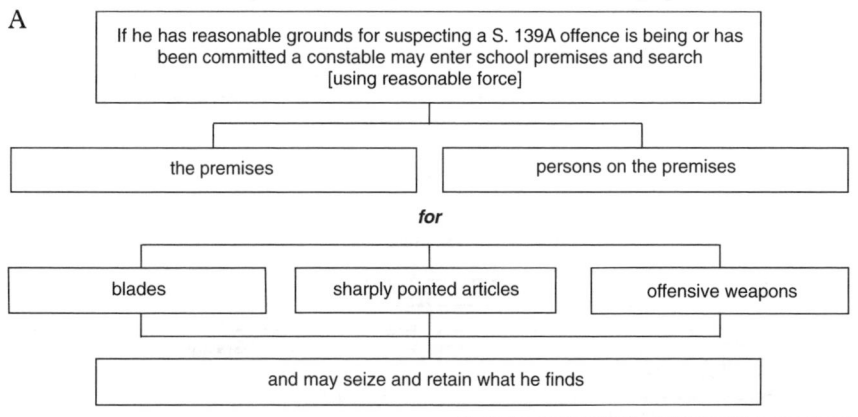

A

```
If he has reasonable grounds for suspecting a S. 139A offence is being or has
been committed a constable may enter school premises and search
              [using reasonable force]
                        │
          ┌─────────────┴─────────────┐
      the premises            persons on the premises
                       for
    ┌──────────────┬─────────────────────┐
  blades   sharply pointed articles   offensive weapons
    └──────────────┴─────────────────────┘
          and may seize and retain what he finds
```

S. 139B CRIMINAL JUSTICE ACT 1988

OFFENSIVE WEAPONS

Q   Outline the offence of trespassing with a weapon of offence

A   A person who is on any premises as a trespasser, after having entered as such, is guilty of an offence if, without lawful authority or reasonable excuse, he has with him on the premises any weapon of offence.

s.8(1) CRIMINAL LAW ACT 1977

Weapon of offence. Any article made or adapted for use for causing injury to or incapacitating a person, or intended by the person having it with them for such use.

Entry as trespasser. The offence is restricted to a person who entered as a trespasser, not someone who entered lawfully but who later became a trespasser.

Premises. Any building; part of a building under separate occupation; any land adjacent to and used/intended for use in connection with a building; the site comprising any building(s) together with ancillary land; any fixed structure; any movable structure, vehicle or vessel designed or adapted for residential purposes.

Q   Define the offence of manufacture, sale/hire of weapons

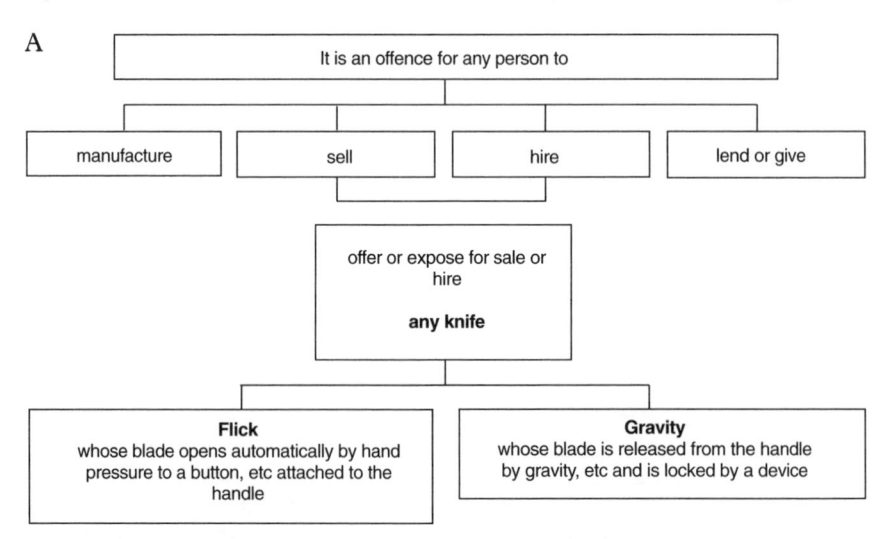

A

```
                    It is an offence for any person to
       ┌─────────────┬──────────────┬──────────────┐
   manufacture      sell           hire        lend or give
                     │              │
                     └──────┬───────┘
                    offer or expose for sale or hire
                            any knife
                     ┌──────┴───────┐
                   Flick          Gravity
```

Flick — whose blade opens automatically by hand pressure to a button, etc attached to the handle

Gravity — whose blade is released from the handle by gravity, etc and is locked by a device

Note 1. This Act (Restriction of Offensive Weapons Act 1959) does not create an offence of possession. The Act was designed to stop trading in such knives only.

OFFENSIVE WEAPONS

Note 2. S. 141 of the Criminal Justice Act 1988 makes similar provisions for a whole range of martial arts weapons.

Q What is the offence of selling knives and articles to under 18s?

A

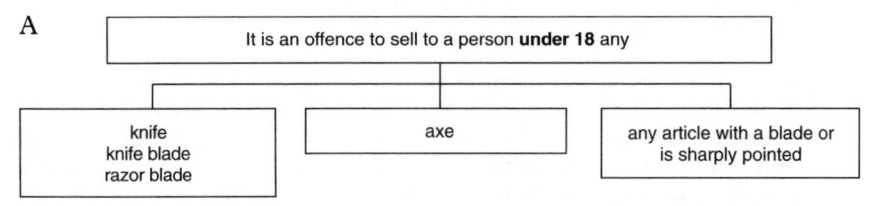

> It is an offence to sell to a person **under 18** any
> - knife / knife blade / razor blade
> - axe
> - any article with a blade or is sharply pointed

S. 141A CRIMINAL JUSTICE ACT 1988

Defence. To prove that he took all reasonable precautions and exercised due diligence to avoid committing the offence.

The offence does not apply to folding pocket knives with a cutting edge not exceeding 3 inches nor to razor blades in cartridges where no more than 2 mm of blade is exposed (e.g. 'Bic' type razors): Criminal Justice Act 1988 (Offensive Weapons) (Exemptions) Order 1996.

Q Outline the offence of unlawful marketing of knives under S. 1 Knives Act 1997

A

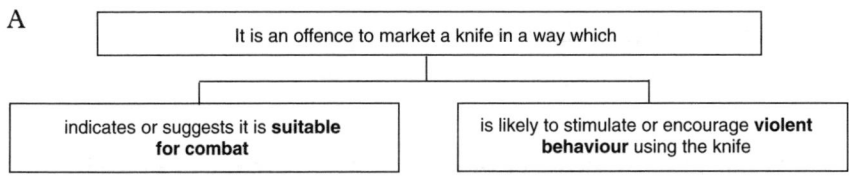

> It is an offence to market a knife in a way which
> - indicates or suggests it is **suitable for combat**
> - is likely to stimulate or encourage **violent behaviour** using the knife

Marketing. Includes selling, hiring [offering or exposing] and possession for marketing.

Q Outline the offence of publishing marketing material under S. 2 Knives Act 1997

A

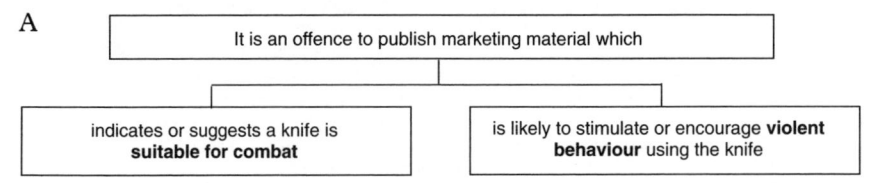

> It is an offence to publish marketing material which
> - indicates or suggests a knife is **suitable for combat**
> - is likely to stimulate or encourage **violent behaviour** using the knife

OFFENSIVE WEAPONS

Q What are the defences to marketing and publishing?

A   [a] The knife was marketed for use by the armed forces of any country or as an antique or curio; and
    [b] it was reasonable to market it that way; and
    [c] there were no reasonable grounds for believing it would be used unlawfully.

It is also a defence to prove that he did not know or suspect that the way in which the knife was marketed [published] indicated that it was **suitable for combat** or would stimulate or encourage **violent behaviour** using the knife as a weapon, or that he took reasonable precautions and exercised due diligence to avoid committing the offence.

SS. 3,4 KNIVES ACT 1997

Q Outline the three offences involving crossbows and persons under 18 years of age

A   [a]
    [b] It is an offence for a person to sell or hire a crossbow or a part of a crossbow to a person **under 18,** unless he believes and has reasonable grounds for believing he is 18 or over.
    [c] A person **under 18** who buys or hires a crossbow or part of a crossbow commits an offence.

Q When is a crossbow not a crossbow?

A   When the draw weight is **less than 1.4 kg.**

SS. 1-3 CROSSBOWS ACT 1987

Q What are the powers of search and seizure of crossbows?

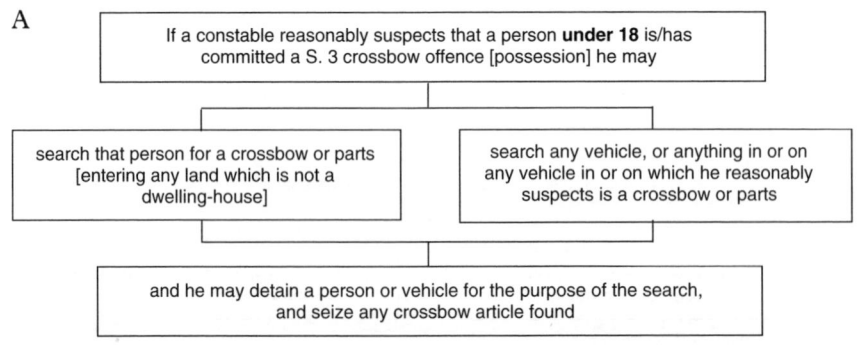

A

| If a constable reasonably suspects that a person **under 18** is/has committed a S. 3 crossbow offence [possession] he may |

| search that person for a crossbow or parts [entering any land which is not a dwelling-house] | search any vehicle, or anything in or on any vehicle in or on which he reasonably suspects is a crossbow or parts |

| and he may detain a person or vehicle for the purpose of the search, and seize any crossbow article found |

S. 4 CROSSBOWS ACT 1987

CIVIL DISPUTES

Q Under the Family Law Act 1996 what is a non-molestation order?

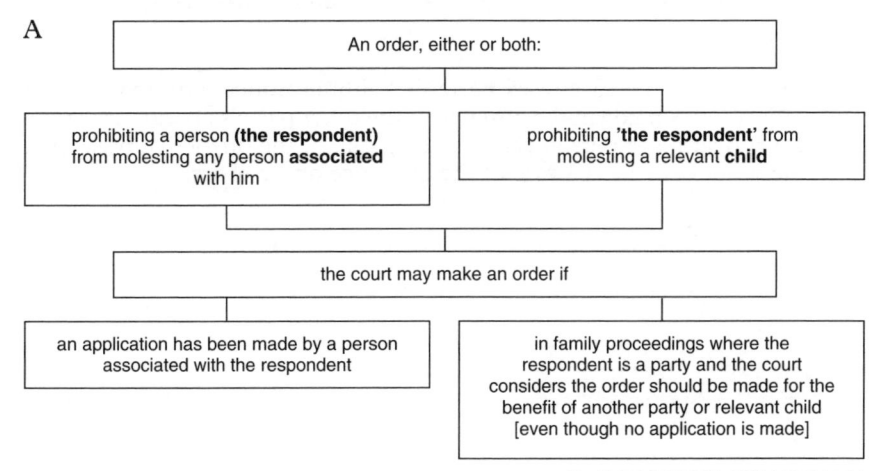

A

An order, either or both:
- prohibiting a person **(the respondent)** from molesting any person **associated** with him
- prohibiting **'the respondent'** from molesting a relevant **child**

the court may make an order if
- an application has been made by a person associated with the respondent
- in family proceedings where the respondent is a party and the court considers the order should be made for the benefit of another party or relevant child [even though no application is made]

S. 42 FAMILY LAW ACT 1996

Associated. Means:

[a] they are or have been married to each other;
[b] they are or have been civil partners of each other;
[c] they are cohabitees, or former cohabitees;
[d] they live or have lived in the same household [but not as employee, tenant, lodger or boarder];
[e] they are relatives;
[f] they have agreed to marry [whether or not the agreement is terminated];
[g] they have entered a civil partnership agreement (whether or not that agreement has been terminated);
[h] they have or have had an intimate personal relationship with each other which is or was of significant duration;
[i] they are parties to the same family proceedings.

In relation to a child they are both:

[i] its parents; or
[ii] have or had parental responsibility.

S. 62 FAMILY LAW ACT 1996

CIVIL DISPUTES

Q   **Outline the offence of breaching a non-molestation order**

A   A person who, without reasonable excuse, does anything that he is prohibited from doing by a non-molestation order is guilty of an offence.

Ex parte. In the case of ex parte or 'without notice' non-molestation orders (ones made in the absence of the other party's attendance at the court hearing) a person can only be guilty of the offence of breaching the order once he is aware of the existence of the order.

TRADE DISPUTES

Q   What is meant by peaceful picketing?

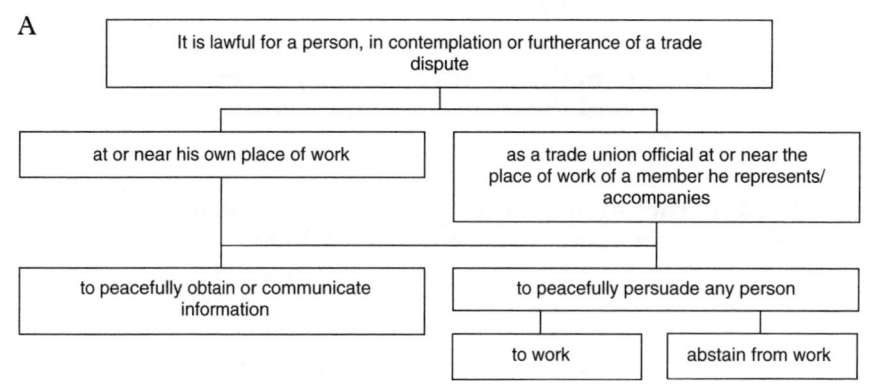

A

It is lawful for a person, in contemplation or furtherance of a trade dispute

- at or near his own place of work
- as a trade union official at or near the place of work of a member he represents/accompanies

- to peacefully obtain or communicate information
- to peacefully persuade any person
  - to work
  - abstain from work

S.220 TRADE UNION AND LABOUR RELATIONS (CONSOLIDATION) ACT 1992

Q   What if he works elsewhere?

A   If he works:

[a]   other than at any one place; or
[b]   it is impracticable to picket there,

then his place of work shall be deemed to be any premises of his employer from which he works or from which his work is administered.

What if he no longer works? If his last employment was terminated in connection with the trade dispute, or gave rise to the dispute, his place of work shall be deemed to be **his last place of work**.

What if the workplace has moved? A person's place of work does not include new premises of an employer who has moved since dismissing him: *News Group Newspapers Ltd. v SOGAT '82 (1987)*.

Q   What is meant by a trade dispute?

A   A dispute between employers and workers relating mainly to:

[a]   terms and conditions of employment, including physical conditions;
[b]   engagement [or not] suspension/termination of employment/duties of one or more workers;
[c]   allocation of work or duties;
[d]   discipline;

TRADE DISPUTES

[e] membership of a trade union;
[f] facilities for union officials; and
[g] machinery for negotiation or consultation.

S. 244(1) 1992 ACT

Q Can a dispute between workers in a government department and the minister come within the section?

A Yes, even though he/she is not the workers' 'employer'.

Q Outline the offence of intimidation by violence or otherwise in relation to labour relations

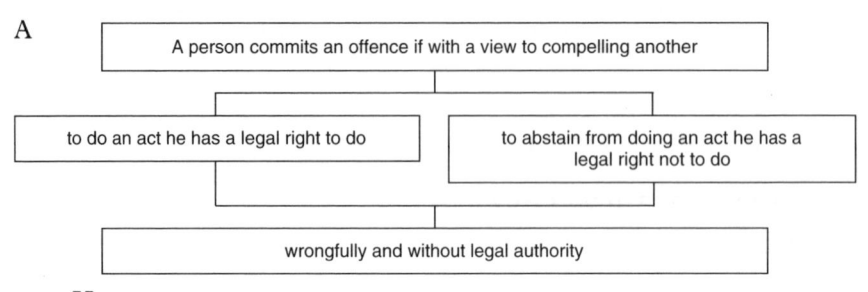

A

```
            A person commits an offence if with a view to compelling another
                            │
          ┌─────────────────┴─────────────────┐
to do an act he has a legal right to do   to abstain from doing an act he has a
                                              legal right not to do
          └─────────────────┬─────────────────┘
                            │
              wrongfully and without legal authority
```

He:

[a] uses violence or intimidates him, his wife or children or damages his property;
[b] persistently follows him;
[c] hides his tools or property or deprives him of their use;
[d] watches or besets his house or work business or where he is [or the approaches];
[e] **three or more** follow him in a disorderly manner in any street or road.

S. 241 TRADE UNION AND LABOUR RELATIONS (CONSOLIDATION) ACT 1992

Seamen. This offence does not apply to seamen.

Intent. 'With a view to compelling' means with intent to compel the other person

OFFENCES RELATED TO LAND

Q What is an interim possession order?

A An order made by a court during proceedings for the recovery of premises occupied by trespassers. Wilful obstruction of anyone executing such an order is a summary offence.

CRIMINAL JUSTICE AND PUBLIC ORDER ACT 1994

Q Outline the interim possession order trespass offence

A When an interim possession order has been made and served then a person commits an offence if he:

[a] is present on the premises as a trespasser during the currency of the order unless:

[i] he leaves **within 24 hours** of its service and does not return; or
[ii] the order is void by reason of not being fixed to the premises;

[b] having been in occupation when the order was served he re-enters as a trespasser after the order expired but **within one year** of it being served.

S. 76 CRIMINAL JUSTICE AND PUBLIC ORDER ACT 1994

Q Define the offence of making false statement to obtain interim possession order

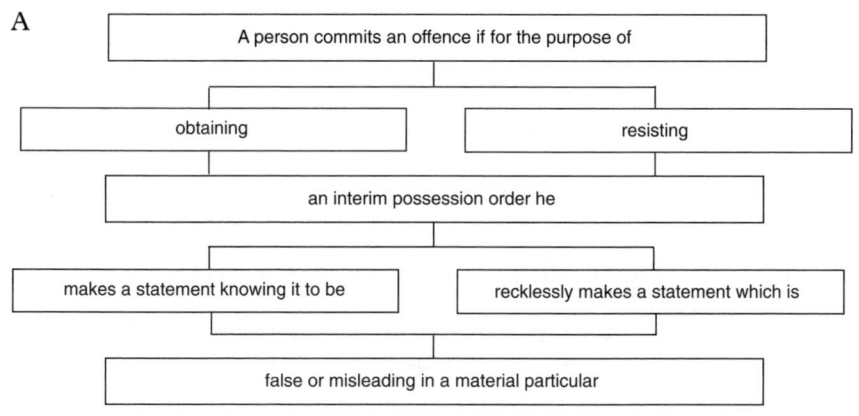

A

```
A person commits an offence if for the purpose of
         │                              │
     obtaining                       resisting
         │                              │
            an interim possession order he
         │                              │
 makes a statement knowing it to be    recklessly makes a statement which is
         │                              │
         false or misleading in a material particular
```

S. 75 CRIMINAL JUSTICE AND PUBLIC ORDER ACT 1994

OFFENCES RELATED TO LAND

Q Outline the offence of aggravated trespass

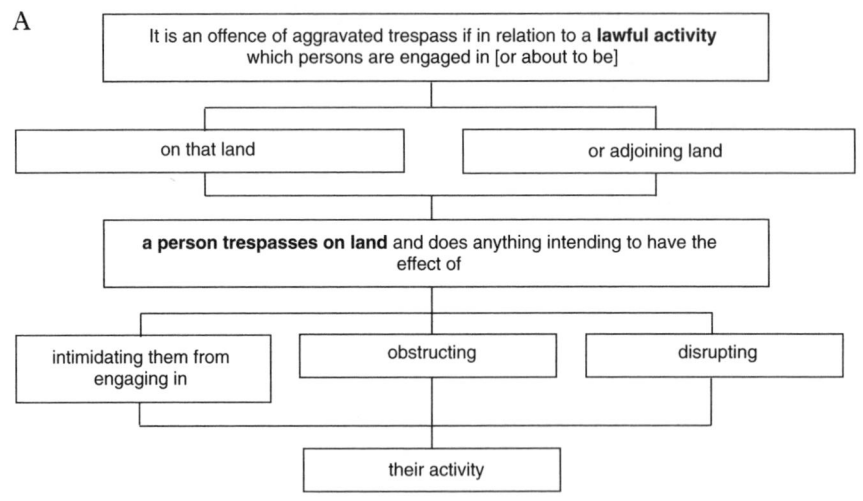

A

```
┌─────────────────────────────────────────────────────────────┐
│ It is an offence of aggravated trespass if in relation to a │
│ lawful activity which persons are engaged in [or about to be]│
└─────────────────────────────────────────────────────────────┘
          │                                  │
┌──────────────────────┐          ┌──────────────────────┐
│    on that land      │          │   or adjoining land  │
└──────────────────────┘          └──────────────────────┘

┌─────────────────────────────────────────────────────────────┐
│ a person trespasses on land and does anything intending to  │
│                    have the effect of                        │
└─────────────────────────────────────────────────────────────┘
      │                       │                      │
┌─────────────────┐   ┌─────────────────┐   ┌─────────────────┐
│ intimidating    │   │   obstructing   │   │   disrupting    │
│ them from       │   │                 │   │                 │
│ engaging in     │   │                 │   │                 │
└─────────────────┘   └─────────────────┘   └─────────────────┘
                            │
                   ┌─────────────────┐
                   │  their activity │
                   └─────────────────┘
```

S. 68 CRIMINAL JUSTICE AND PUBLIC ORDER ACT 1994

Purpose. This offence was primarily intended to cover the activities of protestors. Notice that it only applies to persons who are trespassing on land, and therefore does not encompass protesters who stand on highways or other land where they have permission to be.

Land. Does not include land forming part of the highway unless it is a footpath, bridleway or byway open to traffic or road used as a public path or cycle track. Trespassing in or on buildings as well as on open land is now covered.

Q Outline police powers in relation to aggravated trespass

A The senior police officer present **at the scene** (who need not be in uniform) may direct a person to leave land if he reasonably believes:

[a] he is or is intending to commit the offence of aggravated trespass on land; or

[b] **two or more persons are trespassing** on land with the common purpose of intimidating, obstructing or disrupting a lawful activity.

S. 69 CRIMINAL JUSTICE AND PUBLIC ORDER ACT 1994

Offence. Knowing a direction has been given, fails to leave the land as soon as possible, or having left, re-enters as a trespasser **within three**

OFFENCES RELATED TO LAND

months of the direction being given. Communication of the direction may be made by any officer at the scene (who need not be in uniform).

Defence. To prove he was not a trespasser or that he had reasonable cause for failing to leave, or re-enter.

Q Outline the police powers where two or more people are trespassing for residence

A The senior police officer present **at the scene (who need not be in uniform) may direct persons to leave land if he reasonably believes**:

[a] **two or more persons are trespassing** on land; and
[b] that their common purpose is to **reside there**; and
[c] they have been **asked to leave** [or reasonable steps have been taken by occupier]; and

that any of those persons have:

[a] caused damage to land or property; or
[b] have used threatening, abusive or insulting words or behaviour towards the occupier, his family, employee, or agent; or
[c] they have **six or more vehicles** on the land.

He may direct them to leave the land together with their vehicles and property. The direction may be communicated by any officer at the scene (who need not be in uniform). It is an offence to knowingly:

[a] fail to leave as soon as reasonably practicable; or
[b] having left, to re-enter as a trespasser within three months.

S. 61 CRIMINAL JUSTICE AND PUBLIC ORDER ACT 1994

Trespasser? Where persons were not trespassers at the outset but have subsequently become trespassers the police officer must believe that they have caused damage, used threatening words or behaviour or have six or more vehicles since **becoming trespassers**.

Land. Does not include buildings, except farm buildings or scheduled monuments. Nor does it include a footpath, bridleway or byway open to traffic or road used as a public path or cycle track.

Damage to land. Includes any pollution, e.g. oil from vehicles.

Vehicles. Includes parts, such as a chassis or body appearing to have formed part of a vehicle. Also includes caravans.

OFFENCES RELATED TO LAND

Defence. To prove [a] that he was not trespassing; or [b] that he had a reasonable excuse for failing to leave as soon as reasonably practicable, or for re-entering as a trespasser.

Power of seizure. If a S. 61 direction has been given and an officer reasonably suspects that any person to whom it applies has, without reasonable excuse

[a] failed to remove any vehicle on the land which appears to the officer to belong to him or be in his possession/control; or
[b] entered the land as a trespasser with a vehicle **within three months** of the direction

the officer may seize and remove the vehicle: S. 62.

Q Outline the S. 62A trespassing offence and police powers

A This is a power designed to enable officers to order persons (e.g. 'travellers' or gypsies) to leave land on which they are trespassing with vehicles and to remove any caravan(s), when there is a suitable and legal alternative site available for them to use.

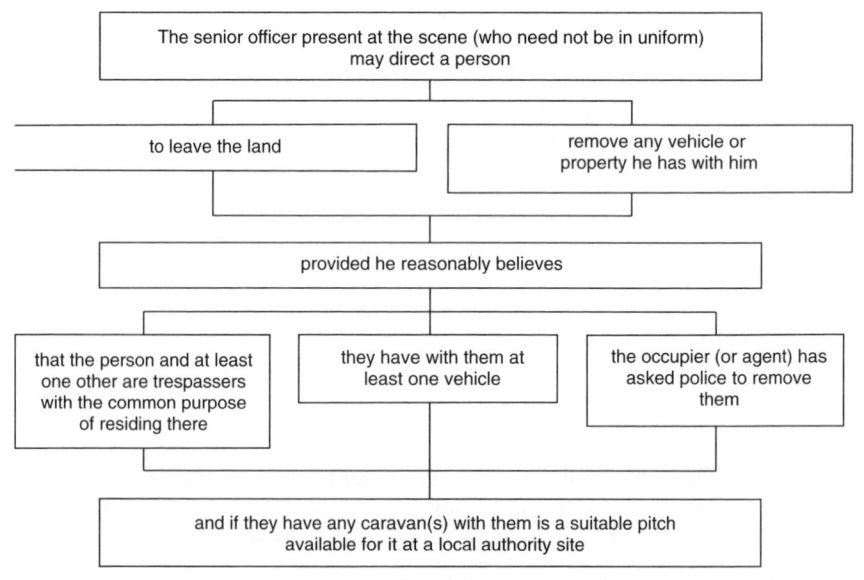

```
The senior officer present at the scene (who need not be in uniform)
                    may direct a person
                            │
         ┌──────────────────┴──────────────────┐
    to leave the land              remove any vehicle or
                                   property he has with him
         └──────────────────┬──────────────────┘
                            │
                provided he reasonably believes
                            │
    ┌───────────────────────┼───────────────────────┐
that the person and at least  they have with them at  the occupier (or agent) has
one other are trespassers       least one vehicle       asked police to remove
with the common purpose                                        them
      of residing there
    └───────────────────────┼───────────────────────┘
                            │
       and if they have any caravan(s) with them is a suitable pitch
                available for it at a local authority site
```

S. 62A CRIMINAL JUSTICE AND PUBLIC ORDER ACT 1994

Offence. It is an offence for anyone who knows of such a direction which applies to him, to fail without reasonable excuse to leave the land

OFFENCES RELATED TO LAND

as soon as reasonably practicable, or re-enter *any land in the local authority area as a trespasser* and with intention to reside **within three months**.

S. 63 CRIMINAL JUSTICE AND PUBLIC ORDER ACT 1994

Q Outline police powers in relation to raves

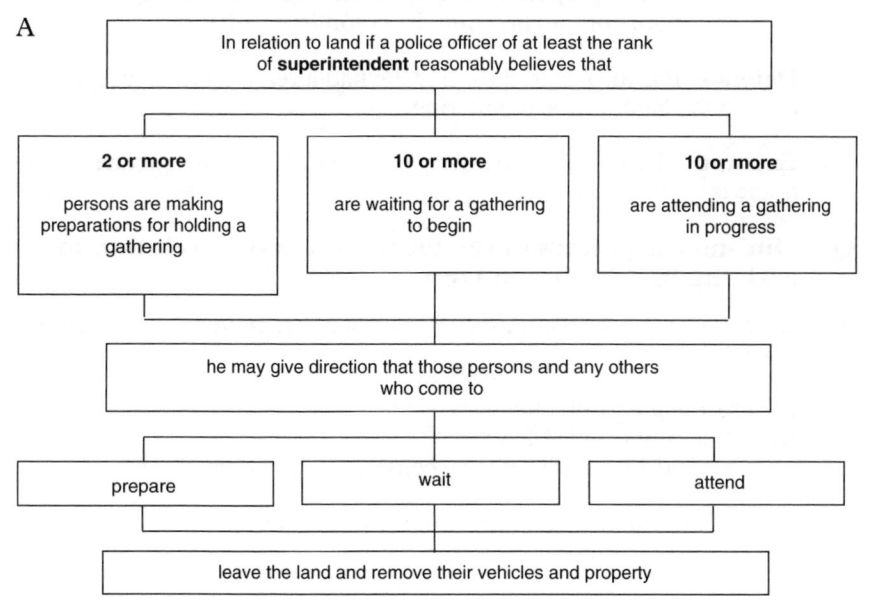

A

In relation to land if a police officer of at least the rank of **superintendent** reasonably believes that

2 or more	10 or more	10 or more
persons are making preparations for holding a gathering	are waiting for a gathering to begin	are attending a gathering in progress

he may give direction that those persons and any others who come to

| prepare | wait | attend |

leave the land and remove their vehicles and property

S. 63 CRIMINAL JUSTICE AND PUBLIC ORDER ACT 1994

Q Who can give the direction at the scene?

A Any constable. He need not be in uniform.

Q What is meant by a gathering?

A [a] On land in the open air
 [b] involving 20 or more persons, trespassing or not, or
 [c] on land, involving 20 or more trespassers (need not be open air)
 [d] at which amplified music is played during the night; and by reason of its loudness, duration and time it is played
 [e] is likely to cause serious distress to the inhabitants of the locality.

The gathering continues during intermissions, and music includes sounds of a succession of repetitive beats.

OFFENCES RELATED TO LAND

Offence. If a person *knows* a direction has been given which applies to him and

- [i] fails to leave the land as soon as reasonably practicable, or
- [ii] having left, re-enters the land **within seven days** of the direction, or
- [iii] makes preparations for, or attends, a gathering within 24 hours of the direction, he commits an offence.

Defence. For the accused to show he had a reasonable excuse for not leaving the land, or for re-entering.

Exempt. The occupier, his family, employees etc or anyone whose home is on the land.

Q Outline the powers of the local authority in relation to residing in vehicles on land

A If it appears to a local authority that persons are residing in a vehicle on any land:

- [a] forming part of a highway;
- [b] other unoccupied land; or
- [c] occupied land without the consent of the occupier,

the authority may give a direction to leave and remove their vehicles and property.

S. 77 CRIMINAL JUSTICE AND PUBLIC ORDER ACT 1994

Offence. If a person *knows* a direction has been given which applies to him and

- [i] fails to leave the land or remove any vehicle or other property which is covered by the direction as soon as reasonably practicable, or
- [ii] having removed any such vehicle/property, re-enters the land with a vehicle **within three months** of the direction,

he commits an offence.

Defence. To prove that his failure to leave/re-entry was due to illness, mechanical breakdown, or other immediate emergency.

Removal order. The local authority can apply to a magistrates' court for a removal order if people ignore the direction. The local authority can enforce the order.

OFFENCES RELATED TO LAND

Notice. 24 hours' notice must be given to the owner of the land and the residents of their intention to enforce the order.

Q **Define the offence of depriving residential occupier of premises - [unlawful eviction]**

A A person shall be guilty of an offence who:

unlawfully deprives the residential occupier of any premises of his occupation of them or any part [or attempts] unless he proves that he believed, and had reasonable cause to believe, that the residential occupier had ceased to reside there.

S. 1(2) PROTECTION FROM EVICTION ACT 1977

Q **Define the offence of harassment of residential occupiers under the Protection from Eviction Act 1977**

A A person commits an offence if, with intent to cause the residential occupier of any premises to:

[a] give up the occupation of the premises [or part]; or
[b] refrain from exercising any right or from pursuing a remedy in respect of the premises,

he does acts likely to interfere with the peace or comfort of the residential occupier or his household, or persistently withdraws or withholds services reasonably required for his occupation, **and in the case of a landlord or his agent,** he knows that his conduct is likely to cause the residential occupier to give up occupation or refrain from exercising any right to pursue any remedy.

S. 1(3) PROTECTION FROM EVICTION ACT 1977

Note. This offence is aimed at acts done by landlords (and others) with the objective of causing occupiers to leave the premises, e.g. cutting off electricity, gas supplies etc.

Residential occupier. Means a person occupying the premises as a resident [under a contract or rule of law] giving him the right to remain in occupation, or restricting the right of any person to recover the premises.

Defence. To prove that he had reasonable grounds for doing the act.

OFFENCES RELATED TO LAND

Q Define the offence of using or threatening violence to enter premises

A It is an offence, without lawful authority, to use or threaten violence to secure entry to premises where **there is someone present** at the time who opposes the entry which the violence is intended to secure, and the person using the violence knows this is the case.

Defence. This section does not apply to a **displaced residential occupier** or a protected intended residential occupier.

S. 6 CRIMINAL LAW ACT 1977

Q Who is a displaced residential occupier?

A Any person who was occupying any premises as a resident immediately before being excluded from occupation by anyone who entered as a trespasser, **but not** a displaced trespasser.

Q Outline the offence of failing to leave premises

A Any trespasser is guilty of an offence if he fails to leave the premises on being required by [or on behalf of]:

[a] a displaced residential occupier; or
[b] a protected intended occupier.

S. 7 CRIMINAL LAW ACT 1977

Defence. To prove that he believed that the person requiring him to leave was not one of the two above.

Non-residential premises. This section does not apply to premises used **mainly** for non-residential premises [e.g. factories, offices etc].

Q Outline the offence of causing or permitting nuisance on educational premises

A Any person who without lawful authority is present on relevant premises and who causes or permits nuisance or disturbance to the annoyance of persons who lawfully use those premises (whether or not any such persons are present at the time) commits an offence.

Which premises? Either premises that provide further or higher education and which are maintained by a local education authority (S. 40(1) Local Government (Misc. Prov.) Act 1982) or premises that provide primary or secondary education and which are LEA or grant maintained (S. 547(1) Education Act 1996). 'Premises' includes playing fields and other outdoor areas.

Police powers. If a constable (or other person authorised by a LEA) has reasonable cause to suspect that a person is committing or has committed an offence under these provisions he may remove him from the premises.

Q   What is the offence of trespassing on a protected site?

A   It is an offence to enter, or be on, any protected site as a trespasser.

S.128(1) SOCAP 2005

Q   What is a 'protected site'?

A   A **nuclear site** (being any premises covered by a nuclear site licence) or a **designated site** (being a site specified in an order made by the Secretary of State). Currently the specified designated sites are certain sites of military significance and certain sites associated with the government, security services and the Royal Family.

Defence. That the person did not know, and had no reasonable cause to suspect, that the site was a protected site.

LICENSING AND OFFENCES RELATED TO ALCOHOL AND GAMBLING

Q   What are the 'licensing objectives'?

A   [a]   The prevention of crime and disorder;
    [b]   public safety;
    [c]   the prevention of public nuisance; and
    [d]   the protection of children from harm.

Q   What are the 'licensable activities'?

A   [a]   The sale by retail of alcohol;
    [b]   the supply of alcohol by or on behalf of a club to, or to the order of, a member of the club (otherwise than a sale by retail);
    [c]   the provision of regulated entertainment; and
    [d]   the provision of late night refreshment.

Q   What does [b] above mean?

A   Members' clubs are organisations where the club property is owned by the members jointly in equal shares. If alcohol is supplied to a member at a price eg. in the club bar, this is not a sale by retail but a release by the other members of their interest in the drink supplied. It would therefore not be covered by [a] above and so a special category has been created to take account of such supplies. If a member's guest is sold alcohol in the club bar this would be an ordinary sale by retail and covered by [a] above.

Q   What is 'late night refreshment'?

A   This means the supply of hot food or hot drink to the public for consumption on or off the premises, between 11 pm and 5 am. It also includes when members of the public (or a section of it) are admitted to any premises, such supply on premises to anyone (or a person of a particular type) on or off those premises.

Q   Which supplies are exempt from being 'late night refreshments'?

A   Exemptions include the supply of food or drink free of charge by a registered charity; provision by way of vending machines; supplies to guests at hotels, guest houses, camp sites etc.

LICENSING AND OFFENCES RELATED TO ALCOHOL AND GAMBLING

Q What are the general exemptions to licensable activities?

A Exemptions include activities:

[a] aboard an aircraft, hovercraft or railway vehicle engaged on a journey;
[b] aboard a vessel engaged on an international journey;
[c] at an approved wharf at a designated port or hoverport;
[d] at an examination station at a designated airport;
[e] at premises which at the time are permanently or temporarily occupied for the purposes of the armed forces of the Crown;
[f] at premises covered by a national security exemption; and
[g] at such other place as may be prescribed.

Q What is the power of entry to investigate licensable activities?

A Where a constable or other authorised person has reason to believe that any premises are being, or are about to be, used for the licensable activity, they may enter the premises (if need be with force) with a view to checking whether the activity is, or is to be, carried on under an authorisation.

S. 179(1) LICENSING ACT 2003

Q What is the power of entry to investigate licensing offences?

A A constable may enter (if need be by force) and search any premises in respect of which s/he has reason to believe that a Licensing Act 2003 offence has been, is being or is about to be committed.

S. 180 LICENSING ACT 2003

Q What is a 'premises licence'?

A A licence granted in respect of any premises which authorises the premises to be used for one or more licensable activities. It lasts until it is revoked or surrendered.

Q Who may apply for a premises licence?

A The following adults over 18 (amongst others):

[a] a person who carries on, or proposes to carry on, a business which involves the use of the premises for the licensable activities to which the application relates;
[b] a recognised club;
[c] a charity;

LICENSING AND OFFENCES RELATED TO ALCOHOL AND GAMBLING

    [d]   the chief officer of police of a police force in England & Wales;
    [e]   the proprietor of an educational institution;
    [f]   a health service body;
    [g]   a person applying under any statutory function or prerogative.

Q   To whom is the application made?

A   To the relevant licensing authority, on a prescribed form, accompanied by a fee. The relevant authority will be the authority (usually the council) in whose area the premises are situated (or mainly situated). If premises straddle more than one area equally, the applicant can nominate the authority from those involved.

Q   What is a 'personal licence'?

A   A personal licence is a licence granted by a licensing authority for the area in which the applicant is normally resident to an individual that authorises him to supply alcohol, or to authorise the supply of alcohol, in accordance with a premises licence. 'Supplying alcohol' means selling by retail or supplying to a club member.

Q   What is 'alcohol'?

A   Spirits, wine, beer, cider or any other fermented, distilled or spirituous liquor, but NOT:

    [a]   alcohol of a strength not exceeding 0.5% at the time of the sale or supply in question;
    [b]   perfume;
    [c]   flavouring essences (including Angostura bitters);
    [d]   medicinal alcohol;
    [e]   denatured, menthyl or naphtha alcohol;
    [f]   liqueur confectionery.

Q   For how long is a personal licence valid?

A   Ten years (unless revoked, suspended or surrendered). At the end of the 10-year period the licensee may apply for a review.

LICENSING AND OFFENCES RELATED TO ALCOHOL AND GAMBLING

Q What are the main conditions which need to be met for a club to be a 'qualifying club'?

A [a] No one may be admitted as a member without an interval of at least two days after his nomination or application for membership;
   [b] persons becoming members without prior nomination or application may not be admitted as a member without an interval of at least two days between their becoming members and admission;
   [c] the club is established and conducted in good faith as a club;
   [d] the club has at least 25 members;
   [e] no alcohol is supplied, or intended to be supplied, to members on the premises except by or on behalf of the club.

Q What is a 'club premises certificate'?

A A certificate which is very similar to a premises licence, and which allows certain 'qualifying club activities' to take place, such as the supply, otherwise than by retail sale, of alcohol to club members; the sale by retail of alcohol to members' guests, and the provision of regulated entertainment.

Q What powers of entry does a constable have in relation to clubs making licensing applications?

A Where a club applies for a club premises certificate, or a variation of an existing certificate, or a review at the end of a certificate period, a constable authorised by the chief officer may (on production of their authority) enter and inspect the premises. Any such entry must take place at a reasonable time on a day which is not more than 14 days after making the application, and upon at least 48 hours' notice to the club. Obstructing a constable or other authorised person in the exercise of this power is a summary offence.

S. 96 LICENSING ACT 2003

Q What other powers of entry to clubs does a constable have?

A Where any club premises certificate is in existence, a constable may enter (if need be by force) and search the premises if s/he has reasonable cause to believe:

   [a] that an offence of supplying (or offering to supply, or being concerned in supplying or making an offer to supply) a controlled drug has been, is being, or is about to be, committed there; or
   [b] that there is likely to be a breach of the peace there.

LICENSING AND OFFENCES RELATED TO ALCOHOL AND GAMBLING

Q What are 'permitted temporary activities'?

A Licensable activities which may be carried out on a temporary basis at premises which do not have a premises licence or club premises certificate (eg. a bar at a wedding reception), provided certain conditions are met. The maximum duration of such temporary activities is 96 hours. A licensable activity is a permitted temporary activity if it is carried on in accordance with a 'temporary events notice' given by a licensing authority.

S. 100 LICENSING ACT 2003

Q Outline the offence of unauthorised licensable activities

A A person commits an offence if

[a] he carries on or attempts to carry on a licensable activity on or from any premises otherwise than under and in accordance with an authorisation, or
[b] he *knowingly* allows a licensable activity to be carried on.

S. 136 LICENSING ACT 2003

Q Outline the offence of exposing alcohol for unauthorised sale

A A person commits an offence if, on any premises, he exposes for sale by retail any alcohol in circumstances where the sale by retail of that alcohol on those premises would be an unauthorised licensable activity.

S. 137 LICENSING ACT 2003

Q What is the defence of 'due diligence'?

A For the offences of unauthorised licensable activities and exposing alcohol for unauthorised sale, it is a defence to prove (on a balance of probabilities) that:

[a] his act was due to a mistake, or to reliance on information given to him, or to an act or omission by another person, or to some other cause beyond his control, **AND**
[b] he took all reasonable precautions and exercised all diligence to avoid committing the offence.

S. 139 LICENSING ACT 2003

Q Outline the offence of allowing disorderly conduct

A It is an offence for a 'specified person' to knowingly allow disorderly conduct on a licensed premises.

S. 140 LICENSING ACT 2003

LICENSING AND OFFENCES RELATED TO ALCOHOL AND GAMBLING

Specified persons. Any person who works at the premises in a capacity which authorises him to prevent the conduct; the holder of the premises licence; the designated premises supervisor; (in respect of clubs) any member or officer of the club present at the time in a capacity which enables him to prevent it, and (in the case of temporary activities) the premises user in relation to the temporary event notice.

Q Outline the offence of selling alcohol to a drunk

A A specified person commits an offence if, on relevant premises, he **knowingly**:

[a] sells or attempts to sell alcohol to a person who is drunk, or
[b] allows alcohol to be sold to such a person

S. 141 LICENSING ACT 2003

Specified persons. As above.

Q Outline the offence of obtaining alcohol for a drunk

A A person commits an offence if, on relevant premises, he knowingly obtains or attempts to obtain alcohol for consumption on those premises by a person who is drunk.

S. 142 LICENSING ACT 2003

Relevant premises. Licensed premises; premises with a club certificate; premises used for a permitted temporary activity.

Q Outline the offence of failure to leave licensed premises

A A person who is drunk or disorderly commits an offence if, without reasonable excuse:

[a] he fails to leave relevant premises when requested to do so by a constable or authorised person, or
[b] he enters or attempts to enter relevant premises after a constable or authorised person has requested him not to enter.

S. 143 LICENSING ACT 2003

Authorised person. Any person who works at the premises in a capacity which authorises him to sell alcohol; (in the case of licensed premises) the premises licence holder, and designated supervisor; (in the case of clubs) any member or officer present on the premises in a capacity which enables him to make such a request; (in the case of temporary activities) the premises user under the temporary events notice.

LICENSING AND OFFENCES RELATED TO ALCOHOL AND GAMBLING

Q   What is the offence of being drunk and disorderly?

A   Any person who in any *public place* is guilty, while drunk, of disorderly behaviour, commits an offence

S. 91(1) CRIMINAL JUSTICE ACT 1967

Drunk *and* Disorderly. Both must be proved. The drunkenness must be a result of excessive alcohol consumption rather than any other form of intoxication, though where there are several causes of the person's drunkenness, one of which is alcohol, a court may find that the offence is made out. 'Drunk' means that the defendant has consumed so much alcohol that it affects his steady self-control.

Q   What if the drunk is only disorderly *after* his arrest?

A   Then the offence is not made out.

Q   What is the offence of being found drunk?

A   Every person found drunk in any highway or other public place, whether a building or not, or on any licensed premises, commits an offence.

S. 12 LICENSING ACT 1872

Q   What is the police duty to help expel disorderly persons?

A   On being requested to do so by any of the authorised persons, a constable MUST help expel the disorderly/drunk person from the premises, or help prevent such a person entering (as applicable).

The duty remains one of assisting the authorised person (as under previous law) rather than simply doing it oneself.

Q   Outline the offence of selling alcohol to children

A   A person (or a club) commits an offence if he sells (or supplies) alcohol to a person under 18.

S. 146 LICENSING ACT 2003

Where? Anywhere (not just on licensed premises).

Defence. To prove that he believed the person was 18 or over **AND** either [a] he had taken all reasonable steps to establish that person's age, **OR** [b] nobody could reasonably have suspected from that person's appearance that he was under 18.

LICENSING AND OFFENCES RELATED TO ALCOHOL AND GAMBLING

Q Outline the offence of selling alcohol to children on licensed premises

A Any person who works at licensed premises, premises with a club premises certificate, or premises used for a permitted temporary activity in a capacity which authorises him to prevent the sale, commits an offence if s/he knowingly allows the sale (supply) of alcohol on the premises to a person under 18.

S. 147 LICENSING ACT 2003

Q It is an offence to sell liqueur confectionery to children below what age?

A 16.

S. 148 LICENSING ACT 2003

Q Outline the offence of purchasing alcohol by children

A A person under 18 commits an offence if he:

[a] buys or attempts to buy alcohol, or
[b] (if a club member) alcohol is supplied to him at his order by or on behalf of the club, or he attempts to have alcohol supplied to him or to his order by or on behalf of the club.

S. 149(1) LICENSING ACT 2003

Exemption. Where the child is a test purchaser acting at the request of a constable or weights and measures inspector.

Q Outline the offence of purchasing alcohol for children

A A person commits an offence if:

[a] he buys or attempts to buy alcohol for a person under 18, or
[b] (where a club member) makes arrangements on behalf of a person under 18 for the supply of alcohol to him or to his order by the club, or attempts to do so.

S. 149(3) LICENSING ACT 2003

Defence. Where the person had no reason to suspect the child was under 18.

LICENSING AND OFFENCES RELATED TO ALCOHOL AND GAMBLING

Q **Outline the offence of purchasing alcohol for a child in licensed premises**

A A person commits an offence if:

[a] he buys or attempts to buy alcohol for consumption on relevant premises by a person under 18, or
[b] (where a club member) by some act or default of his, alcohol is supplied to him, or to his order, by the club for consumption by a person under 18, or he attempts such supply.

S. 149(4) LICENSING ACT 2003

Defence. Where the person had no reason to suspect the child was under 18.

Table meals. This offence does not apply where the following conditions are met:

[a] the relevant person is 18 or over,
[b] the child is 16 or 17,
[c] the alcohol is beer, wine or cider,
[d] its purchase/supply is for consumption at a table meal on the premises, and
[e] the child is accompanied at the meal by a person aged 18 or over.

Q **Outline the offence of consumption of alcohol by child**

A A person under 18 commits an offence if he knowingly consumes alcohol on relevant premises.

S. 150(1) LICENSING ACT 2003

Relevant premises. Licensed premises, premises with a club premises certificate, premises used for a permitted temporary activity.

Table meals. The table meal exception applies.

Q **Outline the offence of sending a child to obtain alcohol**

A A person commits an offence if he knowingly sends an individual under 18 to obtain

[a] alcohol sold or to be sold on relevant premises for consumption on the premises, or
[b] alcohol supplied or to be supplied by or on behalf of a club for such consumption.

S. 152 LICENSING ACT 2003

LICENSING AND OFFENCES RELATED TO ALCOHOL AND GAMBLING

Test purchases. Are exempt.

Working persons under 18. The offence will not be committed where the person under 18 works on the premises in a capacity which involves delivery of alcohol.

Q Outline the offence of persistently possessing alcohol in a public place

A A person under 18 commits an offence if, without reasonable excuse, he/she is in possession of alcohol in any relevant place on **3 or more occasions** within a period of 12 consecutive months.

s.30 POLICING AND CRIME ACT 2009

Relevant place. Any public place (other than places with a premises licence/permitted temporary activity/club premises certificate) or any place, other than a public place, to which that person has unlawfully gained access.

Q Outline the power to confiscate alcohol from children

A Where a constable (who need not be in uniform) reasonably suspects that a person in a relevant place is in possession of alcohol, and that either

[a] he is under 18; or
[b] he intends that any of the alcohol should be consumed by a person under 18 in that or any relevant place; or
[c] a person under 18 who is, or has recently been, with him has recently consumed alcohol in that or any relevant place the constable may require him to surrender anything in his possession which is, or the constable reasonably believes to be, alcohol or a container for such alcohol.

S. I CONFISCATION OF ALCOHOL (YOUNG PERSONS) ACT 1997

Failure to comply. It is an offence to fail to comply without reasonable excuse.

Sealed containers. The constable may only require surrender of sealed containers if he reasonably believes that the person is, or has been, consuming or intends to consume alcohol in a relevant place.

Relevant place. Any public place (not licensed premises), or any place, other than a public place, to which that person has unlawfully gained access.

LICENSING AND OFFENCES RELATED TO ALCOHOL AND GAMBLING

Disposal. The officer may dispose of *anything* surrendered to him (need not actually be alcohol).

Name and address. The constable making the requirement to surrender **must** require the person to state their name and addres.

Under 16? If the constable reasonably suspects that the person is under 16, he may remove him/her to their place of residence or a place of safety.

Q Outline the power to close premises

A Following an application by a **superintendent** or above, where there is or is expected to be any disorder in their area, a magistrates' court for that area may make an order requiring all premises situated at or near the place of disorder and in respect of which a temporary event notice has effect, to be closed for a period not exceeding 24 hours. A constable may use such force as is necessary to close such premises. It is an offence to knowingly contravene the order.

S. 160 LICENSING ACT 2003

Q Outline the offence of keeping smuggled goods

A A person commits an offence if he knowingly keeps or allows to be kept, on any relevant premises, any goods which have been imported without payment of duty or which have otherwise been unlawfully imported.

S. 144 LICENSING ACT 2003

Who commits the offence? Anyone who works at the premises in a capacity which authorises him to prevent the keeping of the goods there; (in the case of licensed premises) the licensee or supervisor; (in the case of clubs) any member or officer present on the premises in a capacity enabling him to prevent them being so kept; (in the case of temporary activities) the premises user under the temporary event notice.

Q What are the 'licensing objectives' under the Gambling Act 2005?

A [a] Protecting children and other vulnerable people from being harmed or exploited by gambling;
   [b] preventing gambling from being a source of crime or disorder, being associated with crime or disorder, or being used to support crime, and
   [c] ensuring that gambling is conducted in a fair and open way.

www.janes.com

LICENSING AND OFFENCES RELATED TO ALCOHOL AND GAMBLING

Q What is 'gambling'?

A Gaming, betting, or participating in a lottery.

Q What is 'gaming'?

A Playing a game of chance for a prize.

Q What is 'betting'?

A Making or accepting a bet on

  [a] the outcome of a race, competition or other event or process,
  [b] the likelihood of anything occurring or not occurring, or
  [c] whether anything is or is not true.

OFFENCES INVOLVING INFORMATION

Q What is the offence of unauthorised access to computers (hacking)?

A A person is guilty of an offence if:

[a] he **causes a computer to perform any function** with intent to secure access to any program or data held in any computer, or to enable any such access to be secured;
[b] the access he intends to secure, or to enable to be secured, is **unauthorised**; and
[c] he **knows** at the time when he causes the computer to perform the function that is the case.

S. 1 COMPUTER MISUSE ACT 1990

Q Outline the offence of unauthorised access with intent to commit an indictable offence

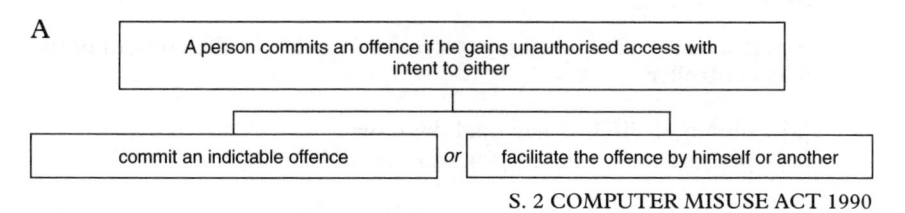

A

```
        A person commits an offence if he gains unauthorised access with
                              intent to either
        ┌──────────────────────────────┬──────────────────────────────┐
        commit an indictable offence   or   facilitate the offence by himself or another
```

S. 2 COMPUTER MISUSE ACT 1990

Q Outline the offence of unauthorised acts with intent to impair computer operation

A A person is guilty of an offence if:

[a] he does any unauthorised act in relation to a computer;
[b] at the time he does the act he knows it is unauthorised; and
[c] *either*he **intends** by doing the act *or* **is reckless**as to whether the act will do, any of the following:

[i] to impair the operation of any computer;
[ii] to prevent or hinder access to any program or data held in any computer;
[iii] to impair the operation/reliability of any such program/data; or
[iv] enable any of the above to be done.

S. 3 COMPUTER MISUSE ACT 1990

OFFENCES INVOLVING INFORMATION

Examples. Implanting computer viruses; sending millions of emails to a computer in order to impair its performance: *DPP v. Lennon* (206) - former employee with grudge.

Q Under the Data Protection Act 1998 what is the meaning of data?

A 'Data' means information recorded in a form in which it can be processed by equipment operating automatically in response to instruction given for that purpose or which is recorded as part of a relevant filing system.

Relevant filing system. Means any set of information relating to **individuals** to the extent that, although not processed by equipment operating automatically, the set is structured in a way that information relating to a **particular individual** is readily accessible.

S. 1 1998 ACT

Q Outline the offence of obtaining, disclosure and sale of personal data

A A person must not knowingly or recklessly, without the consent of the data controller

[a] obtain or disclose personal data; or
[b] procure the disclosure for another, unless:

  [i] it was for preventing or detecting crime; or
  [ii] authorised by an enactment, rule of law, or order of a court; or
  [iii] he believed he had a right in law to obtain, disclose etc; or
  [iv] he believed he would have had the consent of the data controller; or
  [v] it was justified as being in the public interest.

[c] it is an offence **to offer for sale personal data** unlawfully obtained.

S. 55 DATA PROTECTION ACT 1998

Prosecution. Offences under the 1998 Act may not be prosecuted by anyone other than the data protection commissioner or with the consent of the DPP.

OFFENCES INVOLVING INFORMATION

Q What is a covert human intelligence source (CHIS) under the Regulation of Investigatory Powers Act 2000?

A A CHIS is someone who establishes or maintains a relationship with another person for the covert purpose of obtaining information or providing access to information or covertly disclosing information obtained as a result of the relationship. A 'covert' relationship is one which is calculated to ensure that one of the parties is unaware of its true purpose.

Q Who can authorise the use of a CHIS?

A A superintendent (or above). In urgent cases (not involving juveniles or the obtaining of confidential material) an inspector may give authority.

Q Can an inspector give oral authority in an urgent case?

A No. Inspectors' authorities must always be in writing. Only a superintendent (or above) can give oral authority, and then only in urgent cases.

Q For how long can a CHIS authority last?

A A superintendent's written authority will ordinarily last for 12 months. A superintendent's urgent oral authority lasts for 72 hours, as does an inspector's urgent written authority, unless renewed. Strict controls govern the use of juveniles (under 18s) as CHISs. A written authority in such a case will last for one month.

Q For what purposes may the use of a CHIS be authorised?

A When the superintendent/inspector believes it is both necessary and proportionate:

    [a] for the prevention/detection of crime/disorder;
    [b] in the interests of national security, public safety and/or the economic well-being of the UK;
    [c] for protecting health or collecting/assessing taxes, duties etc. or
    [d] for any other purpose specified by order made by the Secretary of State.

Q What is 'covert surveillance'?

A Surveillance which is carried out in a manner calculated to ensure that people subject to it are unaware that it is taking place. 'Surveillance' covers monitoring, observing, listening to and recording people and their conversations, activities and communications.

OFFENCES INVOLVING INFORMATION

Q What is 'directed surveillance'?

A Surveillance which is

[a] covert (but not 'intrusive')
[b] for the purposes of a specific investigation or operation
[c] likely to result in the obtaining of private information about a person (whether or not they have been previously identified for the purposes of the investigation)
[d] not carried out in immediate response to events/circumstances where it would not be reasonably practicable to seek prior authorisation.

Q What is 'intrusive surveillance'?

A Surveillance which is

[a] covert
[b] carried out in relation to anything taking place on any residential premises (including hotel rooms) or in any private vehicle (i.e. for domestic not business use)
[c] involves the presence of an individual on the premises or in the vehicle, or is carried out by means of a surveillance device.

Q What is not intrusive surveillance?

A A location tracking device attached to a vehicle: S. 26(4) (a) RIPA 2000.

Q What is neither directed nor intrusive surveillance?

A Covert TV detector equipment: S.26(6) RIPA 2000.

Q Who can authorise directed surveillance?

A A superintendent (or above). In an urgent case, an inspector. As with CHIS authorities, the superintendent's authority should generally be in writing but a superintendent may give oral authority in an urgent case. Inspectors' urgent authorities must always be in writing. The purposes for which authority can be given are broadly the same as for a CHIS.

Q How long will directed surveillance authorisations last?

A A superintendent's written authority will ordinarily cease to have effect after three months. A superintendent's urgent oral authority will last for 72 hours unless renewed, as will an inspector's urgent written authority.

OFFENCES INVOLVING INFORMATION

Q Who can authorise intrusive surveillance?

A For the police (and military police) it is the 'senior authorising officer' e.g. chief officers, the commissioner/asst commissioner of the Met and City police, and the DG of SOCA [Provost Marshall for the military police]. Authorisation must only be made where it is believed to be necessary and proportionate

[a] in the interests of national security,
[b] for preventing/detecting **serious** crime, or
[c] for safeguarding the economic well-being of the UK.

Any such authority must be notified in writing to a surveillance commissioner as soon as practicable. Except in urgent cases, the authority will only take effect when approval from the surveillance commissioner has been received in writing by the chief officer.

Q How long can intrusive surveillance authorisations last?

A Authorisations last for three months. Urgent authorisations last for 72 hours.

Q What is the offence of unlawful interception of public communications?

A It is an offence to intentionally and without lawful authority intercept, anywhere in the UK, any communication in the course of its transmission by means of:

[a] a public postal service; or
[b] a public telecommunication system.
S. 1(1) REGULATION OF INVESTIGATORY POWERS ACT 2000

Prosecution. The consent of the DPP is required for any prosecution.

Lawful authority. Means:

[a] conduct in accordance with any statutory power;
[b] conduct authorised under the Act (i.e. where both sender and intended recipient consent; the interception is on behalf of the communications provider for its legitimate business purposes; or the interception is authorised under the Wireless Telegraphy Act 1949 S. 5);
[c] conduct in accordance with an interception warrant issued by the Secretary of State.

OFFENCES INVOLVING INFORMATION

Q   When may the Secretary of State issue an interception warrant?

A   Only if he/she believes it is necessary

    [a]   in the interests of national security;
    [b]   for the prevention/detection of serious crime;
    [c]   in order to safeguard the economic well-being of the UK, or
    [d]   for the purposes of international mutual assistance.

Q   For how long does an interception warrant last?

A   Generally three months. (Where a warrant is renewed in the interests of national security or to protect the economic well-being of the UK, it will be valid for a further six months.) In urgent cases a warrant may be signed by a senior official expressly authorised by the Secretary of State, and such urgent warrants are valid for five working days.

Q   What is the indictable offence of making unauthorised disclosures?

A   Where an interception warrant is issued or renewed, it shall be the duty of every specified person to keep secret all matters relating to the warrant. A person who discloses to another anything he is required to keep secret commits an indictable offence.

S. 19 RIPA 2000

Specified persons. Anyone who might legitimately have to know about the warrant eg. persons holding office under the Crown; members of SOCA; everyone employed by or for the purposes of any police force and persons employed by or for the purposes of postal/telecoms services.

DIVERSITY, DISCRIMINATION AND EQUALITY

Q What are the main sources of legislation dealing with equality and discrimination?

A [a] Equal Pay Act 1970
[b] Sex Discrimination Act 1975
[c] Race Relations Act 1976
[d] Disability Discrimination Acts 1995 and 2005

Q Outline the objectives of the Equal Pay Act 1970

A To ensure that men and women who do the same type of work receive the same rewards.

Q The Disability Discrimination Acts make it unlawful to discriminate against people on grounds of disability. What does 'disability' mean?

A A person is considered 'disabled' for the purposes of the Act if they have a physical or mental impairment which has a substantial and long-term effect on their ability to carry out normal daily functions.

Q When does disability discrimination occur in the workplace?

A When -

[a] for reasons which relate to a person's disability, their employer treats them less favourably than they would or do treat others who are not disabled; or
[b] fails to make reasonable adjustments for them; and
[c] this treatment is not justified.

Q What does 'reasonable adjustments' mean?

A Action to try to ensure that disabled people are not put at a substantial disadvantage compared to others. For example, ensuring wheelchair access at entrances and exits or adapting office furniture or computer workstations.

Q What is 'direct discrimination'?

A When someone is treated less favourably than another on the protected grounds (e.g. on the basis of his/her perceived race, colour, sex, religion etc.).

DIVERSITY, DISCRIMINATION AND EQUALITY

Q   What is 'indirect discrimination'?

A   This occurs when an apparently non-discriminatory requirement which applies equally to everyone can only be met by a considerably smaller proportion of people from a particular group, and which is to the detriment of a person from that group because he or she cannot meet it; and the requirement or condition cannot be justified. For example, a condition that all job applicants must work on certain days may indirectly discriminate against someone who cannot work on those days because of their religious beliefs.

Part 2 - Crime

INTRODUCTION

Q What does S. 8 Criminal Justice Act 1967 say about intent?

A A court or jury in deciding whether a person has committed an offence:

[a] shall **not be bound to infer that he intended or foresaw** a result of his actions by reason only of it being a natural and probable consequence; but
[b] shall decide whether **he did intend or foresee** that result by reference to all the evidence, drawing such inferences as appear proper.

Q Define subjective (*Cunningham*) recklessness

A Where the defendant actually foresees that there is a risk of the consequence resulting from his act, and in all the circumstances it is unreasonable for him to take that risk, but he takes it anyway.

Q Give an example of transferred malice

A 'A' throws a rock at 'B' intending him injury, but misses and causes injury to 'C' (So long as the defendant has the required state of mind for a particular offence it does not matter whether the actual target/victim was unintended or unforeseen).

Q What is meant by actus reus and mens rea?

A Actus reus is the physical act of the crime and mens rea is the guilty state of mind, e.g. intent.

Q Distinguish between a principal and an accessory

A The principal is one who has met all the requirements of an offence whilst an accessory is a person who aids, abets, counsels or procures the commission of an offence. An aider and abetter is guilty as a principal.

Q When can an omission amount to an offence?

A When the 'offender' has a **duty of care** to act in favour of the 'victim' e.g. where a police officer voluntarily fails to intervene to prevent an assault.

INTRODUCTION

Q Outline the offence of encouraging or assisting crime

A A person commits an offence if (a) he does an act capable of encouraging or assisting in the commission of an offence; and (b) he intends to encourage or assist its commission.

S. 44 SERIOUS CRIME ACT 2007

Foreseeable consequence. It must be proved that the defendant actually intended to assist or encourage an offence. The Act makes it clear that intention will not be made out simply because such encouragement or assistance was a foreseeable consequence of his act.

Q Outline the offence of encouraging or assisting crime whilst believing it will be committed.

A A person commits an offence if

[a] he does an act capable of encouraging or assisting in the commission of an offence; and
[b] *he believes*

 [i] that the offence will be committed; and
 [ii] that his act will encourage or assist its commission.

S. 45 SERIOUS CRIME ACT 2007

Q Outline the offence of encouraging or assisting crime believing *one or more* will be committed

A A person commits an offence if

[a] he does an act capable of encouraging or assisting the commission of one or more of a number of offences; and
[b] *he believes*

 [i] that *one or more* of those offences will be committed (but has no belief as to which); and
 [ii] that his act will encourage or assist the commission of one or more of them

S. 46 SERIOUS CRIME ACT 2007

Incitement. These offences replace the common law offence of incitement. As with incitement it is not necessary for the substantive offence to be actually committed for the defendant to be guilty of encouraging or assisting it (in other words, it does not matter whether his actions have the effect he intended or believed they would have).

INTRODUCTION

Defence. For all three offences under ss 44, 45 and 46 it will be a defence to prove that he acted reasonably (i.e. that in the circumstances he was aware of, or in the circumstances he reasonably believed existed, it was reasonable for him to act as he did).

Sentence. The defendant is liable to receive any sentence which would be available for the substantive offence. Where the substantive offence is murder, the defendant is liable to life imprisonment.

Q Define statutory conspiracy

A It is an offence to be involved in any agreement between two or more persons to pursue a course of conduct, which, if carried out either:

[a] will involve committing an offence; or
[b] would do so, but in the event it is impossible to commit.

SS. 1, 2 CRIMINAL LAW ACT 1977

No conviction. A defendant cannot be convicted of conspiracy if the only other party to the agreement is his spouse or civil partner, child under 10, or the intended victim. However a husband and wife can both be convicted if they conspire with a third party.

Prosecution. Conspiracy is triable only on indictment even if the substantive offence is summary, but in such a case, the consent of the DPP is required for prosecution.

Q Define conspiracy to defraud at common law

A Any agreement by two or more persons by dishonesty to deprive a person of what is his or to which he is entitled or to harm his proprietary rights: *Scott v Met Police Cmr (1975)*.

Q Define a criminal attempt

A If, with intent to commit an offence, a person **does an act which is more than merely preparatory** to the commission of the offence he is guilty of attempt.

S. 1(1) CRIMINAL ATTEMPTS ACT 1981

Impossible offences. Where the above definition fits, a person may be charged with an attempt even though the offence is impossible. [e.g. searching an empty purse for money].

INTRODUCTION

Q **Define the offence of interfering with motor vehicles**

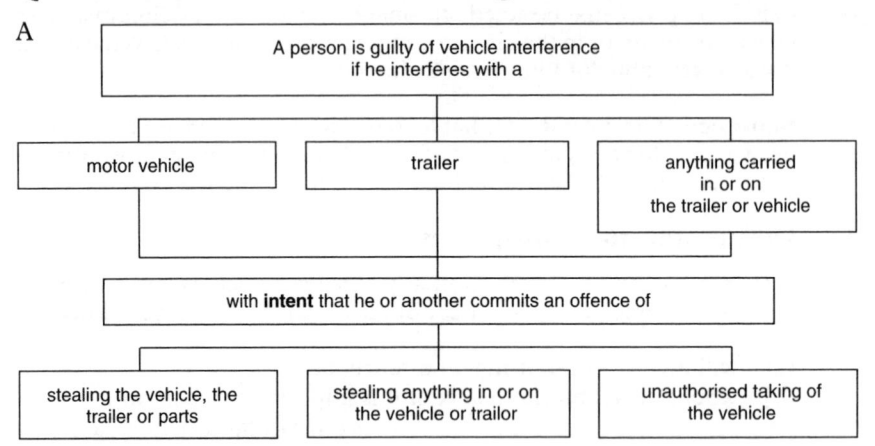

A

> A person is guilty of vehicle interference if he interferes with a
> - motor vehicle
> - trailer
> - anything carried in or on the trailer or vehicle
>
> with **intent** that he or another commits an offence of
> - stealing the vehicle, the trailer or parts
> - stealing anything in or on the vehicle or trailor
> - unauthorised taking of the vehicle

Which charge? Where it is shown that a person accused under this section intended that one of the offences should be committed, it is immaterial that it cannot be shown which one it actually was.

S.9 CRIMINAL ATTEMPTS ACT 1981

DEFENCES

Q Outline the general defences to crime

A **Automatism**. Involuntary reflex action - e.g. a driver being attacked by a swarm of bees.

Intoxication. There is no general defence of intoxication but intoxication (voluntary or involuntary) may be relied upon to negate mens rea in offences of specific intent if the intoxication prevented the offender from forming the specific intent required (unless the offender deliberately became intoxicated simply to give him courage to commit the offence).

Insanity. The test for insanity was established by the **M'Naghten Rules** (1843):

... *to establish a defence on the ground of insanity, it must be clearly proved that, at the time of the committing of the act, the accused was labouring under such a **defect of reason, from disease of mind**, as not to know the nature and quality of the act he was doing, or if he did know it, that he did not know he was doing wrong.*

Mistake. Mistake may be claimed where the mistake would negate the required mens rea for a particular offence e.g. mistakenly picking up someone else's coat and walking off with it may negate the requirement of dishonesty for theft.

Duress by threats. Where a person is threatened with **death or serious physical injury** unless they commit an offence, they may raise this defence, but:

[a] the threat must have caused the defendant to commit the crime;
[b] he must have acted as would a reasonable person with his characteristics;
[c] the threat or injury must be more or less immediate;
[d] he must not have voluntarily exposed himself to an otherwise avoidable risk of duress; and
[e] it is no defence to murder or attempted murder.

Duress of circumstances. Where a person commits an offence to avoid serious consequences because he has no real alternative, e.g. a disqualified driver driving a dying man to hospital, the court will decide the reasonableness of the offender's behaviour.

DEFENCES

Defence of self, another, or property. A person may use such force as is reasonable in the circumstances in the prevention of crime, or in effecting or assisting in the lawful arrest of offenders or suspected offenders or of persons unlawfully at large.

S. 3(1) CRIMINAL LAW ACT 1967

A 'pre-emptive' strike may be justified in all the circumstances. Whether the degree of force used was reasonable in the circumstances will be decided by reference to *the circumstances as the defendant believed them to be*: s.76(3) Criminal Justice and Immigration Act 2008. Force will not be reasonable if it was disproportionate in those circumstances: s.76(6).

Infancy. A child under 10 is presumed incapable of committing crime [*doli incapax*].

HOMICIDE

Q   Define murder

A   Murder is committed when a person

   [a]   unlawfully kills
   [b]   another human being
   [c]   under the Queen's peace
   [d]   with malice aforethought.

COMMON LAW

Sentence. Murder carries the mandatory fixed penalty of life imprisonment ('detention at Her Majesty's pleasure' if under 18).

Unlawfully kills. Actively causes the death of another without lawful justification (and may include omitting an act when a person has a duty to act but fails to, and that failure is a substantial cause of the death). Acting in self-defence, or to prevent crime etc. may amount to justification.

Another human being. Includes a baby who has been born alive and has an existence independent of its mother (in other words, has been fully expelled from the mother's body and has taken its first breath. It is not necessary that the umbilical cord has been cut).

Pre-natal injuries. Where a person injures a baby in the womb and it subsequently dies from those injuries after having being born alive (and therefore become 'another human being'), it may be murder. The defendant's intention at the time of the injury is key. If the defendant intended to kill or seriously injure the baby, then clearly that is sufficient to give rise to murder. If however the defendant only intended to seriously injure the mother, he may be guilty of manslaughter but not murder because his intention (malice) towards the mother is not deemed to transfer fully to the unborn baby: *AG's Ref (No. 3 of 1994)* (1998).

Under the Queen's peace. This excludes deaths caused during the legitimate prosecution of warfare.

Malice aforethought. The required mens rea for murder is intention to kill or cause GBH. Note that for *attempted* murder only intention to kill will suffice.

HOMICIDE

Q What is the position regarding murders committed overseas?

A A British citizen who commits murder (or manslaughter) anywhere in the world may be tried for it in England or Wales: s.9 Offences Against the Person Act 1861.

Q What is the 'year and a day' rule?

A An ancient common law rule which stated that no prosecution for murder could be brought unless the victim died within a year and a day of the defendant's actions. It has now been abolished.

However under the Law Reform (Year and a Day Rule) Act 1996 the Attorney-General's (or Solicitor-General's) consent is required to prosecute in the following cases:

[a] where the victim dies more than 3 years after the injury;
[b] where the defendant has already been convicted of an offence under the circumstances connected with the death (e.g. GBH).

Q What are the 'special defences' to murder?

A Since murder carries a mandatory life sentence (and, in earlier days, the death penalty) certain special defences have been developed to cover circumstances which the law regards as mitigating the gravity of the offence. Unlike general defences (such as self-defence) which if successful would lead to an acquittal, the 'special' defences are 'partial' defences which convert murder to voluntary manslaughter, and allow the sentencing judge to impose a lesser sentence than life imprisonment. A person cannot be *charged* with voluntary manslaughter, such a verdict is only possible where a plea of one of 3 special mitigating circumstances has been successful. They are set out in the Homicide Act 1957 and are (a) diminished responsibility (b) provocation [loss of control] and (c) suicide pact.

Q What effect will the Coroners and Justice Act 2009 have on the special defences?

A Following much criticism of the law relating to diminished responsibility and provocation in particular, the Coroners and Justice Act 2009 when in force (due to be the 4th October 2010) will amend the Homicide Act 1957 special defence of diminished responsibility and replace provocation with 'loss of control'.

Q Outline 'diminished' responsibility

A Section 2 of the Homicide Act 1957 (as amended) states that:

A person ('D') who kills or is a party to a killing of another is not to be convicted of murder if D was suffering from an *abnormality of mental functioning* which -

[a] arose from a recognised medical condition,
[b] *substantially impaired* D's ability to do one or more of the following –

   [i]   understand the nature of D's conduct;
   [ii] form rational judgement;
   [iii] exercise self control;

[c] and *provides an explanation* for D's acts and omissions in doing or being party to the killing.

It is for D to raise this defence and prove it on a balance of probabilities. If the defence is successful D is liable to be convicted of voluntary manslaughter.

Abnormality of mental functioning. The previous wording 'abnormality of mind' was held to amount to 'a state of mind' so different from that of ordinary human beings that the reasonable man would term it abnormal': *R v. Byrne (1960)*. It must arise from a recognised medical condition, substantially impair D's ability to do one of the 3 specified things and should 'provide an explanation' for his acts (or omissions), in other words be of at least a significant contributory factor in his behaviour.

Q Outline 'loss of control'

A This new defence replaces 'provocation'.

Where a person ('D') kills or is party to the killing of another ('V'), D is not to be convicted of murder if –

[a] D's acts and omissions in doing or being a party to the killing resulted from D'S loss of self-control,
[b] the loss of self-control had a qualifying trigger, and
[c] a person of D's sex and age, with a normal degree of tolerance and self-restraint and in the circumstances of D, might have reacted in the same or in a similar way to D.

s.54 Coroners and Justice Act 2009

Sudden loss of control? Previously it had been necessary to prove that D was provoked to a sudden and temporary loss of control (i.e. a 'red mist' moment). This is no longer required.

Revenge? The defence will not apply if D acted 'in a considered desire for revenge': s.54(4)

Qualifying trigger. D's loss of self-control must be attributable to: (a) D's fear of serious violence from V against D or another identified person, and/or (b) to a thing or things done or said (or both) which constituted circumstances of an extremely grave character and caused D to have a justifiable sense of being seriously wronged. What is 'justifiable' will be an objective question for the jury. (It will not be justifiable if D incited the provocative behaviour in the first place as an excuse for violence).

Q Outline 'suicide pact'

A A suicide pact is a common agreement between 2 or more persons having for its object the death of them all, whether or not each is to take his own life. Each participant must have a settled intention of dying. By virtue of s.4 Homicide Act 1957 where 'A' and 'B' form a suicide pact and A, in pursuance of the pact, kill B but does not kill himself, A will be guilty of manslaughter rather than murder.

Q Explain manslaughter

A There are two types of manslaughter. *Voluntary* manslaughter where one of the 3 special, or partial, defences (diminished responsibility, loss of control/provocation, or suicide pact) reduce a murder charge to manslaughter. *Involuntary* manslaughter occurs where the defendant causes the death of another but does not have the required mens rea for murder. Involuntary manslaughter can be divided into two:

[a] killing another by an unlawful act which was likely to cause bodily harm;
[b] killing another by gross negligence.

Unlawful act. Sometimes known as constructive manslaughter. Must be an act (not omission) which is unlawful in itself, rather than simply a lawful act done badly. For example, dropping a slab from a bridge into the path of cars on a motorway is an inherently unlawful act, whereas driving badly is not (driving is lawful, it only becomes unlawful if carried out in a certain way). D must also have the required mens rea for the unlawful act e.g. criminal damage (intention or recklessness).

Gross negligence. D must owe a duty of care towards victim (e.g. doctor towards patient) and commit a very bad negligent breach of that duty. Whether the breach is so bad as to be 'gross' is a question of fact for the jury.

Q   Outline the offence of corporate manslaughter

A   An organisation is guilty of an offence if the way in which its activities are managed or organised –

[a]   causes a person's death, and
[b]   amounts to a gross breach of a relevant duty of care owed by the organisation to the deceased.

However, an organisation will be guilty only if the way in which its activities are managed or organised by its senior management is a substantial element in the breach of the *relevant duty*.
s.1 CORPORATE MANSLAUGHTER AND CORPORATE HOMICIDE ACT 2007

Organisation. Companies; other corporations including public bodies such as local authorities and NHS bodies; organisations incorporated by Royal Charter; limited liability partnerships; Crown bodies such as government departments; police services and authorities.

Senior Management. Those persons who play a significant role in the management of the whole or of a substantial part of the organisation's activities.

Q   What are 'relevant' duties of care?

A   A 'duty of care' is an obligation owed by one person to another to take reasonable care for his health and safety. Duties of care exist in various contexts, for example the duty owed by an employer to his employee to ensure the safe condition of workplaces and equipment. Under the Act 'relevant' duties include employer and occupier duties; duties connected to supplying goods and services; commercial activities; construction and maintenance work, and using or keeping plant, vehicles or other things.

HOMICIDE

Q When are police services and authorities exempt from the relevant duties of care?

A The Act permits exceptions to the relevant duties of care in relation to certain policing and law enforcement activities. These are:

[a] operations for dealing with terrorism, civil unrest or serious disorder that involve the carrying on of policing or law enforcement activities where officers or employees of the public authority in question come under attack, or face the threat of attack or violent resistance, in the course of the operations;
[b] activities carried out in preparation for, or directly in support of, such operations;
[c] training of a hazardous nature or training carried out in a hazardous way in order to improve or maintain the effectiveness of officers or employees of the public authority with respect to such operations.

Q Where can the offence be committed?

A The offence can be prosecuted if the harm resulting in death occurs in the UK, in UK territorial waters, on a British ship, aircraft or hovercraft, or on an oilrig or other offshore installation covered by UK criminal law.

Q Whose consent is required for prosecution?

A Proceedings may only be instituted with the consent of the DPP.

Q Define the offence of causing or allowing the death of a child or vulnerable person

A A person ('D') is guilty of an offence if –

[a] a child or vulnerable adult ('V') dies 'as a result of the unlawful act' of a person who –

[i] was a member of the same household as V, and
[ii] had frequent contact with him,

[b] D was such a person at the time of that act,
[c] at that time there was a significant risk of serious physical harm being caused to V by the unlawful act of such a person, and

HOMICIDE

[d] either D was the person whose act caused V's death or –

   [i] D was, or ought to have been, aware of the risk mentioned in paragraph [c],
   [ii] D failed to take such steps as he could reasonably have been expected to take to protect V from the risk, and
   [iii] the act occurred in circumstances of the kind that D foresaw or ought to have foreseen.
   s.5(1) DOMESTIC VIOLENCE CRIME AND VICTIMS ACT 1994

Child. Person under 16.

Vulnerable adult. Person aged 16 or over whose ability to protect themselves from violence, abuse or neglect is significantly impaired through physical or mental disability or illness, through old age or otherwise.

Same household. Even if D does not actually live in the same house as V he/she may still be considered a member of the same household if they visit it so often and for such periods of time that it is reasonable to regard them as a member of that household.

Q Is it an offence to commit suicide?

A No, nor to attempt to commit suicide. But it is an offence to assist or encourage others to do so.

Q Outline the offence of encouraging or assisting suicide

A A person ('D') commits an offence if –

[a] D does an act capable of encouraging or assisting the suicide or attempted suicide of another person, and
[b] D's act was intended to encourage or assist suicide or an attempt at suicide.
s.2 SUICIDE ACT 1961

Act. Will include a course of conduct.

Another person. Need not be a specific person and D does not have to know or even be able to identify that other person (e.g. author of website promoting suicide and giving guidance on how to achieve it, who intends readers to follow his advice even though he may never know who those readers are).

Impossible acts. The offence may be committed even where suicide would be impossible as a result of the act (e.g. where D believes he/she is supplying the other person with a lethal drug which turns out to be harmless).

Prosecution. The consent of the DPP is required.

Q **Definition solicitation of murder**

A Whosoever shall solicit, encourage, persuade or endeavour to persuade, or shall propose to any person, to murder any other person... shall be guilty of an offence.

s.4 OFFENCES AGAINST THE PERSON ACT 1861

Victim overseas. The proposed victim may be anywhere in the world.

Impossibility. It does not matter whether the person solicited is actually persuaded to carry out the murder, provided there is some form of communication with them. The offence may still be committed even though the proposed killing could never take place (as where the suspect attempts to persuade an undercover police officer to carry out a contract killing).

MISUSE OF DRUGS

Q Give examples of Class A, B and C drugs

A **Class A**, includes the most dangerous drugs e.g. heroin, cocaine, LSD, MDMA ('ecstasy'), methylamphetamine ('crystal meth'), and any form of fungus containing psilocin (e.g. 'magic mushrooms').

Class B, includes cannabis, cannabis resin, cannabis oil, codeine and ritalin.

Class C, includes ketamin, gamma hydroxybutyrate ('GHB') and many commonly abused prescription drugs e.g diazepam.

Q According to the Misuse of Drugs Act 1971, what does cannabis not include?

A [a] Cannabis resin;
[b] the mature stalk of any cannabis plant [or fibre from it]; and
[c] seed from the plant.

Q What two conditions must be satisfied in order to prove possession of a controlled drug?

A [a] That a person has or had a controlled drug under his possession (physical control); and
[b] he knew that he had something in his possession which was in fact a controlled drug.

Q Define the offence of possession

A It is an offence to unlawfully possess a controlled drug.
S. 5(2) MISUSE OF DRUGS ACT 1971

Q Outline the two specific statutory defences to possession of a controlled drug

A [a] **To prevent an offence being committed**:

[i] knowing or suspecting it to be a controlled drug;
[ii] he took possession **to prevent another person committing an offence**; and
[iii] as soon as possible took steps to **destroy the drug**; or
[iv] **to deliver to lawful custody**.

MISUSE OF DRUGS

[b] **To deliver to lawful custody**:

[i] knowing or suspecting it to be a controlled drug;
[ii] he took possession **to deliver it to a person lawfully entitled** to receive the drug; and
[iii] as soon as he took possession he took all steps reasonable **to deliver it to such a person**.

S. 5 MISUSE OF DRUGS ACT 1971

Q   Outline the general defence under S. 28 of the Misuse of Drugs Act 1971

A   In relation to unlawful production, unlawful supply, unlawful possession, possession with intent to supply, unlawful cultivation of cannabis and offences connected with opium, it will be a defence to prove:

[a] **Lack of knowledge of a fact**:

[i] he did not know or suspect, [nor had reason to suspect]
[ii] the existence of a fact alleged by the prosecution which it must prove.

[b] **Who is protected**? E.g. an innocent messenger.
[c] **Lack of knowledge of controlled drug**: Where it is necessary for the prosecution to prove it was a particular controlled drug and it has been proved that it was that drug, it will be a defence to prove:

[i] he thought the substance was **something other than a controlled drug**, and had no reason to believe it to be a controlled drug; or
[ii] he thought it was a controlled drug **which he could lawfully possess**,

but he shall not escape conviction by only proving:

[i] he did not suspect or believe [nor have reason to]
[ii] that the substance was **the particular drug** in question.

Who is protected? E.g. a person mistakenly believing a white substance [heroin] to be salt, or that it was a drug prescribed for him by his doctor (though in fact it was a different drug). **But not** simply that he thought it was one drug when in fact it was another.

MISUSE OF DRUGS

Q Define the offence of producing a controlled drug

A It is an offence to:

[a] unlawfully produce a controlled drug; or
[b] to be concerned in the production of the drug.

S. 4(2) MISUSE OF DRUGS ACT 1971

Produce. Means by manufacture, cultivation or by any other method.

Q Define the offence of supplying controlled drugs

A It is an offence to:

[a] supply or **offer to supply** a controlled drug to another;
[b] to be concerned in the supply; or
[c] to be concerned in the making of an offer to supply.

S. 4(3) MISUSE OF DRUGS ACT 1971

Supply. Includes distribute.

Offer to supply. The offence is complete once the **offer** is made.

Q Define the offence of possession with intent to supply

A It is an offence to possess [lawfully or not] a controlled drug with intent to supply.

S. 5(3) MISUSE OF DRUGS ACT 1971

Intent. A person in lawful possession, e.g. doctor, who intends to unlawfully supply is guilty of this offence.

Q Define the offence of cannabis cultivation

A It is an offence to unlawfully cultivate cannabis.

S. 6 MISUSE OF DRUGS ACT 1971

Cultivate. Includes watering, feeding. It is not necessary for the defendant to know that the plant is cannabis, the offence is complete simply upon proof of cultivation.

MISUSE OF DRUGS

Q Define the offence of supplying articles for administering or preparing drugs

A A person commits an offence who supplies or offers to supply:

[a] any article which may be used or adapted for use [on its own or in conjunction with other articles] in the unlawful **administration** by a person of a controlled drug to himself or another, in the knowledge that the article is to be used unlawfully; or
[b] any article which may be used to **prepare** a controlled drug for unlawful administration by himself or another, in the knowledge that the article is to be used unlawfully.

S. 9A MISUSE OF DRUGS ACT 1971

Unlawful. Any administration of a controlled drug will be unlawful **except** when the

[a] administration to self or another is not an offence of unlawful supply;
[b] administration to himself is not an offence of unlawful possession.

Hypodermic syringes and needles are not covered: S. 9A(2).

Q Outline the offence of drugs misuse by occupiers of premises

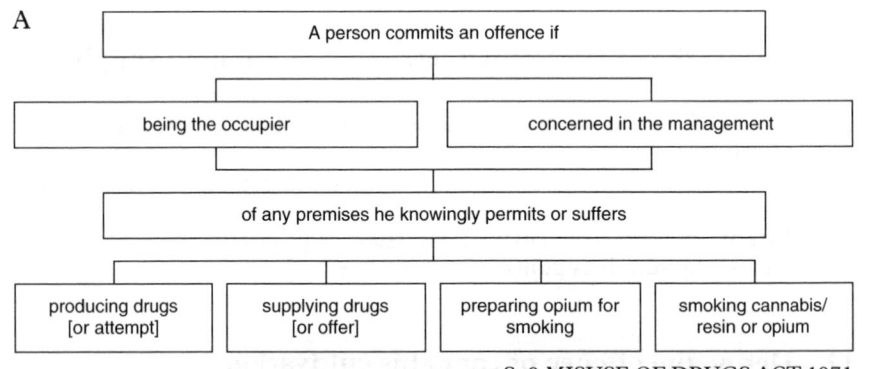

A

```
              A person commits an offence if
            /                                \
   being the occupier              concerned in the management
            \                                /
         of any premises he knowingly permits or suffers
       /            |              |                \
producing drugs  supplying drugs  preparing opium for  smoking cannabis/
[or attempt]     [or offer]       smoking              resin or opium
```

S. 8 MISUSE OF DRUGS ACT 1971

Management. Means someone involved in the planning, organising and actual use of the premises.

Permit/suffer. Turning a 'blind eye' to the activities will do.

MISUSE OF DRUGS

Q What is a 'closure notice'

A This is a power to close 'drug dens', 'crack houses' etc. Under S. 1 of the Anti-Social Behaviour Act 2003, if a superintendent (or above) reasonably believes that premises have been used during the previous three months in connection with the unlawful use, production or supply of a Class A controlled drug, and that the use of the premises is associated with the occurrence of disorder or serious nuisance to members of the public, s/he may authorise the issue of a closure notice in respect of the premises if s/he is satisfied:

[a] that the local authority has been consulted, and
[b] reasonable steps have been taken to discover the identity of anyone residing on the premises, or with control of or responsibility for, or an interest in, the premises.

Q What must the closure notice say?

A The notice must state the following:

[i] that an application will be made to close the premises,
[ii] that access to the premises by any person (other than an habitual resident or owner) is prohibited,
[iii] the date and time and place where the application will be heard,
[iv] the effects of a closure order,
[v] that failure to comply with the notice is an offence, and
[vi] information about housing and legal advisers in the area who may be contacted for assistance.

Q How is a closure notice served?

A It must be served by a police officer, by fixing a copy to

[a] at least one prominent place on the premises,
[b] each normal means of access to the premises,
[c] any outbuildings which appear to the constable to be used with or as part of the premises

and by giving a copy to

[a] at least one person who appears to the constable to have control/responsibility for the premises,
[b] any person who lives on the premises. In order to effect service, the constable may enter the premises, if necessary using reasonable force.

MISUSE OF DRUGS

Q   How is a closure order obtained?

A   Following the issue of a closure notice a police officer must apply to a magistrates' court for a closure order. The application must be heard not later than 48 hours after the notice has been served (although the application may then be adjourned for up to 14 days to allow persons with an interest in the premises to contest the application). A closure order may be made only if the magistrates are satisfied that:

[a]   the premises have been used in connection with the unlawful use, production or supply of a Class A controlled drug,
[b]   use of the premises is associated with the occurrence of disorder or nuisance, and
[c]   making an order is necessary to prevent a reoccurrence of such disorder or nuisance during the period of the notice.

Q   For how long does a closure order last?

A   The order closes the premises (or any specified parts of it) to all persons for such period as decided by the court, but no longer than three months. An extension for a further three months may be applied for at any time before the order expires, with a superindent's authority (following consultation with the local authority). No further extensions may be sought thereafter.

Q   What is the power to enter under a closure order?

A   A police officer (or other authorised person) may enter the premises, using reasonable force if necessary, and/or secure the premises against entry, again using reasonable force if necessary. In addition a police officer (or other authorised person) may enter at any time during the period of the order to carry out essential maintenance or repairs (but must produce evidence of ID and authority if challenged by the owner/occupier).

Q   Outline the breach of closure order offences

A   It is an offence, without reasonable excuse, to remain on or enter premises in contravention of a closure notice or closure order. It is also an offence to obstruct a constable or other authorised person exercising his powers of entry.

S. 4 ANTI-SOCIAL BEHAVIOUR ACT 2003

MISUSE OF DRUGS

Q Define the offence of misuse of drugs outside the UK

A A person commits an offence if **in the UK** he assists or induces the commission in any place **outside the UK** of an offence under the law in force in that other place.

S. 20 MISUSE OF DRUGS ACT 1971

Q Outline police powers of entry etc

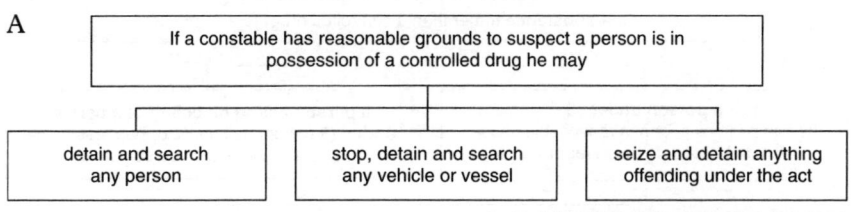

A

> If a constable has reasonable grounds to suspect a person is in possession of a controlled drug he may

- detain and search any person
- stop, detain and search any vehicle or vessel
- seize and detain anything offending under the act

S. 23 MISUSE OF DRUGS ACT 1971

Q What are the grounds for the issue of a warrant?

A A magistrate may issue a warrant if satisfied on information on oath that there are reasonable grounds to suspect:

[a] that any **controlled drug** is unlawfully in the possession of a person on the premises;
[b] or that **a document** relating to an unlawful transaction or dealing is in possession of a person on the premises.

Q What are the powers under the warrant?

A [a] At any time **within one month** from the date of the warrant;
[b] enter, search the premises and persons; and

  [i] if there are grounds for suspecting that an offence has been committed in respect of **controlled drugs found**; or
  [ii] there is reason to believe that **any document found** relates to an unlawful transaction,
  [iii] seize and detain the drugs or document.

S. 23 MISUSE OF DRUGS ACT 1971

Obstruction. It is an offence to intentionally obstruct a constable exercising these powers.

Unlawful transaction. The document is any document in relation to a transaction in the UK or, if carried out abroad, would be an offence under the foreign law.

MISUSE OF DRUGS

Q What is the offence of supply of intoxicating substances?

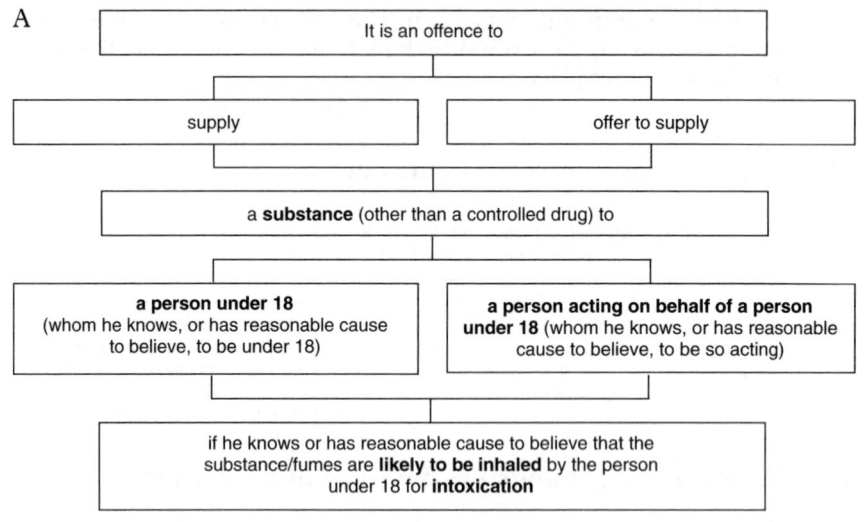

A

It is an offence to

- supply
- offer to supply

a **substance** (other than a controlled drug) to

- **a person under 18** (whom he knows, or has reasonable cause to believe, to be under 18)
- **a person acting on behalf of a person under 18** (whom he knows, or has reasonable cause to believe, to be so acting)

if he knows or has reasonable cause to believe that the substance/fumes are **likely to be inhaled** by the person under 18 for **intoxication**

S. 1 INTOXICATING SUBSTANCES (SUPPLY) ACT 1985

Purpose. Aimed at curbing 'glue sniffing'.

Defence. It is a defence for a person charged with this offence to show that at the time of offer/supply he/she was both:

[a] under 18 and
[b] acting otherwise than in the course or furtherance of a business.

Q What is the offence of supplying butane lighter refills?

A It is an offence to supply any cigarette lighter refill cannister containing butane to any person under 18 years old.

Q What is a travel restriction order?

A The courts may impose travel restrictions on offenders convicted of drug trafficking which may prohibit the offender from leaving the UK at any time during a specified period commencing with the date of his release from custody. The minimum duration of such an order is two years.

S. 36 CRIMINAL JUSTICE AND POLICE ACT 2001

FIREARMS AND GUN CRIME

Q What is a 'firearm'?

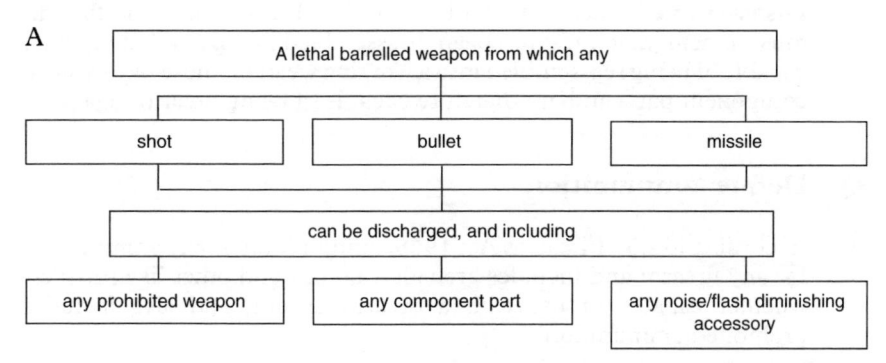

A

```
          A lethal barrelled weapon from which any
                          │
        ┌─────────────────┼─────────────────┐
      shot              bullet            missile
        └─────────────────┼─────────────────┘
                          │
              can be discharged, and including
                          │
        ┌─────────────────┼─────────────────┐
any prohibited weapon  any component part  any noise/flash diminishing
                                                   accessory
```

Lethal. Capable of causing injury.

Component parts. Parts such as triggers or barrels are included, telescopic sights are not. Silencers and flash eliminators feature in the definition but according to *R v Buckfield* (1998) a silencer *on its own* will only be considered a firearm if the prosecution proves that it could be used with a weapon in the defendant's possession and was held for that purpose.

Examples. Air pistols, imitation revolvers and signalling pistols have all been held to be firearms in the past, but each case must be decided on its own merits.

Q When is a firearm not a firearm?

A When it has been deactivated (i.e. rendered incapable of discharging any shot, bullet or missile). This can be proved by establishing:

   [a] it bears a mark (approved by the Secretary of State) denoting the fact that it has been deactivated by one of two approved companies; and
   [b] the company has certified in writing that the work has been carried out in an approved manner.

s.8 FIREARMS (AMENDMENT) ACT 1988

FIREARMS AND GUN CRIME

The approved companies. The Society of the Mystery of Gunmakers of the City of London and the Birmingham Proof House.

Disassembled weapons. To be considered deactivated the firearm must remain intact. If it has been disassembled into parts that are then capable of being reassembled into a working weapon, those parts will be component parts and are therefore capable of being firearms again.

Q   Define 'ammunition'

A   According to s.57 Firearms Act 1968, ammunition is 'any ammunition for any firearm and includes grenades, bombs and other like missiles, whether capable of use with a firearm or not, and also includes prohibited ammunition'.

Ingredients. The definition only covers assembled ammunition and not ingredients, component parts or empty shells (unless they are themselves classified as prohibited).

Q   What are 'imitation' firearms?

A   There are two types: (a) *general* imitations (covered by s.57 Firearms Act 1968), being anything which has the appearance of a firearm, and (b) *imitations of section 1 firearms* (covered by ss.1 and 2 Firearms Act 1982), being those which have both the appearance of a section 1 firearm and which can be readily converted into such a firearm.

Q   What did *R v. Bentham (2005)* decide?

A   In this case the House of Lords held that the definition of firearm in s.57 Firearms Act 1968 requires D to be carrying a 'thing' which is separate from himself and capable of being possessed, so D holding his fingers under a coat to replicate a firearm does not amount to carrying an imitation firearm because one cannot be said to 'possess' attached parts of one's own body (whereas holding a banana or table leg under a coat pretending it to be a firearm may do).

FIREARMS AND GUN CRIME

Q What is a 'prohibited weapon'?

A Certain types of firearm and ammunition are considered so potentially dangerous that they are subject to special laws with greater sentencing potential. The authority of the Secretary of State is required to possess, buy or acquire such a weapon (rather than simply a firearms certificate). Under s.5 Firearms Act 1968 prohibited weapons include:

- [a] automatic weapons;
- [b] most self-loading or pump-action weapons;
- [c] any firearm which has a barrel less than 30 cm long, or is less than 60 cm in length overall (other than an air weapon, a muzzle-loading gun or a firearm designed as signalling apparatus). E.g. most handguns;
- [d] most smooth bore revolvers;
- [e] any weapon, of whatever description, designed or adapted for the discharge of any noxious liquid, gas or other thing;
- [f] any air rifle, air gun or air pistol which uses, or is designed or adapted for use with, a self-contained gas cartridge system;
- [g] military weapons and ammunition including grenades and mortars.

Designed or adapted. Simply filling a washing-up liquid bottle with ammonia or acid does not amount to adapting it for the discharge of noxious liquid because the bottle itself has not been altered in any way, it has merely been filled with liquid.

Q Outline the offence of possessing or distributing prohibited weapons or ammunition

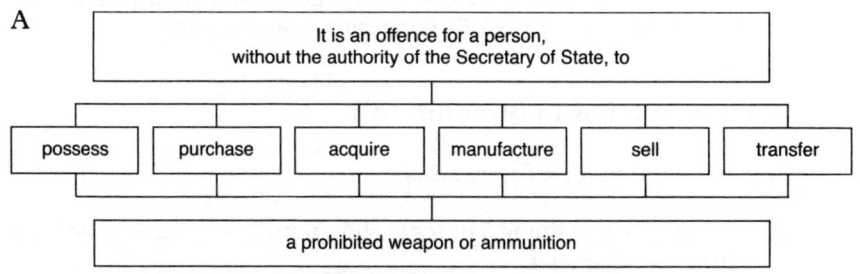

A

It is an offence for a person, without the authority of the Secretary of State, to

- possess
- purchase
- acquire
- manufacture
- sell
- transfer

a prohibited weapon or ammunition

Strict liability. It does not matter whether the person knew they were in possession of the firearm/ammunition or that they knew the nature of the item they were possessing.

FIREARMS AND GUN CRIME

Q   Who is exempt from committing the prohibited weapons offences?

A   Certain categories of persons are exempt by virtue of ss.5 and 5A of the Firearms Act 1968. Section 5A implements exemptions created by the European Weapons Directive and covers authorised collectors and firearms dealers as well as authorised persons involved in transactions of certain ammunition used for lawful shooting and slaughtering of animals, estate management or the protection of other animals and humans. Other 'special exemptions' are provided for by s.5, including:

[a]   slaughtering instruments;
[b]   instruments for the humane killing of animals;
[c]   shot pistols for vermin;
[d]   firearms used for treatment/tranquillising of animals;
[e]   starter pistols for athletics meetings;
[f]   trophies of war (acquired pre 1 January 1946);
[g]   firearms of historic interest;
[h]   air weapons with self-contained gas cartridges owned before 20 January 2004 (provided the owner applied for a firearms certificate before 1 April 2004)

Q   What is a 'section 1 firearm'?

A   This is a term used to describe firearms which are subject to various offences, and in particular section 1 of the Firearms Act 1968. Section 1 firearms include all firearms except shotguns [unless 'sawn-off'] and conventional [i.e. not 'specially dangerous'] air weapons.

Q   What is 'section 1 ammunition'?

A   Any ammunition for a firearm except:

[a]   cartridges containing 5 or more shot, none being bigger than 0.36 inches in diameter;
[b]   ammunition for an airgun, air rifle or air pistol; and
[c]   blank cartridges not more than 1 inch in diameter.

s.1(4) FIREARMS ACT 1968

FIREARMS AND GUN CRIME

Q Outline the offence of possessing a section 1 firearm or ammunition without a certificate

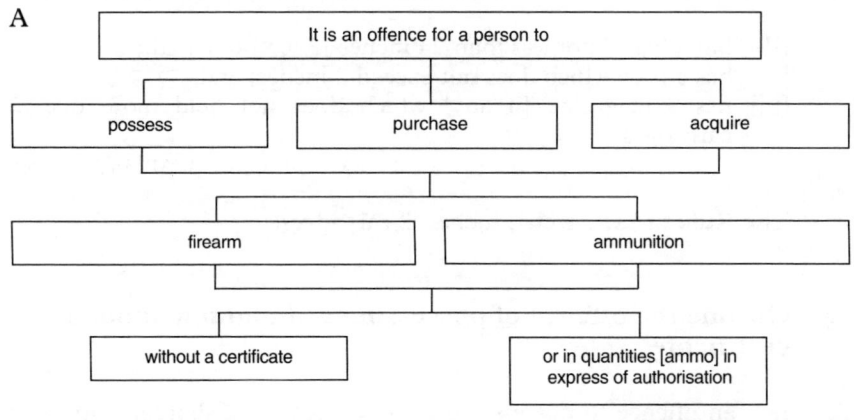

A

```
                It is an offence for a person to
          ┌──────────────┬──────────────┐
       possess         purchase       acquire
          └──────────────┼──────────────┘
                ┌────────┴────────┐
             firearm          ammunition
                │                 │
        without a certificate   or in quantities [ammo] in
                                express of authorisation
```

s1 FIREARMS ACT 1968

Sawn-off shotguns. If the firearm in question is a sawn-off shotgun the offence becomes aggravated (7 years' imprisonment rather than the usual 5).

Imitation firearms. One that has the appearance of a section 1 firearm and which can readily converted into such a firearm.

Q Outline the offence of shortening the barrel of a section 1 firearm

A It is an offence to shorten the barrel of any smooth-bore section 1 firearm which has a bore less than 2 inches to a length **less than 24 inches.**

s.6(1) FIREARMS ACT 1968

Length of barrel. Measure from muzzle to point at which the charge is exploded.

Exempt. Registered firearms dealers who are shortening barrel solely to replace a defective part so as to create a new barrel with an overall length of at least 24 inches.

FIREARMS AND GUN CRIME

Q Define a 'shotgun'

A A shotgun is a smooth-bore gun (not being an airgun or revolver) which

[i] has a barrel not less than 24 inches [2 feet] in length;
[ii] has a bore which does not exceed 2 inches; and
[iii] has a magazine [if any] which does not hold more than 2 cartridges.

s.1(3)(A) FIREARMS ACT 1968

The Rule of 2s. 2 feet, 2 inches, 2 cartridges.

Q Outline the offence of possessing a shotgun without a certificate

A It is an offence to possess, purchase or acquire a shotgun without a holding a shotgun certificate.

s.2(1) FIREARMS ACT 1968

Shotgun certificate. Granted by chief officer of police. May be subject to conditions. It is an offence to fail to comply with any such conditions.

Q Outline the offence of shortening the barrel of a shotgun

A It is an offence to shorten the barrel of a shotgun to a length less than 24 inches.

s.4(1) FIREARMS ACT 1968

Exempt. Registered firearms dealers who are shortening barrel solely to replace a defective part so as to create a new barrel with an overall length of at least 24 inches.

Q When is an air weapon 'specially dangerous'?

A When it is capable of discharging a missile with [a] kinetic energy in excess of 6ft lb (air pistol), or [b] kinetic energy in excess of 12 ft lb (air weapon) [unless it is an underwater gun], or [c] it is disguised as another object.

R.2 FIREARMS (DANGEROUS AIR WEAPONS) RULES 1969

FIREARMS AND GUN CRIME

Q Outline the offence of selling air weapons otherwise than face to face

A A person who sells an air weapon by way of trade or business to an individual in Great Britain who is not a registered firearms dealer commits an offence if the transfer of possession takes place otherwise than at a time when both buyer and seller (or his representative) are present in person.

s.32 VIOLENT CRIME REDUCTION ACT 2006

Q Outline the offence of firing an air weapon beyond premises

A A person commits an offence if:

[a] [a] he has with him an air weapon on any premises; and
[b] [b] he uses it for firing a missile beyond those premises.

s.21A FIREARMS ACT 1968

Defence. To show that he had the consent of the occupier of any premises into or across which the missile was fired.

Age. Note that there are no age limits to this offence, it applies to persons of any age.

Q Summarise the general exemptions from holding a firearms certificate

A [a] Police permit holders;
[b] clubs, athletics and sporting purposes;
[c] borrowed rifle on private premises;
[d] holders of visitors' permits;
[e] antiques as ornaments or curiosities;
[f] authorised firearms dealers;
[g] auctioneers, carriers and warehouse staff;
[h] licensed slaughterers;
[i] theatrical performers;
[j] ships, aircraft or aerodrome equipment;
[k] crown servants;
[l] proof houses; and
[m] holders of a museum licence.

FIREARMS AND GUN CRIME

Q Outline the principal criminal use of firearms offences

A 1. **Possession with intent to endanger life.** It is an offence for a person to have in his possession a firearm or ammunition with intent by means thereof to endanger life [of another] or to enable another person by means thereof to endanger life [of another], whether any injury has been caused or not.

s.16

Imitation firearms? No. This offence cannot be committed by possessing an imitation firearms.

2. **Possession with intent to cause fear of violence.** It is an offence for a person to have in his possession a firearm (or imitation) with intent to cause, or enable another to cause, any person to believe that unlawful violence will be used against him or another.

s.16A

Imitation firearms? Yes, anything which has the appearance of a firearm.

3. **Using a firearm to resist arrest.** It is an offence for a person to make [or attempt to make] use of a firearm (or imitation) to prevent the lawful arrest or detention of himself or another.

s.17(1)

Firearm. 'Firearm' here does not include component parts or silencers/flash eliminators.

Imitation firearms?

Yes, anything which has the appearance of a firearm (but note that because 'firearm' itself here does not include component parts, imitation components will also not be covered).

4. **Possession of a firearm while committing/being arrested for a schedule 1 offence.** If a person, at the time of committing or being arrested for an offence in schedule 1 to the Act, has in his possession a firearm (or imitation) he commits an offence [unless he can show he has it for a lawful object].

s.17(2)

Schedule 1 offences are:

[a] criminal damage;
[b] theft, robbery, blackmail, burglary, taking a conveyance;

FIREARMS AND GUN CRIME

[c] assaults and wounding [but not s.18 GBH];
[d] rape and other sexual offences under the Sexual Offences Act 2003;
[e] child abduction;
[f] aiding, abetting and attempting the above.

Imitation firearms? Yes, anything which has the appearance of a firearm.

5. Having a firearm with intent to commit indictable offence or resist arrest. It is an offence for a person to have with him a firearm (or imitation) with intent to commit an indictable offence, or resist or prevent the arrest of another while in possession of a firearm (or imitation).

s.18(1)

Imitation firearms? Yes, anything which has the appearance of a firearm.

6. Having a firearm in a public place. A person commits an offence if, without lawful authority or reasonable excuse [onus of proof on him] he has with him in a public place –

[a] a loaded shotgun
[b] an air weapon (loaded or not)
[c] any other firearm (loaded or not) together with ammunition suitable for use in that firearm, or
[d] an imitation firearm.

s.19

Imitation firearm? Yes, anything which has the appearance of a firearm.

7. Trespassing with a firearm in a building. A person commits an offence if, while he has a firearm or imitation firearm with him, he enters or is in any building or part of a building as a trespasser and without reasonable excuse [onus of proof on him].

s.20(1)

Imitation firearm? Yes, anything which has the appearance of a firearm.

FIREARMS AND GUN CRIME

8. **Trespassing with a firearm on land.** A person commits an offence if, while he has a firearm or imitation firearm with him, he enters or is on any land as a trespasser and without reasonable excuse [onus of proof on him].

s.20(2)

Imitation firearm? Yes, anything which has the appearance of a firearm.

9. **Using someone to mind a weapon.** A person is guilty of an offence if he uses another to look after, hide or transport a dangerous weapon for him; and he does so under arrangements or in circumstances that facilitate, or are intended to facilitate, the weapon's being available to him for an unlawful purpose.

s.28 VIOLENT CRIME REDUCTION ACT 2006

Available to him. Includes any case where (a) the weapon is available for him to take possession of it at a time and place; and (b) his possession of the weapon at that time and place would constitute, or be likely to lead to, the commission by him of an offence.

Dangerous weapon. A firearm other than an air weapon (or air weapon component/accessory), or a weapon to which ss.141 or 141A Criminal Justice Act 1988 applies (certain offensive weapons, knives and blades).

Q What firearms restrictions are placed on convicted persons?

A Any person who has been sentenced to custody for *life*, or to any form of detention for *3 years or more* is prohibited from having any firearms or ammunition in his/her possession **at any time**. Any person sentenced to any form of detention for between *3 months* and *3 years* is prohibited for **5 years** (beginning on day of release).

s.21 FIREARMS ACT 1968

Imitation firearms? These restrictions do not apply to imitation firearms.

Supplying to prohibited person. It is an offence to sell or transfer a firearm or ammunition to, or repair, test or prove a firearm or ammunition for, a person whom he *knows or has reasonable grounds to believe* to be prohibited by s.21.

FIREARMS AND GUN CRIME

Q **Outline the Firearms Act restrictions which relate to those under 18**

A [a] A person under 18 must not purchase or hire any firearm or ammunition (s.22(1)(a) as amended by the Firearms (Amendment) Regulations 2010; [b] it is an offence to sell or hire any firearm or ammunition to a person under 18 (s.24(1)); [c] a person under 18 must not have with him/her an air weapon or ammunition for an air weapon (s.22(4)) unless under the supervision of a person aged 21 or over (s.23(1)), or (provided he/she is at least 14) on private premises with the consent of the occupier (s.23(3)). If a supervised young person fires the weapon beyond the premises both the young person and their supervisor commit an offence; [d] it is an offence to make a gift or part with possession of an air weapon or ammunition to a person under 18 (save in the permitted circumstances above); [e] it is an offence to sell an imitation firearm to a person under 18 (s.24A(2)), or for a person under 18 to purchase one (s.24A(1)). It is a defence to show that the seller believed that the purchaser was 18 or over and had reasonable grounds for that belief (s.24A(3)).

Q **Outline the Firearms Act restrictions which relate to those under 15**

A [a] A person under 15 must not have with him/her an assembled shotgun unless supervised by a person aged 21 or over, or while the shotgun is securely covered so it cannot be fired; [b] it is an offence to make a gift of a shotgun or ammunition to a person under 15 (ss.22(3) and 24(3)).

Q **Outline the Firearms Act restrictions which relate to those under 14**

A [a] A person under 14 must not have in his/her possession a section 1 firearm or ammunition; [b] It is an offence to make a gift or part with possession of a section 1 firearm or ammunition to a person under 14 (certain sports and shooting club exceptions may apply) (ss.22(2) and 24(2)).

FIREARMS AND GUN CRIME

Q Outline the entry, stop and search powers contained in s.47 Firearms Act 1968

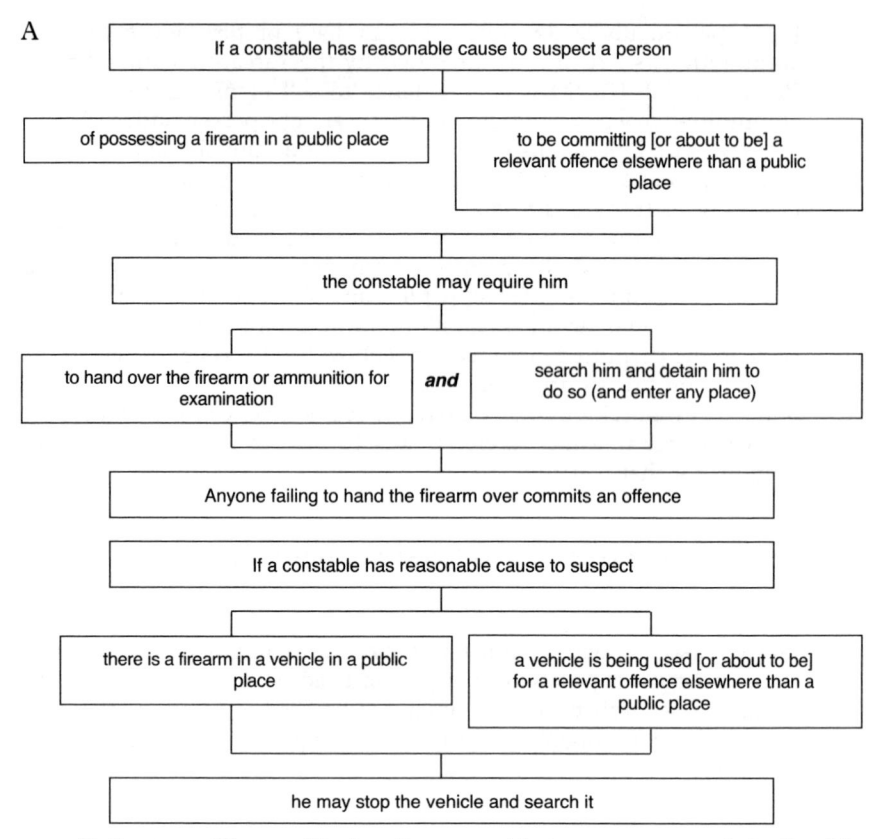

A

```
┌─────────────────────────────────────────────────────────┐
│     If a constable has reasonable cause to suspect a person │
└─────────────────────────────────────────────────────────┘
         │                                    │
┌────────────────────────┐      ┌──────────────────────────────┐
│ of possessing a firearm│      │ to be committing [or about to be] a │
│ in a public place      │      │ relevant offence elsewhere than a   │
│                        │      │ public place                        │
└────────────────────────┘      └──────────────────────────────┘
                    │           │
            ┌─────────────────────────────┐
            │ the constable may require him │
            └─────────────────────────────┘
                    │           │
┌──────────────────────────────┐    ┌──────────────────────────────┐
│ to hand over the firearm or  │ and│ search him and detain him to │
│ ammunition for examination   │    │ do so (and enter any place)  │
└──────────────────────────────┘    └──────────────────────────────┘

┌─────────────────────────────────────────────────────────┐
│  Anyone failing to hand the firearm over commits an offence │
└─────────────────────────────────────────────────────────┘

┌─────────────────────────────────────────────────────────┐
│        If a constable has reasonable cause to suspect        │
└─────────────────────────────────────────────────────────┘
         │                                    │
┌────────────────────────┐      ┌──────────────────────────────┐
│ there is a firearm in a│      │ a vehicle is being used [or about │
│ vehicle in a public    │      │ to be] for a relevant offence     │
│ place                  │      │ elsewhere than a public place     │
└────────────────────────┘      └──────────────────────────────┘

┌─────────────────────────────────────────────────────────┐
│           he may stop the vehicle and search it             │
└─────────────────────────────────────────────────────────┘
```

Relevant offence. Having firearm with intent to commit indictable offence or resist arrest, or trespassing with a firearm.

FIREARMS AND GUN CRIME

Q What are the police powers to demand certificates under s.48 Firearms Act 1968?

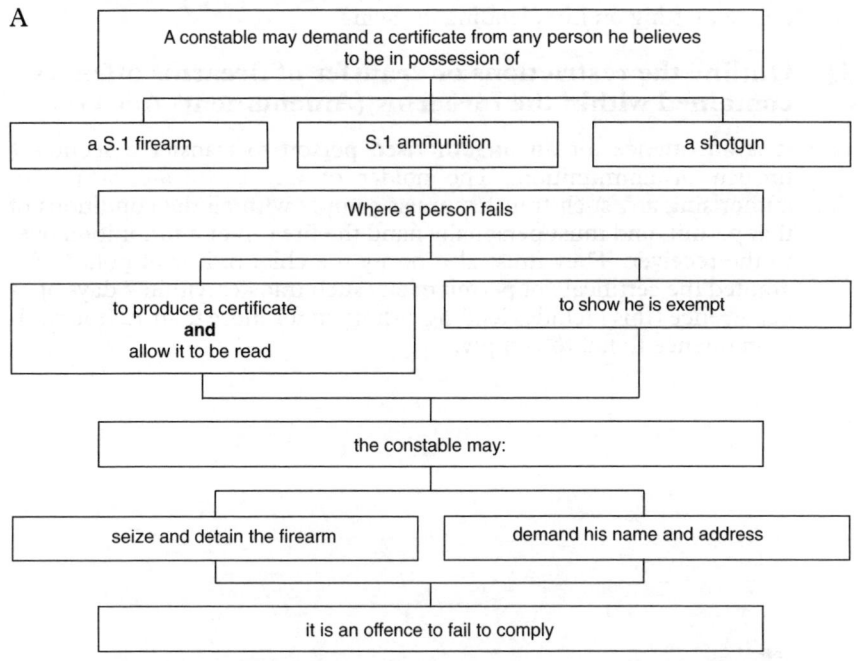

A

```
┌─────────────────────────────────────────────────────────────┐
│  A constable may demand a certificate from any person he    │
│  believes to be in possession of                            │
└─────────────────────────────────────────────────────────────┘
        │                    │                    │
┌───────────────┐   ┌──────────────────┐   ┌───────────────┐
│ a S.1 firearm │   │  S.1 ammunition  │   │   a shotgun   │
└───────────────┘   └──────────────────┘   └───────────────┘
                    ┌──────────────────┐
                    │ Where a person fails │
                    └──────────────────┘
            │                              │
┌───────────────────────┐       ┌───────────────────────┐
│ to produce a certificate│       │ to show he is exempt  │
│        and             │       │                       │
│  allow it to be read   │       │                       │
└───────────────────────┘       └───────────────────────┘
                    ┌──────────────────┐
                    │ the constable may: │
                    └──────────────────┘
            │                              │
┌───────────────────────────┐   ┌───────────────────────────┐
│ seize and detain the firearm│   │ demand his name and address│
└───────────────────────────┘   └───────────────────────────┘
                    ┌───────────────────────────────────┐
                    │ it is an offence to fail to comply │
                    └───────────────────────────────────┘
```

Q Outline the offence of converting an imitation firearm

A It is an offence for a person (other than a registered firearms dealer) to convert an imitation firearm into a firearm.

s.4(3) FIREARMS ACT 1968

Q What is a 'realistic imitation firearm' under the Violent Crime Reduction Act 2006?

A An imitation firearm which has an appearance that is so realistic as to make it indistinguishable, for all practical purposes, from a real firearm.

Q Outline the realistic imitation firearm offences under s.36 Violent Crime Reduction Act 2006

A It is an offence to manufacture or sell a realistic imitation firearm, modify an imitation firearm to become a realistic imitation firearm, or bring or cause to be brought into the UK a realistic imitation firearm. Defences are available in relation to museums and galleries, theatre, film or TV productions, specified historical re-enactments and for crown servants.

Q **In relation to restrictions on 'transferring' firearms, what does 'transferring' mean?**

A Selling, letting on hire, lending or giving.

Q **Outline the restrictions on transfer of firearms offences contained within the Firearms (Amendment) Act 1997**

A It is an offence for an unauthorised person to transfer a section 1 firearm or ammunition. The holder of any certificate or permit authorising any such transfers must comply with all the conditions of that permit, and must personally hand the firearm or ammunition over to the receiver. They must also notify the chief officer of police who granted the certificate or permit of any such transfer within 7 days of its occurrence (this includes lending a shotgun for more than 72 hours). It is an offence to fail to comply.

OFFENCES AGAINST THE PERSON

Q Define common assault and battery

A **Assault** is any act whereby the defendant, intentionally or recklessly, causes another **to apprehend** immediate and unlawful personal violence and **battery** is the actual application of force.

S. 39 CRIMINAL JUSTICE ACT 1988

Q Define assault with intent to resist arrest

A It is an offence to assault any other person with intent to resist or prevent the lawful apprehension of himself or another for any offence.

S. 38 OFFENCES AGAINST THE PERSON ACT 1861

Who is protected? Police, store detectives, bailiffs etc.

The arrest must be lawful and the defendant must be aware of that for the offence to be proved.

Q Define the offence of assault on police

A A person commits an offence who assaults a constable in the execution of his duty or a **person assisting a constable** in the execution of his duty.

S. 89(1) POLICE ACT 1996

Q Define the offence of obstructing police

A Any person who resists or wilfully obstructs a constable in the execution of his duty or a **person assisting a constable** in the execution of his duty, commits an offence.

S. 89(2) POLICE ACT 1996

Obstruction. 'Resistance' suggests physical opposition. Obstruction is wider, and may be interpreted as 'making it more difficult for a constable to carry out his duties'.

Q Outline the offence of obstructing or hindering certain emergency workers

A A person who, without reasonable excuse, obstructs or hinders certain specified emergency workers while that worker is responding to emergency circumstances, commits an offence. Further, a person who without reasonable excuse obstructs or hinders a person assisting such an emergency worker, commits an offence.

SS. 1 & 2 EMERGENCY WORKERS (OBSTRUCTION) ACT 2006

OFFENCES AGAINST THE PERSON

Q Which emergency workers are protected by this offence?

A The following emergency personnel are covered:

[a] A person employed by a fire and rescue authority in England and Wales;
[b] in relation to England and Wales, a person (other than one falling within (a) above) whose duties as an employee or as a servant of the Crown involve -

  [i] extinguishing fires; or
  [ii] protecting life and property in the event of a fire;

[c] a person employed by a relevant NHS body in the provision of ambulance services (including air ambulance services), or of a person providing such services under an NHS arrangement;
[d] a person providing services for the transport of organs, blood, equipment or personnel under an NHS arrangement;
[e] a member of HM Coastguard;
[f] a member of a lifeboat crew, or person who musters such a crew or attends to a lifeboat's launch or recovery.

Q What is an 'emergency' for the purposes of this offence?

A The Act defines an 'emergency circumstance' in s.1(4) as a present or imminent circumstance likely to cause the death of a person, or to cause:

[i] serious injury to or the serious injury (including mental illness) of a person;
[ii] serious harm to the environment (including the life and health of plants and animals);
[iii] serious harm to any building or other property; or
[iv] a worsening of any such injury, illness or harm;

Q Outline the offence of making a threat to kill

A A person who without lawful excuse makes to another a threat, *intending that that other would fear it* would be carried out, to kill that other or a third person shall be guilty of an offence.

S. 16 OFFENCES AGAINST THE PERSON ACT 1861

Without lawful excuse. Defences such as self-defence, or acting to save the life of another, may apply here.

OFFENCES AGAINST THE PERSON

Intention. The essence of this offence lies in the threatener's intention that the person he makes the threat to believes it would be carried out. It does matter whether or not they actually do believe it.

Q Define ABH

A A person commits an offence if he assaults another person so as to cause actual bodily harm.

ABH. Means any hurt or injury calculated to interfere with the health or comfort of the victim, it can include shock and mental 'injury'.

S. 47 OFFENCES AGAINST THE PERSON ACT 1871

Q Define unlawful wounding contrary to S. 20 Offences Against the Person Act 1861

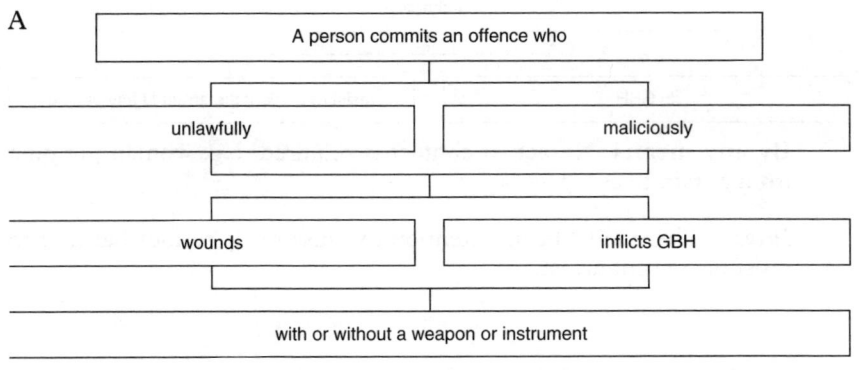

A

```
                A person commits an offence who
               /                                \
         unlawfully                          maliciously
               \                                /
            wounds                          inflicts GBH
               \                                /
              with or without a weapon or instrument
```

Wound. Is the breaking of the whole skin [internally or externally].

GBH. Means really serious harm including psychiatric harm.

Maliciously. Means that the defendant must realise that there is a risk of harm.

Inflicts. The harm may be inflicted indirectly and without physical contact e.g. psychiatric injury following harassment, or infecting someone with a disease.

OFFENCES AGAINST THE PERSON

Q Outline wounding with intent contrary to S. 18 Offences Against the Person Act 1861

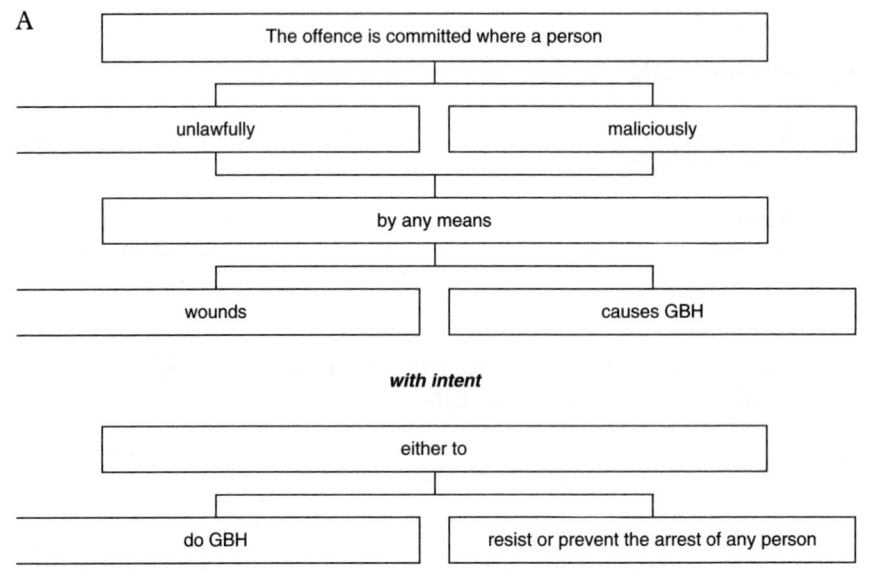

A

```
                The offence is committed where a person
                    |                           |
                unlawfully                  maliciously
                    |                           |
                         by any means
                    |                           |
                 wounds                     causes GBH

                        with intent
                           either to
                    |                           |
                 do GBH          resist or prevent the arrest of any person
```

By any means. No actual contact is required, e.g. woman jumping from a train to escape a rapist.

Intent. There must be an intention to cause really serious harm or to resist or prevent arrest.

OFFENCES AGAINST THE PERSON

Q   Define torture

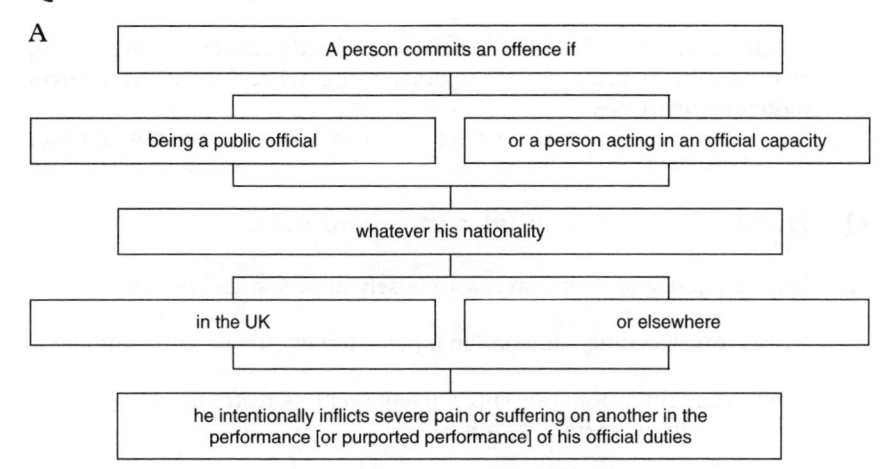

A

```
                  ┌─────────────────────────────────────────┐
                  │     A person commits an offence if      │
                  └─────────────────────────────────────────┘
          ┌───────────────────────┐   ┌───────────────────────────────────┐
          │ being a public official│   │ or a person acting in an official capacity │
          └───────────────────────┘   └───────────────────────────────────┘
                  ┌─────────────────────────────────────────┐
                  │         whatever his nationality        │
                  └─────────────────────────────────────────┘
          ┌───────────────────────┐   ┌───────────────────────────────────┐
          │      in the UK        │   │           or elsewhere            │
          └───────────────────────┘   └───────────────────────────────────┘
      ┌──────────────────────────────────────────────────────────────────┐
      │ he intentionally inflicts severe pain or suffering on another in the │
      │ performance [or purported performance] of his official duties    │
      └──────────────────────────────────────────────────────────────────┘
```

Defence. To prove he had lawful authority, justification or excuse. (But note that in the light of the absolute prohibition against torture under Art. **3 ECHR**, any such defence will be incompatible with the ECHR.)

Prosecution. Consent of Attorney-General (or Solicitor-General) is needed to prosecute.

Non-public officials. Commit this offence if done at the instigation of or with the consent or acquiescence of a public official and the public official was performing [purporting] his duties when he instigated or consented to the offence.

Pain and suffering. It is immaterial whether the pain or suffering is physical/mental or caused by an act or omission.

S. 134 CRIMINAL JUSTICE ACT 1988

Q   Define the offence of poisoning

A   It is an offence to unlawfully and maliciously administer [or cause to be] any poison, destructive or noxious thing so as to **endanger life** or cause **GBH**.

S. 23 OFFENCES AGAINST THE PERSON ACT 1861

Cause to be administered. Covers indirect poisoning and inducing someone to poison themselves.

OFFENCES AGAINST THE PERSON

Q **Define the offence of poisoning with intent**

A It is an offence to unlawfully and maliciously administer [or cause to be] any poison, destructive or noxious thing **with intent to injure, aggrieve or annoy**.

S. 24 OFFENCES AGAINST THE PERSON ACT 1861

Q **Define the offence of false imprisonment**

A It is an offence at common law to falsely imprison any person.

Imprison. Keeping someone in a place unlawfully is imprisonment.

Mens rea. Intentional or subjectively reckless restraint of a person's freedom of movement is required.

Q **Define the offence of kidnapping at common law**

A It is an offence of kidnapping to take or carry away another without their consent and without lawful excuse.

Taking or carrying away. This physical movement must be either by force or fraud. Force need not be physical force, mentally overpowering someone by the exercise of a position of dominance or influence may be enough.

Prosecution. Consent of the DPP is required when the victim is under 16 or where the prosecution is against a parent/guardian (Child Abduction Act 1984 S. 5)

OFFENCES AGAINST THE PERSON

Q Outline the offence of hostage taking

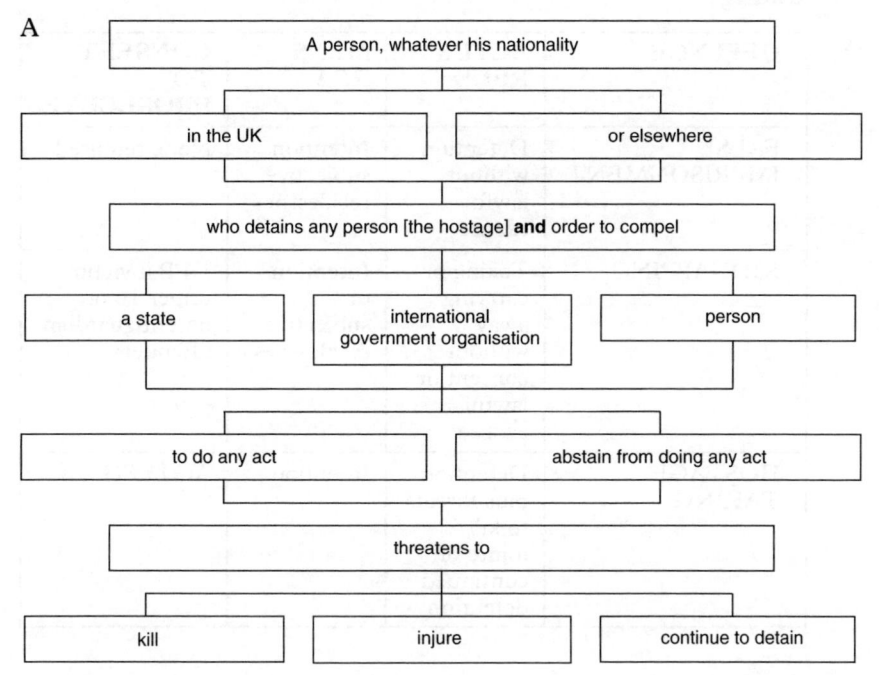

A

```
                A person, whatever his nationality
                            │
        ┌───────────────────┴───────────────────┐
     in the UK                             or elsewhere
        └───────────────────┬───────────────────┘
     who detains any person [the hostage] **and** order to compel
        ┌───────────────────┼───────────────────┐
    a state          international            person
                 government organisation
        └───────────────────┬───────────────────┘
        ┌──────────────────────────────────────┐
     to do any act              abstain from doing any act
        └──────────────────┬───────────────────┘
                    threatens to
        ┌──────────────────┼───────────────────┐
       kill              injure           continue to detain
```

Prosecution. Consent of the Attorney-General (or Solicitor-General) is required to prosecute.

S. 1 TAKING OF HOSTAGES ACT 1982

OFFENCES AGAINST THE PERSON

Q Compare false imprisonment, kidnapping and hostage taking

A

OFFENCE	ACTUS REUS	MENS REA	CONSENT TO PROSECUTE
FALSE IMPRISONMENT	Detention without lawful excuse	Intention subjective recklessness	None required
KIDNAPPING	Taking or carrying away without consent or lawful excuse	Intention or subjective recklessness	DPP if victim under 16 or parent/guardian offender
HOSTAGE TAKING	Detention plus threats to kill injure or continued detention	Intention	AG or SG

SEXUAL OFFENCES

Q What is the definition of 'sexual' under the Sexual Offences Act 2003?

A Penetration, touching or any other activity will be sexual *if a reasonable person would consider that*

[a] whatever its circumstances or any person's purpose in relation to it, **it is sexual by its very nature**, or
[b] because of its nature it may be **sexual** and **because of its circumstances or the purpose** of any person in relation to it, it is sexual.

S. 78 SEXUAL OFFENCES ACT 2003

In other words, category (a) covers those activities which a reasonable person would always consider sexual (e.g. intercourse, masturbation) whilst category (b) covers activities that may or may not be considered sexual by a reasonable person, it will depend on the particular circumstances or intention of the perpetrator (e.g. a doctor inserting a finger into a vagina may be sexual, or it may be non-sexual if it is done simply to carry out a medical inspection). If a reasonable person would not consider the activity to be sexual then it will not be a sexual activity, regardless of any particular sexual gratification an individual may derive from it (e.g. a shoe fetishist deriving pleasure from placing shoes on people's feet in the shoe shop in which he works).

Q What is the definition of 'touching' under the Sexual Offences Act 2003?

A Touching includes touching:

[a] with any part of the body
[b] with anything else
[c] through anything

and in particular, touching amounting to penetration. Touching may include touching clothing.

S. 79(8) SEXUAL OFFENCES ACT 2003

SEXUAL OFFENCES

Q Outline the offence of rape.

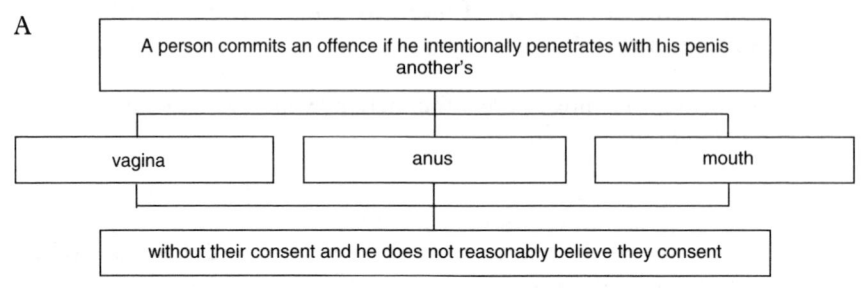

A

> A person commits an offence if he intentionally penetrates with his penis another's
>
> - vagina
> - anus
> - mouth
>
> without their consent and he does not reasonably believe they consent

S. 1 SEXUAL OFFENCES ACT 2003

Reasonable belief in consent. Is to be determined having regard to all the circumstances. Consent is a question of fact.

Victim under 13. If the victim is a child under 13 it is sufficient to prove penetration and the child's age. The issue of consent does not arise: S. 5 Sexual Offences Act 2003.

Q Outline the presumptions about consent

A [a] The 'evidential presumption': the victim can be taken not to have consented where it is proved that the defendant did the act and:

  [i] immediately before, or at the time of the act, any person was using violence against the victim or causing the victim to fear that immediate violence would be used against him/her;
  [ii] immediately before, or at the time of the act, any person was causing the victim to fear that violence was being used, or that immediate violence would be used, against any person;
  [iii] the victim was, and the defendant was not, unlawfully detained at the time of the act;
  [iv] the victim was asleep or unconscious at the time of the act;
  [v] because of the victim's physical disability they would not have been able at the time of the act to communicate consent to the defendant, or
  [vi] any person had administered to or caused to be taken by the victim, without the victim's consent, a substance capable of causing or enabling the victim to be stupefied or overpowered at the time of the act.

SEXUAL OFFENCES

However in any such case the defence is entitled to bring evidence to rebut the presumption.

S. 75 SEXUAL OFFENCES ACT 2003

[i] The 'conclusive presumption': if it is proved that the defendant did the act and that s/he:

[ii] intentionally deceived the victim as to the nature or purpose of the act, or
[iii] intentionally induced the victim to consent by impersonating a person known personally by the victim,

then there will be a conclusive presumption both that the victim did not consent and that the defendant did not believe that s/he consented.

S. 76 SEXUAL OFFENCES ACT 2003

Q Define the offence of assault by penetration

A A person (A) commits an offence if

[a] he intentionally penetrates the vagina or anus of another person (B) with a part of his body or anything else,
[b] the penetration is sexual,
[c] B does not consent to the penetration, and
[d] A does not reasonably believe that B consents.

S. 2 SEXUAL OFFENCES ACT 2003

Victim under 13. Where the victim is a child under 13 it is only necessary to prove intentional sexual penetration and the child's age. The issue of consent does not arise: S. 6 Sexual Offences Act 2003.

Q Define the offence of sexual touching

A A person (A) commits an offence if

[a] he intentionally touches another person (B),
[b] the touching is sexual,
[c] B does not consent to the touching, and
[d] A does not reasonably believe that B consents.

S. 3 SEXUAL OFFENCES ACT 2003

Victim under 13. Where the victim is a child under 13 it is only necessary to prove intentional sexual touching and the child's age. The issue of consent does not arise: S. 7 Sexual Offences Act 2003.

SEXUAL OFFENCES

Q   Define the offence of causing a person to engage in sexual activity without consent

A   A person (A) commits an offence if

   [a] he intentionally causes another person (B) to engage in an activity,
   [b] the activity is sexual,
   [c] B does not consent to engaging in the activity, and
   [d] A does not reasonably believe that B consents.

S. 4 SEXUAL OFFENCES ACT 2003

Victim under 13. Under S. 8 it is an offence to cause or incite a child under 13 to engage in sexual activity. The issue of consent is irrelevant in such cases.

Q   Define the offence of sexual activity with a child under 16

A   A person aged 18 or over (A) commits an offence if

   [a] he intentionally touches another person (B),
   [b] the touching is sexual, and
   [c] either

   [i] B is under 16 and A does not reasonably believe B is 16 or over, or
   [ii] B is under 13.

S. 9 SEXUAL OFFENCES ACT 2003

Age of offender. Must be 18 or over for this offence. If offender is under 18 s/he commits an offence under S. 13, which is punishable (on indictment) by up to five years' imprisonment (rather than 14 years under S. 9).

Q   Define the offence of engaging in sexual activity in the presence of a child under 16

A   A person aged 18 or over (A) commits on offence if

   [a] he intentionally engages in an activity,
   [b] the activity is sexual,
   [c] for the purpose of obtaining sexual gratification, he engages in it

   [i] when another person (B) is present or is in a place from which A can be observed, and
   [ii] knowing or believing that B is aware, or intending that B should be aware, that he is engaging in it, and

[d] either

  [i] B is under 16 and A does not reasonably believe that B is 16 or over, or
  [ii] B is under 13.

S. 11 SEXUAL OFFENCES ACT 2003

Purpose. This offence would cover, for example, a person masturbating in front of a child, or masturbating in the presence of a child to whom he is describing what he is doing, perhaps because the child is covering his face. It would also cover the situation where A performs a sexual act in a place where he knows he can be seen by a child, for example via a webcam.

Q **Define the offence of causing a child under 16 to watch a sexual act**

A A person aged 18 or over (A) commits an offence if

  [a] for the purpose of obtaining sexual gratification, he intentionally causes another person (B) to watch a third person engaging in an activity, or to look at an image of any person engaging in an activity,
  [b] the activity is sexual, and
  [c] either

    [i] B is under 16 and A does not reasonably believe that B is 16 or over, or
    [ii] B is under 13.

S. 12 SEXUAL OFFENCES ACT 2003

Purpose. While the previous offence under S. 11 is concerned with engaging in sexual activity which the person knows, believes or intends to be observed by a child, the S. 12 offence is concerned with intentionally causing a child to watch a third person engaging in such activity, or to look at an image of a person engaging in such activity. For example, a person who forces a child to watch a pornographic film or a couple have sex.

SEXUAL OFFENCES

Q Define the offence of arranging or facilitating child sex offences

A A person (A) commits an offence if

 [a] he intentionally arranges or facilitates something that he intends to do, intends another person to do, or believes that another person will do, in any part of the world, and
 [b] doing it will involve the commission of an offence under SS. 9-11 (i.e. sexual activity with a child, causing or inciting a child to engage in sexual activity or engaging in sexual activity in the presence of a child).

S. 14 SEXUAL OFFENCES ACT 2003

Purpose. The first two limbs of the offence will cover, for example, where A approaches an agency to procure a child for the purpose of sexual activity either with himself or with a friend. The offence is complete whether or not the sex takes place. An example of the third limb of the offence is where A intentionally drives another person (X) to meet a child with whom he knows X is going to have sexual activity. A may not intend X to have child sexual activity, but he believes that X will do so if he meets that child.

Q Define the offence of meeting a child following sexual grooming

A A person aged 18 or over (A) commits an offence if

 [a] A has met or communicated with another person (B) *on at least two occasions* and subsequently –

   [i] A intentionally meets B,
   [ii] A travels with the intention of meeting B in any part of the world or arranges to meet B in any part of the world, or
   [iii] B travels with the intention of meeting A in any part of the world,

 [b] A intends to do anything to or in respect of B, during or after the meeting mentioned in paragraph [a](i) to (iii) and in any part of the world, which if done will involve the commission by A of a relevant offence,
 [c] B is under 16, and
 [d] A does not reasonably believe that B is 16 or over.

s.15 SEXUAL OFFENCES ACT 2003

SEXUAL OFFENCES

Communicated. By any method and in any part of the world e.g internet chat rooms, text messaging, however seemingly innocuous.

Relevant offence. Any offence under Part 1 of the Act (i.e. any of the principal sex offences). Note that the relevant offence does not actually have to take place, it merely needs to be intended by the defendant.

Purpose. To deal with child grooming especially where contact begins via the internet. Evidence of at least two communications will be required, after which the offence is triggered by an intentional meeting with the victim, or the defendant travelling with the intention of such a meeting, or the victim travelling to meet the defendant, in any part of the world (this latter element having been added by the Criminal Justice and Immigration Act 2008).

Q Outline the abuse of position of trust offences

A It is an offence for a person aged 18 or over (A) to

 [a] intentionally sexually touch another person (B); or
 [b] intentionally cause or incite B to engage in a sexual activity; or
 [c] for the purpose of sexual gratification, intentionally engage in any sexual activity when B is present, or in a place from which A can be observed, knowing or believing that B is aware or intending that B should be aware that he is engaging in it; or
 [d] for the purpose of sexual gratification, intentionally cause B to watch a third person engaging in a sexual activity, or look at an image of any person engaging in sexual activity
 [e] if he is in a position of trust in relation to B.

SS. 16-19 SEXUAL OFFENCES ACT 2003

Q What is a 'position of trust'?

A A looks after (i.e. cares for, trains, supervises, is in sole charge of) persons under 18 who are accommodated and cared for in any of the following settings:

 [i] detained in an institution under a court order;
 [ii] local authority accommodation or accommodation provided by a voluntary organisation;
 [iii] hospital;
 [iv] independent clinic;
 [v] care home, residential care home or private hospital;

SEXUAL OFFENCES

[vi] community home, voluntary home or children's home;
[vii] home provided under S. 82 (5) Children Act 1989;
[viii] residential family centre;
[ix] educational establishment.

Q Define the offence of sexual activity with a child family member

A A person (A) commits an offence if

[a] he intentionally touches another person (B),
[b] the touching is sexual,
[c] the relationship of A to B is any of the following:

  [i] parent
  [ii] grandparent
  [iii] brother or sister
  [iv] half-brother or half-sister
  [v] aunt or uncle
  [vi] is or has been foster parent
  [vii] where A and B live or lived in the same household, or A is or has been regularly involved in caring for, training, supervising or being in sole charge of B and
    (a) one of them is or has been the other's step-parent, or
    (b) they are cousins, or
    (c) one of them is or has been the other's step-brother or step-sister, or
    (d) they have the same parent or foster parent

[d] A knows or could reasonably be expected to know that his relation to B is one of the above, and
[e] either

  [i] B is under 18 and A does not reasonably believe that B is 18 or over, or
  [ii] B is under 13.

SS. 25-26 SEXUAL OFFENCES ACT 2003

Q Outline the making indecent photographs offence

A It is an offence for a person

[a] to take, or permit to be taken, or make, any indecent photograph or pseudo-photograph of a child; or

SEXUAL OFFENCES

[b] to distribute or show such indecent photographs or pseudo-photographs; or
[c] to have in his possession such indecent photographs or pseudo-photographs, with a view to their being distributed or shown; or
[d] to publish or cause to be published any advertisement likely to be understood as conveying that the advertiser distributes or shows such indecent photographs or pseudo-photographs, or intends to do so.

S. 1 PROTECTION OF CHILDREN ACT 1978

Defence. It is a defence to prove that he had a legitimate reason for distributing or showing the photos or that he had not himself seen the photos and did not know, nor had any cause to suspect, that they were indecent or they were lawfully married or partners in an enduring family relationship. (There is a further special exception for persons making such photos for crime investigation/prosecution purposes).

Pseudo-photographs. Includes computer images.

Prosecution. The consent of the DDP is required for any prosecution.

Q Outline the possessing indecent photographs offence

A It is an offence for a person to have any indecent photograph or pseudo-photograph of a child in his possession.

S. 160 CRIMINAL JUSTICE ACT 1988

Defence. It is a defence to prove that he had a legitimate reason for having the photograph or pseudo-photograph in his possession or that he had not himself seen the photograph or pseudo-photograph and did not know, nor have any cause to suspect, it to be indecent or that the photograph or pseudo-photograph was sent to him without any prior request made by him or on his behalf and he did not keep it for an unreasonable time or he was married to the child or lived with him as partners in an enduring family relationship.

Q Outline the offence of possessing prohibited images of children

A It is an offence for a person to be in possession of a prohibited image of a child.

s.62 CORONERS AND JUSTICE ACT 2009

Prosecution. The consent of the DPP is required for a prosecution.

Child. Person under 18.

SEXUAL OFFENCES

Prohibited image. To be covered the image must:

[a] be pornographic (i.e. produced principally for the purpose of sexual arousal);
[b] be grossly offensive, disgusting or otherwise of an obscene character, and
[c] be an image which focuses solely or principally on a child's genitals or anal region, or portrays any of the following acts:

  [i] the performance by a person of an act of intercourse or oral sex with or in the presence of a child;
  [ii] an act of masturbation by, of, involving, or in the presence of a child;
  [iii] an act which involves penetration of the vagina or anus of a child with a part of a person's body or with anything else;
  [iv] an act of penetration, in the presence of a child, of the vagina or anus of a person with a part of a person's body or with anything else;
  [v] the performance by a child of an act of intercourse or oral sex with an animal (whether dead or alive or imaginary);
  [vi] the performance by a person of an act of intercourse or oral sex with an animal (whether dead or alive or imaginary) in the presence of a child.

Defences. A number of defences are provided by s.64 of the Act: (a) that the person had a legitimate reason for possessing the image; (b) that the person had not seen the image and therefore neither knew, nor had cause to suspect, that the image was a prohibited image of a child; (c) that the image had been sent to the person without request, and had not been kept for an unreasonable time.

Q Outline the possessing extreme pornographic images offence

A It is an offence for a person to be in possession of an extreme pornographic image.

s.63 CRIMINAL JUSTICE AND IMMIGRATION ACT 2008

Prosecution. The consent of the DPP is required for a prosecution.

Extreme pornographic image. To be covered the image must:

[a] be pornographic (i.e. produced principally for the purpose of sexual arousal);
[b] be grossly offensive, disgusting, or otherwise of an obscene character; and

SEXUAL OFFENCES

[c] portray in an explicit and realistic way, one of the following;

[i] an act which threatens a person's life;
[ii] an act which results in or is likely to result in serious injury to a person's anus, breasts or genitals;
[iii] an act involving sexual intercourse with a human corpse;
[iv] a person performing an act of intercourse or oral sex with an animal (dead or alive);

[d] and a reasonable person looking at the image would think that the people and animals portrayed were real.

Defences. A number of defences are provided by s.65 of the Act: (a) that the person had a legitimate reason for possessing the image; (b) that the person had not seen the image and therefore neither knew, nor had cause to suspect, that the image was an extreme pornographic image; (c) that the image had been sent to the person without request, and had not been kept for an unreasonable time.

Q Define the offence of paying for the sexual services of a child

A A person (A) commits an offence if

[a] he intentionally obtains for himself the sexual services of another person (B),
[b] before obtaining those services, he has made or promised payment for those services to B or a third person, or knows that another person has made or promised such a payment, and
[c] either

[i] B is under 18, and A does not reasonably believe that B is 18 or over, or
[ii] B is under 13.

s.47 SEXUAL OFFENCES ACT 2003

Payment. Includes any financial advantage.

Q Outline the offences of causing, inciting, controlling child etc. prostitution or pornography

A It is an offence for a person (A) to

[a] intentionally cause or incite another person (B) to become a prostitute, or to be involved in pornography *in any part of the world*;

SEXUAL OFFENCES

[b] intentionally control any of the activities of B relating to B's prostitution or involvement in pornography *in any part of the world*;
[c] intentionally arrange or facilitate the prostitution or involvement in pornography *in any part of the world* of B.

SS. 48-50 SEXUAL OFFENCES ACT 2003

Prostitute. Means a person who, on at least one occasion, and whether or not compelled to do so, offers or provides sexual services to another person in return for payment or a promise of payment to themselves or a third person.

Q   What is meant by a 'disqualification order'?

A   An order under the Criminal Justice and Court Services Act 2000 which is aimed at disqualifying people who present a threat to children from working in certain jobs and positions. A court must impose a disqualification order on a person convicted of certain offences against children (such as those involving sexual activity, violence or drugs) unless, having regard to all the evidence, the court is satisfied that it is unlikely that the defendant will commit any further offences against any child. It is an offence for a disqualified person to apply for, offer to do, accept or do any work in a job which involves working with children.

Q   Define the offence of sexual activity with a person with a mental disorder

A   A person (A) commits an offence if

[a] he intentionally touches another person (B),
[b] the touching is sexual,
[c] B is unable to refuse because of or for a reason related to a mental disorder, and
[d] A knows or could reasonably be expected to know that B has a mental disorder and that because of it or for a reason related to it B is likely to be unable to refuse.

S. 30 SEXUAL OFFENCES ACT 2003

Mental disorder. "Mental illness, arrested or incomplete development of mind, psychopathic disorder and any other disorder or disability of mind": S. 1(2) Mental Health Act 1983.

SEXUAL OFFENCES

Q Define the offence of sexual activity in the presence of a person with a mental disorder

A A person (A) commits an offence if

[a] he intentionally engages in an activity,
[b] the activity is sexual,
[c] for the purpose of obtaining sexual gratification, he engages in it

 [i] when another person (B) is present, or is in a place from which A can be observed, and
 [ii] knowing or believing that B is aware, or intending that B should be aware, that he is engaging in it,

[d] B is unable to refuse because of or for a reason related to a mental disorder, and
[e] A knows or could reasonably be expected to know that B has a mental disorder and that because of it or for a reason related to it B is likely to be unable to refuse.

S. 32 SEXUAL OFFENCES ACT 2003

Q Define the offence of causing a person with a mental disorder to watch a sexual act

A A person (A) commits an offence if

[a] for the purpose of obtaining sexual gratification, he *intentionally* causes another person (B) to watch a third person engaging in an activity, or to look at an image of any person engaging in an activity,
[b] the activity is sexual, and
[c] B is unable to refuse because of or for a reason related to a mental disorder, and
[d] A knows or could reasonably be expected to know that B has a mental disorder and that because of it or for a reason related to it B is likely to be unable to refuse.

S. 33 SEXUAL OFFENCES ACT 2003

Inducements. Causing a person with a mental disorder to watch a sexual act by offering inducements, threats or deception is an arrestable offence under S. 37, and is in the same terms as above, except that it is not necessary to show that B was unable to refuse.

SEXUAL OFFENCES

Q   Define the offence of outraging public decency

A   It is an offence at common law to commit an act of a lewd, obscene or disgusting nature and outrage public decency.

COMMON LAW

Deliberate act. The offence requires the deliberate commission of a lewd, obscene or disgusting act. Whether something is lewd etc, is a question of fact. If the act done is not lewd then the defendant's intention or motive in doing the act will not make it so. For example, if the defendant leaves messages in a public toilet asking young boys to contact him and those messages are not lewd etc. themselves, then the offence is not committed, no matter that by leaving the notes the defendant intended to induce boys to commit grossly indecent acts with him.

Q   Define the offence of exposure

A   A person commits an offence if

[a]   s/he intentionally exposes his/her genitals, and
[b]   s/he intends that someone will see them and be caused alarm or distress.

S. 66 SEXUAL OFFENCES ACT 2003

Offence complete. It is not necessary for A's genitals to have been seen by anyone or for anyone to have been alarmed or distressed. The offence is complete upon proof of exposure with the necessary intent.

Q   Outline the offence of voyeurism

A   A person commits an offence if

[a]   for the purpose of obtaining sexual gratification, he observes another person doing a private act, and he knows that that person does not consent to being observed for his sexual gratification; or
[b]   he operates equipment with the intention of enabling another person to observe, for the purpose of obtaining sexual gratification, a third person (B) doing a private act, and he knows that B does not consent to his operating equipment with that intention; or
[c]   he records another person (B) doing a private act, he does so with the intention that he or a third person will, for the purpose of obtaining sexual gratification, look at an image of B doing the act, and he knows B does not consent to his recording the act with that intention; or

SEXUAL OFFENCES

[d] he installs equipment or constructs or adapts a structure or part of a structure, with the intention of enabling himself or another person to commit an offence under (a) above.

S. 67 SEXUAL OFFENCES ACT 2003

Private act. A person is doing a private act if they are in a place which would reasonably be expected to provide privacy and their genitals, buttocks or breasts are exposed or covered only with underwear; or they are using a lavatory; or they are doing a sexual act of a kind not ordinarily done in public.

Examples. (a) Looking through a window or peephole at someone having sex, where A knows the person observed does not consent to being looked at; (b) a landlord (A) operating a webcam to allow people on the internet for their sexual gratification to view live images of his tenant (B) getting undressed, if A knew that B did not consent to this; (c) A secretly films B masturbating in B's bedroom to show to others for their sexual gratification. Proof that the intention was the sexual gratification of others could be obtained by the fact that the images were uploaded to a website, or sent to a pornographic magazine; (d) A drilled a spyhole or installed a two-way mirror in a house with the intention of spying on someone for sexual gratification or allowing others to do so. A would be covered by the offence even if the spyhole or mirror was discovered before it was used.

Q **Define the offence of sexual activity in a public lavatory**

A A person commits an offence if

[a] he is in a lavatory to which the public or a section of the public has or is permitted to have access, whether on payment or otherwise,
[b] he intentionally engages in an activity, and
[c] the activity is sexual.

S. 71 SEXUAL OFFENCES ACT 2003

Sexual activity. The usual definition of sexual activity is replaced for this offence with a narrower test: "an activity is sexual if a reasonable person would, in all the circumstances but regardless of any person's purpose, consider it to be sexual": S. 71(2).

Q **Define the offence of committing a criminal offence with intent to commit a sexual offence**

A It is an offence for a person to commit any offence with the intention of committing a relevant sexual offence.

S. 62 SEXUAL OFFENCES ACT 2003

SEXUAL OFFENCES

Relevant offence. Offences under Part 1 of the Sexual Offences Act 2003 (i.e. the principal sexual offences).

Purpose. This offence is intended to cover the situation where A commits a criminal offence but does so with the intention of committing a subsequent sexual offence, regardless of whether the substantive sexual offence is actually committed. e.g. A kidnaps B so that he can rape him but is caught by the police before committing the rape. Obviously if A does commit the substantive sexual offence he can be charged with that in addition.

Q Define trespassing with intent to commit a sexual offence

A A person commits an offence if

[a] he is a trespasser on any premises,
[b] he intends to commit a relevant sexual offence on the premises, and
[c] he knows that, or is reckless as to whether he is, a trespasser.

S. 63 SEXUAL OFFENCES ACT 2003

Trespasser. On premises without the owner or occupier's consent, whether express or implied.

Premises. Any structure or part of a structure, including tents, vehicles, vessels, or other temporary or movable structures.

Q Define the offence of administering a substance with intent

A A person commits an offence if he intentionally administers a substance to, or causes a substance to be taken by, another person (B)

[a] knowing B does not consent, and
[b] with the intention of stupefying or overpowering B, so as to enable any person to engage in a sexual activity that involves B.

S. 61 SEXUAL OFFENCES ACT 2003

Intent. There is no need for B to actually be stupefied or overpowered or for any sexual activity to take place. The offence is complete at the point of administration with the necessary intent.

SEXUAL OFFENCES

Q **Which persons are subject to notification requirements regulating sex offenders?**

A 'Relevant offenders' under Part 2 of the Sexual Offences Act 2003. These are persons who are

- [a] convicted of a Schedule 3 sexual offence (i.e. the main sexual offences); or
- [b] found not guilty of such an offence by reason of insanity; or
- [c] found to be under a disability and to have done the act charged against them in respect of such an offence; or
- [d] cautioned in respect of such an offence.

Q **What are the notification periods?**

A
- [a] For persons sentenced to imprisonment for life, or thirty months or more: **indefinite**
- [b] For persons admitted to a hospital subject to a restriction order: **indefinite**
- [c] For persons sentenced to between six months and thirty months imprisonment: **ten years**
- [d] For persons sentenced to less than six months imprisonment: **seven years**
- [e] For persons admitted to hospital without a restriction order: **seven years**
- [f] For persons cautioned: **two years**
- [g] For persons given a conditional discharge: **the period of the discharge**
- [h] For any other persons: **five years**

In the case of persons under 18, the ten, seven, five or two year periods are halved.

Q **Outline the notification procedure**

A A relevant offender must, within three days of the date of conviction, finding or caution ('the relevant date') notify the police of (a) their date of birth (b) their national insurance number (c) their name(s) on the relevant date and on the date of notification (d) their home address on the relevant date and on the date of notification (e) the address of any other premises in the UK at which, at the time of notification, they regularly reside or stay. Thereafter, within three days of any change of home address or any use of a name which has not been previously notified to the police, or any stay for a 'qualifying period' at any address which has not been previously notified (i.e. any stay of seven days or more or two or more periods in any 12 months which together amount

SEXUAL OFFENCES

to seven days), or any release from custody, detention or hospital detention, the relevant offender must notify the police of the new details. The relevant offender must then re-notify the police of their details within one year of either the initial notification or notification of change of details (unless they already did so when they notified of the change) i.e. a relevant offender who does not change their details has to re-notify within a year and every year thereafter. Failure to notify without a reasonable excuse is an offence under S. 91 Sexual Offences Act 2003.

Q What is a 'sexual offences prevention order'?

A   A SOPO is a civil order which is designed to prevent offending and provide protection for the public. A court may make a SOPO in certain circumstances (e.g. when dealing with a schedule 3 offence) where it is satisfied that it is necessary to do so for the purpose of protecting the public (or any particular person) from serious sexual harm from the defendant. The order will last for at least five years and can be indefinite, provided that that is specified in the order, and will prohibit the defendant from doing anything specified in the order. Breach of a SOPO, without reasonable excuse, is an offence.

Q What is a 'risk of sexual harm order'?

A   A civil preventative order which may be applied for by a chief officer from a magistrates' court in respect of a person aged 18 or over who resides in his police area or who the chief officer believes is in, or is intending to come to, his police area. The order may only be sought if it appears to the chief officer that the defendant has on at least two occasions done any of the following acts:

[a] engaged in sexual activity involving a child or in the presence of a child,
[b] caused or incited a child to watch a person engaging in sexual activity or to look at a moving or still sexual image,
[c] given a child anything relating to sexual activity or containing references to such activity,
[d] communicated with a child, where any part of the communication is sexual

The court can then make a RSHO if satisfied that the defendant did commit such an act on at least two occasions and that the order is necessary to protect children generally (or a specific child) from harm from the defendant. The order will last for a fixed period not less than two years, or until further order, and prevents the defendant from doing anything specified in the order. Breach of a RSHO, without reasonable excuse, is an offence.

SEXUAL OFFENCES

Q What is a 'prostitute'?

A A man or woman who, on at least one occasion and whether or not compelled to do so, offers or provides sexual services to another person in return for payment or a promise of payment to themselves or another: S. 51(2) Sexual Offences Act 2003.

Q Define the offence of causing, inciting, controlling prostitution for gain

A A person commits an offence if

[a] he intentionally causes or incites another to become a prostitute in any part of the world and he does so for or in the expectation of gain for himself or a third person, or

[b] he intentionally controls any of the activities of another person relating to that person's prostitution in any part of the world, and he does so for or in the expectation of gain for himself or a third person.

SS. 52 & 53 SEXUAL OFFENCES ACT 2003

Q Outline the offence of paying for sexual services of a prostitute subjected to force

A A person ('A') commits an offence if –

[a] A makes or promises payment for the sexual services of a prostitute ('B'),
[b] a third person ('C') has engaged in exploitative conduct of a kind likely to induce or encourage B to provide the sexual services for which A has made or promised payment, and
[c] C engaged in that conduct for or in the expectation of gain for C or another person (apart from A or B).

It is irrelevant where in the world the sexual services are to be provided, or whether they are actually provided.

s. 53A SEXUAL OFFENCES ACT 2003

Exploitative conduct. Force, threats (whether or not relating to violence), any other form of coercion, or any form of deception.

Strict liability. It does not matter whether A is aware that C has engaged in exploitative conduct.

SEXUAL OFFENCES

Q Define the offence of keeping a brothel

A It is an offence for a person to keep, or to manage, or act or assist in the management of, a brothel to which people resort for practices involving prostitution (whether or not also for other practices).

ss. 33A SEXUAL OFFENCES ACT 2003

Q Outline the common law offence of keeping a disorderly house

A It is an offence to keep a disorderly house.

Disorderly. Means unregulated by the restraints of morality, and run in a way that violates law and good order. It is necessary to show a degree of persistence in the behaviour, rather that just a one-off incident, and it is also necessary to prove that the house is open to customers and that the defendant knows it is being so used.

Q Outline the offence of soliciting

A It is an offence for a person, whether male or female, persistently to loiter or solicit in a street or public place for the purpose of prostitution.

s.1 STREET OFFENCES ACT 1959

Persistent. 2 or more occasions in any 3 month period.

Q Outline the offence of soliciting by 'kerb-crawling'

A It is an offence for a person in a street or public place to solicit another ('B') for the purpose of obtaining B's sexual services as a prostitute.

s.51A SEXUAL OFFENCES ACT 2003

Person in a street. Includes a person in a vehicle in a street or public place.

Q Define the offence of placing adverts relating to prostitution

A It is an offence to place an advert relating to prostitution on, or in the immediate vicinity of, a public telephone, with the intention that it should come to the attention of any other person.

S. 46 CRIMINAL JUSTICE AND POLICE ACT 2001

SEXUAL OFFENCES

Q Outline the trafficking offences

A A person commits an offence if he intentionally arranges or facilitates the arrival in (or travel within, or departure from) the UK of another person (B) and either

- [a] he intends to do anything to or in respect of B, after B's arrival but in any part of the world, which, if done will involve the commission of a relevant sexual offence, or
- [b] he believes that another person is likely to do something to or in respect of B, after B's arrival but in any part of the world, which if done will involve the commission of a relevant sexual offence.

SS. 57-59 SEXUAL OFFENCES ACT 2003

Relevant sexual offence. Any of the main sexual offences (Part 1 Sexual Offences Act 2003).

OFFENCES AGAINST CHILDREN AND VULNERABLE PERSONS

Q Outline the offence of child abduction [person connected with the child]

A It is an offence for a person **connected with a child aged under 16 years of age** to take or send the child **outside the UK** without the appropriate consent.

S. 1 CHILD ABDUCTION ACT 1984

Connected with:

[a] parent;
[b] [where not married at the birth] person with reasonable grounds for believing he is the father;
[c] guardian or special guardian;
[d] person with a residence order; or
[e] with custody.

Appropriate consent means the consent of each of the following:

[a] mother;
[b] father [if he has parental responsibility];
[c] guardian or special guardian;
[d] person with a residence order;
[e] person with custody; or
[f] with permission of a court under the Children Act 1989 (if required); or
[g] where a person has custody, permission of the court which awarded custody.

Prosecution. Consent of the DPP is required for a prosecution.

OFFENCES AGAINST CHILDREN AND VULNERABLE PERSONS

Defence.

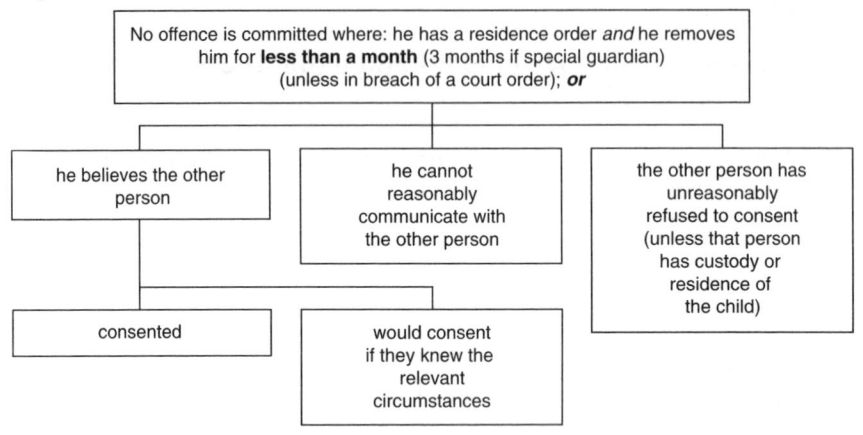

> No offence is committed where: he has a residence order *and* he removes him for **less than a month** (3 months if special guardian) (unless in breach of a court order); *or*

- he believes the other person
  - consented
  - would consent if they knew the relevant circumstances
- he cannot reasonably communicate with the other person
- the other person has unreasonably refused to consent (unless that person has custody or residence of the child)

Q Outline the offence of child abduction [person NOT connected with the child]

A It is an offence for a person **not connected with the child**, without lawful authority or reasonable excuse to take or detain a child **aged under 16 years age of** so as to remove him or keep him from the lawful control of a person entiled to lawful control.

S. 2 CHILD ABDUCTION ACT 1984

Who commits the offence? Anyone who **is not**:

[a] mother;
[b] father [if married at the time of birth];
[c] guardian, person with custody or residence order.

Defence. It shall be a defence to prove:

[a] At the time he believed the child **had attained 16 years of age**;
[b] [where the father and mother were not married at the time of his birth]:

  [i] he is the father; or
  [ii] he believed on reasonable grounds that he was the father.

OFFENCES AGAINST CHILDREN AND VULNERABLE PERSONS

Q Give an example of when both S. 1&2 offences can be committed together

A 'A' and his wife are separated, and the wife has custody. 'A' hires 'B' to collect the child from school and deliver the child to the airport where 'A' takes the child to Belgium. Therefore 'A' commits the S. 1 [connected to] offence and 'B' commits the S. 2 [not connected to] offence.

Q Outline the offence of child cruelty

A Any person who is **at least 16 years old** and who has responsibility for any child or young person under that age who wilfully assaults, neglects, abandons, or exposes him (or causes/procures the same) in a manner likely to cause unnecessary suffering or injury to health, commits an offence.

s.1 CHILDREN AND YOUNG PERSONS ACT 1933

Responsibility. People with parental responsibility or any other legal liability to maintain a child are deemed to have this responsibility at all times (even when not actually caring for the child at the time). Others, such as babysitters, may be deemed to have the required responsibility at the time of the offence as a matter of fact.

Likely to cause. It is not necessary to show that any suffering or injury has actually been caused, simply that the behaviour was *likely* to lead to suffering.

Q Define the offence of harmful publications

A A person who prints, publishes, sells or hires out works likely to fall into the hands of a child or young person, portraying:

[a] the commission of crimes; or
[b] acts of violence or cruelty; or
[c] incidents of a repulsive or horrible nature, in such a way that the work would **tend to corrupt a child or young person**, commits an offence.

S. 2 CHILDREN AND YOUNG PERSONS (HARMFUL PUBLICATIONS) ACT 1955

Prosecution. The consent of the Attorney-General (or Solicitor-General) is required for a prosecution.

OFFENCES AGAINST CHILDREN AND VULNERABLE PERSONS

Q When is a child deemed to be under police protection?

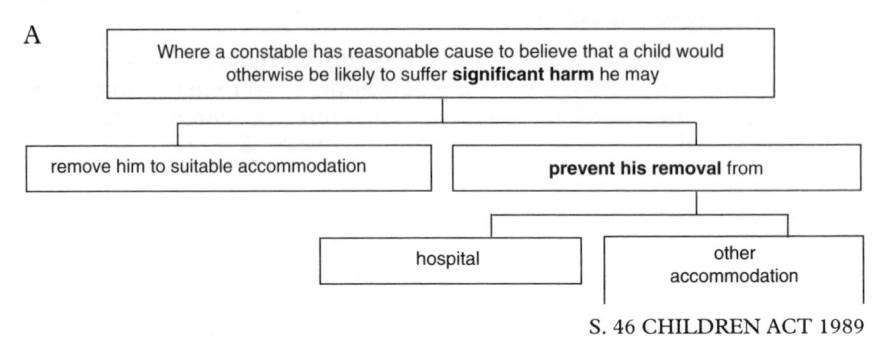

A

Where a constable has reasonable cause to believe that a child would otherwise be likely to suffer **significant harm** he may

- remove him to suitable accommodation
- **prevent his removal** from
  - hospital
  - other accommodation

S. 46 CHILDREN ACT 1989

Q What subsequent action must the constable take?

A [a] Inform local authority [where child found] of action taken/proposed/reasons;
   [b] inform local authority [where child usually lives] of his whereabouts;
   [c] inform the child of steps taken/proposed/reasons;
   [d] discover how the child feels about this;
   [e] tell parents or person with whom he was living of action taken/proposed/reasons;
   [f] if child removed from a place, arrange a refuge or local authority accommodation; and
   [g] inform the **designated officer**.

Q What is the role of the designated officer?

A [a] To enquire into the case, **then release the child unless** he considers that there is still reason to believe that the child would still suffer **significant harm** if released;
   [b] do what is reasonable for the child's welfare;
   [c] allow such contact with the child as he believes is reasonable and in the child's interest [which may be no contact].

   Contact (if considered reasonable and in the child's best interests) may be by:

   [i] the child's parents;
   [ii] a person having parental responsibility;
   [iii] the person the child was living with before police protection;
   [iv] persons who have a right to contact; or
   [v] someone acting on behalf on any of these.

OFFENCES AGAINST CHILDREN AND VULNERABLE PERSONS

Q How old is a 'child' for the purposes of the Children Act 1989?

A Under 18 years of age.

Q What is the maximum duration of police protection?

A 72 hours.

Q Outline the offence of contravention of protection or care order

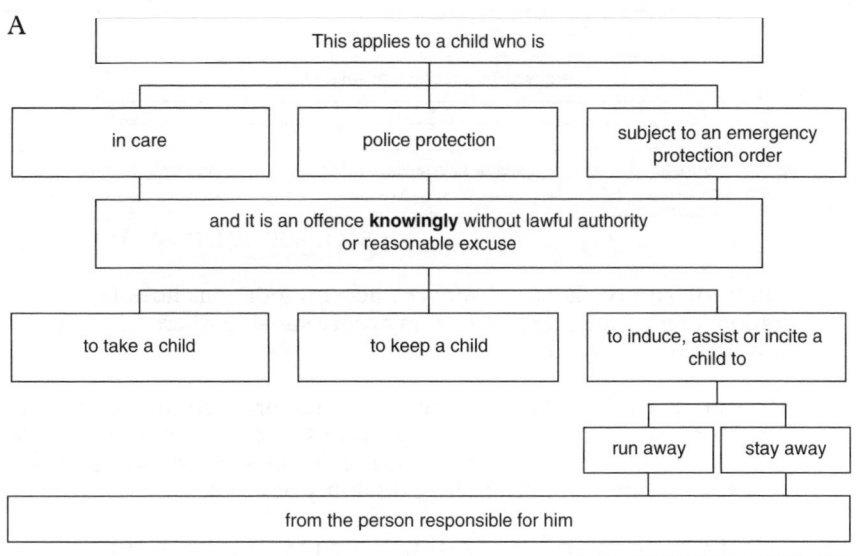

A

This applies to a child who is:
- in care
- police protection
- subject to an emergency protection order

and it is an offence **knowingly** without lawful authority or reasonable excuse:
- to take a child
- to keep a child
- to induce, assist or incite a child to run away / stay away

from the person responsible for him

S. 49 CHILDREN ACT 1989

OFFENCES AGAINST CHILDREN AND VULNERABLE PERSONS

Q Outline police powers to remove mentally disordered people from public places

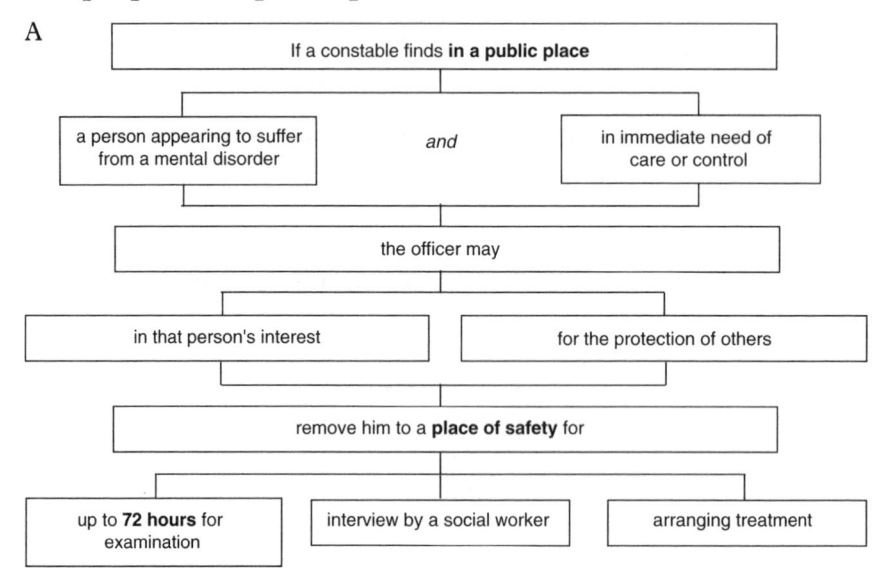

A

```
        ┌─────────────────────────────────────────────┐
        │      If a constable finds in a public place │
        └─────────────────────────────────────────────┘
          │                                     │
┌──────────────────────┐             ┌──────────────────────┐
│ a person appearing   │     and     │  in immediate need   │
│ to suffer from a     │             │  of care or control  │
│ mental disorder      │             │                      │
└──────────────────────┘             └──────────────────────┘
                   │                    │
              ┌─────────────────────────────┐
              │       the officer may       │
              └─────────────────────────────┘
                │                          │
   ┌────────────────────────┐   ┌────────────────────────────┐
   │ in that person's       │   │ for the protection of      │
   │ interest               │   │ others                     │
   └────────────────────────┘   └────────────────────────────┘
                │                          │
              ┌─────────────────────────────┐
              │ remove him to a place of    │
              │ safety for                  │
              └─────────────────────────────┘
        │                    │                    │
┌───────────────┐   ┌──────────────────┐   ┌──────────────────┐
│ up to 72 hours│   │ interview by a   │   │ arranging        │
│ for examination│  │ social worker    │   │ treatment        │
└───────────────┘   └──────────────────┘   └──────────────────┘
```

S. 136 MENTAL HEALTH ACT 1953

Place of safety. Is social services accommodation, hospital, police station, mental nursing home or anywhere suitable where the occupier is willing to receive him.

Mental disorder. Means mental illness, arrested or incomplete development of mind, psychopathic disorder (a persistent disorder or disability resulting in abnormally aggressive or seriously irresponsible conduct) or any other disorder or disability of mind.

Q What are the conditions of a warrant to search for patients?

A Where there is reasonable cause to suspect that a person believed to be suffering from a mental disorder has been, or is being, ill-treated or neglected or is unable to care for himself and is living alone, a warrant may be issued by a magistrate to a constable who may enter the premises and take him to a place of safety and **the officer must be accompanied by a social worker and doctor**.

S. 135 MENTAL HEALTH ACT 1983

OFFENCES AGAINST CHILDREN AND VULNERABLE PERSONS

Q How long do police powers last for the retaking of an escaped patient?

A A person taken to a place of safety by a constable, or under a warrant, who subsequently escapes cannot be retaken after **72 hours**.

Q When does the time begin?

A

At the place of safety	Escape before arrival
Time of arrival	Time of escape

S. 138 MENTAL HEALTH ACT 1983

THEFT AND RELATED OFFENCES

Q Define theft

A A person is guilty of theft if he dishonestly appropriates property belonging to another with the intention of permanently depriving the other of it.

S. 1 THEFT ACT 1968

Q What is the statutory definition of 'dishonesty'?

A There is none. The Theft Act 1968 does not attempt to define what *is* dishonest, rather it provides 3 circumstances which are *not* to be considered dishonest, and one circumstance where behaviour *may be* dishonest. The question of dishonesty is one of fact for the jury or magistrate(s) to decide.

Q What is *not* dishonest?

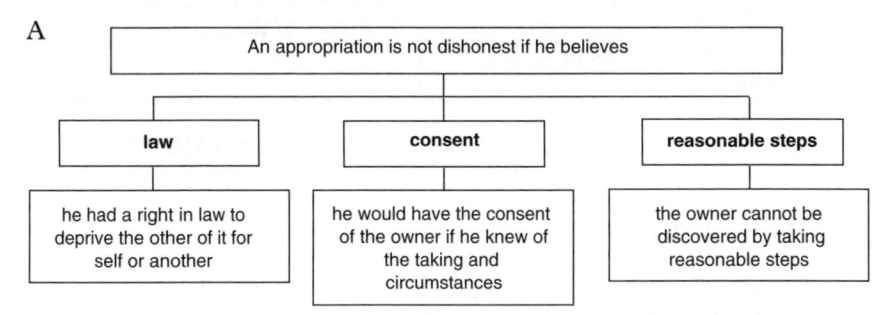

A

An appropriation is not dishonest if he believes

law	consent	reasonable steps
he had a right in law to deprive the other of it for self or another	he would have the consent of the owner if he knew of the taking and circumstances	the owner cannot be discovered by taking reasonable steps

Belief. The belief required of D as to law, consent or reasonable steps is a *subjective* one (i.e. an honestly held belief), it does not need to be a reasonable belief.

Willingness to pay. Behaviour may however be regarded as dishonest notwithstanding a willingness to pay for the goods. [A stranger removing a pint of milk from your doorstep and leaving the money will probably be regarded as dishonest under this section whereas a person removing a pint from an unattended milk float and leaving the money probably will not.]

S. 2 THEFT ACT 1968

THEFT AND RELATED OFFENCES

Q   What *is* dishonest?

A   In cases where the issue of dishonesty is raised but S. 2 does not assist (i.e. the case does not fall within any of the law/consent/reasonable steps/willingness to pay categories) the jury should be directed to decide:

[a] whether, according to the **ordinary standards of reasonable and honest people**, what was done was 'dishonest'; *and* if it was
[b] whether 'the **defendant himself must have realised** that what was done was dishonest' *by those standards.*

R v. GHOSH (1982)

Q   Define what is and what is not an appropriation

A

An appropriation is	An appropriation is not
Any assumption of the rights of the owner, including even if the property was come by innocently, a later assumption by keeping it or dealing with it as an owner.	Where property is transferred **for value** to a person **acting in good faith**, who later assumes the rights of the owner.

S. 3 THEFT ACT 1968

Q   Define property

A   Property includes money [current notes and coins] and all other property, real [land (including soil and cultivated plants), buildings and fixtures] or personal [chattels, moveables] together with things in action and other intangibles.

S. 4 THEFT ACT 1968

Things in action. Means a personal right of property which can only be claimed or enforced by legal action and not by taking physical possession, e.g. copyrights, trade marks, debts, bank accounts in credit.

Other intangible property. Gas, patents.

THEFT AND RELATED OFFENCES

Q   Can land be stolen?

A   No, except by the following:

[a]   **Trustees and personal representatives.** Where a person is in a position of trust or is empowered to dispose of the land he can steal the land if he does something in breach of trust or confidence.
[b]   **Persons who do not possess the land [strangers].** They steal land if they sever it e.g. dig gravel, cut turf, dig up cultivated plants, chop down trees etc.
[c]   **Tenants.** They steal land only by taking fixtures [wall sockets etc] or structures let for use with the land, e.g. garden sheds, coal bunkers. So, a tenant who removes topsoil does not steal land as he is not a stranger to it.

Q   When can things growing wild (i.e. uncultivated plants) be stolen?

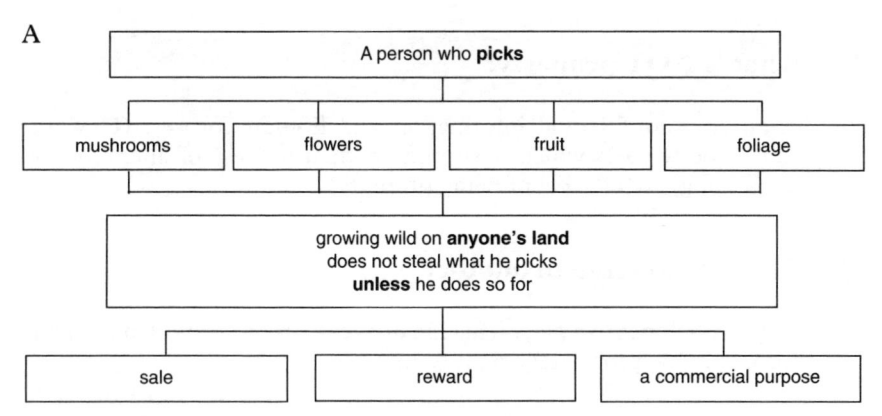

A

```
                    A person who picks
   ┌────────────┬────────────┬────────────┐
 mushrooms    flowers       fruit       foliage
   └────────────┴────────────┴────────────┘
           growing wild on anyone's land
            does not steal what he picks
                unless he does so for
   ┌────────────────┬──────────────────────┐
      sale           reward        a commercial purpose
```

Digging up. Would amount to an offence as this section is limited to **picking**.

www.janes.com   207

THEFT AND RELATED OFFENCES

Q When can wild creatures be stolen?

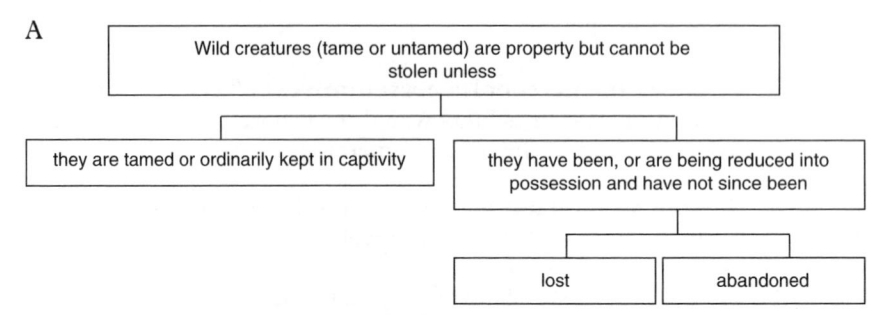

A

```
        Wild creatures (tame or untamed) are property but cannot be
                              stolen unless
    ┌──────────────────────────────┴──────────────────────────────┐
 they are tamed or ordinarily kept in captivity    they have been, or are being reduced into
                                                   possession and have not since been
                                                        ┌──────────┴──────────┐
                                                       lost              abandoned
```

Ordinarily kept in captivity means that a zoo creature can be stolen, and **reduction into possession** means that a person who has, for example, snared a rabbit, is its new owner and that rabbit can be stolen from him. If however he forgets where the snare is or simply abandons the snare [and rabbit], it then reverts to its wild state and cannot be stolen.

S. 4 THEFT ACT 1968

Q What is NOT property?

A Electricity, confidential information and human corpses. (However human body parts which have undergone a process of alteration eg. embalming, are capable of being property).

Q Define belonging to another

A Property belongs to a person having **possession or control** of it, or any non-equitable proprietary right or interest.

S. 5(1) THEFT ACT 1968

Can you steal your own property? Yes, where another has possession or control at the time of your appropriation, e.g. say a garage has completed an MOT on your vehicle and you sneak in and remove the vehicle then you are guilty of theft because the vehicle 'belonged to another' at that time.

THEFT AND RELATED OFFENCES

Q What is the meaning of obligations regarding another's property?

A Where a person receives property or its proceeds and is under a legal obligation to deal with it in a particular way (not simply a moral obligation) the property shall be regarded as belonging to another.

E.g. Where monies thrown into a fountain for charitable purpose are removed by the owner for himself, he would be guilty under this section.

S. 5(3) THEFT ACT 1968

Q What is meant by an obligation to restore another's property?

A Where a person gets property by another's mistake, and is under a legal obligation to restore it (or its proceeds), then that property shall be regarded as belonging to that other, and an intention not to restore it shall be regarded as an intention to deprive.

E.g. Money mistakenly credited to an account must be returned.

S. 5(4) THEFT ACT 1968

Q According to S. 6 which two circumstances may amount to an intention to permanently deprive?

A [a] If a person treats property as his own to dispose of, regardless of the owner's rights, and a borrowing or lending amounts to a permanent deprivation if done for a period or under circumstances that make it an outright taking.

S. 6(1) THEFT ACT 1968

E.g. Borrowing property and then 'lending' it to a total stranger in the 'hope' that he will return the goods! Or borrowing a season ticket and using it for more than the permitted number of times.

[b] Where a person parts with property [of another] **under a condition for its return** which he may not be able to perform, this amounts to treating the property as his own regardless of the other's rights.

S. 6(2) THEFT ACT 1968

E.g. Pawning another's property without his consent. If there is a likelihood he may not be able to redeem it, then S. 6(2) will help to prove an intention to permanently deprive.

www.janes.com 209

THEFT AND RELATED OFFENCES

Q Define robbery

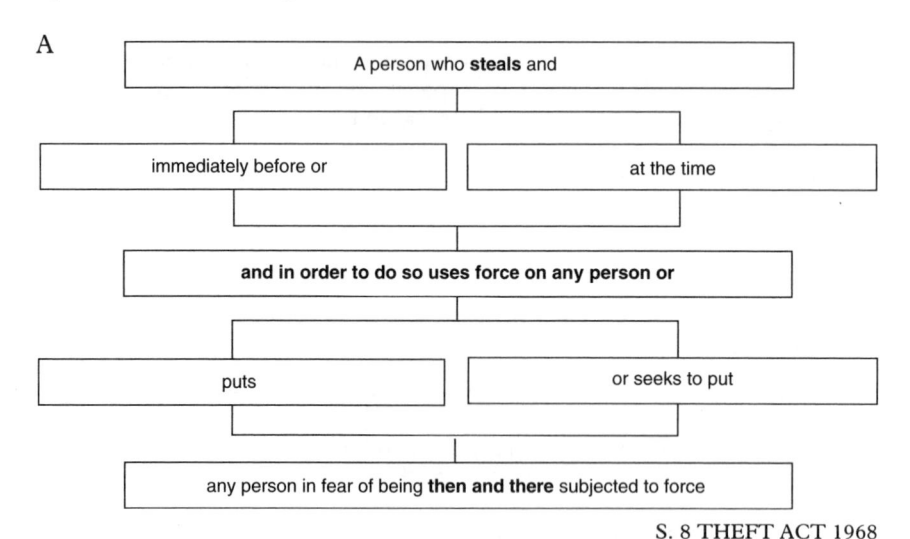

A

```
                    A person who steals and
        ┌──────────────────────┬──────────────────────┐
        immediately before or          at the time
        └──────────────────────┴──────────────────────┘
              and in order to do so uses force on any person or
        ┌──────────────────────┬──────────────────────┐
                puts                    or seeks to put
        └──────────────────────┴──────────────────────┘
          any person in fear of being then and there subjected to force
```

S. 8 THEFT ACT 1968

Steals. Means contrary to SS. 1-6 Theft Act 1968. No theft, no robbery.

Force. Robbery is simply stealing aggravated by the use of force or the threat of force. The force may be indirectly applied (e.g. pulling a handbag from someone's grasp) but must be applied in order to steal. Where the defendant has used force on another (or put another in fear of immediate force) in order to steal but has not achieved the appropriation of any property (and is therefore not guilty of robbery) he can be convicted of assault with intent to rob.

S. 8(2) THEFT ACT 1968

THEFT AND RELATED OFFENCES

Q Define burglary

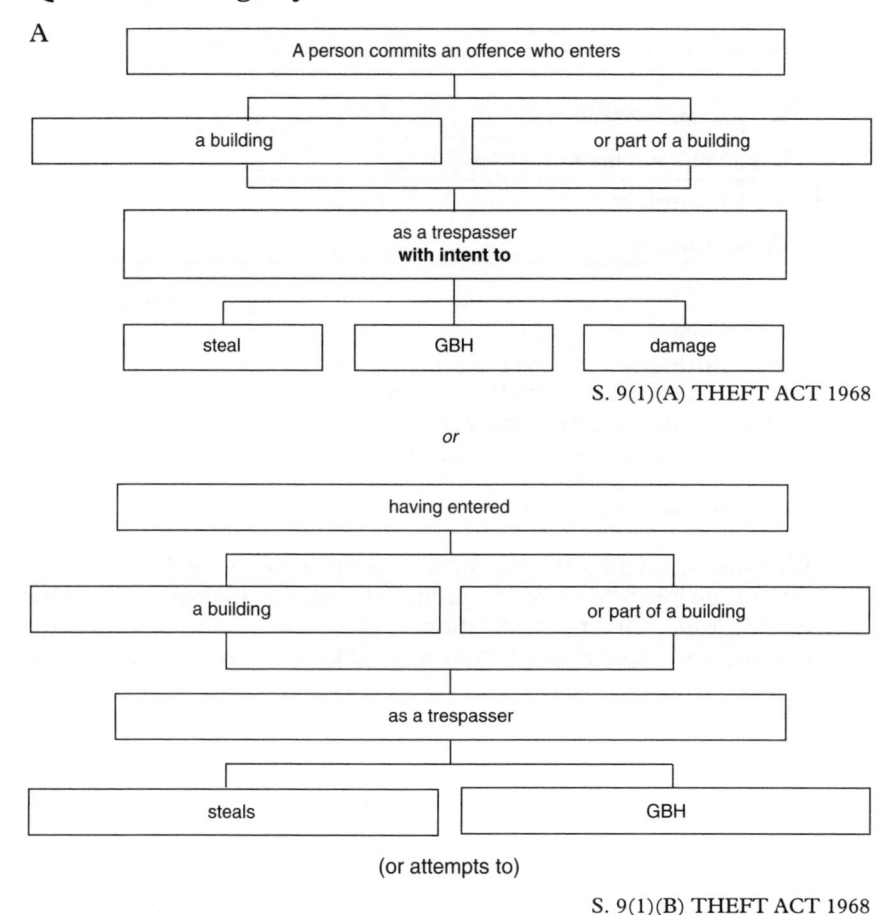

A

```
        A person commits an offence who enters
        ┌──────────────────┴──────────────────┐
      a building                      or part of a building
        └──────────────────┬──────────────────┘
                  as a trespasser
                   **with intent to**
        ┌─────────────────┼─────────────────┐
       steal             GBH              damage
```

S. 9(1)(A) THEFT ACT 1968

or

```
                having entered
        ┌──────────────────┴──────────────────┐
      a building                      or part of a building
        └──────────────────┬──────────────────┘
                  as a trespasser
        ┌─────────────────┴─────────────────┐
       steals                              GBH
```

(or attempts to)

S. 9(1)(B) THEFT ACT 1968

Building. Includes inhabited vehicle or vessel [whether occupant there or not].

Steal. Theft contrary to SS. 1-6 Theft Act 1968. This does not include abstracting electricity (S. 13) or taking a conveyance (S. 12), or pedal cycle (S. 12(5)).

THEFT AND RELATED OFFENCES

Q When does burglary become aggravated?

A   If he commits any burglary and **at the time** has with him any:

W	weapon of offence;
I	imitation firearm;
F	firearm; or
E	explosive.

S. 10 THEFT ACT 1968

At the time. For the S. 9(1)(a) offence (entering **with intent** it must be shown that he had his **WIFE** with him at the **point of entry**. The S. 9(1)(b) offence (**having entered**) requires him to have his **WIFE** at the time of stealing or causing GBH.

Has with him. Means readily at hand.

Weapon of offence. Means any article made or adapted or intended for causing injury to or for incapacitating a person and would therefore include rope, binding tape, sticking plaster etc [used for tying up victims], but not poisoned meat intended for incapacitating a guard dog.

Q Define the offence of taking a conveyance without authority

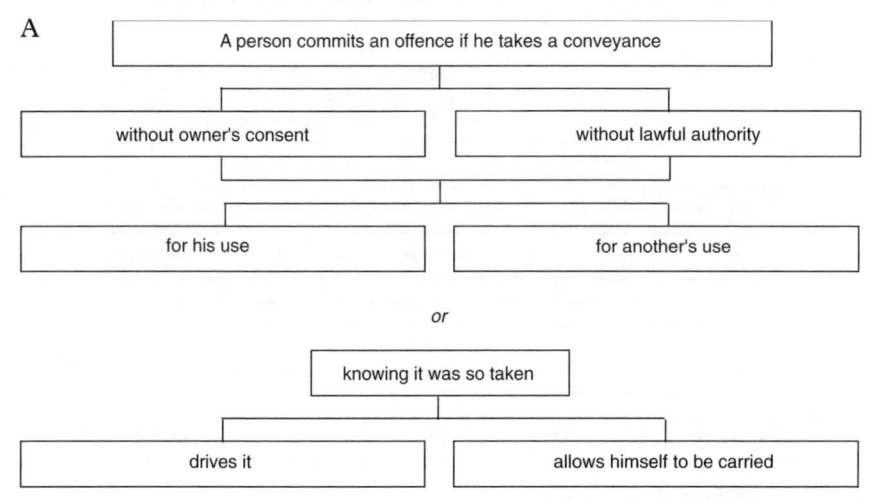

A

```
                A person commits an offence if he takes a conveyance
   without owner's consent                            without lawful authority
        for his use                                       for another's use
                                   or
                         knowing it was so taken
          drives it                                 allows himself to be carried
```

S. 12 THEFT ACT 1968

Conveyance. Means any conveyance constructed or adapted for carriage of persons by land, water or air. Not animals used for carriage, or pedestrian-controlled handcarts etc. used only for goods.

Taking for use as a conveyance. Both elements must be satisfied so if, for example, a person 'takes' a vehicle simply by pushing it elsewhere for a practical joke on its owner, the offence is not committed: it has not been taken for use as a conveyance.

THEFT AND RELATED OFFENCES

Q When does this offence become aggravated?

A

The offence becomes aggravated when he commits the above offence

and

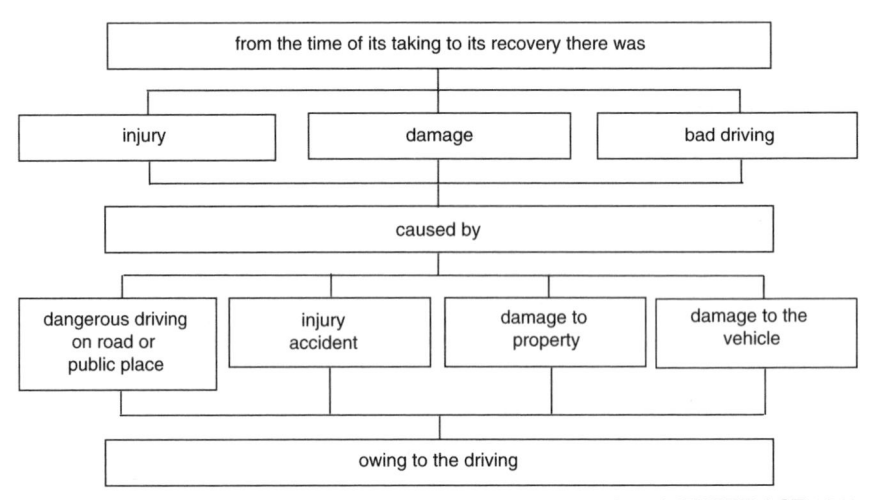

from the time of its taking to its recovery there was:
- injury
- damage
- bad driving

caused by:
- dangerous driving on road or public place
- injury accident
- damage to property
- damage to the vehicle

owing to the driving

S. 12A THEFT ACT 1968

Defence. The driving, accident or damage occurred:

[a] **before** taking; or
[b] when the driving, accident or damage occurred, he was **not in or in the immediate vicinity** of the vehicle.

Q Define taking a pedal cycle without authority

A It is an offence for a person, without having the consent of the owner or other lawful authority, to take a pedal cycle for his/her own or another's use, or to ride a pedal cycle knowing it to have been taken without such authority.

S. 12(5) THEFT ACT 1968

Q Define abstracting electricity

A A person who dishonestly uses without due authority, or dishonestly causes to be wasted or diverted any electricity, commits an offence.

S. 13 THEFT ACT 1968

THEFT AND RELATED OFFENCES

Q Define handling stolen goods

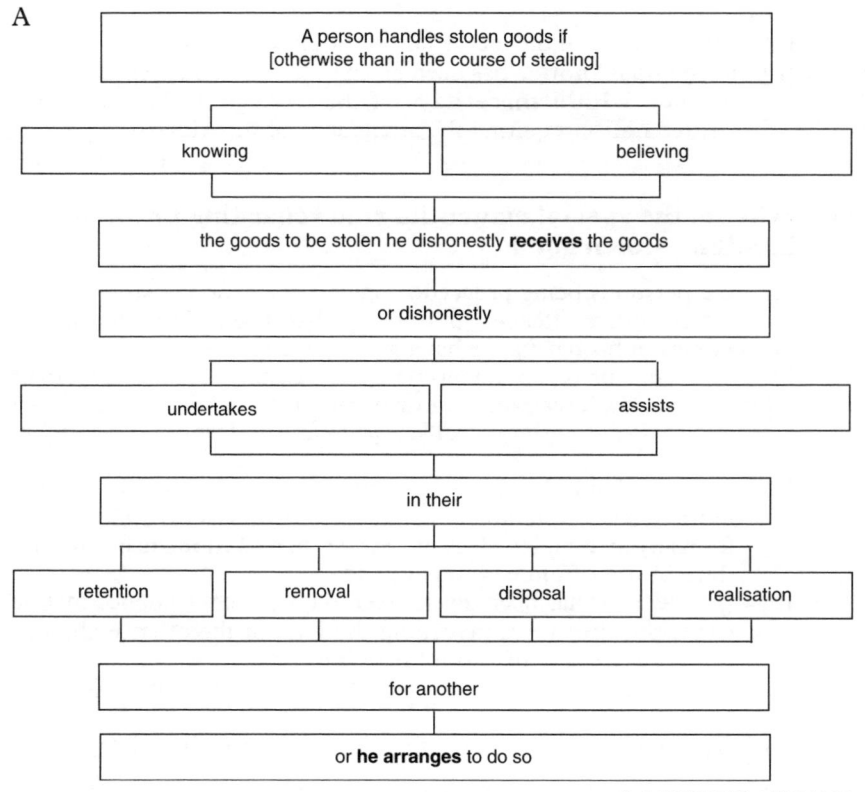

A

```
A person handles stolen goods if
[otherwise than in the course of stealing]
   │                           │
knowing                    believing
   │                           │
the goods to be stolen he dishonestly receives the goods
              or dishonestly
   │                           │
undertakes                  assists
              in their
   │         │         │         │
retention  removal  disposal  realisation
              for another
           or he arranges to do so
```

S. 22 THEFT ACT 1968

Stolen goods:

[a] a person can be convicted of handling if the goods were stolen **anywhere in the world** so long as the stealing (if not an offence under the Theft Act) was an offence in that other country;
[b] goods are classed as stolen if they are the original goods or now represent **the proceeds** of the goods;
[c] goods cease to be stolen when they are restored to lawful possession.

S. 24 THEFT ACT 1968

Proof that goods were stolen. In relation to proceedings for the theft of anything in the course of transmission (whether by post or otherwise), a statutory declaration that a person despatched, received,

THEFT AND RELATED OFFENCES

or failed to receive any goods, or they were in a particular state or condition shall be evidence of the fact providing:

[a] oral evidence of the fact would be admissible; and
[b] **seven days' notice** has been given to the person charged, and he has not, **within three days** of the trial, given the prosecutor written notice requiring the attendance of the witness.

S. 27(4) THEFT ACT 1968

Q What is the special evidential rule regarding proof of handling stolen goods?

A Where a person is being proceeded against for handling stolen goods (but for no other offence), if evidence has been given during the proceedings of his having, or having arranged to have, those goods in his possession, or of his undertaking or assisting or arranging their retention, removal, realisation or disposal, then the following evidence is admissible *in order to prove that he knew or believed the goods to be stolen:*

[a] evidence that he had in possession (or had undertaken or assisted in the retention, removal realisation or disposal of) stolen goods from any theft taking place not earlier than **12 months before the date of the offence charged**; and
[b] (provided he has been given seven days notice) evidence that he has within five years preceding the date of the offence charged been convicted of theft or of handling.

S. 27 (3) THEFT ACT 1968

Q Define the offence of re-programming mobile phones

A A person (not being the manufacturer, or having the written consent of the manufacturer) commits an offence if he (a) changes a unique device identifier (UDI), or (b) interferes with the operation of a UDI.

S. 1 MOBILE TELEPHONES (RE-PROGRAMMING) ACT 2002

UDI. The IMEI number indentifying the mobile phone.

Facilitating re-programming. It is also an offence for anyone to have in his custody or control, or to supply or offer to supply, anything which may be used for changing or interfering with a UDI if he knows or believes that it will be used unlawfully for that purpose.

S. 2 2002 ACT

THEFT AND RELATED OFFENCES

Q **Define the offence of advertising a reward**

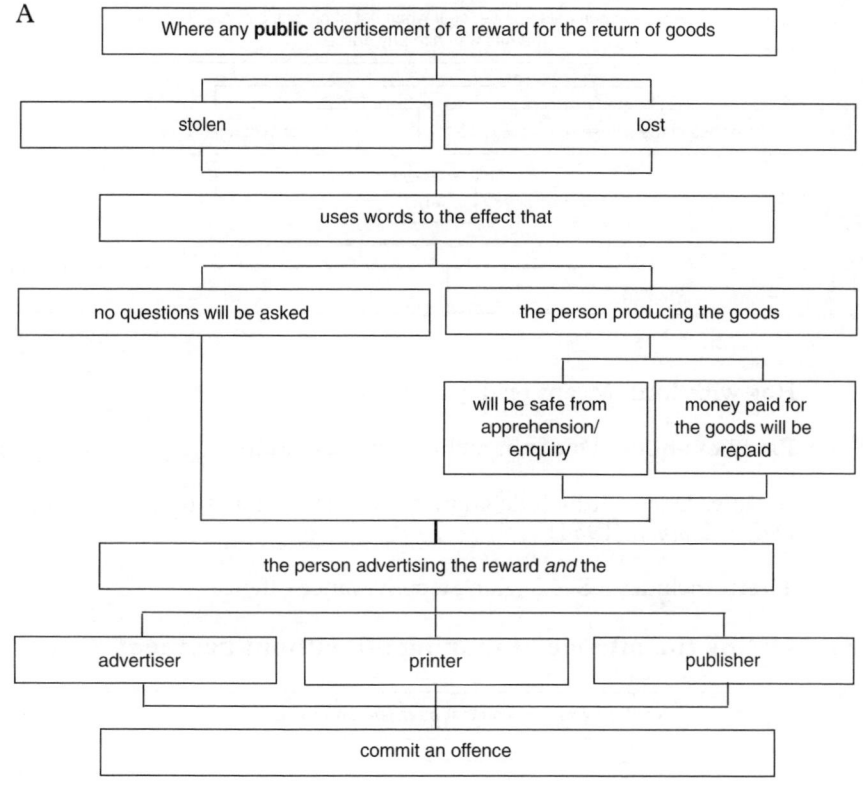

A

Where any **public** advertisement of a reward for the return of goods
- stolen
- lost

uses words to the effect that
- no questions will be asked
- the person producing the goods
  - will be safe from apprehension/enquiry
  - money paid for the goods will be repaid

the person advertising the reward *and* the
- advertiser
- printer
- publisher

commit an offence

S. 23 THEFT ACT 1968

THEFT AND RELATED OFFENCES

Q Define going equipped for stealing

A

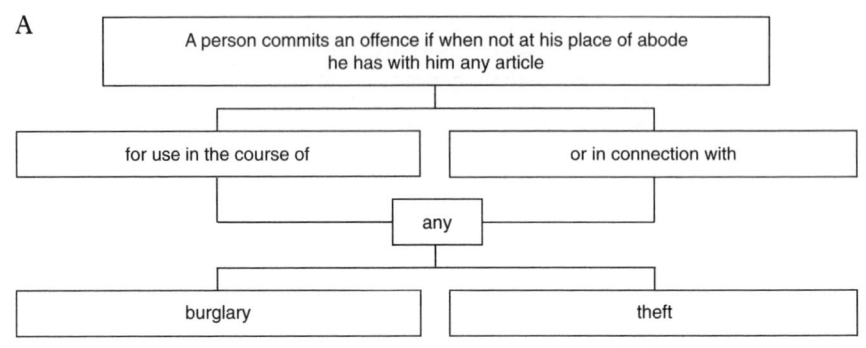

```
┌─────────────────────────────────────────────────────────┐
│ A person commits an offence if when not at his place of  │
│ abode he has with him any article                        │
└─────────────────────────────────────────────────────────┘
        │                                    │
┌───────────────────────┐           ┌───────────────────────┐
│ for use in the course │           │ or in connection with │
│ of                    │           │                       │
└───────────────────────┘           └───────────────────────┘
              │                               │
              │        ┌─────────┐            │
              └────────│   any   │────────────┘
                       └─────────┘
              │                               │
┌───────────────────────┐           ┌───────────────────────┐
│       burglary        │           │         theft         │
└───────────────────────┘           └───────────────────────┘
```

S. 25 THEFT ACT 1968

Has with him. Means readily to hand.

Place of abode. Does not include business address.

Article. Does not include animate objects such as a trained monkey: *Daly v Cannon* (1954).

Theft. Includes a S. 12 taking a conveyance offence.

Q Define the offence of making off without payment

A

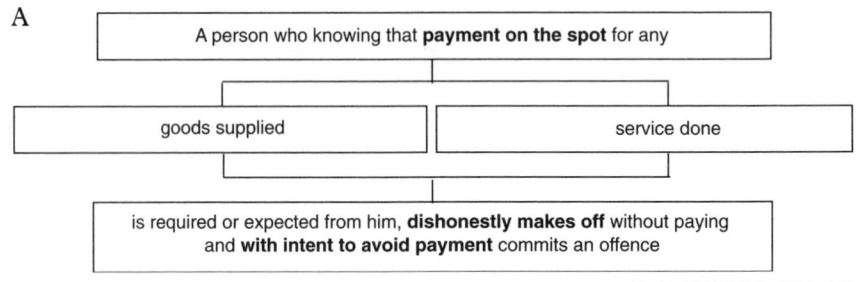

```
┌─────────────────────────────────────────────────────────┐
│ A person who knowing that payment on the spot for any   │
└─────────────────────────────────────────────────────────┘
        │                                    │
┌───────────────────────┐           ┌───────────────────────┐
│    goods supplied     │           │      service done     │
└───────────────────────┘           └───────────────────────┘
        │                                    │
┌─────────────────────────────────────────────────────────┐
│ is required or expected from him, dishonestly makes off  │
│ without paying and with intent to avoid payment commits  │
│ an offence                                               │
└─────────────────────────────────────────────────────────┘
```

S. 3 THEFT ACT 1978

Contrary to law. This section does not apply to anything which is contrary to law, eg. prostitution, drugs, unlawful gaming etc.

Makes off. Refers to making off from the spot where payment is required or expected, then and there.

Mens rea. Knowledge that payment is required then and there coupled with dishonest making off with intent to permanently avoid payment.

THEFT AND RELATED OFFENCES

Q   Define blackmail

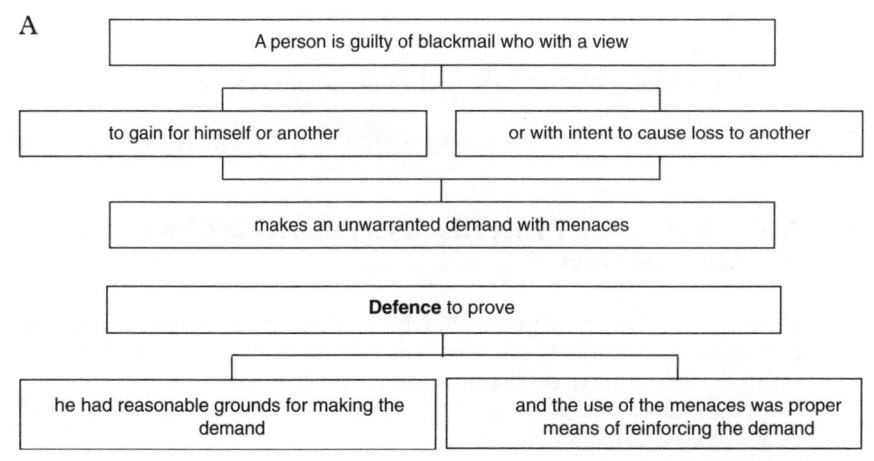

A

```
             A person is guilty of blackmail who with a view
             ┌──────────────────────────┴──────────────────────────┐
   to gain for himself or another              or with intent to cause loss to another
             └──────────────────────────┬──────────────────────────┘
              makes an unwarranted demand with menaces
                              │
                       Defence to prove
             ┌──────────────────────────┴──────────────────────────┐
  he had reasonable grounds for making the       and the use of the menaces was proper
              demand                                means of reinforcing the demand
```

S. 21 THEFT ACT 1968

Blackmail letters. The offence is complete at the time of posting.

Gain. Includes keeping what one has and getting what one has not.

Loss. Includes parting with what one has and not getting what one might get.

Unwarranted/menaces. The standard 'red' bill of a last demand from say the Gas Board, threatening to cut you off unless you pay up, is a 'proper' menace attached to a 'reasonable' demand (i.e. the defence would apply).

Q   Define the offence of retaining a wrongful credit

A   A person is guilty of an offence if:

   [a]   a **wrongful credit** has been **paid into his account** [or in which he has an interest];
   [b]   **he knows** it is wrongful; and
   [c]   he dishonestly **fails to cancel** that credit.

THEFT AND RELATED OFFENCES

A credit to an account is wrongful to the extent that it derives from:

[a] theft;
[b] blackmail;
[c] fraud (contrary to section 1 Fraud Act 2006); or
[d] stolen goods.

S. 24A THEFT ACT 1968

Q According to the Proceeds of Crime Act 2002 what is 'criminal conduct'?

A Criminal conduct is conduct which (a) constitutes an offence in any part of the UK, or (b) *would* constitute an offence in any part of the UK *if it occurred there*. It does not matter whether the conduct occurred before or after the passing of the Act, nor who carried it out, or benefited from it: s.340(2) & (4)

Q According to the Proceeds of Crime Act 2002 what is 'criminal property'?

A Property is criminal property if (a) it constitutes a person's benefit from criminal conduct or it represents such a benefit (in whole or in part and whether directly or indirectly) and (b) the alleged offender *knows or suspects* that it constitutes or represents such a benefit: s.340(3)

Q Outline the offence of concealing criminal property

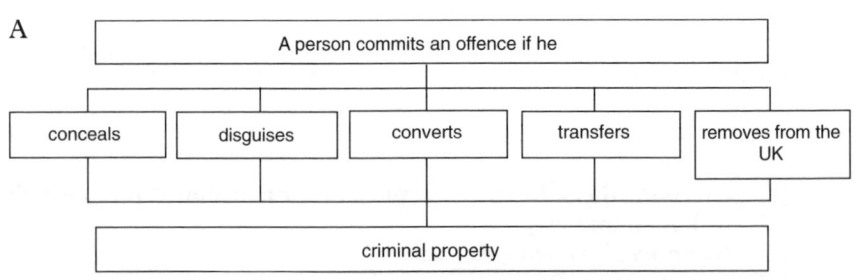

A

```
         A person commits an offence if he
┌──────────┬──────────┬──────────┬──────────┬──────────────┐
│ conceals │ disguises│ converts │ transfers│ removes from │
│          │          │          │          │    the UK    │
└──────────┴──────────┴──────────┴──────────┴──────────────┘
              criminal property
```

S.327 PROCEEDS OF CRIME ACT 2002

Conceals/disguises. Includes concealing or disguising its nature, source, location, disposition, movement or ownership or any rights with respect to it.

THEFT AND RELATED OFFENCES

Property. This offence is often referred to as 'money laundering' but it is not just money that is covered. 'Property' here means *all* property wherever situated, including money, all other forms of property, real or personal, heritable or movable, and things in action and other intangible or incorporeal property.

Q Outline the offence concerning arrangements in relation to criminal property

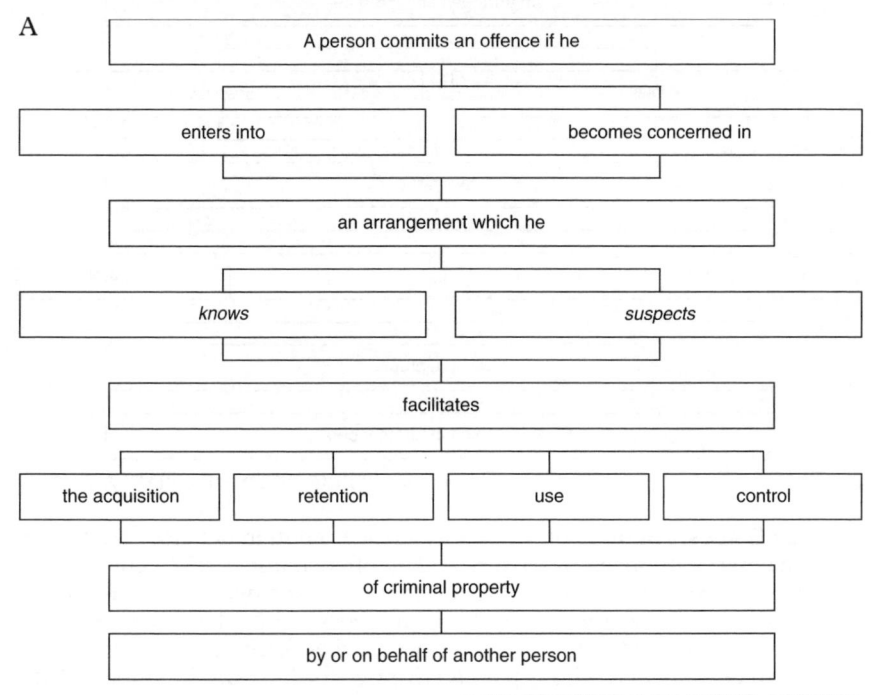

A

```
A person commits an offence if he
    ├── enters into
    └── becomes concerned in
an arrangement which he
    ├── knows
    └── suspects
facilitates
    ├── the acquisition
    ├── retention
    ├── use
    └── control
of criminal property
by or on behalf of another person
```

S.328 PROCEEDS OF CRIME ACT 2002

THEFT AND RELATED OFFENCES

Q Outline the offence concerning acquisition, use and possession of criminal property

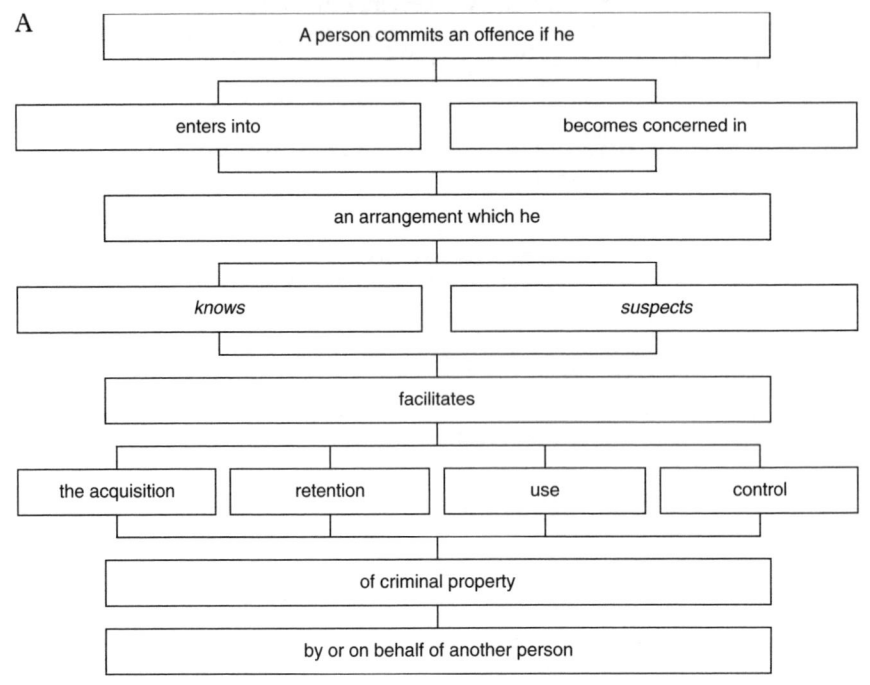

A

```
A person commits an offence if he
    ├── enters into
    └── becomes concerned in
        an arrangement which he
            ├── knows
            └── suspects
        facilitates
            ├── the acquisition
            ├── retention
            ├── use
            └── control
        of criminal property
        by or on behalf of another person
```

S.329 PROCEEDS OF CRIME ACT 2002

Defences. All three of the above offences contain defences relating to making 'authorised disclosures'. The offence under s.329 contains an additional defence which states that a person will not commit the offence if he acquired, used or had possession of the property for adequate consideration i.e. a proper market price. Thus a tradesman, such as a builder, who is paid a fair price for his work in money which comes from the proceeds of crime is not under an obligation to question the source of that money.

FRAUD

Q Outline the offence of Fraud

A A person commits fraud if he commits any of the following:

[a] fraud by false representation;
[b] fraud by failing to disclose information;
[c] fraud by abuse of position

S. 1 FRAUD ACT 2006

Q What is 'fraud by false representation'?

A A person commits fraud by false representation if he:

[a] dishonestly makes a false representation, and
[b] intends, by making the representation:
  [i] to make a gain for himself or another; or
  [ii] to cause loss to another or to expose another to the risk of loss.

S. 2 FRAUD ACT 2006

Representation. Any statement (made in any form whatsoever, by words or conduct) as to fact or law, including a representation as to the state of mind of (a) the person making the statement or (b) any other person. Representations may be express or implied.

'False' representation. A representation is false if (a) it is untrue or misleading, *and* (b) the person making it knows that it is, or might be, untrue or misleading.

Dishonestly. The test for dishonesty in fraud is the same as that for theft (*R v Ghosh* (1982)).

Machines. Whereas under the old deception law it was not possible to deceive a machine, there is no such restriction under the Fraud Act 2006, so entering a false PIN number into a machine may lead to this offence.

FRAUD

Q What is 'fraud by failing to disclose'?

A A person commits fraud by failing to disclose information if he:

[a] dishonestly fails to disclose to another person information which he is under a legal duty to disclose; and
[b] intends, by failing to disclose the information:
  [i] to make a gain for himself or another; or
  [ii] to cause loss to another or to expose another to the risk of loss.

S. 3 FRAUD ACT 2006

Legal duty. D must be under a **legal** duty to disclose the information rather than simply a moral one. This is undefined, but may include duties under both written and oral contracts, statute, trade custom and where fiduciary relationships exist (i.e. relationships of utmost loyalty and confidentiality)

Q What is 'fraud by abuse of position'?

A A person commits fraud by abuse of position if he:

[a] occupies a position in which he is expected to safeguard, or not act against, the financial interests of another person,
[b] dishonestly abuses that position (by act or omission), and
[c] intends, by means of the abuse of that position:
  [i] to make a gain for himself or another; or
  [ii] to cause loss to another or to expose another to the risk of loss.

S. 4 FRAUD ACT 2006

Q What does 'gain' and 'loss' mean?

A Section 5 of the Fraud Act 2006 states that 'gain' and 'loss' in sections 2, 3 and 4 extend only to gain and loss in *money* or *other property* (whether real or personal, tangible or intangible), whether such gain/loss be temporary or permanent. 'Gain' includes a gain by keeping what one has, as well as getting what one does not have. 'Loss' includes a loss by not getting what one might get, as well as a loss by parting with what one has.

Q Outline the offence of possession or control of articles for use in fraud

A A person is guilty of an offence if he has in his possession or under his control any article for use in the course of or in connection with any fraud.

S. 6 FRAUD ACT 2006

FRAUD

Any fraud. This offence applies to all fraud offences under the 2006 Act.

Where? The offence can be committed anywhere at all; it does not contain the 'not at his place of abode' restrictions of the offence of 'going equipped' under s.25 Theft Act 1968.

Article. Anything, including any form of electronic program or data.

Q Outline the offence of making or supplying articles for use in frauds

A A person is guilty of an offence if he makes, adapts, supplies or offers to supply any article:

[a] knowing that it is designed or adapted for use in the course of or in connection with fraud, or
[b] intending it to be used to commit, or assist in the commission of, fraud.

S. 7 FRAUD ACT 2006

Q Outline the offence of obtaining services dishonestly

A A person is guilty of an offence if he obtains services for himself or another by a dishonest act, and:

[a] the services are made available on the basis that payment has been, is being or will be made for, or in respect of, them,
[b] he obtains them without any payment having been made in respect of them or without payment having been made in full, and
[c] when he obtains them, he knows:
  [i] that they are being made available in return for payment as in (a) above, or
  [ii] that they might be,

but intends that payment will not be made, or will not be made in full.

S. 11 FRAUD ACT 2006

Note. There is no requirement for any fraudulent representation here; D must simply obtain a service dishonestly, in the knowledge that some payment is expected e.g. slipping through a back door into an event in order to avoid paying the required entrance fee.

FRAUD

Q Define the offence of false accounting

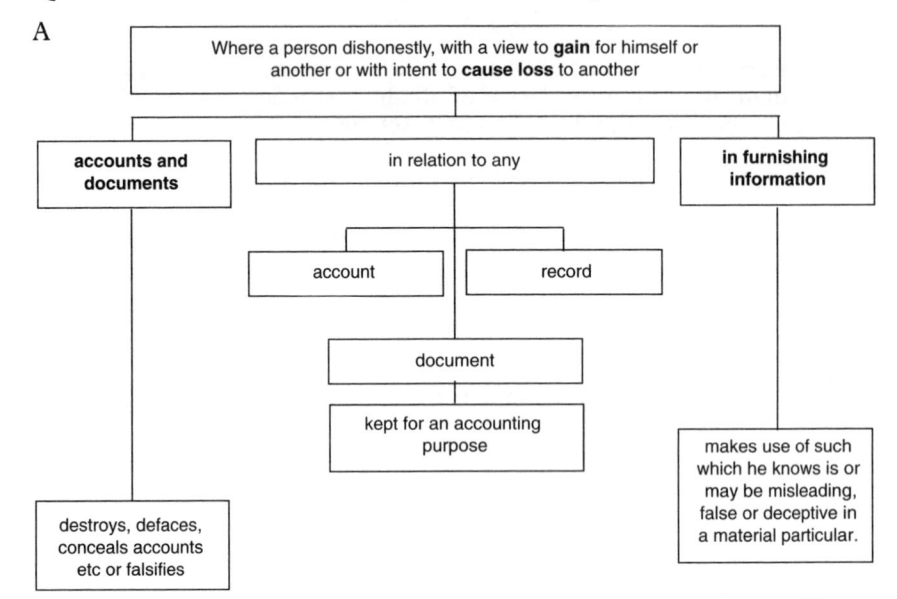

A

```
Where a person dishonestly, with a view to gain for himself or
another or with intent to cause loss to another
```

- accounts and documents
- in relation to any
  - account
  - record
  - document
  - kept for an accounting purpose
- in furnishing information

destroys, defaces, conceals accounts etc or falsifies

makes use of such which he knows is or may be misleading, false or deceptive in a material particular.

S. 17 THEFT ACT 1968

Falsifies. May be by omission as well as by act. Eg. failing to make an entry on a ledger.

A person concurring. In making the account etc, is also guilty.

Q Forgery, what is a false instrument?

A A document which tells a lie about itself.

Not false, if a constable makes out a claim for overtime he did not work and signs it, the claim is not a forgery because it does not purport to be something it is not.

False, if a constable makes out a claim for overtime and signs his supervisor's signature as having checked the claim to be correct, the document is a lie and therefore forged.

Bank notes. Are not forged, but are counterfeited.

FRAUD

Q Define making a false instrument with intent

A A person is guilty of forgery if he makes a false instrument, with intent that he or another use it **to induce someone to accept it as genuine** and as a result someone is prejudiced.

S. 1 FORGERY AND COUNTERFEITING ACT 1981

Q Define using a false instrument with intent

A It is an offence for a person to use an instrument which is [and he knows or believes] to be false with the intention **of inducing someone to accept it as genuine** and as a result someone is prejudiced.

S. 3 FORGERY AND COUNTERFEITING ACT 1981

Q Define the offence of copying a false instrument with intent

A It is an offence for a person to make a copy of an instrument which is [and he knows or believes] to be false with the intention that he or another shall use it **to induce someone to accept it as a copy of a genuine instrument,** resulting in someone being prejudiced.

S. 2 FORGERY AND COUNTERFEITING ACT 1981

Q Define the offence of using a copy of a false instrument with intent

A It is an offence for a person to use a copy of an instrument which is [and he knows or believes] to be false with the intention of **inducing someone to accept it as a copy of a genuine instrument** resulting in someone being prejudiced.

S. 4 FORGERY AND COUNTERFEITING ACT 1981

Q Define an instrument

A [a] Any document;
[b] any stamp issued or sold by a postal operator;
[c] any Inland Revenue stamp;
[d] any disc, tape, sound track or device on which information is stored or recorded by any means (e.g. a tachograph record sheet); and
[e] a mark used by a postal operator in lieu of a stamp.

S. 8 FORGERY AND COUNTERFEITING ACT 1981

FRAUD

Q Define having specific instruments with intent

A [a] It is an offence for a person to **have in his custody** or under his control an **instrument** which is false [and he knows or believes] with the intention that he or another shall use it to **induce someone to accept it as genuine**, resulting in someone being prejudiced; and
 [b] it is an offence for a person **to make** or have in his custody or control a **machine or implement, or paper or material** which is false [and he knows or believes] with the intention that he or another shall make an instrument which is false and use it **to induce someone to accept it as genuine** resulting in someone being prejudiced.

S. 5(1), (3) FORGERY AND COUNTERFEITING ACT 1981

Instruments are: Money orders, postal orders, UK postage stamps, Inland Revenue stamps, share certificates, cheques and other bills of exchange, travellers' cheques, bankers' drafts, promissory notes, cheque cards, debit cards, credit cards, certified copies relating to entry in a register of births, adoptions, marriages, civil partnerships or deaths.

Q Define the offence of acknowledging bail in the name of another

A Any person, without lawful authority or excuse who acknowledges bail by a court or the police, in the name of another person, commits an offence.

S. 34 FORGERY ACT 1861

Q What is meant by counterfeiting?

A [a] It is an offence for a person to make a counterfeit of a **currency note or protected coin** intending that he or another pass it as genuine; and
 [b] it is an offence for a person to make a counterfeit **currency note or protected coin** without lawful authority or reasonable excuse.

S.14(1), (2) FORGERY AND COUNTERFEITING ACT 1981

FRAUD

Q **Define the offence of passing or tendering counterfeit coins and notes with intent**

A It is an offence for a person:

[a] **to pass or tender** as genuine any thing which is [or he knows or believes] to be a counterfeit note or protected coin; or
[b] to deliver to another any thing which is [or he knows or believes] to be counterfeit intending that **that person pass or tender it as genuine**.

S. 15(1)(A), (B) FORGERY AND COUNTERFEITING ACT 1981

Protected coin. Any coin customarily used as money in any country, or otherwise specified as such by the Treasury.

Q **Define the offence of reproducing a British currency note**

A It is an offence for a person, without the written consent of the relevant authority, to reproduce on any substance whatsoever, and whether or not on the correct scale, any British currency note or any part of a British currency note.

S. 18 FORGERY AND COUNTERFEITING ACT 1981

Relevant authority. The authority empowered by law to issue notes of that description [e.g. Bank of England].

CRIMINAL DAMAGE

Q Define simple damage

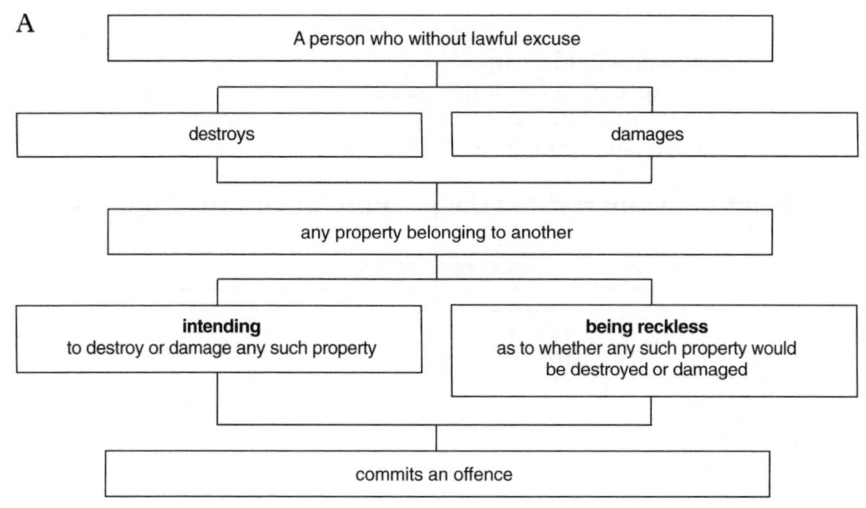

A

```
┌─────────────────────────────────────────────┐
│      A person who without lawful excuse     │
└─────────────────────────────────────────────┘
         │                         │
┌──────────────────┐    ┌──────────────────┐
│     destroys     │    │     damages      │
└──────────────────┘    └──────────────────┘
         │                         │
┌─────────────────────────────────────────────┐
│       any property belonging to another     │
└─────────────────────────────────────────────┘
         │                         │
┌──────────────────────┐  ┌──────────────────────────┐
│     intending        │  │      being reckless      │
│ to destroy or damage │  │ as to whether any such   │
│   any such property  │  │ property would be        │
│                      │  │ destroyed or damaged     │
└──────────────────────┘  └──────────────────────────┘
         │                         │
         └────────────┬────────────┘
         ┌─────────────────────────┐
         │   commits an offence    │
         └─────────────────────────┘
```

S. 1(1) CRIMINAL DAMAGE ACT 1971

Arson. Where the damage or destruction is caused by fire it shall be charged as *arson*.

Which court? The offence is triable either way (maximum sentence 10 years) but, except in cases of arson or where the offence is racially or religiously aggravated, if the value of the property destroyed or the damage done is less than £5000, it is to be tried summarily: s.22 Magistrates' Court Act 1980. Where it is to be tried summarily because of the value of the damage, the offence is not considered to be a 'summary' offence (so it can still be *attempted*).

Racially or religiously aggravated. This offence is covered by the Crime and Disorder Act 1998, so can be racially or religiously aggravated if the defendant demonstrates hostility towards the victim at the time of or immediately before or after committing the offence, and that hostility is based on the victim's membership or presumed membership of a racial or religious group. Maximum sentence in such cases is 14 years.

Destroy or damage. Not defined. Whether property has been destroyed or damaged is a question of fact for the court. Temporary and minor damage has been held to be 'damage' e.g. defacing a pavement with water-soluble paint, and graffiti smeared in mud.

CRIMINAL DAMAGE

Reckless. Following the decision of the House of Lords in *R v. G&R* (2003) this means *subjective* recklessness. Thus a person acts recklessly for the purposes of criminal damage:

- with respect to a circumstance when he/she is aware of a risk that existed or would exist;
- with respect to a result or consequence when he/she is aware of a risk that it would occur and it is, in the circumstances known to him/her, unreasonable to take the risk.

Q What is 'property' for the purpose of criminal damage?

A

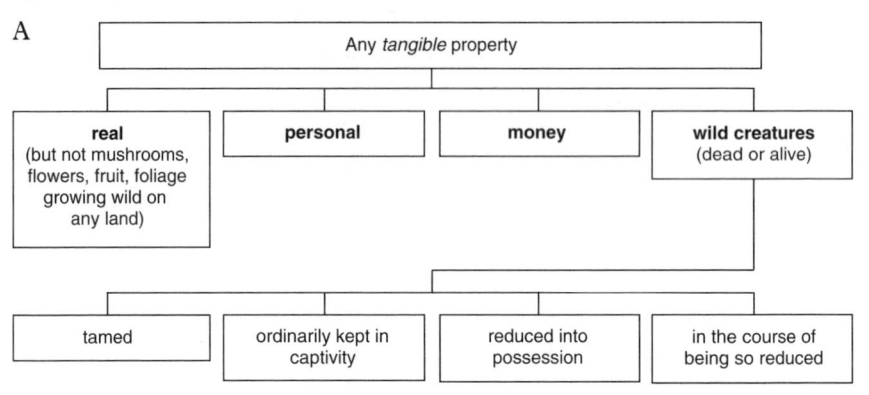

```
                    Any tangible property
   ┌──────────────┬──────────────┬──────────────┐
   real         personal        money      wild creatures
(but not mushrooms,                        (dead or alive)
flowers, fruit, foliage
 growing wild on
   any land)
   ┌──────────────┬──────────────┬──────────────┐
  tamed      ordinarily kept    reduced into   in the course of
              in captivity       possession    being so reduced
```

S.10(1) CRIMINAL DAMAGE ACT 1971

Q What does 'belonging to another' mean here?

A

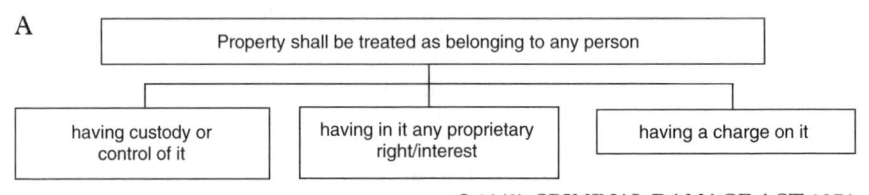

```
        Property shall be treated as belonging to any person
   ┌──────────────────┬──────────────────┬──────────────────┐
having custody or    having in it any        having a charge on it
  control of it      proprietary right/interest
```

S.10(2) CRIMINAL DAMAGE ACT 1971

Q What does 'lawful excuse' mean?

A As well as general defences which might apply, there are two lawful excuses set out in s.5 of the Act. The defendant would have a lawful excuse if

   [a] at the time of the act of damage *he believed* that he had or would have the consent of the property's owner (or other person entitled to consent) or

CRIMINAL DAMAGE

[b] he acted to protect property *believing* that there was an immediate need to do so and that the means of protection adopted or proposed to be adopted were reasonable in all the circumstances.

Q **Outline the aggravated damage offence**

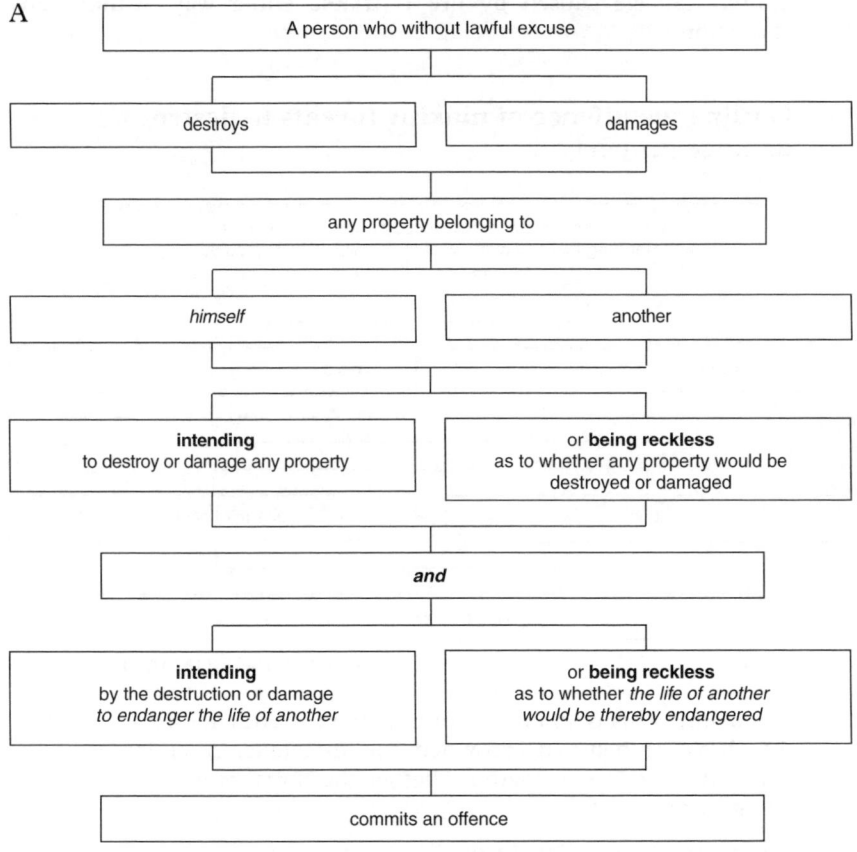

A

```
                A person who without lawful excuse
                            │
         ┌──────────────────┴──────────────────┐
      destroys                              damages
         └──────────────────┬──────────────────┘
                            │
                any property belonging to
                            │
         ┌──────────────────┴──────────────────┐
      himself                               another
         └──────────────────┬──────────────────┘
                            │
         ┌──────────────────┴──────────────────────────┐
      intending                          or being reckless
  to destroy or damage             as to whether any property would be
     any property                       destroyed or damaged
         └──────────────────┬──────────────────────────┘
                            │
                           and
                            │
         ┌──────────────────┴──────────────────────────┐
      intending                          or being reckless
 by the destruction or damage         as to whether *the life of another*
  *to endanger the life of another*    *would be thereby endangered*
         └──────────────────┬──────────────────────────┘
                            │
                   commits an offence
```

S.1 (2) CRIMINAL DAMAGE ACT 1971

Lawful excuse. The two statutory lawful excuses under s.5 (above) do not apply to aggravated damage. The lawful excuse referred to here is lawful excuse under the general law e.g. self-defence or prevention of crime

CRIMINAL DAMAGE

Q What is 'arson'?

A Arson is simply criminal damage (whether simple or aggravated) caused by fire. Aggravated damage caused by fire is triable only on indictment and carries a maximum penalty of life imprisonment. Simple damage caused by fire is triable either way, without any restriction.

Q Outline the offence of making threats to destroy or damage property

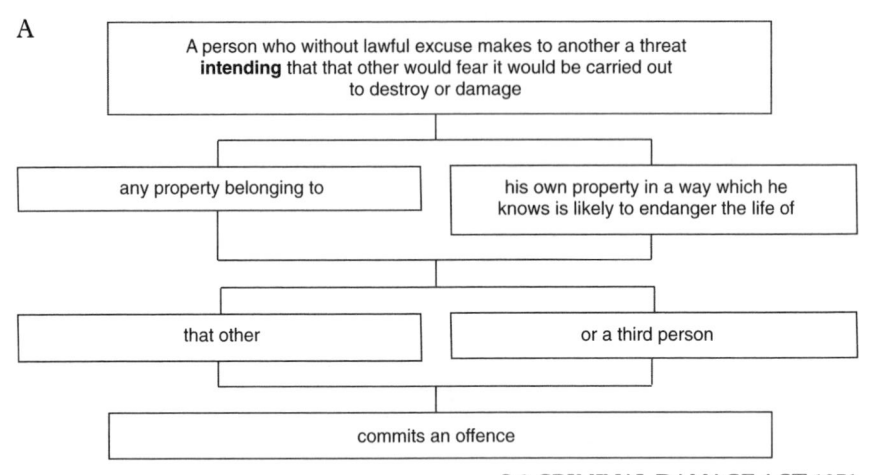

A

```
       A person who without lawful excuse makes to another a threat
       intending that that other would fear it would be carried out
                        to destroy or damage

   ┌─────────────────────────────┬─────────────────────────────┐
   any property belonging to       his own property in a way which he
                                   knows is likely to endanger the life of

   ┌─────────────────────────────┬─────────────────────────────┐
          that other                      or a third person

                        commits an offence
```

S.2 CRIMINAL DAMAGE ACT 1971

Intention. This is an offence of intention. It does not matter whether the threat is believed, provided the threatener intended it to be believed. Nor does it matter whether the threat is in fact capable of being carried out.

CRIMINAL DAMAGE

Q Outline the offence of having articles with intent to destroy or damage property

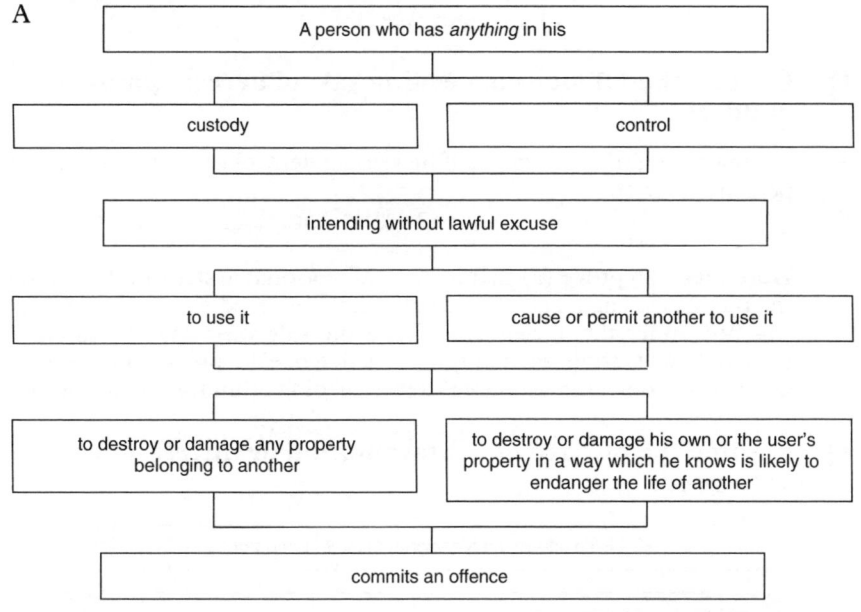

A

```
        ┌─────────────────────────────────────────────┐
        │     A person who has *anything* in his      │
        └─────────────────────────────────────────────┘
              │                               │
        ┌───────────┐                   ┌───────────┐
        │  custody  │                   │  control  │
        └───────────┘                   └───────────┘
              │                               │
        ┌─────────────────────────────────────────────┐
        │        intending without lawful excuse      │
        └─────────────────────────────────────────────┘
              │                               │
        ┌───────────┐                   ┌──────────────────────────────┐
        │ to use it │                   │ cause or permit another to   │
        │           │                   │           use it             │
        └───────────┘                   └──────────────────────────────┘
              │                               │
   ┌──────────────────────────┐   ┌──────────────────────────────────────┐
   │ to destroy or damage any │   │ to destroy or damage his own or the  │
   │ property belonging to    │   │ user's property in a way which he    │
   │ another                  │   │ knows is likely to endanger the life │
   │                          │   │ of another                           │
   └──────────────────────────┘   └──────────────────────────────────────┘
              │                               │
        ┌─────────────────────────────────────────────┐
        │             commits an offence              │
        └─────────────────────────────────────────────┘
```

S.3 CRIMINAL DAMAGE ACT 1971

Search warrant. There is a statutory power to apply to a magistrate for a search warrant under s.6

Q What is a 'graffiti penalty notice'?

A Where an authorised officer of a local authority has reason to believe that a person has committed a relevant offence (which is not racially or religiously aggravated) in that local authority area, s/he may give that person a penalty notice under s.43 Anti-social Behaviour Act 2003. 'Relevant offences' include simple damage involving painting, writing on, soiling or otherwise defacing property; painting or affixing things on structures on the highway; affixing posters; defacing streets with slogans; displaying adverts in contravention of planning regulations.

Q What is a 'defacement removal notice'?

A Where a local authority is satisfied that a relevant surface in its area has been defaced by graffiti and that defacement is offensive or detrimental to the amenity of the area, it may serve a defacement removal notice upon any person who is responsible. 'Relevant surface' means the

CRIMINAL DAMAGE

surface of any street or of any building, structure or other object in or on any street, or the surface of any land owned, occupied or controlled by an educational establishment or any building or structure on any such land: s.48 Anti-social Behaviour Act 2003

Q Outline the offence concerning sale of aerosol paint to children

A A person commits an offence if he sells an aerosol paint container to a person under 16.

s.54 ANTI-SOCIAL BEHAVIOUR ACT 2003

Defences. To prove (a) that he took all reasonable steps to determine the purchaser's age, and (b) he reasonably believed that the purchaser was not under the age of 16. Where the sale was made by another person (e.g. a shop assistant) it is a defence to prove that he (the defendant) took all reasonable steps to avoid committing the offence.

Q Outline the offence of contamination or interference with goods

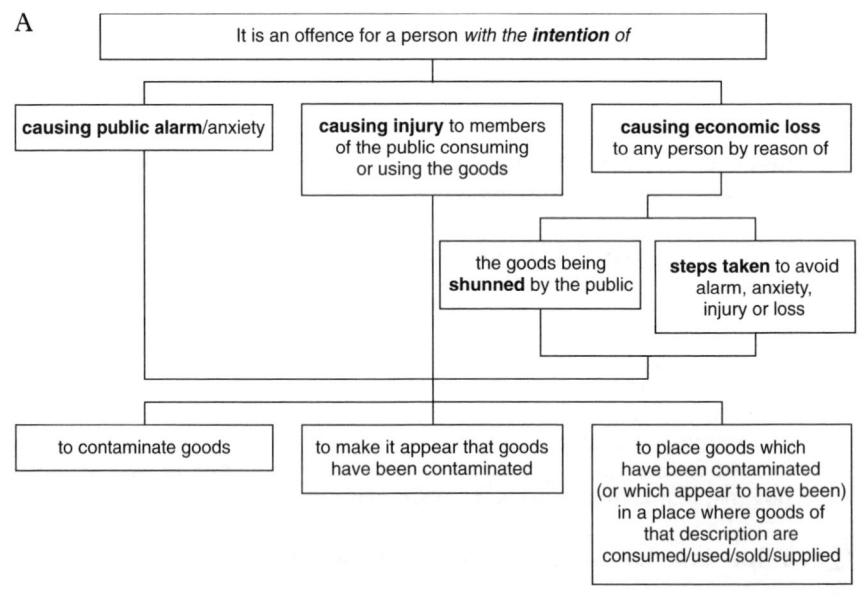

A

It is an offence for a person *with the* **intention** *of*

- **causing public alarm**/anxiety
- **causing injury** to members of the public consuming or using the goods
  - the goods being **shunned** by the public
- **causing economic loss** to any person by reason of
  - **steps taken** to avoid alarm, anxiety, injury or loss

- to contaminate goods
- to make it appear that goods have been contaminated
- to place goods which have been contaminated (or which appear to have been) in a place where goods of that description are consumed/used/sold/supplied

S.38(1) PUBLIC ORDER ACT 1986

Goods. Includes 'substances whether natural or manufactured and whether or not incorporated in or mixed with other goods'.

CRIMINAL DAMAGE

Q Outline the offence of making threats about contamination

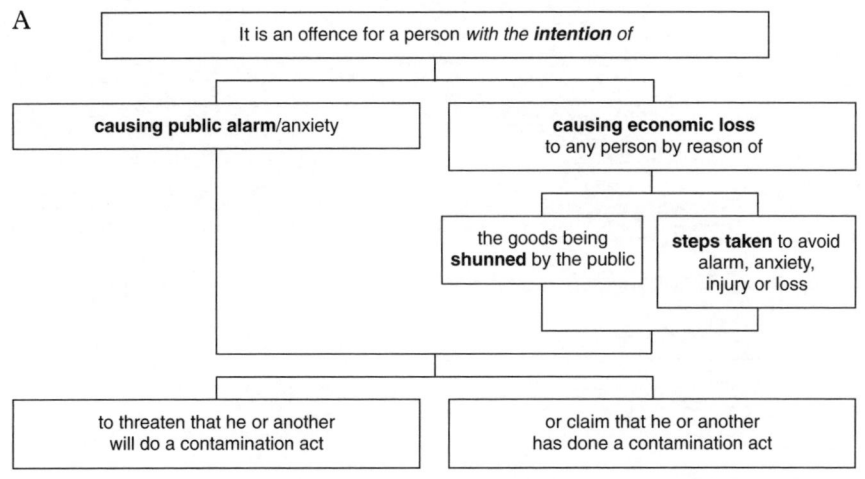

A

It is an offence for a person *with the* **intention** *of*

- causing public alarm/anxiety
- causing economic loss to any person by reason of
  - the goods being **shunned** by the public
  - **steps taken** to avoid alarm, anxiety, injury or loss

- to threaten that he or another will do a contamination act
- or claim that he or another has done a contamination act

S.38(2) PUBLIC ORDER ACT 1986

Warnings. The reference to a person claiming that a contamination act has been committed does not include a person who in good faith communicates a warning or reports that such acts appear to have been committed.

Q Outline the offence of possessing articles for contamination

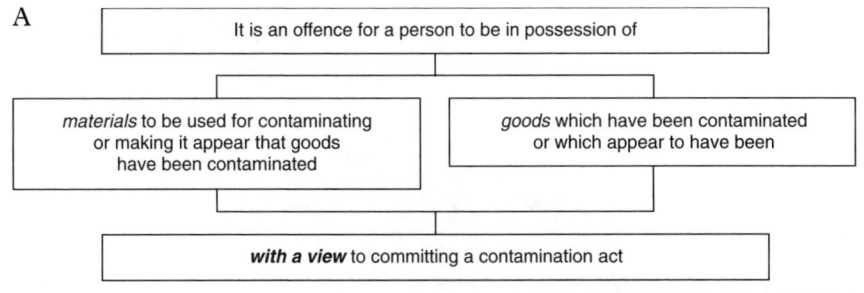

A

It is an offence for a person to be in possession of

- *materials* to be used for contaminating or making it appear that goods have been contaminated
- *goods* which have been contaminated or which appear to have been

with a view to committing a contamination act

S.38(3) PUBLIC ORDER ACT 1986

OFFENCES AGAINST THE ADMINISTRATION OF JUSTICE

Q Define perjury

A If any person **lawfully sworn** as a witness or interpreter in a judicial proceeding wilfully makes a statement material in that proceeding, which he knows to be false or does not believe to be true, he commits an offence.

S.1 PERJURY ACT 1911

Wilful. Deliberate (not accidental).

Material. The statement must be important to the case. Whether a statement is material is a question of law for the judge.

Q Define the offence of aiding and abetting perjury

A Every person who aids, abets, counsels, or procures another to commit an offence of perjury, or incites the offence, commits an offence.

Q Which other offences are similar to perjury?

A [a] If any child wilfully gives false evidence which, had it been given on oath would be perjury, he commits an offence: S. 38(2) Children & Young Persons Act 1933 (False Testimony of Unsworn Child Witness).
   [b] If any person in a **written statement** tendered in criminal proceedings wilfully makes a statement which is material, and which he knows to be false or does not believe to be true, he commits an offence: S. 89 Criminal Justice Act 1967 (False Statements in Criminal Proceedings).
   [c] If any person being required or authorised by law to make any statement on oath and being lawfully sworn [**otherwise than in judicial proceedings**] wilfully makes a statement which is material for that purpose and which he knows to be false or does not believe to be true, he commits an offence: S. 2 Perjury Act 1911 (False Statements on Oath).

Q Define the offence of perverting the course of justice

A It is an offence at common law to do an act tending and intended to pervert the course of public justice.

COMMON LAW

Requires a positive act and not a mere omission or failure to take steps to prevent an injustice.

OFFENCES AGAINST THE ADMINISTRATION OF JUSTICE

Q Outline the offence of intimidating witnesses and jurors in proceedings for criminal offences

A [a] A person who does to another:

[i] an act which intimidates, and is intended to **intimidate**, another person;
[ii] knowing or believing that that person is assisting in the investigation of an offence as a witness, or juror; and
[iii] intending thereby to cause the investigation to be **obstructed, perverted or interfered with**, commits an offence.

[b] A person who does or threatens to do to another:

[i] an act which **harms him**, and is intended to harm him; or is intended to make him fear harm;
[ii] knowing or believing that that person, or another, **has assisted in** an investigation into an offence or has **given evidence** or acted as a **juror**; and
[iii] does or threatens to do it because of that knowledge or belief.

S. 51 CRIMINAL JUSTICE AND PUBLIC ORDER ACT 1994

Q Outline the offence of intimidation of witnesses in any proceedings

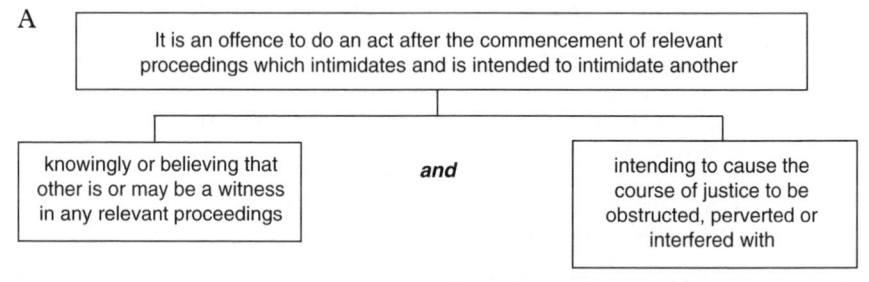

A

```
It is an offence to do an act after the commencement of relevant
proceedings which intimidates and is intended to intimidate another
```

knowingly or believing that other is or may be a witness in any relevant proceedings	**and**	intending to cause the course of justice to be obstructed, perverted or interfered with

S. 39 CRIMINAL JUSTICE AND POLICE ACT 2001

Relevant proceedings. Any proceedings in any court save the House of Lords which are not for a criminal offence.

OFFENCES AGAINST THE ADMINISTRATION OF JUSTICE

Q Define the offence of assisting offenders

A Where a person has committed a relevant offence any other person who, knowing or believing him to be guilty of the offence, or some other arrestable offence, without lawful authority or reasonable excuse, **does any act with intent to impede** his arrest or prosecution, commits an offence.

S. 4 CRIMINAL LAW ACT 1967

Prosecution. DPP's permission is required to prosecute.

Q Define the offence of concealing relevant offences

A Where a person has committed a **relevant offence**, any other person, knowing or believing the offence or some other relevant offence has been committed and **he has information which might be material** in securing the prosecution or conviction of an offender, **accepts** or agrees to accept **for not disclosing that information any consideration** [but not making good loss or injury caused by the offence/compensation] commits an offence.

S. 5 CRIMINAL LAW ACT 1967

Prosecution. DPP's permission is required to prosecute.

Q Define the offence of escaping

A It is an offence at common law to escape from legal custody.

COMMON LAW

Assisting escape. A person who assists a prisoner in escaping or attempting to escape from a prison, or (intending to facilitate the escape of a prisoner) brings, throws or otherwise conveys anything into prison, or causes another person so to do, or gives anything to a prisoner or leaves anything in any place (whether inside or outside a prison) commits an offence.

s.39 PRISON ACT 1952

Q Define the offence of harbouring offenders

A Any person who **knowingly harbours** an escapee or person unlawfully at large or **gives assistance with intent to prevent, hinder or interfere** with his arrest commits an offence.

S. 22 CRIMINAL JUSTICE ACT 1961

OFFENCES AGAINST THE ADMINISTRATION OF JUSTICE

Q **Outline the offence of wasting police time**

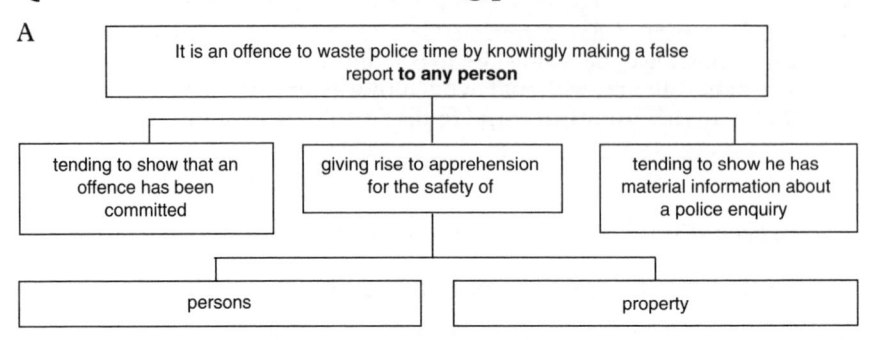

A

It is an offence to waste police time by knowingly making a false report **to any person**

- tending to show that an offence has been committed
- giving rise to apprehension for the safety of
  - persons
  - property
- tending to show he has material information about a police enquiry

IMMIGRATION OFFENCES

Q Outline the offence of illegal entry

A A non-British citizen commits an offence in any of the following circumstances:

[a] if he knowingly enters the UK in breach of a deportation order or without leave;
[b] if, having only a limited permission to enter or remain in the UK, he knowingly either

   [i] remains beyond the time limited by the permission ('overstays') or
   [ii] fails to observe a condition of the permission;

[c] if, having lawfully entered without leave, he remains beyond any permitted time;
[d] if, without reasonable excuse, he fails to comply with any requirement to report to a medical officer or attend or submit to any medical test or examination;
[e] if, without reasonable excuse, he fails to observe any residence, employment, occupation or reporting restrictions imposed on him;
[f] if he disembarks in the UK from a ship or aircraft after being placed on board with a view to his deportation;
[g] if he leaves or seeks to leave the UK through the Channel Tunnel in contravention of an imposed restriction.

S. 24 IMMIGRATION ACT 1971

Q Outline the offence of using deception to enter or remain

A A person who is not a British citizen is guilty of an offence if, by means which include deception by him

[a] he obtains or seeks to obtain leave to enter or remain in the UK; or
[b] he secures or seeks to secure the avoidance, postponement or revocation of enforcement action against him

S. 24A IMMIGRATION ACT 1971

Part 3 - Road Policing

STANDARDS OF DRIVING

Q Define 'motor vehicle'

A   For most road traffic offences S. 185 Road Traffic Act 1988 defines a motor vehicle as a mechanically propelled vehicle intended or adapted for **use on roads**. Whether it is so adapted is a question of fact in each case, e.g. a 'Go-ped' motorised scooter. (However, for the purposes of powers under S. 59 of the Police Reform Act 2002, a motor vehicle is defined as any mechanically propelled vehicle whether or not it is intended or adapted for use on roads.)

Q Define 'mechanically propelled vehicle'

A   A wider term than motor vehicle which means a vehicle constructed so it can be propelled mechanically. The test is one of construction rather than use. It must derive its power from an engine which may be powered by internal combustion, steam or battery. It can include a vehicle whose engine has been removed (where there is a possibility that it may soon be replaced) and a vehicle which has broken down because of mechanical failure. Eg. dumper trucks, fork lifts, cranes, quad bikes.

Q Define the offence of causing death by dangerous driving

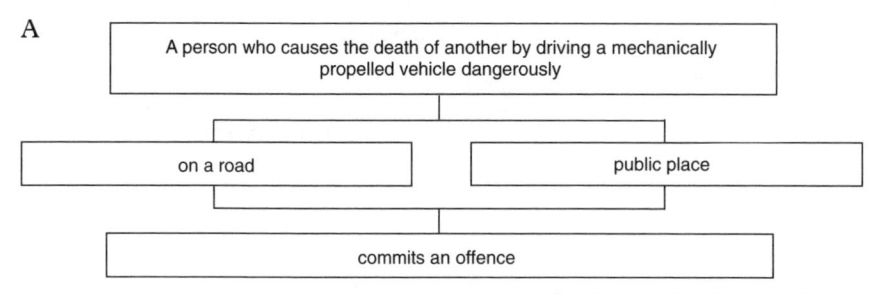

A

```
           A person who causes the death of another by driving a mechanically
                              propelled vehicle dangerously
        ┌──────────────────────────────┴──────────────────────────────┐
                on a road                              public place
        └──────────────────────────────┬──────────────────────────────┘
                              commits an offence
```

S. 1 ROAD TRAFFIC ACT 1988

Death. The driving must be 'a' cause, it need not be the sole or substantial cause. The death must be of another, not the defendant himself.

Driving. Must control both **direction and movement** of the vehicle. Pushing a car whilst steering has been held not to be driving (in England and Wales). Straddling a motorcycle and pushing it along using feet is driving. It is also driving to 'free-wheel' down a hill in a car.

STANDARDS OF DRIVING

Road. Means any highway or road to which the public have access. Vehicles 'half on, half-off' a road, are on the road.

Not a road. If only a restricted section of the public has access [say, members of a club] it is not a road. Equally, it is not a road if members of the public have to overcome physical barriers or defy prohibitions to gain access.

Public place. Includes driving off-road, in places to which the public have access and includes bridleways and footpaths. If the public have access, it is a public place.

How wide is the offence? A man free-wheeling [controlling the brakes and steering wheel] down a multi-storey car park in a dumper truck, whose driving is dangerous and results in the death of another, can be guilty of this offence.

Manslaughter. The offence also amounts to manslaughter, though it is rarely charged as such.

Q   Define the offence of dangerous driving

A   A person commits an offence who:

   [a]   drives;
   [b]   a mechanically propelled vehicle;
   [c]   dangerously;
   [d]   on a road or public place.

S. 2 ROAD TRAFFIC ACT 1988

STANDARDS OF DRIVING

Q What is the test of dangerous driving

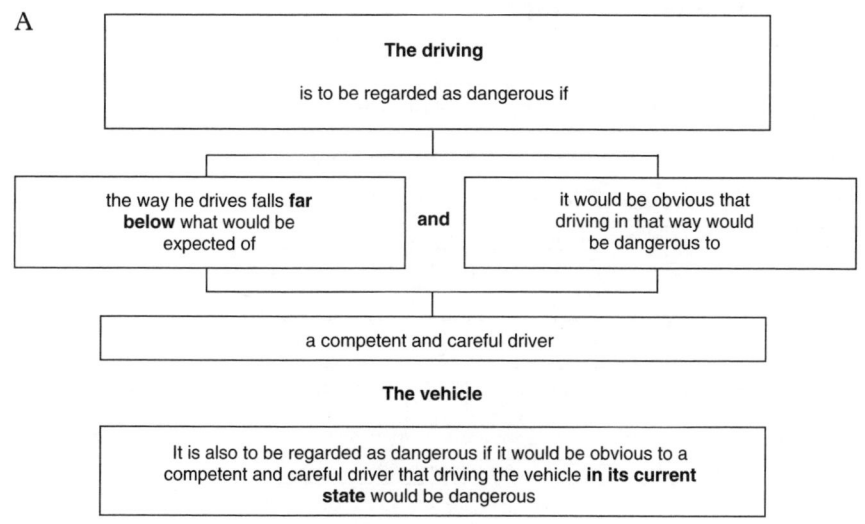

A

> **The driving** is to be regarded as dangerous if

- the way he drives falls **far below** what would be expected of

and

- it would be obvious that driving in that way would be dangerous to

→ a competent and careful driver

The vehicle

> It is also to be regarded as dangerous if it would be obvious to a competent and careful driver that driving the vehicle **in its current state** would be dangerous

Current state of the vehicle. Case law indicates that this implies a state different from the original state of the vehicle. Regard may be given to anything attached to, and carried on, the vehicle and to 'how' it is attached or carried.

Q Define 'careless and inconsiderate driving'

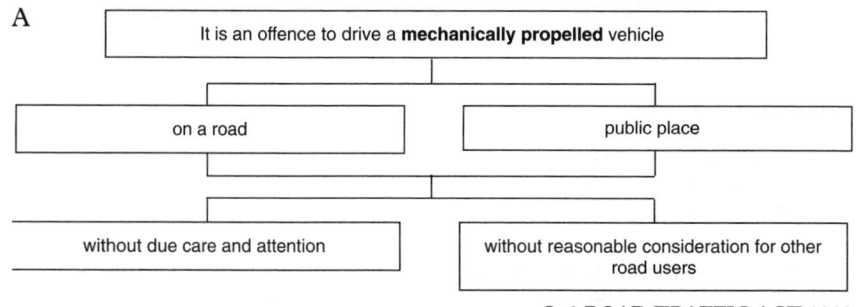

A

> It is an offence to drive a **mechanically propelled** vehicle

- on a road
- public place

- without due care and attention
- without reasonable consideration for other road users

S. 3 ROAD TRAFFIC ACT 1988

Due care and attention. The standard of driving that would be expected of a competent and careful driver: S. 32A RTA 1988

Inconsiderate driving. e.g. driving through a puddle and splashing a bus queue.

STANDARDS OF DRIVING

Q What powers exist to order careless drivers (or unlawful off-Roaders) to Stop?

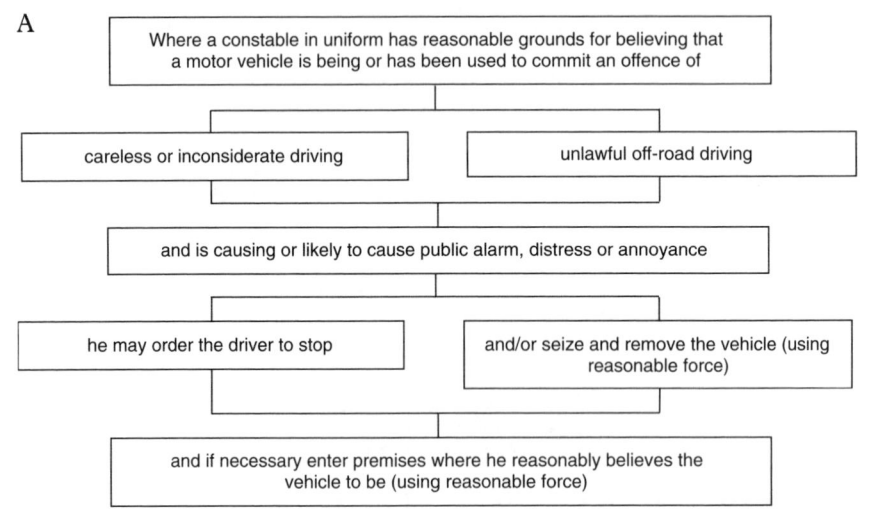

A

```
Where a constable in uniform has reasonable grounds for believing that
a motor vehicle is being or has been used to commit an offence of
```
↓
```
careless or inconsiderate driving        unlawful off-road driving
```
↓
```
and is causing or likely to cause public alarm, distress or annoyance
```
↓
```
he may order the driver to stop    and/or seize and remove the vehicle (using
                                   reasonable force)
```
↓
```
and if necessary enter premises where he reasonably believes the
vehicle to be (using reasonable force)
```

S. 59 POLICE REFORM ACT 2002

Premises. Not private dwelling-houses (though this does not include garages, driveways etc. occupied with the dwelling).

Motor vehicle. Note that motor vehicle for this offence is a wider concept than usual: any mechanically propelled vehicle *whether or not it is intended or adapted for use on roads: s.59(9)*.

Warnings. In order to exercise the power to seize/remove a vehicle it is necessary in most cases to first warn the driver not to continue the behaviour. However a warning need not be given in the following circumstances:

[a] where it is impracticable to do so;
[b] where a warning has already been given on that occasion;
[c] where the officer has reasonable grounds for believing that a warning has already been given on that occasion by someone else; or
[d] where the officer has reasonable grounds for believing that a warning has already been given to that person during the previous 12 months.

Failure to stop. Failing to comply with any order to stop is an offence.

STANDARDS OF DRIVING

Q Outline the defence to bad driving of automatism

A Automatism occurs when a driver's movements are beyond his control or his movements are brought about involuntarily, e.g. a driver being attacked by a swarm of bees or losing control as a result of lapsing into a coma. The defence is not available to a person who knows that he is subject to a condition which will result in his losing control, e.g. a diabetic who begins to feel the effects of a hypoglycaemic episode but continues to drive.

Q Outline the offence of causing death by careless driving whilst under the influence

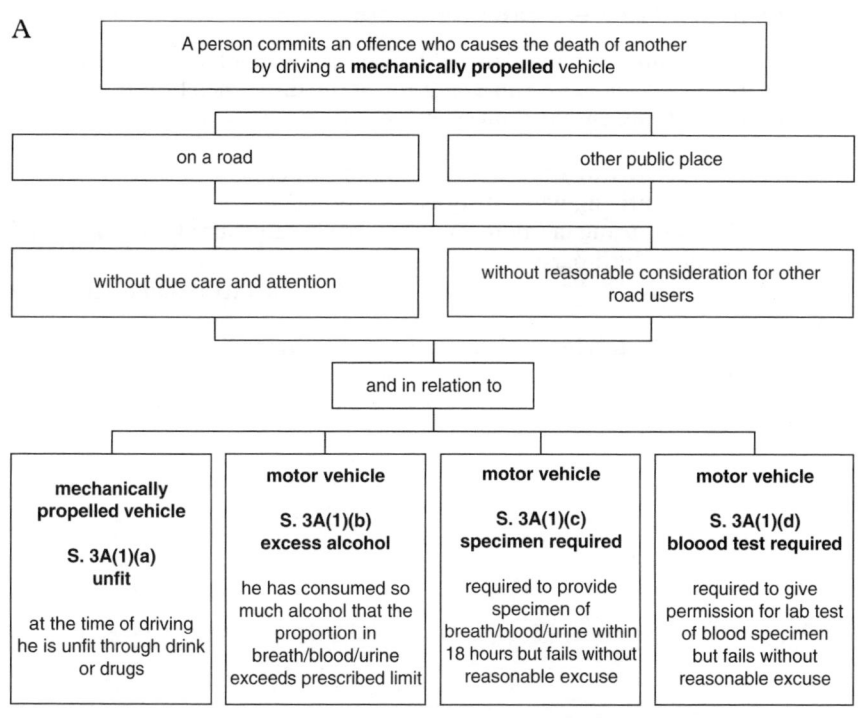

A

```
              A person commits an offence who causes the death of another
                    by driving a mechanically propelled vehicle

          ┌───────────────────────────┴───────────────────────────┐
       on a road                                            other public place

   without due care and attention          without reasonable consideration for other
                                                        road users

                              and in relation to

  ┌──────────────┬──────────────────┬──────────────────┬──────────────────┐
  mechanically      motor vehicle      motor vehicle      motor vehicle
  propelled vehicle   S. 3A(1)(b)       S. 3A(1)(c)        S. 3A(1)(d)
                     excess alcohol    specimen required  bloood test required
   S. 3A(1)(a)
      unfit        he has consumed so   required to provide   required to give
                  much alcohol that the    specimen of      permission for lab test
  at the time of driving  proportion in  breath/blood/urine within  of blood specimen
  he is unfit through drink  breath/blood/urine  18 hours but fails without   but fails without
      or drugs    exceeds prescribed limit  reasonable excuse   reasonable excuse
```

s.3A ROAD TRAFFIC ACT 1988

Power of entry. Unfit - power of entry always. Excess alcohol - injury accident.

S. 3A (1)(a). Relates to a mechanically propelled vehicle. Power of arrest and entry.

STANDARDS OF DRIVING

S. 3A (1)(b), (c) & (d). Relate to a **motor vehicle** [intended or adapted for use on a road] and the '18 hours' requirement under (c) relates only to police station procedures.

Q **Outline the offence of causing death by careless or inconsiderate driving**

A A person who causes the death of another person by driving a **mechanically propelled** vehicle on a road or other public place without due care and attention, or without reasonable consideration for other persons using the road or place, is guilty of an offence.

S. 2B ROAD TRAFFIC ACT 1988

Q **Outline the offence of unlicensed, disqualified or uninsured drivers causing death**

A A person is guilty of an offence if he causes the death of another person by driving a *motor vehicle* on a *road* and at the time when he is driving any of the following circumstances apply –

[a] he was driving otherwise than in accordance with a licence,
[b] he was driving while disqualified, or
[c] he was using a motor vehicle while uninsured or unsecured against third party risks.

s.3ZB ROAD TRAFFIC ACT 1988

Standard of driving. There is no requirement that the standard of driving be poor, merely that a motor vehicle was driven in one of the specified circumstances and the driving caused the death of another.

NOTICE OF INTENDED PROSECUTION

Q What is a notice of intended prosecution (NIP)?

A A warning notice which must be served upon offenders before certain offences can be prosecuted.

Q Which offences are subject to NIP?

A

Section	Offence
S. 2 RTA 1988	Dangerous driving
S. 3	Careless and inconsiderate driving
S. 22	Leaving vehicle in dangerous position
S. 28 and S. 29	Dangerous, careless and inconsiderate cycling
S. 35	Failure to comply with traffic directions
S. 36	Failure to comply with traffic signs
S. 16 RT Regulation Act 1984	Speeding [temporary restrictions]
S. 17 RT Regulation Act 1984	Speeding [special roads]

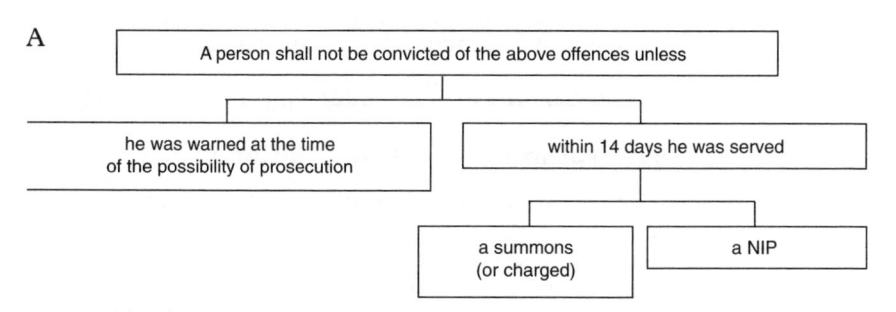

Q When is a NIP required?

A

A person shall not be convicted of the above offences unless

- he was warned at the time of the possibility of prosecution
- within 14 days he was served
  - a summons (or charged)
  - a NIP

www.janes.com   251

NOTICE OF INTENDED PROSECUTION

Q How is service of a NIP proved?

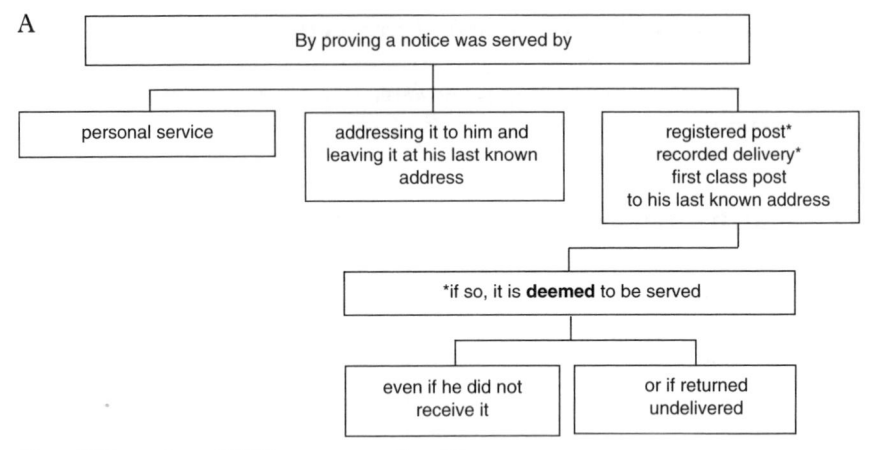

A

By proving a notice was served by:
- personal service
- addressing it to him and leaving it at his last known address
- registered post*, recorded delivery*, first class post to his last known address

*if so, it is **deemed** to be served
- even if he did not receive it
- or if returned undelivered

Q When is a NIP not required?

A [a] In relation to an offence if at the time, or immediately afterwards, and owing to the presence of the vehicle concerned on a road an accident occurred (S. 2(1) RT Amendment Act 1988); or
[b] when a **fixed penalty** has been issued in respect of the offence (S. 2(2)).

Where the accident is so minor that the driver is unaware of its occurrence then a NIP will have to be served (although if it was so severe that the driver has no recollection of it, there is no need to serve a NIP).

Q What if you are unable to trace the offender?

A A lack of a warning notice **will not be a bar to conviction** where:

[a] neither the offender's name and address, nor that of the registered keeper (if any), could be ascertained, despite reasonable diligence, in time for a summons or a complaint to be served or for a notice to be served or sent in compliance with the requirement to do so; or
[b] that the accused **by his own conduct** contributed to the failure.

Q What is the presumption in law in relation to NIPs?

A They shall be deemed to have been served unless the contrary is proved by the defence.

ACCIDENTS

Q Define a reportable accident

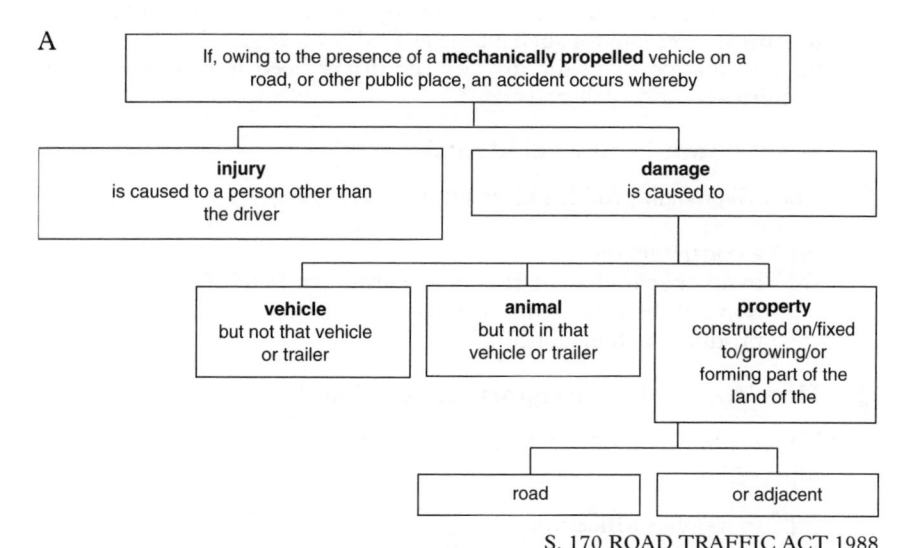

A

```
If, owing to the presence of a mechanically propelled vehicle on a
road, or other public place, an accident occurs whereby
```

- **injury** is caused to a person other than the driver
- **damage** is caused to
  - **vehicle** but not that vehicle or trailer
  - **animal** but not in that vehicle or trailer
  - **property** constructed on/fixed to/growing/or forming part of the land of the
    - road
    - or adjacent

S. 170 ROAD TRAFFIC ACT 1988

Animal. Means horse, cattle, ass, mule, sheep, pig, goat or dog.

Q What are the driver's duties and responsibilities in such a case?

A The driver shall:

[a] stop; and
[b] if required to do so by any person having reasonable grounds for doing so, give

   [i] his name and address; and
   [ii] the name and address of the owner; and
   [iii] the identification mark of the vehicle.

[c] if for any reason the driver does not give his name and address, he must **report** the accident.

ACCIDENTS

This is, essentially, a duty 'to exchange details' with any other parties involved (including owners of any property damaged) and as such case law states that providing a solicitor's address for further correspondence is sufficient to discharge the duty. The requirement is to **stop** and remain for such a time as to allow interested persons to ask for information from the driver - the driver need not make his own enquiries to find such persons.

Q What about injury accidents?

A The driver shall produce his insurance to:

[a] a constable; or
[b] to any person having reasonable grounds. [And if he is unable to do so at the time of the accident, he must report the accident and produce such evidence].

Q How does a driver report an accident?

A Where the driver does not give his name and address at the time he must report:

[a] to a police officer; or
[b] at a police station [personally]; and it must be done

[i] as soon as reasonably practicable; and in any case
[ii] within 24 hours.

24 hours. This does not give the driver 24 hours to report the accident, it must be done as soon as is reasonably practicable **and in any** case within 24 hours.

Q Define the offence of failing to stop or report an accident

A A person who fails to stop or report an accident commits an offence. [Two offences].

S. 170(4) ROAD TRAFFIC ACT 1988

Q Is failing to stop or report also the offence of perverting the course of justice?

A No. In *R v Clark (2003)* the Court of Appeal held that the failure to report the accident could not amount to perverting the course of justice since that requires an act rather than an omission.

ACCIDENTS

Q **What is the defence to not producing insurance at the time of the accident?**

A To prove that he produced it at a police station specified by him at the time of the accident within **seven days**.

S. 170(7) ROAD TRAFFIC ACT 1988

Q **Define the offence of giving false details**

A In the case of an allegation of dangerous or careless driving or cycling, the driver/rider **who refuses, or gives a false name and address**, to any person with reasonable grounds for requiring it, commits an offence.

S. 168 ROAD TRAFFIC ACT 1988

There is no requirement for an accident to have occurred, only for an allegation of such driving to have been made.

DRINK, DRUGS AND DRIVING

Q Outline the offence of being unfit to drive through drink or drugs

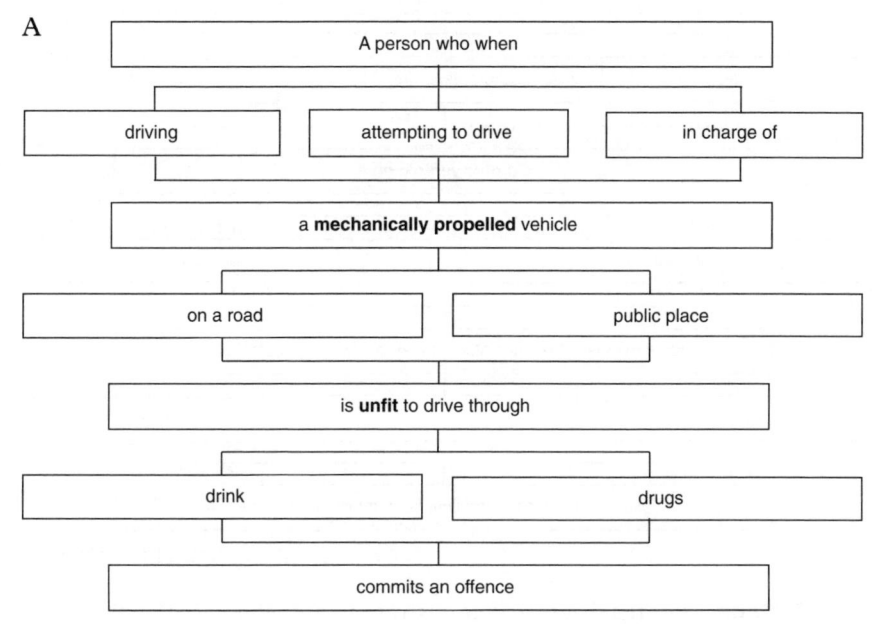

A

```
            A person who when
    ┌───────────────┼───────────────┐
  driving    attempting to drive   in charge of
    └───────────────┼───────────────┘
         a mechanically propelled vehicle
                    │
         ┌──────────┴──────────┐
      on a road           public place
         └──────────┬──────────┘
              is unfit to drive through
                    │
         ┌──────────┴──────────┐
       drink                 drugs
         └──────────┬──────────┘
              commits an offence
```

S. 4 ROAD TRAFFIC ACT 1988

Police Powers. If a constable reasonably suspects that a person **is or has been** committing this offence he may arrest, **and may enter [if need be by force]**, the place where he is or the constable reasonably suspects him to be.

Does the constable need to be in uniform? No

Unfit. Means his ability to drive is for the time being impaired.

When is a driver not in charge? When he can prove that there was no likelihood of his driving so long as he remained unfit.

What if the driver is injured? In determining whether the defendant was likely to drive while unfit the court may disregard any injury to the driver or damage to the vehicle.

Drugs. Means any intoxicant that is not alcohol.

DRINK, DRUGS AND DRIVING

Q Outline the offences of driving and being in charge whilst over the prescribed limit

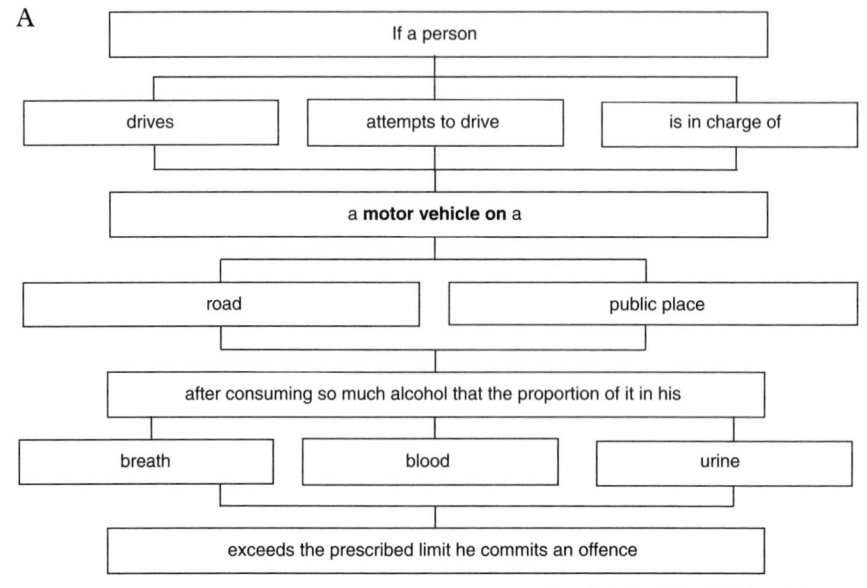

A

```
                          If a person
                               │
        ┌──────────────────────┼──────────────────────┐
      drives              attempts to drive         is in charge of
        └──────────────────────┼──────────────────────┘
                               │
                      a **motor vehicle on** a
                               │
                    ┌──────────┴──────────┐
                   road               public place
                    └──────────┬──────────┘
                               │
        after consuming so much alcohol that the proportion of it in his
                               │
        ┌──────────────────────┼──────────────────────┐
      breath                 blood                   urine
        └──────────────────────┼──────────────────────┘
                               │
            exceeds the prescribed limit he commits an offence
```

S. 5 ROAD TRAFFIC ACT 1988

Defence. For the driver to demonstrate an arguable case that there was no likelihood of his driving whilst he remained over the prescribed limit. The prosecution must then prove beyond reasonable doubt that there was such a likelihood to defeat this defence: *Sheldrake v DPP (2003)*.

What if the driver is injured? In determining whether the driver was likely to drive whilst over the prescribed limit the court may disregard any injury to the driver and damage to the vehicle.

Q What are the 'prescribed limits'?

A [a] 35 microgrammes of alcohol in 100 millilitres of breath;
[b] 80 milligrammes of alcohol in 100 millilitres of blood, and
[c] 107 milligrammes of alcohol in 100 millilitres of urine.

DRINK, DRUGS AND DRIVING

Q Outline the requirement to co-operate with a preliminary test

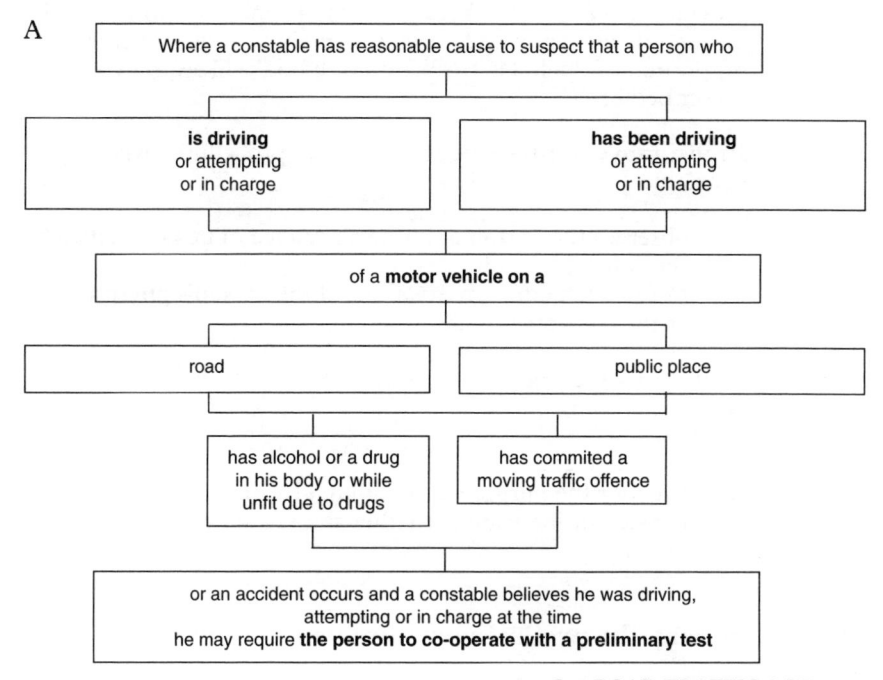

A

```
Where a constable has reasonable cause to suspect that a person who
```

| **is driving** or attempting or in charge | **has been driving** or attempting or in charge |

of a **motor vehicle on a**

| road | public place |

| has alcohol or a drug in his body or while unfit due to drugs | has committed a moving traffic offence |

or an accident occurs and a constable believes he was driving, attempting or in charge at the time
he may require **the person to co-operate with a preliminary test**

S. 6 ROAD TRAFFIC ACT 1988

Uniform. Except in the case of preliminary tests following an accident, the officer *administering* the tests must be in uniform. The officer *making the requirement* need not be. What amounts to 'uniform' for these purposes is not clear but it is likely that the requirement is satisfied if the constable can be clearly identified from his dress as a police officer.

DRINK, DRUGS AND DRIVING

Q Outline the three preliminary tests

A 1. **Preliminary breath test.** A procedure whereby a person provides a specimen of breath for the purpose of obtaining, by means of an approved device, an indication whether the proportion of alcohol in the breath or blood is likely to exceed the prescribed limit.

2. **Preliminary impairment test.** A procedure whereby a constable

   [a] observes the person in his performance of tasks specified by the constable, and
   [b] makes such other observations of the person's physical state as the constable thinks expedient.

3. **Preliminary drug test.** A procedure by which a specimen of sweat or saliva is

   [a] obtained, and
   [b] used for the purpose of obtaining, by means of an approved device, an indication whether the person has a drug in his body.

   S. 6A-C ROAD TRAFFIC ACT 1988

Q Where may the preliminary tests be administered?

A Preliminary breath tests may only be administered at or near the place where the requirement to co-operate with the test is imposed. (But see below for tests following accidents). Preliminary impairment and drug tests may be administered either at that place, or if the constable who imposes the requirement thinks it expedient, at a police station specified by him.

Q What is the purpose of a preliminary test?

A To obtain an indication of the likelihood of an offence having been committed (rather than to prove the offence).

Q Who can administer a preliminary test?

A In the case of preliminary breath and drug tests, any officer. Impairment tests may only be administered by those approved by their chief officer for this purpose.

DRINK, DRUGS AND DRIVING

Q What is the procedure following an accident?

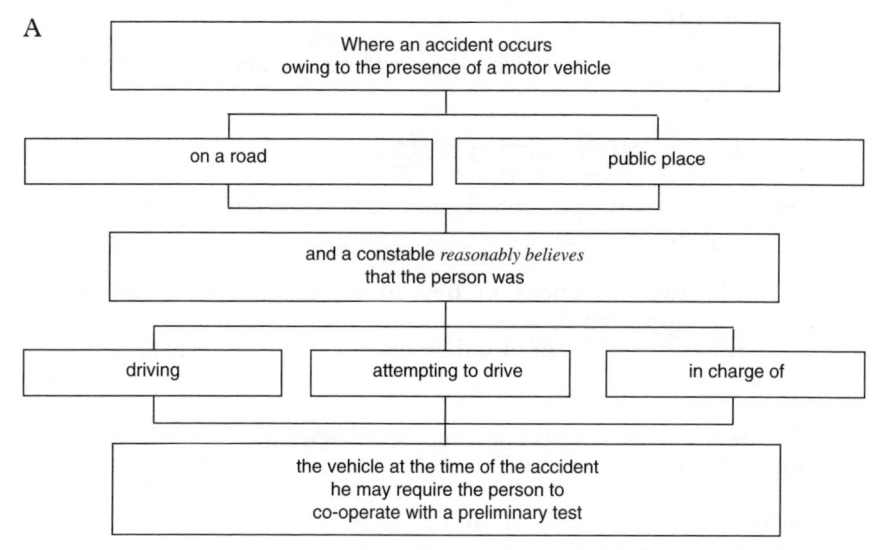

A

```
┌─────────────────────────────────────────┐
│        Where an accident occurs         │
│   owing to the presence of a motor vehicle │
└─────────────────────────────────────────┘
        │                       │
┌───────────────┐       ┌───────────────┐
│  on a road    │       │ public place  │
└───────────────┘       └───────────────┘
        │                       │
┌─────────────────────────────────────────┐
│       and a constable *reasonably believes* │
│           that the person was           │
└─────────────────────────────────────────┘
        │              │              │
┌───────────┐  ┌──────────────────┐  ┌──────────────┐
│  driving  │  │ attempting to drive │  │ in charge of │
└───────────┘  └──────────────────┘  └──────────────┘
                       │
┌─────────────────────────────────────────┐
│  the vehicle at the time of the accident │
│    he may require the person to         │
│    co-operate with a preliminary test    │
└─────────────────────────────────────────┘
```

S. 6 ROAD TRAFFIC ACT 1988

Location of breath test. Note that where an accident has occurred all 3 preliminary tests (including breath tests) may be administered either at the place where the requirement is made or at a specified police station (where there is no accident breath tests can only be administered at the scene).

Power of entry. S.6E Road Traffic Act 1988 provides a power of entry (using reasonable force) to impose the requirement in case of **injury** accidents.

Q Outline the offence of failing to co-operate with a preliminary test

A A person commits an offence if, without reasonable excuse, he fails to co-operate with a preliminary test.

S. 6(6) ROAD TRAFFIC ACT 1988

Arrest. A constable may arrest if the person fails to co-operate with a preliminary test requirement and the constable reasonably suspects that the person has alcohol or a drug in his body or is under the influence of a drug.

DRINK, DRUGS AND DRIVING

Q Outline the provision of specimens for analysis requirement

A   In the course of an investigation into whether a person has committed an offence of:

[a] death by careless driving [S. 3A];
[b] drunk in charge [S. 4]; or
[c] being over the prescribed limit [S. 5] a constable may require him to provide:

  [i] two specimens of **breath** for analysis by means of an approved device; or
  [ii] a specimen of **blood or urine** for a laboratory test.

S. 7 ROAD TRAFFIC ACT 1988

Failure. The provision of only one breath specimen is a failure. Failure includes a refusal.

Where may the requirement be made? Breath specimen: at a police station, hospital or (if constable is in uniform or requirement follows an accident) at or near scene where breath test administered. Blood/urine: hospital or (provided certain conditions satisfied, see later) police station.

What if no one admits to driving? The requirement can be made of more than one person in respect of the same vehicle.

Q Which are the approved devices?

A   The CAMIC Datamaster; the Lion Intoxylizer 6000UK and the EC/IR Intoximeter.

Q When can a driver choose to replace a breath test with a specimen of blood/urine?

A   Of the two breath specimens provided the one with the lower proportion of alcohol shall be used and the other disregarded. If the one used contains no more than 50 mcg of alcohol in 100 ml of breath, the provider may request that a blood or urine sample be used, and if he provides such a sample then neither breath specimen may be used.

S. 8(2) ROAD TRAFFIC ACT 1988

Option. If the driver chooses the option of blood/urine and subsequently fails or refuses he commits no offence - revert to the original breath specimen.

DRINK, DRUGS AND DRIVING

Q Can you make a request for blood or urine at a police station?

A Only in the following circumstances:

[a] for medical reasons a breath test cannot be provided or should not be required;
[b] a breath test device is not available or it is not practicable to use;
[c] in relation to **causing death by careless driving (S. 3A) or unfit (S. 4)** a doctor has advised that his condition might be due to a drug.

Who decides, blood or urine? The constable, unless a doctor is of the opinion that blood cannot or should not be taken, then it shall be urine.

Doctor's advice. May be given over the telephone if appropriate.

Urine. Two specimens within one hour, the first being discarded.

Blood. Shall be divided into two parts, one being supplied to the defendant.

Q Define the offence of failing to provide evidential specimens

A A person who, without reasonable excuse, fails to provide a specimen when required to do so commits an offence.

S. 7(6) ROAD TRAFFIC ACT 1988

Reasonable excuse. What amounts to a reasonable excuse is a question of law. Whether the defendant actually had a reasonable excuse is a question of fact for the court. In *DDP v Falzarano (2001)*, where the defendant was suffering from panic attacks and shortness of breath, it was held that the reasonable excuse had to arise out of a physical or mental inability to provide a specimen or a substantial risk to health in its provision. Being drunk or under stress is not enough in itself to provide a reasonable excuse. It is not reasonable to refuse to provide a specimen until one's legal adviser is present since the public interest requires that specimens be given without delay.

DRINK, DRUGS AND DRIVING

Q Outline the hospital procedure

A A breath test or blood/urine specimens cannot be taken from a patient in hospital unless the doctor in immediate charge of his case has been notified of the proposal and:

[a] if the requirement is made, it shall be for the provision of a specimen at the hospital; but
[b] if the doctor objects the requirement may not be made. The doctor may object on the grounds that the patient's care and treatment will be adversely affected by any one of:

[i] the requirement to provide a specimen; or
[ii] the provision of the specimen itself; or
[iii] the warning [i.e. failure to provide may lead to prosecution].

S. 9 ROAD TRAFFIC ACT 1988

Patient. A person continues to be a patient until his treatment is finished. (But once a person is discharged he ceases to be a patient even if he has to return later for further treatment).

Q Outline the evidence required for offences under Sections 3A, 4 and 5

A Evidence of the proportion of alcohol or drug in breath, blood or urine **shall in all cases be taken into account** unless the accused proves:

[a] he consumed alcohol between ceasing to drive; and
[b] before providing a specimen; **and**
[c] had he not done so he would have not exceeded the limit or been impaired.

DRINK, DRUGS AND DRIVING

Q **Distinguish between Sections 4 and 5**

A   constable [in uniform *or out of uniform]*

1. May arrest a person following a positive breath test or where he has failed to supply a breath test **and** the constable suspects he has alcohol in his body.

2. May **enter** [if need be by force] any place where he is or the constable suspects him to be to:

    [a] require him to provide a breath test following an **injury accident**; or
    [b] to arrest under S. 5 following an **injury accident**.

	Unfit – S. 4	Over prescribed limit – S. 5
Driving	driving, attempting, in charge	driving, attempting, in charge
Vehicle	**mechanically propelled vehicle**	motor vehicle
Where	road or public place	road or public place
Uniform	No	Yes
Power to arrest or to require a breath test	a constable may arrest [see breath test powers below]	Breath test where a constable suspects: 1. has alcohol in his body or has committed a moving traffic offence 2. has had alcohol in his body and still has alcohol in his body 3. has committed a moving traffic offence
Offence	unfit through drink or drugs	breath, blood, urine, exceeds the prescribed limit
Entry	Yes where he is or suspected to be	conditional 1. to require breath test 2. to arrest following an injury accident
Defence	no likelihood of him driving whilst he remained unfit	no likelihood of him driving whilst he remained over the limit

INSURANCE

Q Define the offence of having no insurance

A It is an offence to use, [cause/permit] a motor vehicle on a road or public place without insurance.

S. 143(2) ROAD TRAFFIC ACT 1988

Q What is the defence to having no insurance?

A [a] The vehicle did not belong to him and was not in his possession under contract of hire or loan;
[b] he was using the vehicle in the course of his employment; and
[c] that he neither knew nor had reason to believe that there was no insurance.

S. 143(3) ROAD TRAFFIC ACT 1988

Q What restrictions in a policy of insurance are void?

A Breach of the following restrictions does not make the policy void for the purposes of S. 143:

[a] the age or physical or mental condition of the driver;
[b] the condition of the vehicle;
[c] the number of persons carried;
[d] the weight or physical characteristics of the goods carried;
[e] the times or areas in which the vehicle is used;
[f] the horsepower or cc or value of the vehicle;
[g] carrying any particular apparatus; or
[h] carrying any particular means of identification of the vehicle.

Q Outline police powers to demand the production of insurance

A [a] A person driving a motor vehicle **on a road** [not an invalid carriage];
[b] a person whom a constable [or vehicle examiner] reasonably believes to have been the driver when an **accident** occurred owing to its presence on a road or public place; or
[c] a person whom a constable [or vehicle examiner] reasonably believes to have **committed an offence** in relation to the use of the vehicle on a road, shall, on being required by a constable or vehicle examiner:

[i] give his name and address; and
[ii] the name and address of the owner; and
[iii] produce the certificate of insurance of that vehicle (and any required test certificate).

INSURANCE

Not produced at time. In proceedings for an offence, it is a defence to prove that the insurance was produced within **seven days** at a police station specified by him, or it was produced as soon as was reasonably practicable, or it was not practicable to produce it before the proceedings began.

Q **What is the purpose of the Motor Insurers' Bureau?**

A   To provide compensation in cases where a person suffers injury or damage following a RTA but is unable to pursue a claim against the other party because s/he is not insured, unknown or untraceable, or is an insured company now in liquidation.

TRAFFIC SAFETY MEASURES

Q Define the law relating to seat belts

A Where a person is aged **14 years old** and over, it is an offence to:

[a] **drive** a motor vehicle; or
[b] ride as a **front seat passenger**; or
[c] ride in the **rear seat** of a motor car or passenger car without wearing an adult seat belt.

S. 14(3) ROAD TRAFFIC ACT 1988

Aiding and abetting. There is no offence of aiding and abetting adult offenders. Only the person actually committing the contravention is guilty.

Q Outline the law relating to children in front seats

A Section 15 of the RTA 1988 states that, where a child under the age of 14 is in the *front* of a motor vehicle, a person must not without reasonable excuse drive the motor vehicle on a road unless the child is wearing a seat belt. In addition, where a child is in the front of a motor vehicle (other than a bus), is in a rear-facing restraining device, and the passenger seat where the child is placed is protected by a front air bag, a person must not without reasonable excuse drive the vehicle on a road unless the air bag is deactivated: S. 15 (1A)

Q Outline the law relating to children in rear seats

A Where a child under 3 is in the *rear* of a motor vehicle, or a child over 3 but under 14 and a rear seat belt is fitted, a person must not without reasonable excuse drive the vehicle on a road unless the child is wearing a seat belt: S. 15 (3).

Q Outline the law on motor cycle helmets

A A motor cycle means a two-wheeled motor cycle [with or without sidecar] and it is an offence to ride a motor cycle without protective headgear, except

[a] mowing machines;
[b] it is being pushed [not straddled]; or
[c] a Sikh wearing a turban.

S. 16 ROAD TRAFFIC ACT 1988

TRAFFIC SAFETY MEASURES

Who commits the offence? Only the person actually failing to wear a helmet i.e. helmeted drivers are not responsible for bare-headed passengers, except in the case of persons under 16, in which case both driver and passenger commit the offence.

Q What is the law in relation to passengers on motor cycles?

A   [a]   Only one passenger may be carried
    [b]   sitting astride, on a secure seat, behind the driver.

S. 23 ROAD TRAFFIC ACT 1988

Who commits the offence? The driver. The passenger can be convicted of aiding and abetting.

Q Who is exempt from speed restrictions?

A   Drivers of the under-mentioned vehicles are exempt if the observance of the speed limit would be **likely to hinder** its use on that occasion:

Fire Brigade, Ambulance Service, Police

S. 87 RT REGULATION ACT 1984

Q How do you prove someone's speed?

A   A person prosecuted for speeding shall not be convicted only on the evidence of one witness to the effect that, in his opinion, the defendant was exceeding the speed limit. Corroboration may be provided by:

[a] equipment in a police vehicle or other speed measuring equipment; or
[b] evidence of two police officers (although the court will decide how much weight to place on such evidence).

Q Define the obstruction offences

A   **Highway**. A person who without lawful authority or excuse, wilfully obstructs the highway commits an offence.

S. 137 HIGHWAYS ACT 1980

Road. A person in charge of a motor vehicle or trailer who causes or permits it to stand on a road so as to cause an unnecessary obstruction of the road commits an offence.

Reg. 103 ROAD VEHICLES (CONSTRUCTION AND USE) REGS 1986

TRAFFIC SAFETY MEASURES

Street. Any person in any street who, to the obstruction, annoyance, danger of residents or passengers, wilfully interrupts any public crossing, or causes any wilful obstruction in any public footpath commits an offence.

S. 28 TOWN POLICE CLAUSES ACT 1847

Q Define the offence of parking heavy vehicles on verges

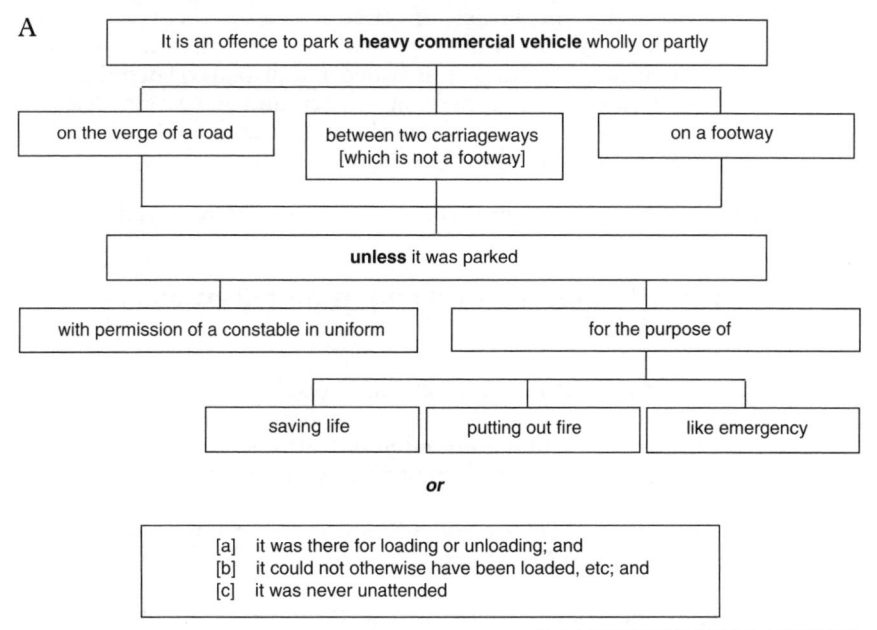

A

It is an offence to park a **heavy commercial vehicle** wholly or partly
- on the verge of a road
- between two carriageways [which is not a footway]
- on a footway

unless it was parked
- with permission of a constable in uniform
- for the purpose of
  - saving life
  - putting out fire
  - like emergency

or

[a] it was there for loading or unloading; and
[b] it could not otherwise have been loaded, etc; and
[c] it was never unattended

S. 19 ROAD TRAFFIC ACT 1988

Heavy commercial vehicle. Means its operating weight exceeds 7.5 tonnes.

Q Define the offence of leaving a vehicle in a dangerous position

A A person in charge of a vehicle/trailer, who causes or permits it to remain at rest in a road in such a position or in such condition or in such circumstances as to involve a **danger of injury** to other road users commits an offence.

S. 22 ROAD TRAFFIC ACT 1988

Moving vehicle. This offence applies to moving as well as stationary vehicles e.g. failing to set a handbrake properly so that the vehicle rolls down a hill.

TRAFFIC SAFETY MEASURES

Q Define the offence of wrongful use of disabled person's badge under S. 117 Road Traffic Regulation Act 1984

A A person who fails to comply with, or contravenes, any provision in relation to parking also commits an offence if at the time:

[a] a disabled badge sticker was displayed; and
[b] he was using the vehicle in circumstances where a disabled person's concession would be available to a disabled person's vehicle, **unless** the badge was issued and displayed lawfully. [So a driver who commits a parking offence and misuses a disabled badge at the same time commits both the parking offence **and** an offence under S. 117].

Removal of badge. On third conviction, it may be removed.

Q What is the law on removal and immobilisation of parked vehicles?

A Where a vehicle is permitted to remain at rest on a road:

[a] in contravention of a prohibition or restriction; or
[b] in a position or under circumstances as to obstruct or cause danger;
[c] or any **land in the open air** so as to appear to have been **abandoned/broken down**,

then a constable may arrange for it to be moved from that road to another position on that road or another road.

REG. 4 REMOVAL AND DISPOSAL OF VEHICLES REGS 1986

Q Outline the offence of causing danger to road users

A It is an offence if a person, intentionally and without lawful authority or reasonable cause:

[a] causes anything to be on or over a road; or
[b] interferes with a motor vehicle, trailer or cycle; or
[c] interferes with traffic equipment,

in such circumstances that it would be obvious to a reasonable person **that to do so would be dangerous.**

S. 22A ROAD TRAFFIC ACT 1988

TRAFFIC SAFETY MEASURES

Traffic equipment. Means anything placed on or near a road by the highway authority, a traffic sign lawfully placed on or near a road by any person and any fence, barrier or light lawfully placed on or near a road, or by a constable or anyone acting under his instructions.

Dangerous. Refers to danger either of injury to a person on or near a road or serious damage to property on or near a road and regard will be given to the circumstances of which he could be expected to be aware, but also to circumstances within the accused's knowledge.

Q Define the offence of tampering with and getting on to vehicles

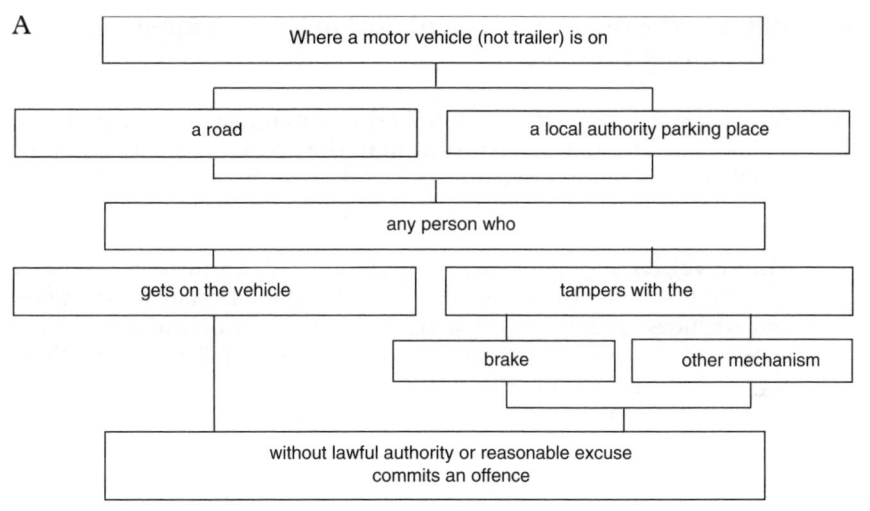

A

Where a motor vehicle (not trailer) is on
- a road
- a local authority parking place

any person who
- gets on the vehicle
- tampers with the
  - brake
  - other mechanism

without lawful authority or reasonable excuse commits an offence

S. 25 ROAD TRAFFIC ACT 1988

Q Define the offence of holding/getting on to a vehicle in motion

A 1. If, for the purpose of being carried, a person without lawful authority or reasonable cause takes or retains holds of, or gets on to a motor vehicle or trailer *while in motion on a road* he is guilty of an offence.

2. If, for the purpose of being drawn, a person takes or retains hold of a motor vehicle or trailer *while in motion on a road* he is guilty of an offence.

s.26 ROAD TRAFFIC ACT 1988

TRAFFIC SAFETY MEASURES

Q   Define the offence of abandoning motor vehicles

A   A person is guilty of an offence who, without lawful authority:

[a]   abandons **on any land in the open air**, or on a highway, a motor vehicle or anything which formed part of a motor vehicle and was removed from it whilst dismantling the vehicle on land; or

[b]   abandons on such land anything [not a motor vehicle] brought there for the purpose of abandoning it.

S. 2(1) REFUSE DISPOSAL (AMENITY) ACT 1978

Q   What is the duty of the local authority to remove abandoned vehicles?

A   Where it appears to a local authority that a motor vehicle is abandoned without lawful authority **on any land in the open air**, or on a highway, it is their duty to remove it.

S. 3 REFUSE DISPOSAL (AMENITY) ACT 1978

Motor vehicle. Means a mechanically propelled vehicle intended or adapted for use on roads, whether or not it is in a fit state for such use, and includes trailers, any chassis or body, with or without wheels, appearing to have formed part of the vehicle or trailer, and anything attached to such a vehicle or trailer.

TRAFFIC SAFETY MEASURES

Q Outline police powers to remove vehicles from roads

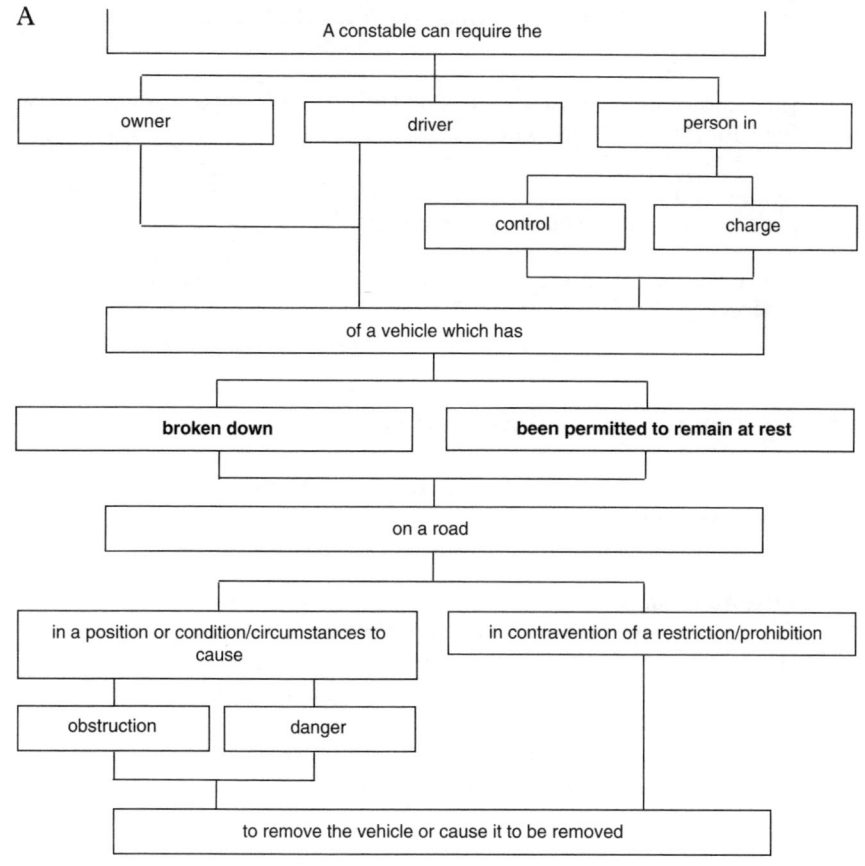

A

A constable can require the

- owner
- driver
- person in
  - control
  - charge

of a vehicle which has

- broken down
- been permitted to remain at rest

on a road

- in a position or condition/circumstances to cause
  - obstruction
  - danger
- in contravention of a restriction/prohibition

to remove the vehicle or cause it to be removed

REG. 3 REMOVAL AND DISPOSAL OF VEHICLES REGS 1986

TRAFFIC SAFETY MEASURES

Q Define the offence of off-road driving

A It is an offence to drive a mechanically propelled vehicle without lawful authority on:

[a] common or moorland, or any land (not being part of a road); or
[b] footpath or bridleway;

except, it may be driven on any land within **15 yards** of a road which may lawfully be driven on for parking only.

No offence. If done for saving life, extinguishing fire, or like emergency.

S. 34(1) ROAD TRAFFIC ACT 1988

Q Outline the law on builders' skips

A A skip can only be deposited with the written permission of the Highway Authority.

Offences:
[a] placing on a highway without permission;
[b] not properly lit during the hours of darkness;
[c] it does not bear the owner's name and address **or** telephone number;
[d] it is not removed as soon as possible after it has been filled;
[e] there is a failure to comply with a condition of the Highway Authority.

S. 139 HIGHWAYS ACT 1980

Who is liable? Both the owner of the skip and the offender.

Defence for owner. To prove that the offence arose due to the action or default of another **and** he had taken all reasonable precautions and exercised due diligence to prevent the offence.

Police powers. A constable **in uniform** may require the removal of the skip and failure to do so is an offence. The requirement must be made **in person.**

TRAFFIC SAFETY MEASURES

Q Outline the law in relation to school crossings

A Where a vehicle is approaching a place on a road where a person is crossing or seeking to cross the road, a school crossing patrol wearing an approved uniform shall have power by exhibiting a prescribed sign to require a driver to stop. Thereafter he shall stop so as not to stop or impede the person(s) crossing and remain stopped until the sign is not exhibited.

S. 28 RT REGULATION ACT 1984

Offence. To fail to conform.

Presumptions. Unless the contrary is proven, it is presumed that he was in uniform, the prescribed sign was exhibited and that people were crossing or seeking to cross.

Traffic wardens. May exercise this function and they do not have to wear the uniform but they must exhibit the sign.

Q Outline the law on 'street playgrounds'

A The local traffic authority may prohibit or restrict vehicular access to certain roads so that they may be used as street playgrounds. A person who uses a vehicle, or causes or permits a vehicle to be used, in contravention of any such prohibition shall be guilty of an offence.

S. 29(3) ROAD TRAFFIC ACT 1984

Crown servants. Vehicles or drivers in the public service of the Crown are exempt from this provision.

Q Outline the law governing the safety and security of road works

A Those responsible for undertaking street/road works are required to ensure that their works sites are properly guarded, signed and lit. Removing, taking down or altering any fence, barrier, traffic sign or light (or extinguishing a light) at such a site without lawful authority or excuse is a summary offence.

S. 65(6) NEW ROADS AND STREET WORKS ACT 1991

CONSTRUCTION AND USE

Q Outline the law in relation to maintaining brakes

A   Every part of every braking system and of the means of operation fitted to a vehicle shall be maintained in a good and efficient working order.
REGS. 15-18 ROAD VEHICLES (CONSTRUCTION AND USE) REGS 1986

Can a constable check brakes? Yes, he may be able to give evidence that when the handbrake was applied he could push the vehicle along.

Q Outline the law in relation to defective tyres

A   A tyre is defective when:

[a] it is unsuitable for use;
[b] it is under or over inflated;
[c] it has a cut in excess of **25 mm** or **10%** of its section width [whichever is greater] and deep enough to reach the ply or cord;
[d] it has any lump, bulge or tear caused by failure of the structure;
[e] ply or cord is exposed;
[f] the base of a groove in a tread is not visible; either:

  [i]   The grooves of the tread of the tyre do not have a depth of at least 1 mm [1.6mm for motor cars, light goods vehicles, light trailers] throughout a continuous band measuring at least three-quarters of the breadth of the tread round the entire outer circumference; or
  [ii] if the grooves of the original tread did not extend beyond three-quarters of the breadth of the tread, any groove which showed in the original tread does not have a depth of at least 1 mm [1.6mm for motor cars, light goods vehicles, light trailers]; or

[g] it is not maintained in a condition fit for its use; or
[h] it has a defect which might cause damage to the road or to persons.

REG. 27

Exemptions. Certain specialised vehicles are exempt e.g. agricultural vehicles travelling below 20mph.

CONSTRUCTION AND USE

Q   Outline the law in relation to mirrors

A   With certain exceptions every passenger vehicle, goods vehicle or dual purpose vehicle first used on or after 1 June 1978, must be equipped with:

[a]   an interior rear view mirror; and
[b]   at least one exterior mirror fitted to the off-side.

If the interior rear view mirror is obscured the driver must have an exterior rear view mirror attached to the near-side of the vehicle.

REG. 33

Q   Outline the law in relation to silencers

A   Every vehicle propelled by an internal combustion engine must be fitted with an exhaust system including a silencer and the exhaust gases from the engine must not escape without passing through the silencer.

REGS. 54,57

Q   Define the offence of quitting

A   It is an offence to leave a motor vehicle unattended on a road unless **both** the engine has been stopped **and** the brake set.

REG. 107

Unattended. If there is a person with the vehicle, he must be licensed to drive it.

Q   Outline the law relating to stopping of engine

A   The driver of every vehicle when stationary shall stop the action of any machinery attached to or forming part of the vehicle so far as may be necessary for the prevention of noise or exhaust emissions. (This does not apply if the vehicle is only stationary due to traffic; or where it is necessary to examine machinery following its failure; or where it is required to be worked for a purpose other than driving the vehicle; or where a vehicle is propelled by gas produced in plant carried on the vehicle (in which case the exception applies to the plant itself).

REG. 98

CONSTRUCTION AND USE

Q Outline the offence of dangerous vehicle

A Every **motor vehicle**, trailer, parts and accessories must at all times be in such a condition that no danger is caused to any person in or on the vehicle or trailer or on a road. The number of **passengers** carried, or the manner of their carriage, must be such that no danger is caused or likely to be caused to any person in or on the vehicle or trailer or on a road. The **load** carried by a motor vehicle or trailer must at all times be so secure and be in such a position, that neither danger nor nuisance is likely to be caused to any person or property by reason of the load or part of it falling or being blown from, or by reason of any other movement of the load or part. It is an offence to use, cause or permit another to use any vehicle contravening the above.

S. 40A ROAD TRAFFIC ACT 1988

Q Define the offence of breach of brake, steering gear, tyres requirements

A A person commits an offence who:

[a] fails to comply with regulations as to brakes, steering gear or tyres; or
[b] uses on a road a motor vehicle or trailer [or causes or permits], which does not comply with the regulations.

S. 41A ROAD TRAFFIC ACT 1988

Q Define the offence of breach of weight requirements for goods and passenger vehicles

A A person commits an offence who:

[a] fails to comply with regulations in relation to weights applicable to:

　　[i] a goods vehicle; or
　　[ii] a motor vehicle or trailer adapted to carry **more than eight passengers**; or

[b] uses on a road a vehicle [or causes or permits] which does not comply with the regulations.

S. 41B ROAD TRAFFIC ACT 1988

CONSTRUCTION AND USE

Defence. It is a defence to prove:

[a] that at the time the vehicle was being used on a road

  [i] it was proceeding to the nearest weighbridge to be weighed, or
  [ii] it was proceeding from a weighbridge to the nearest point at which it was reasonably practicable to reduce the weight to the relevant limit, without causing an obstruction on any road, or

[b] in a case where it was not more than 5% overweight, that limit was not exceeded at the time of original loading and no person has subsequently added to the weight.

DRIVING LICENSING

Q What are police powers in relation to driving licences?

A   Any person:

[a] **driving** a motor vehicle on a road;
[b] whom a constable or vehicle examiner has reasonable cause to believe has been the driver of a motor vehicle at the time when an **accident** occurred owing to its presence on a road;
[c] whom a constable or vehicle examiner has reasonable cause to believe **committed an offence** in relation to the use of the motor vehicle on a road; or
[d] **a supervisor** of a provisional licence holder driving a motor vehicle on a road or a person whom a constable or vehicle examiner reasonably believes was supervising such a driver at the time of an accident or offence relating to that vehiclemust, on being required to do so by a constable or vehicle examiner:

[i] produce his licence;
[ii] and its counterpart so as to enable the constable or vehicle examiner to examine it and ascertain:
 1. name and address of the holder;
 2. date of issue; and
 3. the authority by which issued.

S. 164 ROAD TRAFFIC ACT 1988

Defence. It is a defence for him to show that:

[a] he produced the licence and counterpart at a police station specified by him at the time the production was required **within seven days**;
[b] he produced them in person there as soon as was reasonably practicable; or
[c] it was not reasonably practicable for him to produce them there before the day the proceedings were commenced.

In person. Driving licences must be produced in person by the holder.

DRIVING LICENSING

Q What are the grounds for demanding date of birth?

A [a] The person **fails** to produce his licence forthwith; **or**
[b] the driver number has been altered, removed or defaced; or
[c] the person is a supervisor for a provisional licence holder and the constable has reason to suspect he is under 21; or
[d] the constable has reason to suspect that the licence was not granted to him, was granted in error or contains an alteration made with intent to deceive.

S. 164(2) ROAD TRAFFIC ACT 1988

Q Define the offence of failing to produce and state date of birth

A A person who fails, when required, to produce his licence or state his date of birth (or produce his certificate of completion of a training course for motor cyclists) commits an offence.

S. 164(6) ROAD TRAFFIC ACT 1988

Q Define the offence of disqualified driving

A A person is guilty of an offence if, while disqualified from holding or obtaining a licence, he drives a motor vehicle on a road.

S. 103(1) (B) ROAD TRAFFIC ACT 1988

Licence obtained by person disqualified. Has no effect.

Q Outline the law in relation to provisional licences and motor bicycles

A The granting of provisional licences is governed by S. 97(3) RTA 1988, which states:

[a] a provisional licence shall not authorise a **person aged under 21 years**:

  [i] to ride a solo motor cycle unless it is a 'learner motor cycle', or it was first used before 1 January 1982 and does not exceed 125 cc; or
  [ii] to ride a motor cycle with a sidecar unless its power to weight ratio is less than or equal to 0.16 kilowatts per kilogram;

[b] or authorise a person to ride a motor cycle or moped on a road unless he has successfully completed an approved training course, or is driving while undergoing training on such a course.

DRIVING LICENSING

How long does the licence last? Two years. No licence will then be issued for one year.

Q **What are the general conditions for a provisional licence holder?**

A **Supervision.** A provisional licence holder shall not drive a motor vehicle [nor a motor cycle] otherwise than under the supervision of a qualified driver who is present with him in or on the vehicle, who is:

[a] **aged 21 years or over; and**
[b] **has held a full licence for at least three years.**

'L'&'D' plates. Plates are required to be clearly visible to other road users within a reasonable distance from the back and front of the vehicle. In Wales there is an option to use 'D' plates.

Towing trailers. The licence holder must not draw a trailer.

If a provisional licence holder fails to observe these conditions he commits an offence under S. 91 Road Traffic Offenders Act 1988. If the person has no provisional licence the offence is under S. 87 (driving otherwise than in accordance with a licence).

Q **Define the offence of supervisors failing to give details**

A A person who:

[a] supervises the holder of a provisional licence who is driving a motor vehicle (other than an invalid carriage) on a road; or
[b] whom a constable or vehicle examiner has reasonable cause to believe was supervising a provisional licence holder:

[i] when an **accident** occurred; or
[ii] when **an offence** is suspected to have been committed by the holder of the provisional licence,

must, on being so required by a constable or vehicle examiner:

[a] give his name and address; and
[b] the name and address of the owner.

DRIVING LICENSING

Q What is the law in relation to driving instruction?

A It is an offence to give motor car driving lessons **for money** or money's worth unless the tutor is a registered approved instructor. (Registered in accordance with the provisions of Part V RTA 1988). [Police driving instructors are exempt from this regulation].

S. 123 ROAD TRAFFIC ACT 1988

'Free' driving lessons. Offered by a person in the business of buying and selling cars will be deemed to be given for payment if the lessons are a condition of buying the vehicle.

S. 132(3) ROAD TRAFFIC ACT 1988

Q How long can foreign nationals drive in this country under their own licence?

A 12 months.

Q Define the offence of driving with uncorrected defective eyesight

A If a person drives a motor vehicle on a road with uncorrected defective eyesight he commits an offence.

S. 96(1) ROAD TRAFFIC ACT 1988

Test. A constable, having reasonable cause to suspect that a person driving a motor vehicle may be guilty of this offence, may require him to submit to an eyesight test. Refusal to do so is an offence.

Defective eyesight. The requirements as to eyesight are contained in Regs. 72–73 and Sch. 8 to the Motor Vehicles (Driving Licences) Regs 1999, which *generally* require a potential driver to be able to read:

[a] letters and figures 79.4 mm high and 57 mm wide;
[b] on a registration plate;
[c] fixed to a vehicle;
[d] at 20.5 m;
[e] in good light.

(Spectacles may be worn at the time).

[Where plates with narrower 50 mm wide characters are used, the distance is 20 m]

Q What is the law in relation to new drivers?

A A newly qualified driver is a new driver for a probationary period of **two years** and if he sustains **six or more penalty points** the full entitlement to drive is lost until they pass a further test of competence.

FIXED PENALTY SYSTEMS

Q What is a fixed penalty?

A   A fixed penalty notice means a notice offering the opportunity of the discharge of any liability to conviction of the offence to which the notice relates by payment of a fixed penalty.

S. 52(1) ROAD TRAFFIC OFFENDERS ACT 1988

Q When can a fixed penalty not be issued?

A   [a] Where the penalty points would involve disqualification; or
    [b] Where the driver does not consent to surrendering his licence.

Q Outline the procedure where the driver is present

A

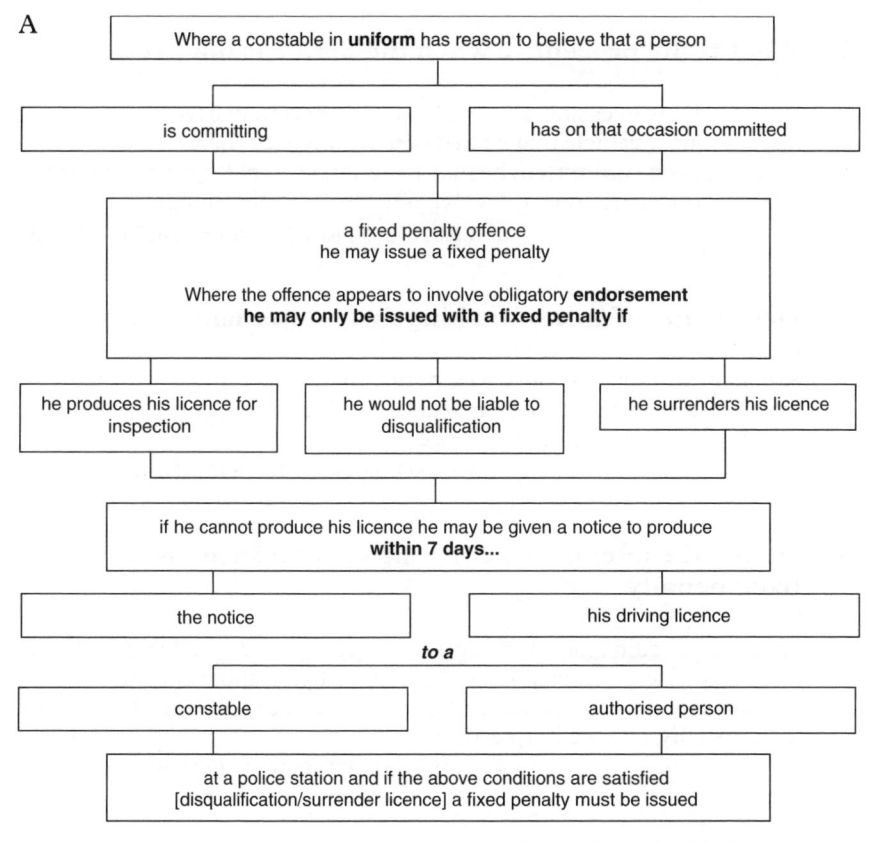

Where a constable in **uniform** has reason to believe that a person

- is committing
- has on that occasion committed

a fixed penalty offence
he may issue a fixed penalty

Where the offence appears to involve obligatory **endorsement**
he may only be issued with a fixed penalty if

- he produces his licence for inspection
- he would not be liable to disqualification
- he surrenders his licence

if he cannot produce his licence he may be given a notice to produce
within 7 days...

- the notice
- his driving licence

to a

- constable
- authorised person

at a police station and if the above conditions are satisfied
[disqualification/surrender licence] a fixed penalty must be issued

S. 54 ROAD TRAFFIC OFFENDERS ACT 1988

FIXED PENALTY SYSTEMS

Q What is the procedure if the person does not pay the penalty?

A If a person has not paid the fixed penalty, or given notice requesting a court hearing, the police can register a sum equal to 1.5 times the amount of the penalty for enforcement against that person. Where this happens the justices' clerk will notify him. Where a person receives such a notice he can serve a statutory declaration to the effect that either:

[a] he was not the person who was given the fixed penalty; or
[b] he has given notice requesting a court hearing.

He must serve this notice on the clerk **within 21 days** of receiving his notification.

Q What is the procedure when the driver is not present?

A Where on any occasion a constable has reason to believe in the case of any stationary vehicle that a fixed penalty offence is being or has on that occasion been committed, he may issue a fixed penalty notice unless the offence appears to him to involve obligatory endorsement.

S. 62 ROAD TRAFFIC OFFENDERS ACT 1988

Q Define the offence of making false statements etc

A A person who, in response to a notice to owner, provides a statement which is false in a material particular and does so recklessly or knowing it to be false is guilty of an offence.

S. 67 ROAD TRAFFIC OFFENDERS ACT 1988

Q Define the offence of removing or interfering with a fixed penalty

A A person is guilty of an offence if he removes or interferes with any notice fixed to a vehicle, unless he does so by or under the authority of the driver or person in charge of the vehicle, or the person liable for the fixed penalty offence in question.

S. 62(2) ROAD TRAFFIC OFFENDERS ACT 1988

FIXED PENALTY SYSTEMS

Q What is a conditional offer?

A Where a constable has reason to believe that a fixed penalty offence has been committed and no notice has been issued, then a notice can be sent to the alleged offender. A conditional offer must:

[a] outline the offence;
[b] state the amount payable; and
[c] state that no proceedings will take place before **28 days**.

The conditional offer must indicate that if:

[a] **within 28 days** the alleged offender:

  [i] makes payment to the fixed penalty clerk; and
  [ii] where the offence involves obligatory endorsement, at the same time delivers his licence, and its counterpart to the clerk, and;

[b] where his licence and its counterpart are so delivered, that clerk is satisfied on inspecting them that, if the alleged offender were convicted of the offence, he would not be liable to disqualification, any liability to conviction of the offence shall be discharged.

Failure to pay. If the defendant fails to pay the fixed penalty and/or surrender his licence, the police will be notified. The police will also be notified in any case where the defendant does pay (and surrender his licence) but it turns out that he is in fact liable to disqualification. The defendant's licence and payment should then be returned to him.

S. 75 ROAD TRAFFIC OFFENDERS ACT 1988

FORGERY AND FALSIFICATION OF DOCUMENTS

Q Define the offence of forgery of documents

A A person who, with intent to deceive:

  [a] forges, alters or uses a relevant document or other thing, or
  [b] lends, or allows to be used by another a relevant document or thing, or
  [c] makes or has in his possession any document or thing so closely resembling a relevant document or thing as to be calculated to deceive, commits an offence.

  S. 173 ROAD TRAFFIC ACT 1988

  Relevant documents or 'things'. Includes: licences, test certificates, insurance, certificates of exemption from seat belts, haulage permits, documents evidencing successful completion of a driver training course and goods vehicle plates.

Q Outline the offence of false statements and withholding information

A [a] A person who knowingly makes a **false statement** for the purpose of:

  [i] obtaining a licence;
  [ii] preventing the grant of a licence;
  [iii] procuring a provision or condition on a licence;
  [iv] obtaining the grant of an international road haulage permit;
  [v] securing the entry or retention of the name of any person on the register of approved instructors; or

  [b] **in supplying information** or producing documents:

  [i] makes a statement which he knows to be false or is reckless in so doing;
  [ii] makes use of a document he knows to be false or is reckless in so doing

  [c] knowingly produces false evidence or statement in a declaration; or
  [d] wilfully makes a false entry in a record required to be kept or with intent to deceive makes use of such an entry; or

FORGERY AND FALSIFICATION OF DOCUMENTS

[e] makes a false statement or withholds any information for the purpose of the issue:

[i] of insurance; or
[ii] any document issued under the Act commits an offence.

S. 174 ROAD TRAFFIC ACT 1988

Issue of documents. It is also an offence to knowingly issue such documents (S. 175).

Q Outline police powers in relation to false documents/forgery

A If a constable has reasonable cause to believe that a document produced to him is a document in relation to which an offence has been committed, he may seize the document.

S. 176 ROAD TRAFFIC ACT 1988

Q Define the offence of forging/altering registration documents

A A person is guilty of an offence if he forges, fraudulently alters, fraudulently uses, lends or allows to be used a registration document.

SS. 44-45 VEHICLE EXCISE AND REGISTRATION ACT 1994

Q Define the offence of forgery of certain documents relating to PSVs

A A person who, with intent to deceive:

[a] forges or alters, or uses or lends to, or allows to be used; or
[b] makes or has in his possession any document or other thing so closely resembling a document or other thing as to be calculated to deceive,

commits an offence.

Which documents? Licences, certificates of fitness, certificates of type, operator's disc certificates of competence of any person.

Q Define the offence of forgery relating to goods vehicles

A A person is guilty of an offence if, with intent to deceive, he forges, alters or uses a document or thing, lends to or allows to be used, or has in his possession a document or thing so closely resembling a document or other things as to be calculated to deceive.

S. 38 GOODS VEHICLES (LICENSING OF OPERATORS) ACT 1995

FORGERY AND FALSIFICATION OF DOCUMENTS

Q   Define the offence of misuse of parking documents and apparatus

A   A person shall be guilty of an offence if, with intent to deceive:

[a] he uses, lends or allows to be used:

[i] any parking device or apparatus designed to be used in connection with parking devices;
[ii] any ticket issued by a parking meter, parking device or apparatus;
[iii] any authorisation by a certificate or other means of identification; or
[iv] any permit or token.

[b] makes or has in his possession anything so closely resembling any such thing as to be calculated to deceive.
[c] a person who knowingly makes a false statement for the purposes of procuring the grant or issue of any such authorisation commits an offence.

S. 115 ROAD TRAFFIC REGULATION ACT 1984

Part 4 - Evidence and Procedure

INSTITUTING CRIMINAL PROCEEDINGS

Q   The appearance of a defendant before a magistrates' court can be secured in a number of ways. What are they?

A   [a]   by his arrest without warrant, followed by being charged with an offence and bailed to attend at court on a specified day to answer the charge;
[b]   by his arrest without warrant, followed by being charged with an offence and brought before the court in police custody;
[c]   by his arrest without warrant, followed by being bailed to await the decision of the CPS over how to proceed (the written charge and requisition procedure);
[d]   (in the case of private prosecutions) by the laying of an information by the prosecutor before a magistrate resulting in a summons to attend court on a specified day to answer the allegation in the information; or
[e]   by the laying of information by a prosecutor before a magistrate resulting in the issue of a warrant for the defendant to be arrested and brought before the court (or arrested and bailed to attend on a specified day.)

Q   Outline the written charge and requisition procedure

A   Under the provisions of the Criminal Justice Act 2003 a public prosecutor may issue a document called a written charge, charging a person with an offence. The person must then be served with a 'requisition' (a document that requires the person to appear before a magistrates' court to answer the written charge). Both the written charge and the requisition must be served on the person and a copy served on the court. The written charge must describe the offence charged, in ordinary layman's language so far as is possible, and refer to any relevant statutory provision. It must also give sufficient particulars to provide reasonable information about the nature of the charge.

INSTITUTING CRIMINAL PROCEEDINGS

Q Can the written charge and requisition procedure be used in private prosecutions?

A No. In private prosecutions a person may 'lay an information' (a written or verbal allegation to a magistrate alleging that a person has committed, or is suspected of having committed, an offence or a breach of law, such as a breach of the peace). Following an information being laid, a magistrate or clerk may either issue a summons requiring attendance at court to answer the allegation, or a warrant of arrest to secure a attendance.

Q What must a summons or requisition contain?

A It must state the name of the magistrate or prosecutor responsible for issuing it, provide brief details of the information or charge, and state the time and place at which the defendant is required to attend at court.

Q How may a summons or requisition be served?

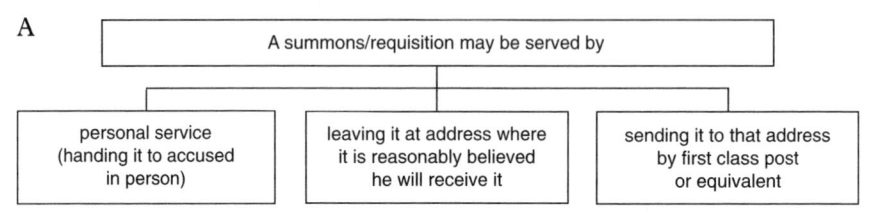

A

A summons/requisition may be served by:
- personal service (handing it to accused in person)
- leaving it at address where it is reasonably believed he will receive it
- sending it to that address by first class post or equivalent

R.4 CRIMINAL PROCEDURE RULES 2010

Service on corporations. May be by personal service on a person holding a senior position in that corporation, or by leaving it at, or sending it by first class post to, its principal office (where no such principal office is readily identifiable, any place where it carries on business will suffice). Where the corporation is legally represented, service may alternatively be on the representative or to his address.

Q Can summonses or requisitions be served in Scotland and Northern Ireland?

A Yes, but the rules as to service are different. Summonses/requisitions issued in England and Wales may be served anywhere, but NI summonses/requisitions may only be personally served. Scottish summonses are called 'citations' and may be 'effected' (served) by post in England and Wales.

s.39 CRIMINAL LAW ACT 1977

INSTITUTING CRIMINAL PROCEEDINGS

Q   Define the five types of warrant

A   1. **Arrest warrant.** Where a magistrate can issue a summons they may issue a warrant instead if:

   [a]   the information is in writing and on oath; and either
   [b]   the offence is indictable or imprisonable, or
   [c]   the accused's address is insufficient to serve a summons.

   Can the clerk issue a warrant? No. The information must be on oath and made to a magistrate.

   2. **Warrant to arrest a witness.** Where a magistrate is satisfied that a person who could give material evidence would not voluntarily attend court he may issue a warrant.

   3. **Warrant to arrest in default.** Issued for non-payment of fine etc.

   4. **Warrant to commit to prison.** This warrant authorises a constable to take a person directly to prison [and obtain a receipt].

   5. **Warrant to distrain property.** This warrant is issued to collect money in the form of goods to be seized and sold.

Q   Which warrants do not need to be in the possession of a constable at the time of their execution?

A   Any warrant of arrest, commitment, detention or distress which falls into the following categories:

   [a]   warrants to arrest for an offence;
   [b]   warrants under the Armed Forces Act 2006;
   [c]   warrants under the General Rate Act 1967 [insufficiency of distress];
   [d]   warrants under the Family Law Act 1996 [breach of occupation orders/non-molestation orders]
   [e]   warrants under the Crime & Disorder Act 1988 [unwilling witnesses]
   [f]   warrants to bring offenders before a youth offender panel;
   [g]   witness arrest warrants.

INSTITUTING CRIMINAL PROCEEDINGS

Q   What must a constable do when executing a warrant?

A   When executing a warrant of arrest, commitment or detention a constable must

  [a]   show the warrant to the relevant person (if he has it with him) or tell the person where the warrant is and how he can inspect it;
  [b]   explain the charge and reason for arrest; and
  [c]   (unless in uniform) produce documentary proof of identity.

R.18.11(1) 2010 RULES

What about entry? A constable may enter and search if he has reasonable grounds for believing the person is on the premises in order to execute the warrant. Reasonable force may be used if necessary, but the search must only be to the extent required and is restricted to those parts of the premises where the constable genuinely has reason to believe the suspect to be.

Q   Outline the law on the execution of warrants throughout the UK

A

Warrant issued in	Can be executed in	By
Scotland or Northern Ireland	England or Wales	a constable
England, Wales or Northern Ireland	Scotland	a constable
England, Wales or Scotland	Northern Ireland	PSNI constable or reserve PSNI constable

S 38 CRIMINAL LAW ACT 1977

Q   Which warrants may be executed by civilian enforcement officers?

A   In England and Wales CEOs may execute any warrant of arrest, commitment, detention or distress issued by a magistrate. The arrested/committed person is entitled to demand a written statement from the officer which must state (a) the officer's name; (b) the authority by which s/he is employed (c) s/he is authorised to execute warrants.

S. 125A MAGISTRATES' COURTS ACT 1980

BAIL

Q What is 'bail'?

A A process whereby an accused person may be temporarily released from custody (whether conditionally or otherwise).

Q What is 'street bail'?

A A discretionary power introduced by S. 4 Criminal Justice Act 2003 (S. 30A-30D PACE Act 1984) whereby constables may grant an arrested person immediate bail at the scene of arrest.

Q Outline the street bail procedure

A A constable may, at his/her discretion, release on bail any person arrested or taken into custody, at any time before he arrives at a police station. The bailed person must be required to attend at a police station at a subsequent date, and to secure such attendance conditions similar to those which may be imposed by a custody officer at a police station (save for the taking of security/sureties) may be attached. The bailed person must be given a written notice before he is released stating (a) the offence for which he was arrested (b) the grounds on which he was arrested (c) that he is required to attend a specified police station at a specified time (if this time/place information is not given in the notice at the time it must be given subsequently in a further notice in writing). Any later change to the specified venue/time must be notified in writing to the bailed person. A verbal explanation of the procedure should also be given at the time of bail. If bail was granted subject to conditions the written notice must specify the requirements imposed by those conditions and explain the procedure for applying to vary them.

Q Once a person is given street bail, can he be re-arrested?

A Yes. Officers can re-arrest a person released on bail anytime before he is due to attend a police station if new evidence justifying arrest comes to light.

Q What if the bailed person fails to attend at the required time?

A A constable may arrest anyone bailed under S. 30A if they fail to answer their bail. They should be taken to a police station as soon as practicable.

BAIL

Q What if s/he is no longer required to attend?

A S/he must be given a notice in writing that his attendance is no longer required.

Q What are the criteria for granting street bail?

A In addition to being satisfied that a correct name and address have been provided, the bailing officer should consider:

  [a] the severity or nature of the offence committed
  [b] the need to preserve vital evidence
  [c] the person's fitness to be released back on to the streets
  [d] the person's ability to understand what is being said/happening
  [e] the likelihood that the person may continue to commit the offence or a further offence.

Q At a police station, when should bail be given without charge?

A The custody officer must release a detainee either unconditionally or on bail in the following circumstances:

  [a] there is insufficient evidence to charge and the officer is not willing to authorise detention for questioning (s.37(2) PACE 1984);
  [b] there is sufficient evidence to charge and a decision is awaited from the DPP [i.e. CPS] under s.37B as to how to proceed with the case (s.37(7)(a) [bail in this case can be with or without conditions];
  [c] there is sufficient evidence to charge but not for the purpose in [b] above (usually, further enquiries are to be made) (s.37(7)(b);
  [d] the review officer concludes that detention without charge can no longer be justified (s.40(8));
  [e] at the end of 24 hours' detention without charge (or 36 hours where the detainee is suspected of an indictable offence and continued detention up to 36 hours is authorised by a superintendent (s.41(7)).

Q What happens after charge?

A Once a person is charged at a police station the custody officer must decide whether to detain that person in custody pending attendance at a magistrates' court, or to release that person, and if so, whether unconditionally or on bail (S. 38 PACE). The general presumption is in favour of bail.

BAIL

Q **In which circumstances should bail usually not be granted?**

A Under S. 25 Criminal Justice and Public Order Act 1984 bail should only exceptionally be granted in cases where the charge is

[a] murder
[b] attempted murder
[c] manslaughter
[d] rape
[e] assault by penetration
[f] causing a person to engage in sexual activity without consent [where activity involves penetration]
[g] rape of a child under 13
[h] assault of a child under 13 by penetration
[i] causing/inciting a child under 13 to engage in sexual activity [where activity involves penetration]
[j] sexual activity with a person with a mental disorder [where activity involves penetration]
[k] attempts to commit any of the above sexual offences

and the charged person has **previously been convicted** of any such offence.

Q **When can communication of a bail decision be delayed?**

A Detainees should be informed of the bail decision as soon as it is made. However, communication of the decision may be delayed in the following circumstances (in which case the detainee should be informed as soon as practicable):

- the detainee is incapable of understanding what is said; or
- the detainee is violent, or likely to become so; or
- the detainee is in urgent need of medical attention

CODE C PARA 1.8

Q **Outline the general grounds for refusing bail**

A
[a] name and address are doubted or cannot be ascertained;
[b] there is a risk of absconding;
[c] there is a risk of interference with witnesses/evidence;
[d] in the case of imprisonable offences, there is a risk of commission of further offences;
[e] in the case of non-imprisonable offences, there is a risk of injury to others or damage to property;
[f] the detainee's own protection requires it;

BAIL

[g] detention is necessary for the welfare of a juvenile (S. 38 PACE).

Q   What conditions may be attached to bail?

A   Where it appears necessary to prevent the person

[a] failing to surrender to custody; or
[b] committing an offence while on bail; or
[c] interfering with witnesses/evidence; or
[d] in the interests of his own protection/welfare

then any of the following conditions may be imposed:

[a] live and sleep at a specified address
[b] notify any changes of address
[c] report periodically at his local police station
[d] geographical restrictions
[e] contact restrictions
[f] surrender passport
[g] curfews
[h] provision of surety/security.

Any conditions imposed must be noted in the custody record and a copy given to the bailed person. An application to vary/remove conditions may be made at any time to the custody officer who imposed them or to any custody officer at the same station. The custody officer must consider the application on the merits and may either remove the conditions, vary them (to make them more/less onerous, whichever is justified) or leave them unchanged. This must be noted in the custody record. Applications may also be made to a magistrates' court.

Q   What is a 'surety'?

A   A person who is prepared to offer financial security for the bailed person's promise to surrender to custody.

Q   What is 'security'?

A   A sum of money or other valuable item given by the accused person or someone on their behalf to secure their promise to surrender to custody.

BAIL

Q What happens when a juvenile is refused bail?

A The custody officer must try to make arrangements for them to be taken into local authority care for detention pending their appearance in court. The only exceptions are where the custody officer certifies that it is impracticable to obtain such accommodation or (in the case of a 12 year old or over) where no secure accommodation is available and there is a risk of serious harm to the public from that juvenile.

Q When must detention be reviewed?

A Detention of a person refused bail must be reviewed by the custody officer within nine hours of the last decision to refuse bail. This may only be delayed when the custody officer is unavailable to carry it out and in such a case the review must be carried out as soon as practicable thereafter. If detention can no longer be justified, the person must be released: S. 40 PACE.

Q When must such a person be brought before the court?

A A person charged but refused bail must be brought before a magistrates' court at the next available session: S. 46 PACE.

Q Outline the offences of failing to surrender

A It is an offence for any person released on bail to fail, without reasonable cause, to surrender to custody.

S. 6 BAIL ACT 1976

A person **with** reasonable cause for failing to surrender at the appointed time must still surrender as soon as practicable after the appointed time. Failure to do so is an offence.

S. 6(2) BAIL ACT 1976

COURT PROCEDURE AND WITNESSES

Q   Who is competent and compellable to give evidence?

A   'Competence' relates to whether a person is legally able to provide testimony. 'Compellability' relates to whether competent persons can be made to provide testimony. In short, all people are competent and all competent witnesses are compellable but there are special rules relating to accused persons, their spouses, children, persons of impaired intellect and certain other groups.

Q   What is the law in relation to accused persons?

A   **On behalf of the prosecution**; the accused is not competent to give evidence on behalf of the prosecution unless:

[a]   he pleads guilty;
[b]   he is convicted;
[c]   the charges against him are dropped.

Therefore, if the prosecution wish an accused to give evidence against a co-accused (i.e. a person charged with him at the same trial) they must make him competent to give evidence, either by dropping the charges against him, or by obtaining a conviction or a guilty plea.[The admission of the guilty plea of a co-defendant has been found not to violate the accused's rights to a fair trial under Art. 6 ECHR].

On behalf of the defence. Every person charged with an offence shall be a competent witness for the defence at every stage of the proceedings, whether charged solely or jointly, but shall not be called except on his own application.

COURT PROCEDURE AND WITNESSES

Q When is a spouse/civil partner competent and compellable to give evidence?

A

Competent	Compellable
A spouse/civil partner (other than when husband and wife/civil partner are jointly charged) is competent to give evidence FOR THE PROSECUTION	and is compellable (unless jointly charged) when the offence charged: [a] involves assault on, or injury or threat of injury to, the other spouse/civil partner; [b] involves assault on, or injury or threat of injury to, a person under 16; [c] involves a sexual offence against a person under 16; [d] involves aiding, abetting, conspiring to commit etc. any of the above
A spouse/civil partner (other than when jointly charged) is competent to give evidence **FOR THE DEFENCE**	Yes
A spouse/civil partner is competent to give evidence **FOR ANY CO-ACCUSED**	Yes

Q Outline the position of children as witnesses in criminal proceedings

A The evidence of any child **under 14** shall be unsworn. A deposition of a child's unsworn evidence may be taken for criminal proceedings as though it had been given on oath. Witnesses over 14 are to be sworn provided they have a sufficient appreciation of the solemnity of the occasion and of the particular responsibility to tell the truth when on oath.
S. 55 YOUTH JUSTICE AND CRIMINAL EVIDENCE ACT 1999

Q How is a child's age determined?

A By all the evidence available to the court at the time, usually by the production of a birth certificate.

Q Outline the position of people with impaired intellect

A Expert evidence can be received as to the person's competence, i.e. whether they can give 'intelligible testimony' and understand questions put to them and give answers which can be understood.

Q Outline the law in relation to hostile witnesses

A A hostile witness is a witness who does not give evidence fairly or shows no regard for the truth **as against the side calling him to give evidence**. [Not simply a witness who happens to give unfavourable evidence]. In such cases the judge may deem the witness to be hostile whereupon the party calling him can;

[a] ask leading question;
[b] contradict him with other evidence;
[c] prove that on another occasion he made a statement inconsistent with the present testimony.

Q What are 'witness anonymity orders'?

A These are orders allowing evidence to be given anonymously during criminal trials. They may be granted by the court if the following conditions are satisfied:

- the order is necessary to protect the safety of the witness, or another person, or the prevention of serious damage to property, or to prevent real harm to the public interest;
- having regard to all the circumstances, the taking of these measures would be consistent with the defendant receiving a fair trial; and
- it is in the interests of justice by reason of the fact that it appears to the court that the witness should testify and the witness would not testify if the order was not made.

s.86 CORONERS AND JUSTICE ACT 2009

COURT PROCEDURE AND WITNESSES

Q When can live television links be used for giving evidence?

A They may be used [other than for the accused] for witnesses who:

[a] are outside the UK; or
[b] a child; or

in the case of trials on indictment, appeals to the Court of Appeal, proceedings in youth courts and appeals to the Crown Court arising from offences of:

[a] assault on, or injury or threat of injury, to a person;
[b] cruelty to a person under 16;
[c] certain sexual offences;
[d] offences under the Protection of Children Act 1978; and
[e] aiding and abetting the above.

S. 32 CRIMINAL JUSTICE ACT 1988

It may also be used in certain other proceedings, such as summary trials, by virtue of the Criminal Justice Act 2003.

Q When can a witness refresh his memory?

A A person giving oral evidence in criminal proceedings may, at any stage, refresh his memory of it from a document made or verified by him at an earlier time if:

[a] he states in his oral evidence that the document records his recollection of the matter at that earlier time, and
[b] his recollection of the matter is likely to have been significantly better at that time than it is at the time of his oral evidence.

Transcripts of tape recordings of previously given oral accounts may also be used in the same way.

S. 139 CRIMINAL JUSTICE ACT 2003

Q Can a constable give oral evidence of conversations held via an interpreter?

A No, the only valid evidence of such a conversation is that of the interpreter.

Q What is a leading question?

A A question which suggests or 'leads' the respondent into giving the desired answer. Leading questions are generally forbidden in examination-in-chief (the evidence of a party's own witness) unless they relate to matters not in dispute, refreshing memory, identification or where the witness has been declared hostile.

YOUTH CRIME AND DISORDER

Q   Under the Crime and Disorder Act 1998 summarise a parenting order

A   The order requires a parent to:

[a] comply with the requirements of the order for not more than 12 months; and
[b] to attend counselling and guidance sessions specified by the responsible officer. These shall **not exceed three months and not be more than one a week**.

The order shall not infringe on the parents':

[i] religious beliefs, or
[ii] times of work, or
[iii] attendance at an educational establishment.

SS. 8-9 CRIME AND DISORDER ACT 1998

Q   Who can the order be made against?

A   [a] One or both biological parents, and
[b] a guardian (being any person who, in the opinion of the court, was for the time being the carer of a child or young person).

Q   Which court can discharge or vary the order?

A   The original court making the order.

Q   When shall an order be made?

A   Where a person **under 16** is convicted of **an offence**.

Q   Who is the responsible officer?

A   [a] A probation officer;
[b] a social worker, or
[c] a person nominated by the chief education officer or by a person appointed as director of children's services under the Children Act 2004
[d] a member of a youth offending team.

S. 8(8) CRIME AND DISORDER ACT 1998

YOUTH CRIME AND DISORDER

Q What is the position if the terms of the order are breached?

A The parent who breaches the order without reasonable excuse commits an offence.

S.9(7) 1998 ACT

Q What is the purpose of a child safety order?

A To help prevent children **under 10** from turning to crime.

Q When can a child safety order be made?

A If a magistrates' court, on the application of a local authority, is satisfied that a **child under 10**:

[a] has committed an offence; or
[b] that an order is necessary to stop him committing offences; or
[c] that the child has breached a curfew notice; or
[d] the child has caused harassment, alarm or distress, to someone other than a person in his own household.

S. 11 1998 ACT

Q Which magistrates' court makes the order?

A The family proceedings court. This is to ensure that the order is not seen to be 'criminal' in nature.

Q What if the child breaches the order?

A The court can:

[a] vary the order, or
[b] cancel the order and make a care order.

S. 12(6) 1998 ACT

YOUTH CRIME AND DISORDER

Q What is a child curfew scheme?

A These are designed to tackle unsupervised young children engaging in anti-social and offending behaviour. Where the scheme is in force, a local authority or a chief officer of police (having consulted with each other) may:

[a] ban children **under 16**,
[b] for up to **90 days**,
[c] from being in specified areas:

  [i] **between 9 pm and 6 am**, and
  [ii] without a responsible person **aged 18 or over**.

S. 14 1998 ACT

Q When does such a scheme become effective?

A Generally one month after confirmation by the Home Secretary.

Q What if the child breaches the ban?

A A constable with reasonable cause to believe that a child is in contravention of a ban shall:

[a] inform the local authority as soon as possible, and
[b] take the child home [unless he is likely to suffer significant harm].

Q What are police powers to deal with truants?

A If following a direction by a superintendent (or above) that the powers contained in S. 16 Crime & Disorder Act 1988 are to apply, a constable has reasonable cause to believe that a child he finds in a public place in a specified area is:

[a] of school age, and
[b] is absent from school without lawful authority, the constable can remove him to:

  [i] a designated place, or
  [ii] back to his school.

S. 16 CRIME AND DISORDER ACT 1988

Lawful authority. Means leave, sickness, unavoidable cause or day set apart for religious observance.

Designated place. Any premises designated by a local authority as premises to which children of school age may be taken by a constable following a superintendent's direction to deal with truants.

Specified area. Any area specified in the superintendent's direction.

Absent from school. The powers only apply to children registered at a school, not those educated at home.

Q   What is a truancy penalty notice?

A   The Anti-Social Behaviour Act 2003 provides for a penalty notice scheme under the Education Act 1996 whereby parents or guardians of persistent truants may be issued with a penalty notice by a constable, senior teacher (head, deputy or assistant head, or other authorised staff member) or local education officer. The amount of the penalty is currently GBP50 if paid within 28 days (or GBP100 if paid between 28–42 days).

SENTENCING

Q Outline the procedure for release of short-term prisoners on licence

A   The Secretary of State may order the release of a prisoner on licence when s/he has served the 'requisite period' of their sentence. For those imprisoned for between four-18 months, this period is one quarter of their term, for those with sentences of 18 months or more the period is 135 days less than one half of their term. Release may be subject to conditions such as electronic monitoring.

S. 246 CRIMINAL JUSTICE ACT 2003

Q Outline the procedure for release of short-term prisoners on home curfew

A   Some prisoners may be permitted to complete part of their sentence under the home curfew scheme. This runs for between 14-60 days, and will only apply where the prisoner agrees to the curfew conditions (which are to be determined by the prison governor). Generally the curfew will be from 7 pm to 7 am, with a minimum curfew duration of nine hours. The Parole Service is responsible for monitoring the scheme. The police must be notified of curfews at least 14 days prior to release, and may subsequently request, *with a superintendent's authority*, information as to the prisoner's compliance with his curfew. Such requests for information must be answered within 24 hours.

Q What happens if a curfew is broken?

A   If it appears to the Secretary of State that a person released on licence has broken his curfew conditions, or his whereabouts can no longer be electronically monitored, or that it is necessary to do so in order to protect the public from serious harm, the Secretary of State may revoke the licence and recall the person to prison. Following revocation of the licence the person shall be liable to be detained and, if at large shall be deemed to be unlawfully at large.

SENTENCING

Q What types of detention are applicable to young offenders?

A [a] Detention at Her Majesty's Pleasure (murder sentences for under 18s);
[b] life sentences (murder sentences for those aged 18-21 years old);
[c] detention for specific periods (certain serious offences, where the court may sentence the offender to detention for a term not exceeding the maximum available when it is of the opinion that there is no other way of dealing with the case);
[d] detention in young offenders institutions (for those aged 18-21 years old);
[e] detention and training orders (under 18s).

Q Outline the community order requirements

A [a] **Unpaid work** requirement (of between 40-300 hours within a 12-month period);
[b] **activity** requirement (for a specific number of days not exceeding 60 in total);
[c] **programme** requirement (such as anger management or substance abuse courses);
[d] **prohibited activity** requirement (refrain from certain activities during a specified period);
[e] **curfew** requirement (remain at a specified place for a specified time, which must be between two and 12 hours a day);
[f] **exclusion** requirement (not to enter a specified place for a specified time, up to two years);
[g] **residence** requirement (to reside at a specified place for a specified period);
[h] **mental health treatment** requirement (to submit to treatment);
[i] **drug rehabilitation** requirement (to submit to treatment for at least six months);
[j] **alcohol treatment** requirement (to submit to treatment for at least six months);
[k] **supervision** requirement (to attend appointments with the responsible officer for the promotion of rehabilitation);
[l] **attendance centre** requirement (to attend an attendance centre for between 12-36 hours in total). This requirement may only be imposed upon those over 18 but under 25.

EVIDENCE

Q   What two questions are applied to any evidence?

A   [a]   Admissibility (i.e. is the evidence relevant to a fact in issue?); and
    [b]   weight (i.e. what weight should be attached to the evidence - how far does it prove or disprove the case?).

Q   What reasons exist for excluding admissible evidence?

A   A trial judge may exclude evidence if he believes its prejudicial effect outweighs its probative value, and in cases of admissions and confessions they may be excluded if obtained by improper or unfair means [inducements and oppression]. Evidence may also be excluded for the following reasons:

   [a]   the incompetence of the witness;
   [b]   it relates to previous convictions or character of the accused;
   [c]   it is hearsay;
   [d]   it is non-expert opinion evidence;
   [e]   it is privileged information; or
   [f]   as a matter of public policy.

Q   What is meant by the facts in issue?

A   The facts which must be proved to establish guilt. e.g.;

   [a]   the identity of the defendant;
   [b]   the *actus reus* [the physical act or criminal conduct]; and
   [c]   the *mens rea* [the state of mind - knowingly, wilfully etc].

Q   On whom lies the burden of proof?

A   Generally the prosecution, to a standard of *beyond all reasonable doubt*. Exceptionally the defence, e.g. when raising a defence such as diminished responsibility or proving a lawful excuse. This standard is known as *the balance of probabilities, i.e. more probable than not*.

Q   What is a formal admission?

A   A formal admission dispenses with the need to prove a fact because it is admitted. Any fact may be admitted by the prosecutor or defendant, and admissions:

   [a]   may be made before or at the proceedings;
   [b]   if not made in court, shall be in writing;

EVIDENCE

[c] if made by an individual;

[i] shall be signed; and
[ii] shall be made by his counsel or solicitor (or approved by them, if made before trial).

S. 10 CRIMINAL JUSTICE ACT 1967

Q What is meant by drawing inferences?

A The courts are permitted to draw 'such inferences as appear proper' against the accused in circumstances relating to the accused's silence. They relate to:

[a] silence when questioned or charged by a constable;
[b] silence when questioned by a person charged with a duty to investigate offences;
[c] silence in court; and
[d] failure to give evidence in his defence.

SS. 34-38 CRIMINAL JUSTICE AND PUBLIC ORDER ACT 1994

Q When can a court draw such inferences as appear proper?

A Where in proceedings against a person for an offence evidence is given that he:

[a] on being questioned under caution by a constable; or
[b] on being charged or reported; he

failed to mention any fact relied on in his defence then:

a court or jury may draw such inferences as appear proper.

This does not prejudice:

[a] the admissibility in evidence of the silence of the accused in the face of anything **said in his presence** in so far as evidence would in any case be admissible; or
[b] the drawing of any inference from such silence.

EVIDENCE

Q When can an inference be drawn at court?

A At a trial of a person who has attained 14 years and the court is satisfied that the accused is aware that the stage has been reached at which evidence can be given for the defence

[a] if he refuses to answer questions; or
[b] does not give evidence;

the court or jury may draw such inferences as appear proper from his refusal without good cause, to answer questions.

This does not prejudice:

[a] the admissibility in evidence of the silence of the accused in the face of anything **said in his presence** in so far as evidence would in any case be admissible; or
[b] the drawing of any inference from such silence.

Q When must a special warning be given?

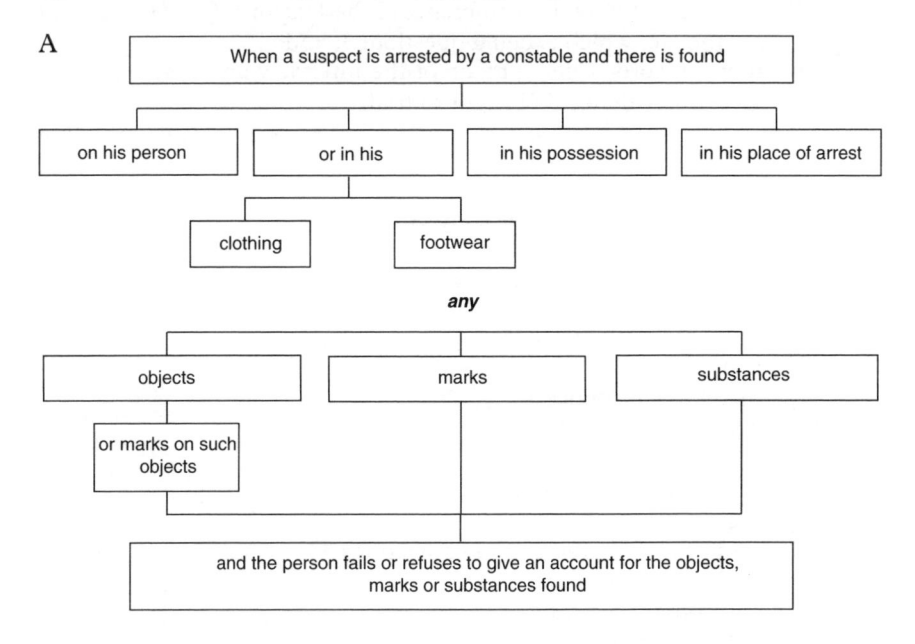

A

When a suspect is arrested by a constable and there is found

- on his person
- or in his
  - clothing
  - footwear
- in his possession
- in his place of arrest

any

- objects
  - or marks on such objects
- marks
- substances

and the person fails or refuses to give an account for the objects, marks or substances found

EVIDENCE

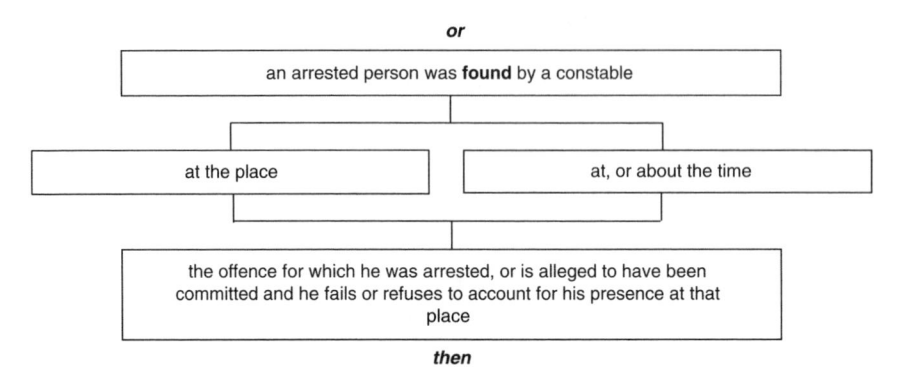

```
                              or
        ┌─────────────────────────────────────────────┐
        │  an arrested person was **found** by a constable │
        └─────────────────────────────────────────────┘
         ┌──────────────────┬──────────────────────┐
    ┌────┴─────────┐                    ┌──────────┴──────────┐
    │ at the place │                    │ at, or about the time │
    └──────────────┘                    └─────────────────────┘
                   └──────────┬──────────┘
        ┌─────────────────────────────────────────────────────┐
        │ the offence for which he was arrested, or is alleged to have been │
        │ committed and he fails or refuses to account for his presence at that │
        │                          place                      │
        └─────────────────────────────────────────────────────┘
                              *then*
```

for an inference to be drawn from the suspect's failure or refusal to answer a question about one of the matters, or to answer in a satisfactory manner, the investigating officer must tell the suspect in ordinary language;

[a] what offence he is investigating;
[b] what fact he is asking the suspect to account for;
[c] that he believes this fact may be due to his taking part in the crime;
[d] that a court may draw inferences if he fails or refuses to account for the fact which is being questioned; and
[e] that a record is being made of the interview and that it may be given in evidence if brought to trial.

S. 36-37 PACE ACT 1984

Q **What are the sources of evidence?**

A   Evidence is classified as follows:

[a] original [oral] evidence;
[b] real evidence;
[c] secondary evidence;
[d] documentary evidence;
[e] hearsay evidence;
[f] circumstantial evidence;
[g] presumptions;
[h] evidence of character and convictions;
[i] evidence of opinion;
[j] corroboration; and
[k] judicial notice.

EVIDENCE

A. **Original or primary [oral] evidence**. Is evidence given to a court from the witness box which is evidence of the first-hand knowledge of the witness about a fact or facts, and which is subject to cross-examination.

B. **Real evidence**. Usually takes the form of a material object, e.g. exhibits. Also evidence about a person's behaviour, appearance or demeanour.

C. **Secondary evidence**. Is evidence which is not the best evidence, e.g. copy of a document. It may be produced when:

   [a] a party fails to produce evidence in court when required to do so;
   [b] where a stranger to the case lawfully refuses to produce a document, eg. where he could claim privilege;
   [c] where a document has been lost or destroyed;
   [d] where the production of the original document is impossible, e.g. painting on a wall;
   [e] where a public document is concerned, where its production would be illegal or inconvenient.

D. **Documentary evidence**. E.g. documents, maps, plans, graphs, drawings, photographs, discs, tapes, video tapes and films. They include CCTV video. **Evidence by certificate of plan or drawing**. In criminal proceedings, a plan or drawing signed by a constable or person with prescribed qualifications [architect, engineer etc], as a plan or drawing made by him which is drawn to a scale specified shall be evidence of the things shown on the plan or drawing. Before this can be adduced in evidence a copy must be served on the defendant **not less than seven days** before the hearing and the defendant may serve notice **not less than three days** before the hearing that he wishes the witness to attend the trial to give evidence. Otherwise the evidence may be adduced without the witness appearing. (S. 41 Criminal Justice Act 1948). **Admissibility of S. 9 Criminal Justice Act 1967 written statements**. Written statements shall be admissible as evidence to the same extent as oral evidence if:

   [a] signed by the maker;
   [b] it contains a declaration that it is true to the best of his knowledge and belief and that he made it knowing that, if it

were tendered in evidence, he would be liable to prosecution if he wilfully stated in it anything which he knew to be false or did not believe to be true;
- [c] before the hearing copies are served on the other parties; and
- [d] none of the other parties **within seven days** from the service, serves a notice requiring attendance of the witness. (Parties may agree to waive this provision before or during the hearing);
- [e] if under 18, it shall give his age;
- [f] if he cannot read, it shall be read to him before he signs it and contain a declaration by the person who read it to him to that effect;
- [g] exhibits shall be served on the other parties;

Service of S. 9 statements. S. 9 Statements may be served:

- [a] by delivering it to him or his solicitor;
- [b] by addressing it to him and by leaving it at his usual or last known place of abode or place of business or by addressing it to his solicitor and leaving it at his office;
- [c] by sending it by registered letter or recorded delivery addressed to him at his usual or last known place of abode, or addressed to his solicitor at his office; or
- [d] in the case of a company, addressed to the secretary at their registered office or by registered letter or recorded delivery.

Documentary records. A statement made by a person in a document shall be admissible if:

- [a] he is dead or by reason of bodily or mental condition is unfit to attend as a witness; or
- [b] the person is outside the UK and it is not practicable to secure his attendance; or
- [c] that all reasonable steps have been taken to find him without success; or
- [d] the statement was made to a police officer or person charged with the duty of investigating offences or charging offenders, and that the person does not give evidence through fear or because he is kept out of the way.

Business documents. A statement in a document shall be admissible in criminal proceedings of any fact of which oral evidence would be admissible if:

- [a] the document was created or received by a person in the course of a trade, business, profession or other occupation, or as the holder of a paid or unpaid office, and
- [b] the information contained in the document was supplied by a person who had personal knowledge of the matter dealt with, but it will only be admissible if:

  - [i] the information was supplied directly or indirectly, but if indirectly only if each person through whom it was supplied received it in the course of a trade, business, profession or other occupation or is the holder of a paid or unpaid office, or
  - [ii] a confession which would be inadmissible is not rendered admissible by virtue of the above.

Computer records. In any proceedings a statement in a document produced by a computer shall not be admissible as evidence unless it is shown:

- [a] that there are no reasonable grounds for believing that the statements are inaccurate because of improper use of the computer;
- [b] that at all material times the computer was operating properly, or if not that any aspect in which it was not operating properly, or was out of operation, was not such as to affect the production of the documents or accuracy of the contents; and
- [c] the relevant conditions in the rules of the court are satisfied.

E. **Hearsay.** Hearsay evidence is 'second-hand' evidence consisting of something someone else said, or wrote, or did. Since it is not as good as direct evidence it is generally inadmissible in criminal proceedings, unless it is permitted by virtue of a number of rules. The admissibility of hearsay is now primarily dealt with by the Criminal Justice Act 2003, S. 114, which states that a statement not made in oral evidence in the proceedings is admissible as evidence of any matter stated if, but only if:

[a] a statutory provision makes it admissible;
[b] a rule of law makes it admissible;
[c] all parties to the proceedings agree to it being admissible; or
[d] the court is satisfied that it is in the interests of justice for it to be admissible.

In deciding whether to admit evidence under [d] above, the court must consider the following factors (and any others it considers relevant):

[i] how much probative value the statement has [ie. to what extent it goes towards proving issues in the case], or how valuable it is for understanding other evidence;
[ii] what other evidence has been, or can be, given on the matter;
[iii] how important the matter is in the context of the case;
[iv] the circumstances in which it was made;
[v] how reliable the maker of the statement appears to be;
[vi] how reliable the evidence of the making of the statement appears to be;
[vii] whether oral evidence of the matter can be given, and if not, why not;
[viii] the difficulty in challenging the statement; and
[ix] the extent to which that difficulty would prejudice the party facing it.

Other rules of law are preserved by the 2003 Act concerning the admissibility of public information, reputation evidence, *res gestae*, confessions, admission by agents, common enterprise and expert evidence.

Public information. S. 118 preserves the common law rule which permits the admissibility of facts of a public nature stated in published works dealing with matters of a public nature which have been recorded by authorised public agents in the course of their official duties eg. court records, registers of births, baptisms, deaths, marriages etc.

Reputation or family tradition. Another preserved common law rule allows evidence to be admitted to establish pedigree, the existence of a marriage, any public or general right, or the identity of a person or thing.

EVIDENCE

Res gestae Is evidence which would ordinarily be hearsay but is so *closely connected with a specific event that it ought to be admitted in evidence under the res gestae rule.*

The trial judge must be satisfied that:

[a] the event was so unusual or startling or dramatic as to dominate the thoughts of the victim; and
[b] that very effect on the thoughts of the victim exclude the possibility of their lying or being mistaken; and
[c] the statement was made at approximately the same time as the event.

E.g. Suppose that A and B are standing drinking at a bar when the door opens. A shouts 'don't shoot Bob' whereupon a shot rings out and A falls to the floor mortally wounded. From B's position he could not see who fired the shot and the assassin has now made off. Whilst B is comforting A who is dying A says, 'I can't believe it, Bob Russell shot me'. Although hearsay, these facts would fit the *res gestae* rule and be admitted as evidence.

F. **Circumstantial evidence.** Is evidence not of the fact to be proved, but of other facts from which that fact may be proved with more or less certainty.

G. **Presumptions.** Fall into three categories:

[a] **irrebuttable presumption of law**. E.g. A child under 10 cannot be guilty of an offence.
[b] **rebuttable presumption of law**. E.g. presumption of regularity. Until it is rebutted, it is assumed that officials have been properly appointed, police officers are acting in the execution of their duty, etc.
[c] **presumption of facts**. A court *may* presume, in the absence of evidence to the contrary, a fact from the evidence of other facts. Where evidence that a person was alive on a certain date is given to the court, it may be presumed that the person was still alive on a subsequent date.

H. **Character.** Character evidence is now dealt with by the Criminal Justice Act 2003. A person's reputation is admissible in order to prove his 'bad character'. Bad character is defined as evidence of, or a disposition towards, misconduct on his part (other than evidence relating to the alleged facts of the offence for which he is charged, or evidence of misconduct in connection with the investigation of that offence).

[a] **Non-defendant's bad character**. Evidence can be given of the previous misconduct of a person other than the defendant if three conditions are satisfied:

[i] it is important explanatory evidence,
[ii] it has substantial probative value in relation to an issue in the case, and is of substantial importance in the context of the case as a whole, and
[iii] all parties agree to the evidence being admissible.

Previous convictions of witnesses. By virtue of S. 6 Criminal Procedure Act 1865 if a witness, upon being questioned about previous convictions, either denies or does not admit them, or refuses to answer, it shall be lawful to prove such a conviction [by production of a certificate of conviction].

[b] **Defendant's bad character**. S. 101 of the 2003 Act makes evidence of the defendant's bad character admissible if, but only if:

[i] all parties agree to the evidence being admissible,
[ii] the evidence is adduced by the defendant himself or given in answer to a question in cross-examination,
[iii] it is important explanatory evidence,
[iv] it is relevant to an important matter in issue between the defendant and prosecution,
[v] it has substantial probative value in relation to an important matter in issue between the defendant and co-defendant,
[vi] it is evidence to correct a false impression given by the defendant, or
[vii] the defendant has made an attack on another person's character.

[c] **Defendant's good character**. The defendant is entitled to adduce this in order to demonstrate his credibility or to dispel the liklihood that he would commit the crime in question.

I. **Opinion**. May be given by non-expert and expert witnesses.

Non-expert evidence. May be given in relation to such matters as the time of day, temperature, the value of an item, whether a person was drunk etc;

Expert evidence. Usually arises in relation to such issues as:

[a] medical;
[b] science;
[c] determining mental illness;
[d] handwriting samples;
[e] facial mapping.

Full disclosure requires any party intending to produce an expert to furnish the other party with written statements of the expert's findings.

J. **Corroboration**. Must be independent testimony which affects the accused by connecting him with the crime. *"In other words, it must be evidence which implicates him, that is, which confirms in some material particular not only the evidence that the crime has been committed, but also that the prisoner committed it."* per Lord Reid in *R v Baskerville (1916)*.**Corroboration required as a matter of law**. For the offences of treason, perjury and speeding (corroboration as to the speed the vehicle was travelling).**Identification evidence**. In *R v Turnbull (1976)* it was held that the factors that should be considered in identification evidence include:

[a] how long did the witness have the accused under observation?
[b] at what distance?
[c] in what light?
[d] was the observation impeded? [e.g. passing traffic];
[e] had the witness seen the accused before?
[f] how often?
[g] if only occasionally, had he any special reason for remembering him?
[h] how long elapsed between the original observation and subsequent identification?
[i] was there a material discrepancy between first description and the accused's actual appearance?

EVIDENCE

K. **Judicial notice**. The courts may take notice of facts that are so well known that they need no further proof, e.g. night follows day, the grass is green, Glasgow is in Scotland.

EXCLUSION OF ADMISSIBLE EVIDENCE

Q When should confessions be excluded in evidence?

A When they are:

[a] obtained by oppression; or
[b] considered unreliable.

S. 76 PACE ACT 1984

Oppression. In any proceedings where the prosecution proposes to give in evidence a confession made by an accused, if it is represented to the court that it may have been obtained by oppression, the court may exclude the evidence. **Oppression is** *'the exercise of authority or power in a burdensome, harsh or wrongful manner; unjust or cruel treatment... the imposition of unreasonable or unjust burdens'. R v. Fulling (1987).*

Unreliable. Means the confession was obtained in consequence of anything said or done which was likely to render it unreliable and the court shall not allow the confession to be given. In *R v Fulling (1987)* it was suggested that *"... questioning which by its nature, duration, or other attendant circumstances (including the fact of custody) excites hopes (such as the hope of release) or fears, or so affects the mind of the subject that his will crumbles and he speaks when otherwise he would have stayed silent ".* Courts have held the following confessions to be unreliable:

[a] no caution was given, the suspect was not asked if he wanted his solicitor present and he was not shown the notes of the interview;
[b] flagrant breach of the Codes of Practice;
[c] interviewing a suspect who had just vomited [should have been seen by a doctor];
[d] where the appropriate adult had a low IQ and was unable to assist the detained person;
[e] suggested to a suspect of a sexual assault that it would be better for them to receive treatment than go to prison;
[f] where a person had been kept in custody for 14 hours, had been interviewed four times before confessing and had been refused any visits from his family;
[g] where the officers had a 'warm-up chat' with the suspect before the interview and the 'chat' lasted over two hours;
[h] an offer of bail if the suspect admits the offence or conversely telling the suspect that be will be kept in custody until he admits the offence.

EXCLUSION OF ADMISSIBLE EVIDENCE

Q What is the effect of excluding confessions?

A While additional evidence obtained after a confession may be admissible, its value may be lost as S. 76 of the PACE Act 1984 prevents the prosecution from linking the discovery of the additional evidence to any confession which has been excluded.

Q What is the law in relation to the exclusion of evidence generally?

A In any proceedings the court may refuse to allow evidence on which the prosecution rely to be given if it appears to the court that, having regard to all the circumstances, the admission of the evidence would have such an adverse effect on the fairness of the proceedings that the court ought not to admit it.

S. 78 PACE ACT 1984

Evidence that has been excluded includes:

[a] informing the suspect [wrongly] that his fingerprints had been found at the scene;
[b] undercover operations where the police failed to record conversations in accordance with PACE;
[c] failure by custody officer to inform a detained person of his rights;
[d] interviewing without informing the detained person of his rights;
[e] failing to provide the detained person with adequate meals;
[f] 'off the record' interviews which were not recorded;
[g] failing to make contemporaneous notes of conversations;
[h] failing to get an interpreter or appropriate adult.

DISCLOSURE OF EVIDENCE

Q Define a criminal investigation

A Is an investigation which police officers or other persons have a duty to conduct with a view to it being ascertained:

[a] whether a person should be charged with an offence; or
[b] whether a person charged with an offence is guilty of it.

S. 1(4) CRIMINAL PROCEDURE AND INVESTIGATIONS ACT 1996

Q To whom do the disclosure provisions apply?

A All not guilty pleas.

Q What is meant by primary disclosure?

A Relates to the duty of the prosecutor to disclose material which is in his possession or which he has inspected and which in his opinion **might undermine the case** against the accused, i.e. which might be helpful to the defence. Material is material of any kind, including information and objects which are obtained in the course of a criminal investigation and which may be relevant to the investigation.

S. 3 1996 ACT

Q What is disclosure by the defence?

A This duty only arises **after** the prosecution's primary disclosure and may be:

[a] compulsory; or
[b] voluntary.

Compulsory. [This does not apply to cases being tried at magistrates' court.] The statement would outline the defence in general terms. It should include those issues which the accused disputes with the prosecution and any alibi evidence. This must be done **within 14 days of primary disclosure**.

S. 5 1996 ACT

Voluntary. This applies to cases being tried at magistrates' court. This happens where:

[a] the defence is not satisfied with the material disclosed at the primary disclosure;
[b] where they wish to examine items listed in the schedule of non-sensitive material; or

DISCLOSURE OF EVIDENCE

[c] they wish to show the strength of their case in order to persuade the prosecution not to proceed.

S. 6 1996 ACT

Q What is meant by secondary disclosure by the prosecutor?

A Once a defence statement has been provided [compulsory or voluntarily], the prosecution must disclose any material which:

[a] has not already been disclosed; and
[b] might be reasonably expected to **assist the accused's defence** as disclosed by the defence statement. If the prosecutor, having reviewed the defence, considers that there is no further material to disclose, a written statement to that effect must be given to the defence.

S. 6E 1996 ACT

Q What is the continuing duty of prosecution to disclose?

A The prosecution must continue to review the disclosure of material right up until the case is completed. The duty falls in two stages:

[a] after primary disclosure the prosecutor **must** review material not disclosed in terms of whether it might undermine the prosecution case; and
[b] after secondary prosecution disclosure.

S. 7A 1996 ACT

Q Outline those with roles and responsibilities under the 1996 Act

A **Prosecutor**. Means any person acting as a prosecutor whether an individual or a body.

Officer in charge of the case. Is the police officer responsible for directing a criminal investigation. He is also responsible for ensuring that proper procedures are in place for the recording of information, and retaining records of information and other material at the request of the prosecutor.

DISCLOSURE OF EVIDENCE

Disclosure officer. Is the link between the investigation team and the CPS. He is the person responsible for examining material retained by the police during the investigation; revealing material to the prosecutor during the investigation and any criminal proceedings resulting from it, and certifying that he has done this, and disclosing material to the accused at the request of the prosecutor.

Supervisor. There must be an officer in charge and a disclosure officer. If either can no longer perform his task his supervisor must assign another person to take over his duties.

Q What are the duties of the disclosure officer in relation to primary disclosure?

A First, to create a schedule of all *non-sensitive material* and secondly a schedule of *sensitive material*. He must then decide what material might undermine the prosecution case. In addition to the schedules and copies of material which undermine the prosecution case he must provide a copy of certain material **whether or not it undermines the prosecution case**. This is:

[a] first description of the alleged offender;
[b] the alleged offender's explanation for the offence;
[c] material casting doubt on the reliability of a confession;
[d] any material casting doubt on the reliability of a witness; and any other material which may satisfy the test for prosecution disclosure.

Q What are the duties of the disclosure officer in relation to secondary disclosure?

A After primary disclosure the defence may provide a defence statement setting out their case, together with reasons why they wish to inspect additional items of the schedule which have not been disclosed. Once the defence statement has been provided, the disclosure officer must:

[a] review the material contained in the schedules; and
[b] inform the prosecutor of any material which might reasonably be expected **to assist the defence** as disclosed by the defence statement.

Secondary disclosure may then be made to the defence.

DISCLOSURE OF EVIDENCE

Q What is the continuing duty of the disclosure officer?

A His continuing duty is to review material for items that should be disclosed to the defence **as undermining the prosecution** or which might assist the defence case.

Q What are the duties of investigators?

A Investigators are required to pursue all reasonable lines of inquiry, *whether they point towards or away* from the *suspect*. All material that is relevant to the case must be recorded and retained.

Q What is sensitive material?

A Material which is not in the public interest to disclose, e.g.

[a] material given in confidence;
[b] observation posts;
[c] informants;
[d] police communications, etc. [many such items would be covered by public interest immunity].

Q What did the Johnson ruling state in relation to observation posts?

A In *R v Johnson (1988)* the following guidance as to the *minimum evidential requirements* was outlined:

[a] The police officer in charge of the observations (not lower than the rank of **sergeant**) must be able to give evidence that beforehand he visited all observation posts to be used to ascertain the attitude of the occupiers of premises, not only as to the use to be made of them, but also as to the possible **disclosure of their use** and other facts which could lead to the identification of the premises and occupiers.

[b] A police officer (of no lower rank than **chief inspector**) must be able to testify that, immediately before the trial he visited the places used for observations and ascertained whether the occupiers are the same as when the observations took place and what attitude the current occupiers have as to the **possible disclosure** of the use made of the premises and of other facts which could lead to the identification of the premises and occupiers.

Q What are the retention periods for material?

A Material must be retained until a decision is taken whether to prosecute and then until the case has been dealt with. In the event of a conviction it must be retained at least until:

[a] the person is released from custody; otherwise
[b] six months from the date of conviction.

In the case of an appeal, until:

[a] the appeal is concluded; or
[b] the appeal does not go ahead.

CUSTODY OFFICER DUTIES

Q Which prisoners must be taken to a designated police station?

A Persons who are to be detained [or likely to be] for **more than six hours** must be taken to a designated police station, otherwise they may be taken to a non-designated police station.

S. 35 PACE ACT 1984

Designated. One that has enough facilities for detaining arrested people. Stations are 'designated' by the chief officer.

Q Who shall act as a custody officer?

A

Designated police station
Sergeant – designated custody officer, or, where the custody officer is not available any officer

Non-designated police station
any officer who is not involved in the investigation of the offence, if readily available; or, if not available
the arresting officer who took him to the police station; or
officer who granted him street bail; or
any officer involved in the investigation
and in all cases If he is the officer who took him to the station, he must inform an inspector at a designated police station.

S. 36 PACE ACT 1984

Q What is meant by police detention?

A A person is in police detention when:

[a] he has been taken to a police station after being arrested for an offence; or
[b] he is arrested at a police station; or
[c] he has been taken to a police station after being arrested under the Terrorism Act 2000.

and is detained there [or elsewhere] in the charge of a constable.

S. 118 PACE ACT 1984

CUSTODY OFFICER DUTIES

Not in detention. A person charged and who is at court is not in police detention. Nor is a person who has been removed to a police station as a place of safety under the Mental Health Act 1983.

Being transferred. Under the Police Reform Act 2002, where persons are being transferred into the custody of investigating officers, or where designated escort officers are taking an arrested person to a police station or transferring a detainee between stations, such persons are deemed to be in police detention.

Q What is the right to have someone informed of arrest?

A Any person arrested and held in custody may on request have:

[a] one person known to him; or
[b] who is likely to take an interest in his welfare, informed at public expense of his whereabouts.

S. 56 PACE ACT 1984

Alternatives. If the requested person cannot be contacted two alternatives may be chosen, thereafter the custody officer or officer in charge of the investigation has discretion to allow further attempts.

Change of police station. The above rights apply to every move to another police station, even if someone was already informed at the former station.

Q Who can delay this right?

A An inspector or above, but only in relation to an indictable offence. The delay can be for a maximum of 36 hours (48 in terrorism cases) calculated from the 'relevant time.'

Q What about juveniles?

A In the case of juveniles the person responsible for their welfare must be informed that the juvenile is in detention, but should the juvenile wish any other person to be informed, this right may be delayed in the same circumstances as it may for adults.

Q What other rights of communication does a detainee have?

A The right to speak to a person on the telephone for a reasonable time, or be supplied [on request] with writing materials for sending letters. Interpreters may do this on the detainee's behalf.

CUSTODY OFFICER DUTIES

Q **When can an inspector delay this additional right to communicate?**

A Where he is detained for an indictable offence the right can be denied or delayed if an **inspector** [or above] considers that it would result in:

[a] **interference with or harm** to evidence connected with an indictable offence or interference with, or physical injury to, other people; or
[b] will lead to the **alerting of other people** suspected of having committed such an offence but not yet arrested for it; or
[c] will **hinder the recovery** of property obtained as a result of such an offence.

They may also be delayed where the indictable offence is either:

[a] **a drug trafficking offence** and the officer has reasonable grounds for believing that the detained person has benefited from it and that the recovery of the value of that person's proceeds will be hindered; or
[b] an offence covering **confiscation orders** applies and the officer has reasonable grounds for believing that the detained person has benefited from the offence and that the recovery of the value of the property or anything connected with it will be hindered.

S. 56 PACE ACT 1984

Q **What is the right to legal advice?**

A A person arrested and held in custody at a police station or other premises has the right to consult privately with a solicitor free of charge if he requests it and must be informed of the right when he first arrives at the police station.

S. 58 PACE ACT 1984

What if he declines? The custody officer shall ask the reasons.

What if he changes his mind? Where a suspect first requires a solicitor then changes his mind the interview may proceed providing he has given his agreement in writing or on tape to being interviewed without legal advice and an **inspector** or above has inquired into his reasons and given authority to proceed.

Superintendents. May delay access to legal advice in cases of indictable offences, for a maximum of 36 hours (from the 'relevant time'), or until the time the person will first appear at court, whichever is sooner. Authorisation to delay may be made orally at first, but must be recorded in writing as soon as practicable. Note that any such delay will restrict the drawing of adverse inferences from silence.

Terrorism cases. The right may also be delayed under the Terrorism Act 2000, for a maximum of 48 hours from the time of arrest.

Q What is meant by a solicitor?

A This means a solicitor who holds a current practising certificate, a trainee, a duty solicitor representative or an accredited representative.

Q Who can refuse to admit an accredited or probationary representative?

A Both may give advice unless an officer of **inspector** or above considers that such a visit will hinder the investigation of crime and directs otherwise. If admitted he should be treated as any other legal adviser.

Q What should the inspector have regard to in deciding whether to admit a probationary or accredited person?

A [a] That his identity and status has been established;
[b] is he a suitable character to give legal advice [a person with a criminal record is unlikely to be suitable, unless minor and not recent]; and
[c] any other matters in a letter of authorisation provided by the solicitor on whose behalf he is acting.

Q Can a person be interviewed in the absence of a solicitor who has been requested?

A A **superintendent** (or above) may authorise an interview to continue without a solicitor being present if he has reasonable grounds for believing that to wait for a solicitor might:

[a] lead to interference with, or harm to, evidence connected with an offence;
[b] lead to interference with, or physical harm to, other persons;
[c] lead to serious loss of, or damage to, property;
[d] lead to alerting others suspected of having committed an offence but who are not yet arrested for it;
[e] hinder the recovery of property obtained in consequence of an offence.

CUSTODY OFFICER DUTIES

An **inspector** (or above) may authorise an interview to continue without a solicitor being present in the following cases:

[a] the solictor nominated by the detainee cannot be contacted; or
[b] the nominated solicitor has previously indicated that he/she does not wish to be contacted; or
[c] the nominated solicitor declines to attend after having been contacted; **and**
[d] the detainee has been advised of the duty solicitor scheme but has declined to ask for a duty solicitor.

Q What should not be delayed until a solicitor arrives?

A It is not necessary to delay taking breath, blood or urine samples.

Q Distinguish relevant time from review time

A

Relevant time	Review time
Calculates the 24 hours that the detainee is permitted to be kept in police custody and runs from the time of arrival at the police **station**	Calculates the times when reviews of detention must be carried out and runs from the time detention is authorised
Note: Invariably the relevant time runs before the review time. This has the effect of having two clocks ticking at the same time!	

The Relevant time		
Prisoner's status	Conditions	Relevant time begins
Attends police station voluntarily or accompanies a constable there voluntarily	is arrested at the police station	on arrest
Brought to police station under arrest		on arrival at police station

www.janes.com 343

CUSTODY OFFICER DUTIES

The Relevant time		
Prisoner's status	**Conditions**	**Relevant time begins**
Arrested outside England and Wales		*the earlier* of time of arrival at the first police station at the police area where the offence is being investigated, or 24 hours **after entry** into England and Wales
Arrested by Force 1 for Force 2	he is not wanted by Force 1 and not questioned about the Force 2 offence	time of arrival at the police station in the area where he is wanted by Force 2, or 24 hours **after arrest** by Force 1
Arrested by Force 1 for their offence and is also wanted by Force 2	he is dealt with by Force 1 for their offence and not questioned about the offence in Force 2	the earlier of time of the arrival at the first police station in the area where he is wanted by Force 2, or 24 hours after leaving the police station where he is detained by Force 1
Hospitals. The relevant time clock stops when he is on his way to, whilst at, and on his way back from hospital so long as he is **not questioned** to obtain evidence of the offence.		

Suppose that Smith is arrested by Thames Valley Police for an offence and he is being dealt with for that offence by Thames Valley. Before release a Police National Computer check reveals he is also wanted for an offence by Devon & Cornwall Constabulary. He is not questioned by Thames Valley about the Devon & Cornwall offence. The relevant time clock for Devon & Cornwall will start at the

earlier time of	
His arrival at the first police station where he is wanted in Devon & Cornwall	24 hours **after leaving** the police station in Thames Valley

CUSTODY OFFICER DUTIES

Q Who is responsible for conducting reviews of detention?

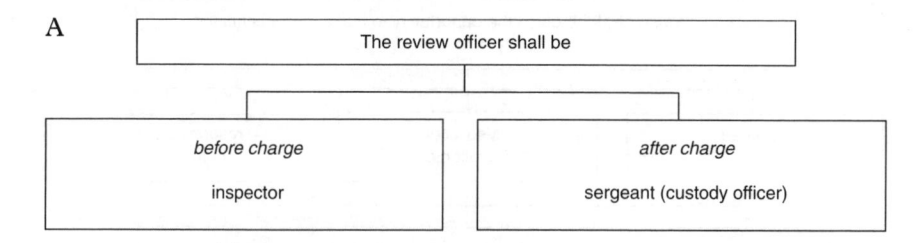

A

The review officer shall be:
- before charge: inspector
- after charge: sergeant (custody officer)

Q When does the review time begin?

A From the time the custody officer authorises detention.

Q When shall review be carried out?

A

Reviews			
1st	not more than	Six hours	from first authorisation
2nd	not more than	Nine hours	after the first
3rd	not more than	Nine hours	intervals

S. 40 PACE ACT 1984

Terrorism Act 2000 reviews: First, as soon as reasonably practicable after arrest, then at least every 12 hours; after 24 hours it must be conducted by a superintendent (or above).

Q When can a review be delayed?

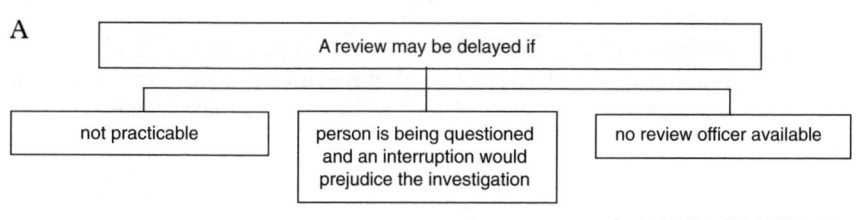

A

A review may be delayed if:
- not practicable
- person is being questioned and an interruption would prejudice the investigation
- no review officer available

S. 40(4) PACE ACT 1984

www.janes.com   345

CUSTODY OFFICER DUTIES

Q Who can make representations to the review officer?

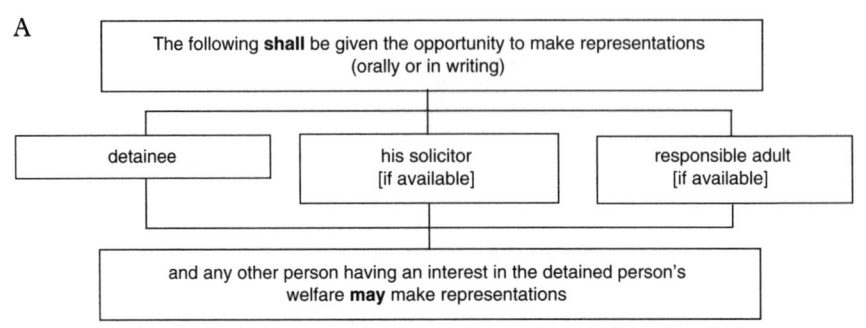

A

```
┌─────────────────────────────────────────────────────────┐
│ The following shall be given the opportunity to make    │
│ representations (orally or in writing)                  │
└─────────────────────────────────────────────────────────┘
        │                    │                    │
┌──────────────┐    ┌──────────────────┐   ┌──────────────────┐
│   detainee   │    │   his solicitor  │   │ responsible adult│
│              │    │   [if available] │   │  [if available]  │
└──────────────┘    └──────────────────┘   └──────────────────┘
        │                    │                    │
┌─────────────────────────────────────────────────────────┐
│ and any other person having an interest in the detained │
│ person's welfare may make representations               │
└─────────────────────────────────────────────────────────┘
```

S. 40(4) PACE ACT 1984

Q Can a review be conducted over the telephone?

A Where a review is due and the detainee has not been charged, the review may be conducted by telephone if:

[a] the use of video conferencing facilities is not applicable, or not reasonably practicable **and**
[b] it is not reasonably practicable for the review officer to attend the station.

Q What if a review falls at the time when a person is likely to be asleep?

A Bring the review forward, so the detainee can be present: Code C, note 15C.

Q When can detention be authorised beyond 24 hours?

A Detention may be authorised for up to **36 hours** where the offence is an indictable offence and a **superintendent** or above responsible for the station is satisfied:

[a] there is not sufficient evidence to charge; and
[b] the investigation is being conducted diligently and expeditiously; and
[c] the person's detention is necessary to secure or preserve evidence relating to the offence or to obtain evidence by questioning him.

S. 42(1) PACE ACT 1984

CUSTODY OFFICER DUTIES

Q When can the decision to keep a person in detention for over 24 hours be made?

A [a] Within 24 hours of the relevant time; and
[b] not before the second review.

S. 42(2) PACE ACT 1984

Q Who is the review officer during the 24 - 36 hour period?

A The superintendent.

Q What about terrorism cases?

A Where a person has been arrested under S. 41 Terrorism Act 2000 s/he can be kept in police detention for up to 48 hours without court authorisation.

Q How long can a court authorise further detention?

A A total of 96 hours. (Once the 36-hour limit is reached, further detention must be authorised by a court through the issue of a warrant of further detention.)

Q Outline the procedure for applying for a warrant of further detention

A The application is made under oath in court by the police. The detainee must be present. The information must set out:

[a] the nature of the offence (which must be an indictable offence);
[b] the general evidence on which the person was arrested;
[c] what inquiries have been made;
[d] what further inquiries are proposed; and
[e] why it is believed that continuing detention is necessary for the enquiries.

S. 43 PACE ACT 1984

Q When should the application be made?

A Within 36 hours [may be extended by six hours if there is no court sitting]. An application for a warrant or its extension should be made between 10 am and 9 pm, and if possible during normal court hours.

CUSTODY OFFICER DUTIES

Q When can a person be cautioned?

A [a] Where there is evidence of guilt with a realistic prospect of conviction; and
[b] he admits the offence; and
[c] he agrees to be cautioned.

Who administers the caution? A uniformed inspector.

Q Outline the custody officer's duties on arrival of arrested persons

A [a] Open custody record;
[b] inform him of his rights;
[c] provide a written notice of rights;
[d] ask for signature on custody record of receipt of rights;
[e] undertake a risk assessment of detainee.

Q What must be noted about the author of entries in the custody record?

A All entries must have the person's name and rank except for officers dealing with Terrorism Act 2000 offences.

Q What other duties are there in relation to special groups?

A [a] If the person is deaf or has difficulty with English, use an interpreter;
[b] if blind or seriously visually impaired, he should have help from his representative;
[c] if a juvenile, obtain an appropriate adult;
[d] if mentally impaired, obtain an appropriate adult.

Q What is the procedure for authorising detention?

A [a] The arresting officer must give reasons for arrest (in the presence of arrested person];
[b] The alleged offence(s) and reason(s) for arrest must be recorded on the custody record;
[c] The custody officer must decide whether to authorise detention, and (unless he is violent, unable to understand or in need of urgent medical attention) the detainee must be informed of the grounds as soon as reasonably practicable, and before being questioned about any offence;
[d] Any comment made by the detainee must be recorded.

CUSTODY OFFICER DUTIES

Q Who can authorise a search at the police station?

A   The custody officer. He shall:

[a] ascertain what property he has on his arrival at the police station;
[b] ascertain what property he might have for a **harmful or unlawful purpose**;
[c] decide what property to keep and what to let the detained person keep;
[d] inform him of the reasons why any property is being retained.

Record? The custody officer is not required by PACE to record all property in the custody record, but may choose to do so at his discretion [bearing in mind force orders].

Sex. The search must be carried out by a person of the same sex.

Force. Reasonable force may be used.

Q What property cannot be seized?

A   Items subject to legal privilege.

Q When does a search become a strip search?

A   Where the custody officer authorised removal of more than the outer clothing.

Q When may a strip search take place?

A   Only if the custody officer reasonably considers that the detainee might have concealed an article which might be used to:

[a] harm himself or others;
[b] damage property;
[c] effect an escape; or
[d] which might be evidence of an offence **and** it is necessary to remove such an article.

Q What is an intimate search?

A   A search consisting of the physical examination of a person's body orifices other than the mouth.

CUSTODY OFFICER DUTIES

Q When can an search take place?

A Only if authorised by an inspector (or above) who has reasonable grounds for believing:

[a] that an article which could cause physical injury to the detainee or others has been concealed; or
[b] the detainee has concealed a Class A drug which he intends to supply to another or to export.

The authorising officer must also believe that an search is the only practicable means of removing the item.

Q What about intimate or strip searches of juveniles?

A Where a juvenile is the subject of an intimate search or a strip search, an appropriate adult must generally be present. Where an appropriate adult is required:

- the appropriate adult may be of the opposite sex *if the detainee specifically requests it* and the adult is readily available;
- where there is a risk of serious harm to the detainee or others, the search may be conducted without the appropriate adult being present;
- a search of a juvenile may take place in the absence of the appropriate adult only if the juvenile signifies in the presence of the appropriate adult that he/she prefers the search to be done in his/her absence and the appropriate adult agrees. A record should be made of this decision and signed by the appropriate adult.

CODE C, ANNEX A PARAS 5 AND 11

Q How often should detainees be visited in cells?

A Every hour and drunks every half hour. Drunks should be roused and spoken to on each visit.

Q Can juveniles be placed in cells?

A A juvenile should only be placed in a police cell if no other secure accommodation is available and the custody officer considers it is not practicable to supervise them if they are not placed in a cell, or that a cell provides more comfortable accommodation than other secure accommodation in the station.

CUSTODY OFFICER DUTIES

Q Can more than one person be placed in a cell?

A This is not specifically prohibited by the Codes of Practice but should be avoided so far as is practicable. In no circumstances must a juvenile be placed in a cell or detention room with an adult, and where detainees have to share a cell they must be of the same sex. Where a custody officer is considering placing more than one person in a cell, he/she must consider the following:

- there must be sufficient bedding available for each person;
- he/she is responsible for the safety of all prisoners and there may be a risk of assault in the cells;
- he/she is responsible for the safety of police staff and other visitors to the police station who may be overpowered by more than one prisoner;
- the dignity of the prisoners;
- security of evidence.

Q Before handing over a detainee, what should the custody officer consider?

A [a] Whether he is in need of a rest period;
[b] whether he is unfit through drink or drugs; and
[c] whether the right of access to legal advice is being complied with.

Q What is meant by rest period?

A In any 24 hours he shall have at least **eight hours for rest**, free from questioning, travel or any interruption by police officers in connection with the investigation. His rest may not be interrupted unless there are reasonable grounds for believing that it would:

[a] involve a risk or harm to people or serious loss of, or damage to property;
[b] delay unnecessarily the person's release from custody; or
[c] otherwise prejudice the outcome of the investigation.

CODE C 12.2

Q When must an appropriate adult be informed?

A In cases where the detained person is:

[a] a juvenile [under 17];
[b] mentally vulnerable; or
[c] appears to be suffering from a mental disorder.

Juveniles held incommunicado. Must have an appropriate adult.

CUSTODY OFFICER DUTIES

Q **What is meant by an appropriate adult?**

A **In the case of a juvenile:**

- [a] parent or guardian;
- [b] social worker; or
- [c] failing above, an adult [aged 18 or over].

In the case of the mentally ill:

- [a] a relative, guardian or person responsible for his care;
- [b] a person experienced with the mentally ill;
- [c] failing above, an adult [aged 18 or over].

What about police employees? A police officer or police employee cannot act as an appropriate adult.

Q **Who should not act as an appropriate adult?**

A Any person who is suspected of involvement in the offence, is a victim, witness or a **person receiving admissions** prior to attending as an appropriate adult. If a juvenile is estranged from a parent and expressly objects to the parent's presence.

Q **When should an interpreter be used?**

A Whenever a detainee is unable to speak or understand English effectively.

IDENTIFICATION

Q Outline identification methods where the suspect is known

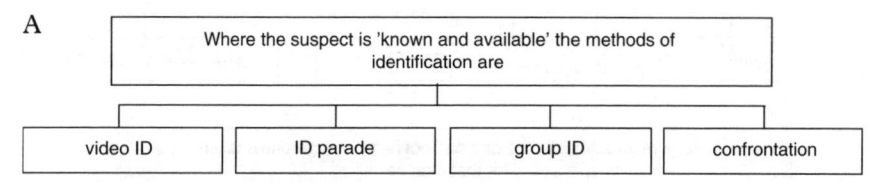

A

```
        Where the suspect is 'known and available' the methods of
                         identification are
```

| video ID | ID parade | group ID | confrontation |

Priority. The revised Code D indicates that a suspect should initially be offered a video ID unless video ID is not practicable or an ID parade is both practicable and more suitable. A group ID may initially be offered if the officer in charge considers it is more suitable than either video or ID parade.

Who is the identification officer? A uniformed inspector.

Known and available. Means available for arrest *(R v Kitchen (1994))*. Do not go to photograph ID if the suspect is known and available.

Q Who may not take part in the procedures?

A Officers involved in the investigation of the offence.

Q What if the suspect refuses the method offered?

A The suspect must be asked to state their reasons for refusal and may seek advice from their solicitor and/or appropriate adult. Any of these persons may then make representations about why another method is preferred. This should be recorded. If the officer considers an alternative is suitable and practicable then that should be offered. If s/he does not consider an alternative is suitable the reasons must be recorded.

Q What is meant by first description?

A The first description provided of a person suspected of a crime must be recorded. It must be disclosed to the defence in the pre-trial procedure in all cases and, in particular, before any identification procedures take place.

Media publicity. Before any procedures take place, witnesses must be asked if they have seen any material previously released to the media.

IDENTIFICATION

Q When can fingerprints be taken without consent?

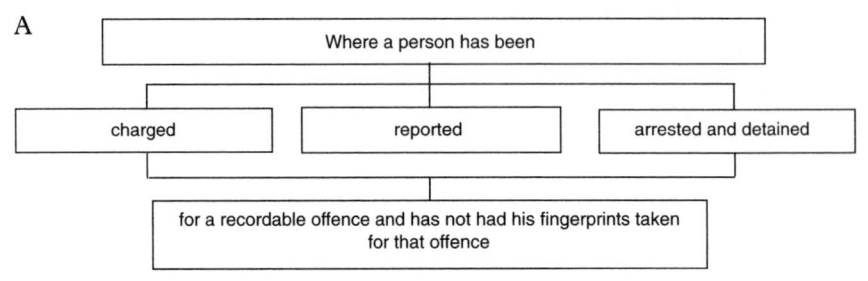

A

```
                    Where a person has been
         ┌──────────────────┼──────────────────┐
      charged             reported       arrested and detained
         └──────────────────┼──────────────────┘
     for a recordable offence and has not had his fingerprints taken
                          for that offence
```

S. 61 PACE ACT 1984

Q When can fingerprints be taken following conviction?

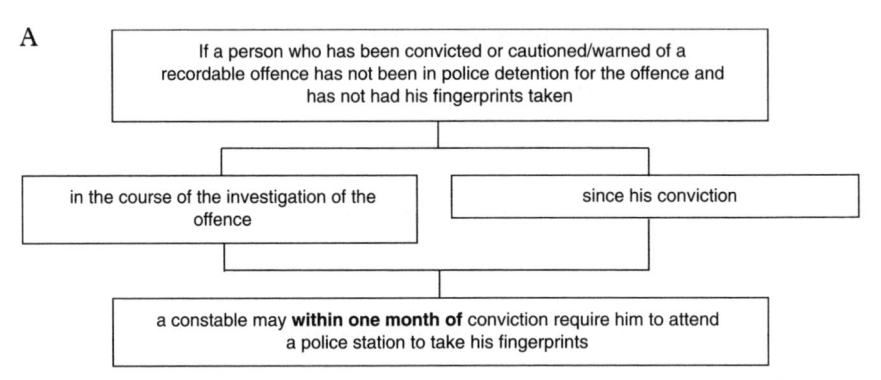

A

```
   If a person who has been convicted or cautioned/warned of a
   recordable offence has not been in police detention for the offence and
                    has not had his fingerprints taken

   ┌─────────────────────────────┬─────────────────────────────┐
  in the course of the investigation        since his conviction
              of the offence
   └─────────────────────────────┴─────────────────────────────┘
   a constable may within one month of conviction require him to attend
                 a police station to take his fingerprints
```

Notice. He must be given **seven days' notice** of the requirement and it may direct that he attends at a specific time of day or between specific times.

Arrest. In the event of failure to comply a constable may arrest.

S. 27 PACE ACT 1984

Why this power? This power fits the position where a person is reported for an offence, e.g. shoplifting, and is not taken to the police station resulting in fingerprints not being taken, but subsequently is convicted for the offence.

IDENTIFICATION

Q Define an intimate sample

A Intimate sample means:

[a] blood;
[b] semen;
[c] tissue fluid;
[d] urine; or
[e] pubic hair; and
[f] a dental impression;
[g] a swab from any part of a person's genitals or from a body orifice other than the mouth.

S. 65(2) PACE ACT 1984

Q Define a non-intimate sample

A Non-intimate samples include:

[a] hair [not pubic];
[b] nails [from a nail or under a nail];
[c] swabs from any part of the body other than a part from which a swab taken would be an intimate sample
[d] footprints and other impressions of the body [but not fingerprints]; and saliva.

Q Can an intimate sample be taken without consent?

A No.

Q Whose consent is required?

A **Both** the suspect and an inspector (or above). The taking of such a sample without consent is a serious matter and may give rise to both criminal (assault) and civil liability. It may also amount to a breach of Art. 3 ECHR (inhuman or degrading treatment).

Q Whose consent is required in the case of juveniles?

A

under 14	Over 14 but under 17
parents or guardian only	**both** the juvenile and the parents or guardian
and the inspector	

IDENTIFICATION

Q **What happens where a sample proves 'insufficient for analysis'?**

A   Retake them [again with both consents].

Q **When can an inspector authorise the taking of intimate samples?**

A

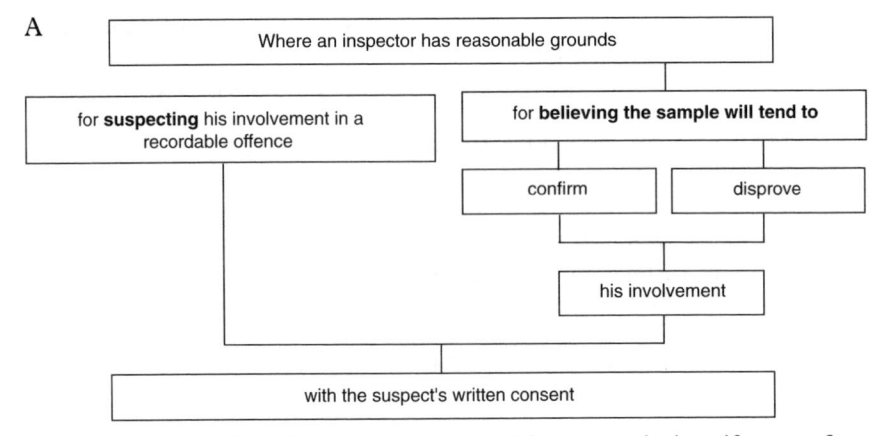

```
                    ┌─────────────────────────────────────────┐
                    │ Where an inspector has reasonable grounds│
                    └─────────────────────────────────────────┘
        ┌──────────────────────────┐   ┌──────────────────────────────────┐
        │ for suspecting his        │   │ for believing the sample will tend to │
        │ involvement in a          │   └──────────────────────────────────┘
        │ recordable offence        │       ┌──────────┐   ┌──────────┐
        └──────────────────────────┘       │ confirm  │   │ disprove │
                                            └──────────┘   └──────────┘
                                                ┌──────────────────┐
                                                │ his involvement  │
                                                └──────────────────┘
                    ┌─────────────────────────────────────────┐
                    │ with the suspect's written consent       │
                    └─────────────────────────────────────────┘
```

Warning. 'You do not have to provide a sample but if you refuse without good cause your refusal may harm your case if it comes to trial.'

S. 62 PACE ACT 1984

Q **What information has to be recorded?**

A   The inspector's authority may be given orally but if so must be confirmed in writing as soon as practicable. The suspect's authority must be in writing. Also the following:

[a]   the authorisation;
[b]   the grounds;
[c]   the suspect consented;
[d]   at a police station the suspect was informed the sample would be subject to a speculative search; and
[e]   the warning had been given.

IDENTIFICATION

Q **When can non-intimate samples be taken without the suspect's consent?**

A When a suspect is in police detention, a non-intimate sample can be taken without his consent when he is in detention in consequence of his arrest for a recordable offence and either

> [a] he has not had a non-intimate sample of the same type and from the same part of the body taken in the course of the investigation; or
> [b] he had such a sample taken but it proved insufficient.

Non-intimate samples may also be taken without consent, whether or not the suspect is in police detention, if the suspect has been

- charged with a recordable offence or informed that he will be reported for such an offence; and either he has not had a non-intimate sample taken from him in the course of the investigation, or one was taken but proved insufficient or unsuitable for analysis;
- convicted of a recordable offence.
- detained following acquittal on grounds of insanity/unfitness to plead.

Q **When is an inspector's authority required to take a non-intimate sample?**

A When the suspect is being held in custody by the police on the authority of a court. Such authority can be given where the inspector has *reasonable grounds for believing* the suspect's involvement in a recordable offence and *believes* that the sample will tend to confirm or disprove his involvement.

Q **Can samples be retained?**

A Yes, but they can only be used for purposes related to the prevention or detection of crime, the investigation of any offence or the conduct of a prosecution. Where a person has provided a sample voluntarily (e.g. for elimination purposes) he must consent to its retention. If he does not, it must be destroyed and information derived from it cannot be used as evidence against him for any offence or for the investigation of any offence.

INTERVIEWS

Q Define an interview

A An interview is the questioning of a person regarding his involvement or suspected involvement in a criminal offence.

Questions of identification. Do not amount to an interview, e.g. to establish his identity or ownership of a vehicle etc.

Q When should a person be cautioned?

A A caution should be administered to all people who are:

[a] arrested for an offence;
[b] whom there are grounds to suspect of an offence,

before any questions about it are put to them if their answers or silence may be given in evidence.

CODE C

The caution. 'You do not have to say anything but it may harm your defence if you do not mention, when questioned, something which you later rely on in court. Anything you say may be given in evidence.'

CODE C PARA 10.5

Q What questions may be asked without caution?

A Where the questions are

[a] solely to establish identity or ownership of any vehicle;
[b] to obtain information in accordance with any statutory requirement (e.g. under the Road Traffic Act 1988);
[c] in furtherance of the proper and effective conduct of a search (e.g. to determine the need to search in the [d] exercise of stop and search powers);
[d] to seek verification of a written record; or
[e] in certain Terrorism Act matters.

Q What should be told to a person cautioned, but not under arrest?

A That he is not under arrest and is not obliged to remain with the officer.

INTERVIEWS

Q   When can an arrested person be interviewed not at a police station?

A   If the delay in taking him to a police station would be likely to:

   [a] lead to interference with or **harm** to **evidence** connected with an offence or interference with or physical harm to other **people or serious loss/damage to property**; or
   [b] lead to the **alerting of others** suspected of having committed an offence but not yet arrested; or
   [c] **hinder the recovery of property** obtained in consequence of the offence.

   CODE C PARA 11.1

When must it cease? When the relevant risk has been averted.

Q   When can a person be interviewed after charge?

A   If it is necessary to:

   [a] prevent or minimise harm or loss to some other person or the public; or
   [b] clear up an ambiguity in a previous answer or statement; or
   [c] in the interest of justice to allow him to comment on information that has come to light since he was charged or reported.

Q   When must an interview be taped?

A   [a] where a person has been cautioned for an indictable offence;
   [b] when further questions, after charge, are put in relation to [a] above;
   [c] when bringing to the notice of a person at [a] the contents of:

      [i]   an interview; or
      [ii] a statement made by another person.

   CODE E

INTERVIEWS

Q When can a custody officer authorise an interview not to be taped?

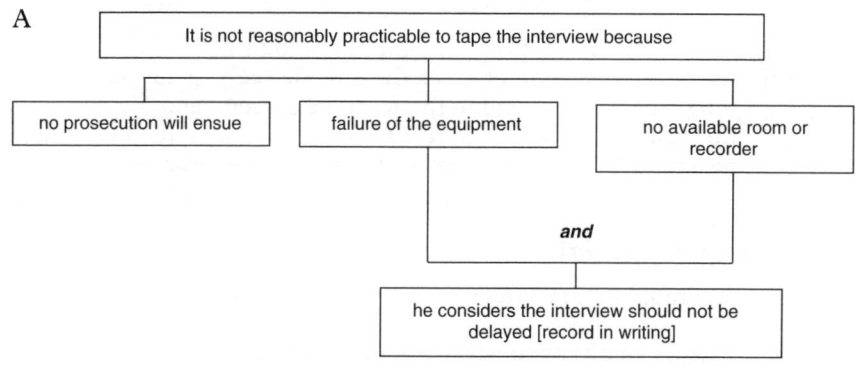

A It is not reasonably practicable to tape the interview because:
- no prosecution will ensue
- failure of the equipment
- no available room or recorder

and

he considers the interview should not be delayed [record in writing]

Q Outline the position of solicitors and legal advice

A [a] A suspect must not be dissuaded from obtaining legal advice;
[b] if a request for legal advice is made during interview, the interview shall stop and legal advice be sought;
[c] if a solicitor arrives at a police station to see a suspect, the suspect must be asked if he wants to see the solicitor, regardless of what legal advice has already been received. The custody officer must be informed and the attendance and suspect's decision recorded.

CODE C PARA 6.15

Excluding a solicitor. If the investigating officer considers that a solicitor is acting in a way that he is unable properly to put questions to the suspect he will stop the interview and consult a **superintendent**, or if not available, an **inspector** who will decide whether or not to exclude the solicitor from the interview.

CODE C PARA 6.10

Unacceptable conduct by solicitor. Include answering questions on his client's behalf and providing written replies for him to quote.

Q When should questioning cease?

A If it is considered that:

[a] there is enough evidence to prosecute; and
[b] there is enough evidence for a prosecution to succeed; and
[c] that the person **has said all he wishes** about the offence.

INTERVIEWS

Q When is an interpreter required?

A An interpreter is required when:

[a] the suspect has difficulty in understanding English;
[b] the interviewer cannot speak the interviewee's language;
[c] the suspect wishes an interpreter to be present; and
[d] the suspect appears to have a hearing/speaking difficulty, unless he agrees **in writing** to proceed without an interpreter.

CODE C PARA 13.2

Q When are special warnings required?

A They are required in relation to questions put to suspects about:

[a] objects, marks or substances found on them; or
[b] in or on their clothing or footwear, or
[c] in their possession; or
[d] in the place where they were arrested, and in relation to why
[e] they were at the scene at or near the time of their arrest; and
[f] their failure to account for their presence.

CODE C PARA 10.10

Q What is the procedure when a person makes a statement in a foreign language?

A [a] The interpreter shall take the statement in the foreign language,
[b] the person making it shall sign it; and
[c] a translation shall then be made.

CODE C PARA 13.4

QUICK CHECKLIST OFFENCES REQUIRING CONSENT FOR PROSECUTION ATTORNEY-GENERAL (OR SOLICITOR-GENERAL)

1. **Homicide** where victim dies more than three years after injury or where D has already been convicted of an offence connected with the death (Law Reform (Year and a Day Rule) Act 1996 S. 22)

2. **Torture** (Criminal Justice Act 1988 S. 134)

3. **Hostage taking** (Taking of Hostages Act 1982 S. 1)

4. **Conspiracy to commit offences outside the UK** (Criminal Law Act 1977 S. 1A and Criminal Justice (Terrorism and Conspiracy) Act 1998)

5. **Offences under the Explosive Substances Act 1883**

6. **Offences of racial hatred** (Public Order Act 1986)

7. **Wearing political uniform in public places** (Public Order Act 1936 SS.1 & 2)

8. **Corruption** (Public Bodies Corrupt Practices Act 1889 S. 1)

9. **Corruption of Agents** (Prevention of Corruption Act 1906 S. 1)

10. **Harmful Publications** (Children and Young Persons (Harmful Publications) Act 1955)

11. **Trespassing on Protected Site** (Serious Organised Crime & Police Act 2005 S. 128(1))

OFFENCES REQUIRING DPP CONSENT FOR PROSECUTION

1. **War crimes** (War Crimes Act 1991)

2. **Encouraging or assisting suicide** (Suicide Act 1961 s.2)

3. **Riot** (Public Order Act 1986 S. 7)

4. **Theft or criminal damage** where the property in question belongs to D's spouse (Theft Act 1968 S. 30(4))

5. **Concealing relevant offences and assisting offenders** (Criminal Law Act s. 4(4)

6. **Sexual intercourse with patients** (Mental Health Act 1959 S. 128)

7. **Incest** (Sexual Offences Act 1956 SS. 10 and 11)

8. **Child abduction** (person connected with child) and **kidnapping** where victim is under 16 or parent/guardian offender (Child Abduction Act 1984 SS. 4(2) and 5)

9. **Indecent photographs** (Protection of Children Act 1978)

10. **Unlawful interception of public and private communications** (Regulation of Investigatory Powers Act 2000 SS. 1(1) and 1(2))

11. **Data protection offences** unless prosecuted by information commissioner (Data Protection Act 1998)

12. **Terrorism Act 2006 Offences** [where an offence has been committed for a purpose at least partly connected with the affairs of another country, the DPP's consent may only be given with the permission of the AG]

13. **Corporate manslaughter** (Corporate Manslaughter and Corporate Homicide Act 2007)

14. **Possession of extreme pornographic images** (Criminal Justice and Immigration Act 2008)

15. **Possession of prohibited images of children** (Coroners and Justice Act 2009 s.62)

NOTES

NOTES

NOTES